FASHION
THE CENTURY OF THE DESIGNER

1900–1999

© 1999 Könemann Verlagsgesellschaft mbH
Bonner Straße 126, D – 50968 Cologne

Publishing director: Peter Feierabend
Art direction & design: Sabine Vonderstein
Project management: Franziska Sörgel
Assistant: Freia Schleyerbach
Picture editing: Elisabeth Alric-Schnee
Editor of the original text: Astrid Roth
Illustrations (Glossary): Yris Kayser

Production: Mark Voges
Reproduction: Niemann + Steggemann, Oldenburg

Original title: Mode, Das Jahrhundert der Designer
1900–1999

© 2000 for this English edition:
Könemann Verlagsgesellschaft mbH
Bonner Straße 126, D – 50968 Cologne

Translation: Neil and Ting Morris, Karen Waloschek for
Book Creation Services Ltd
Editing: Lucilla Watson for Book Creation Services Ltd
Typesetting: Gene Ferber for Book Creation Services Ltd
Project management: Tamiko Rex for Book Creation Services Ltd
Project coordination: Nadja Bremse
Production: Ursula Schümer
Printing and binding: Mateu Cromo, Madrid

Printed in Spain
ISBN 3-8290-2980-2
10 9 8 7 6 5 4 3 2 1

CHARLOTTE SEELING

FASHION
THE CENTURY OF THE DESIGNER
1900–1999

KÖNEMANN

Table of contents

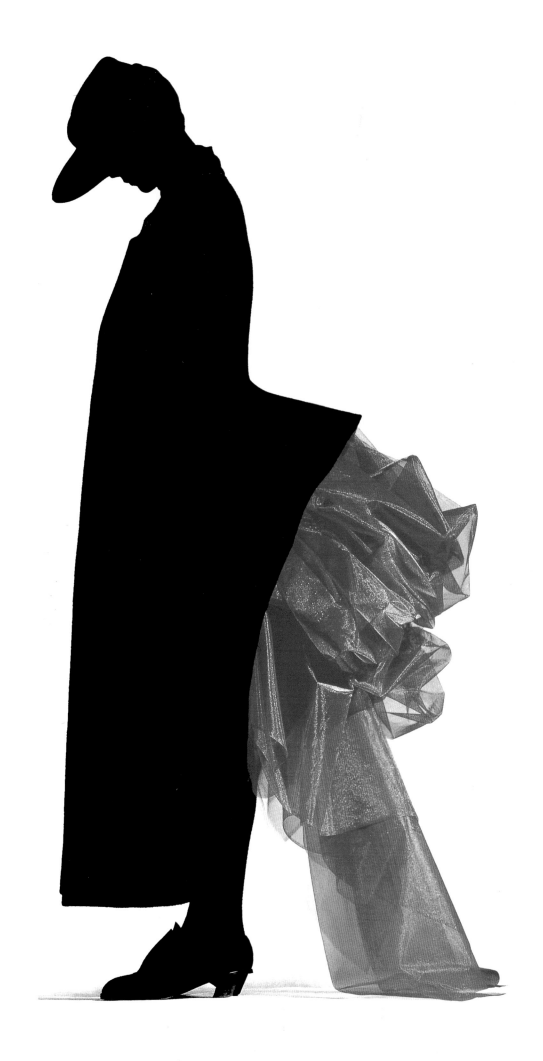

How fashion came about

There have been beautiful clothes throughout history, but FASHION is a 20th-century phenomenon. In earlier periods there were many different ways of dressing, and these varied between countries and social classes. People at court dressed very differently from the bourgeoisie, and the French differently from the British, Italians, or Germans. Things changed when Charles Frederick Worth decided that he wanted to be more than simply a supplier to Her Imperial Highness Eugénie of France and began to "sign" his creations as if he were an artist. This signaled the birth of the trade mark. The fournisseur became a couturier, and what he created was FASHION.

Fashion comes from Paris, and one of its greatest characteristics is that it changes. No sooner is something "in fashion" than it is "out of fashion" again. It may seem as if couturiers make these changes on a personal whim and mood, but in reality their creations only really catch on if they capture the spirit of the age. In this way the couturier can justifiably be compared to an artist, especially since his works are handmade originals.

Fashion was only really brought into fashion by the designers of the 1960s. In an age of mass reproduction they realized that clothes did not have to be unique in order to be seen as creations. Since then the trade mark has become an independent force. It appears not only on clothes but on items such as sunglasses, underwear, ashtrays, and vases, and the design often no longer comes from the designer himself; it is enough that the work carries the designer's signature, and that it does so all over the world.

Today the same fashion language is spoken everywhere, from New York to Tokyo, and it has moved away from its French origins. The latest thing may come from London, Milan, or Hamburg. It may not even stem from a couturier or designer. A good marketing department can always polish a name until it becomes fashionable. Everything from T-shirts to trainers can become a cult, just as if they had been created by Worth.

The spirits that Worth once called upon to protect his exclusive works have taken their revenge on fashion designers. At the end of the century in which they acquired so much fame, it seems as if designers have almost become superfluous. Some are no longer even putting their own name to their designs, which is a sign of their intuitive knowledge.

Where have a hundred years of haute couture led us? One might almost say that they have led us back to the very beginning. Today we can again see the corsets and bustles that dominated the beginning of the 20th century, with bosoms and bottoms leading to a new kind of seduction. And yet fashion has changed: when today's women put on corsets and today's designers remain anonymous, they choose to do so. Things have come full circle, and in the 21st century people will surely continue to take great pleasure in fashion.

Charlotte Seeling

1900–1909

Down with the corset

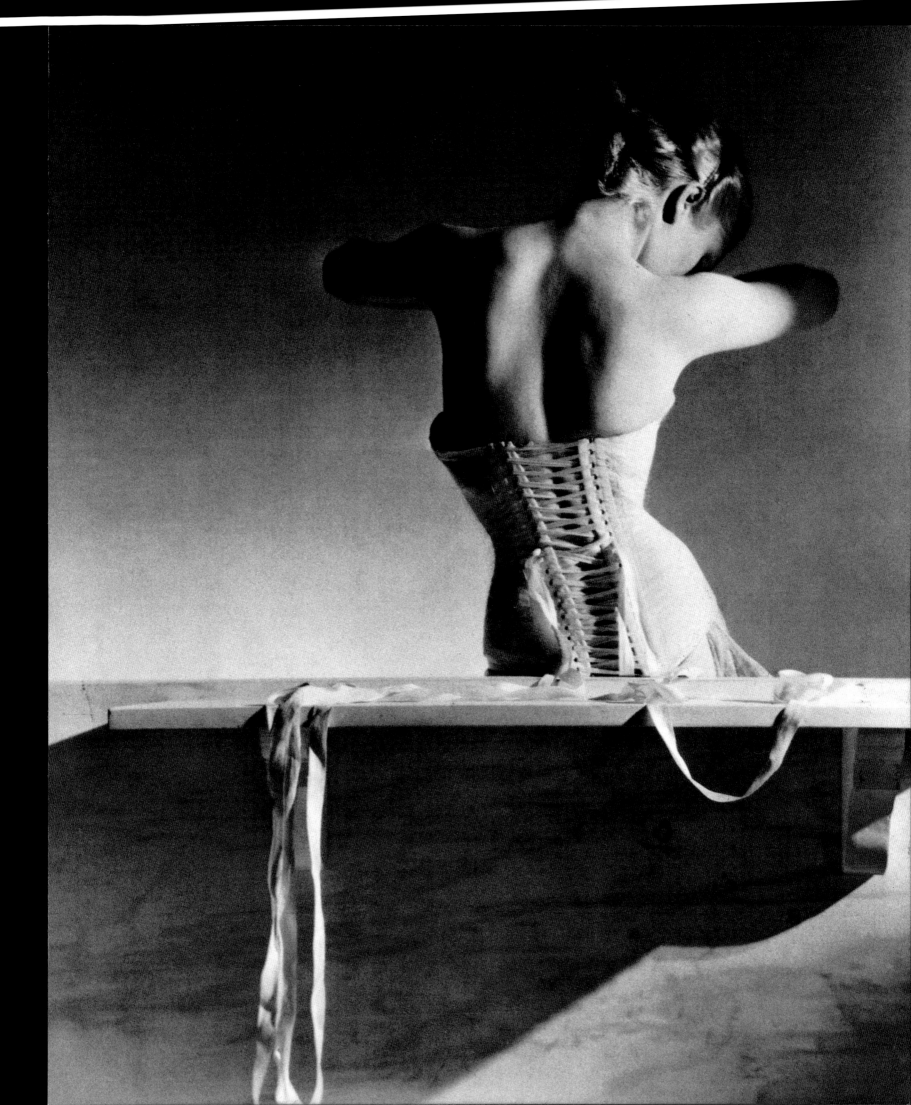

1900–1909

French *haute couture* made its first triumphant appearance at the 1900 World Fair in Paris. In the Pavilion of Elegance a few chosen fashion houses, including Worth and Doucet, who dressed stage stars such as Eleonora Duse and Sarah Bernhardt, showed their lavish and spectacular creations to an amazed international audience.

"For all those who offer sacrifice at the altars of elegance, brilliance, splendor, and beauty," read a subsequent newspaper review, "for all those Paris was, is, and always will be the only truly blessed place of pilgrimage."

A truly prophetic judgment! Paris was to be the world's fashion center for an entire century, and it is no coincidence that this reputation began with the rise of the designers – and perhaps it will end with their decline. At that time they were, of course, still known as couturiers and they saw themselves as guardians of the high art of tailoring and dressmaking. However, they had to be creators and artists, public relations geniuses and entertainers, self-promoters and directors all rolled into one if they wished to rise from the mass of gifted craftsmen.

Strangely enough, it is an Englishman who is regarded as the founder of French *haute couture*. Charles Frederick Worth came to Paris at the age of 20, after a seven-year apprenticeship in the London textile trade. Thirteen years later, in 1858, he founded his own couture house in the Rue de la Paix with his Swedish partner Boberg. From 1871 he ran the business on his own. Worth was the first to see how to attain star status, which he did quite simply by adopting the practise of signing his garments as if they were works of art. He also presented a new collection every year, and this introduced into fashion the constant factor of change, a pioneering innovation which promoted sales and from which all designers still profit to this day.

The line of fashion which Worth developed was much less revolutionary than his marketing.

Charles Frederick Worth (1825–95)

Two empresses made the English dressmaker famous: Elisabeth of Austria (the tragic "Sisi"), and Eugénie, elegant wife of Napoleon III, at whose court Worth began his illustrious career. Both ladies were captured for posterity in paintings by Franz Xaver Winterhalter, wearing Worth's creations of silk tulle with gold embroidery. The term "haute couture" was coined for Worth's luxurious fashions.

Previous page:
Finally the corset is unlaced, but when will it fall? This photograph of a woman in a corset by Mainbocher has a highly symbolic content. It is one of the most famous images by the great German photographer Horst P. Horst.

Opposite:
The Eiffel Tower – wonder of the 1889 World Fair and subsequently symbol of the most important fashion fair – watches over Paris.

Above, left and right:
Hand embroidery in pastel tones on a cream evening gown with train, designed by Jean-Philippe Worth, who took up his father's artistic heritage and continued his tradition of great elegance. The gown is owned by Mrs. Walter H. Page.

Worth had simply made the crinoline, which had become increasingly extensive, somewhat more moderate by flattening the skirt at the front as well as gathering the fullness of the material at the back. This developed into the bustle, which together with the hooped skirt became exaggerated and provoked biting ridicule.

However, it was the 18th rather than the 19th century which influenced style and prompted endless imitations, and so no new lines were presented at the 1900 World Fair. The real sensation lay in the optimistic sense of mission shown by the new class of couturiers. They were all oriented toward Worth, who had already been dead for five years and had been succeeded by his sons Gaston and Jean-Philippe. The word *couturier* was created for Worth, who knew how

to combine English dressmaking technique with French display of splendor. Previously there had only been simple female dressmakers, or *couturières*.

Jeanne Paquin, the woman who had the honor of selecting the participants for the Pavilion of Elegance, traded as a fashion designer rather than as a dressmaker. She also presented nothing new, but did so with great allure. A wax model, which faithfully reproduced her beautiful features, was dressed up in the finest lace and silk, and this clever presentation deflected attention from the absence of innovation. The only shockingly new thing was the fact that a woman had been given the chairmanship of the fashion fair, for the world of couture was – and still is – dominated by men. They were very much of the opinion that the female body should be both laced up and padded, in

Opposite:
This very low-cut ball gown made of black tulle over white silk duchesse exemplifies classic turn-of-the-century style, with its extravagant use of sumptuous materials. The wearer, with her loose hairstyle and shy posture, is wrapped in her delicate veil like a butterfly in a luxurious cocoon.

Ostrich feathers, ruches, and fans were instruments of seduction at the turn of the century. A carefree smile, a laced-up waist, and a heavy bosom were considered irresistible. In 1997 Jean-Paul Gaultier rediscovered the coquettishness of the *belle époque* (*bottom right*).

order to approach the ideal of the hourglass – delicately fragile at the waist, spreading out voluptuously above and below. In profile the line followed the shape of an S, more or less sharply curved according to the corset and bustle.

Jean Cocteau is supposed to have said at the time that undressing a woman "is an undertaking similar to the capture of a fortress." Someone must have told the homoerotic writer, perhaps his colleague Colette, who was a vehement champion of all physical pleasures and showed an equal interest in both sexes.

A broad-brimmed hat with abundant feathers on pinned-up curly hair. With so much to support, the neck needed the extra support of a choker. It is difficult to comprehend how much weight a woman had to balance on her head in those days.

slight train. To give the silhouette greater balance and to act as a counterweight to the emphasized derrière, the hat was tilted slightly forward on the lady's pinned-up hair.

The matching ankle boots or shoes were pointed and had a slightly curved baroque heel. Silk stockings were indispensable accessories, though of course they could only be guessed at by others, and tight gloves ensured that not even the hands were bare outside the house. With a low-cut evening dress, gloves had to be long enough to cover the upper arms, so it was no wonder that a glimpse of bare skin or a slim ankle drove men wild. The obligatory parasol might seem coquettish from today's viewpoint, but then it was the only way to protect a pale complexion from taking on a rustic tan, which in the higher social classes was seen as extremely unrefined.

Although Worth had moderated it somewhat, women's clothing still had something of the straitjacket about it. High, narrow stand-up collars, preferably of firm lace, demanded that the head be held upright, especially since a sumptuously decorated hat was balanced on top. Heavy ostrich feathers were especially favored, since they were the most expensive and were an important status symbol. Narrowly cut tops, worn over whalebone corsets that were themselves hidden by "cache-corsets," had inset gigot sleeves in the shape of a leg of mutton. They were wide and puffed at the shoulder, and narrowed from the elbow to the hand. The sleeves ended only at the fingers, since proper ladies kept themselves covered as much as possible, preferably from head to toe. The skirt was full-length, loose at the hips, flared toward the hem in a bell shape, gathered and pleated toward the back, and often ending in a

Materials such as linen, velvet, and wool were used for daywear. Popular colors were subdued dark or pale pastel shades, such as pink, blue, or mauve. Lavish ornaments were used in an attempt to make up for a lack of imagination in the cut itself; braids and ribbons, tucks and bows, appliqués and flounces were all used as decoration.

In the evening it had to be silk and lace, muslin, tulle, chiffon, satin, and crêpe de Chine, richly embroidered and decorated, and often cut with a very low neckline. Pearls were the jewelry of the decade, worn as droplet earrings, loosely around the neck in a

At Longchamp racecourse, 1910. High society women and the demimondaines were to be seen at the Sunday races, weighed down by their heavy hats and dresses, which particularly emphasized the derrière. The first couturiers used this social event to introduce their latest creations into the fashion race.

Just a few years later, female racegoers at Longchamp look much more relaxed. Their clothes no longer cut into the waist, the materials are lighter, and the skirts have become shorter. Even the hats are free of plush and plumes.

single long string, or tightly in several rows as a choker. A woman of refinement always looked as if she were on her way to a garden party, even if she were spending the season, as was fitting, at the Côte d'Azur. In Paris, however, she preferred to be taken to the theater, where she could show off her dainty opera glasses and broad fan.

This was how the *femme ornée* of the *belle époque* was dressed. But the *femme libérée* was already waiting in the wings. Many people helped to liberate her, yet no one was better at espousing this revolution in the world of fashion than Paul Poiret.

Opposite:
Isadora Duncan did more for the liberation of women than any couturier. Even Paul Poiret would never have taken up his fight against the corset if dancers such as Duncan, Mata Hari, and Lois Fuller had not displayed their lithe bodies in expressive veiled dances.

Paul Poiret: The first designer

"Fashion needs a tyrant," proclaimed Paul Poiret, and with that he identified exactly what was needed in fashion at the turn of the century. Poiret's motives were purely self-centered, as he obviously saw only himself in the role of the liberating tyrant. Amid so much indecisiveness and nonsense, someone plainly had to come and lead the way, and this person must have new ideas. He must love life, love the arts, and love women. He must have an unquenchable thirst for beauty and self-realization. In short, this could only be Paul Poiret.

Paul Poiret was born on April 8, 1879 into a world of physical pleasures. His parents were drapers in the Les Halles district, which thanks to its famous covered market was still regarded as the food center of Paris and which has remained to this day the hub of the French textile industry. From an early age he knew that he was destined for greater things. Anyone with too much imagination and not enough discipline for a normal day's work must be a born artist. This view of the tubby, jolly daydreamer was lovingly fostered by his mother and his three sisters. Only the father showed resistance to his son's charm and forced him to stay on at school and take his exams. After that he sent him to a famous umbrella-maker to work as an errand boy, hoping that he might learn something of the serious side of life.

"I might have forgotten to wash my neck now and then," Poiret recalled of this humiliating time, "but I changed my white collar every day." The one thing of which he was totally convinced was that there is nothing more important than external appearance, and so he took from his employer the one and only thing that could help him to get on: silk remnants. At home in the evening, using scraps from mundane umbrella production, he designed extravagant couture creations, draping them on a 15-inch wooden doll given to him by his sisters, whose passionate admiration for his designs was an attitude that he demanded of women throughout his life.

It is extraordinary that to this day Poiret is celebrated as the fashion liberator of women, since he was interested only in his own glory and the only standard he accepted was his own taste. This attitude, together with his talent for drawing, secured him a position as an assistant to the successful couturier Jacques Doucet, a great art collector and connoisseur. From him the versatile and gifted Poiret learnt not only the dressmaker's craft and a sophisticated lifestyle, but also how to pay court effectively to the stars of the stage.

In 1901, after completing his military service, Poiret was employed by Worth, the leading fashion house of his time. But Jean-Philippe and Gaston Worth, the two sons who succeeded their father, the founder of the couture house, failed properly to appreciate Poiret's talent – or did they? – and did not give him a chance.

Fortunately there were women who had an unquestioning faith in him. Mama Poiret parted with 50,000 francs so that her son could set up on his own, opening his first fashion salon in 1903. The much admired actress Réjane deserted Poiret's former employers and became his first client; the apprentice must have outshone his master as far as flattery was concerned. Réjane was like a magnet: wherever she arrived with her two white donkeys – a present from the King of Portugal – admirers and imitators gathered.

Just three years later, Poiret himself was a star. He was recognized in the street and in restaurants, and the whole of Paris thronged to his parties. Poiret knew how to surround himself with the most talented illustrators, painters, and designers: Paul Iribe, Georges

PAUL POIRET
a Paris

Parasols and umbrellas were among the indispensable accessories of the decade. Paul Poiret knew how to give them a certain lively style.

Denise Poiret in the marital bedroom. As usual she is dressed in Poiret.

Lepape, Erté (Romain de Tertoff), Mariano Fortuny, Maurice de Vlaminck, André Derain, Raoul Dufy. He celebrated and worked with them, and felt himself one of them. "Am I a fool because I claim to be an artist?" he asked in his 1930 autobiography, which with characteristic self-confidence he called *I Dressed My Epoch*. But by this time his glory had long faded and other fixed stars shone in the fashion firmament. First and foremost among them was Coco Chanel, who knew from her own experience what was wrong with women's fashion.

Poiret might rightly have claimed that "I've gone to war against the corset," but his revolutionary deeds had purely aesthetic motives. He considered the division of the female body into two – a heavy bosom at the front and a jutting derrière at the back – simply ridiculous. Inspired by contemporary Art Nouveau and

18th-century Directoire style, possibly even influenced by the search of English designers and suffragettes for a "reform dress," Poiret designed a simple, narrow robe with a long skirt that began below the bust and fell sheathlike to the floor in a straight line. With this he created a design that made him immortal. He christened the dress La Vague, because it swirled around the body like a gentle wave.

Compared with the laced, dressed-up beauties of the *belle époque*, the new Poiret woman looked modest, young, and outrageously supple. Hidden beneath her light dress was quite obviously a good figure instead of a good corset. One wonders whether Poiret would ever have dared create this sensational design if his own wife had been less slim and graceful. In 1905 he married Denise Boulet, a close childhood friend. He made her the mother of five children and,

Paul Poiret

moreover, one of the most elegant women in Paris. "She was plain," he wrote in his autobiography, "but I saw her hidden beauty." No one could show off his straight, hanging dresses better than Denise. "Slim, dark, young, unlaced, and untouched by makeup or powder," as Poiret himself described her in *Vogue* in 1913.

Suddenly all Parisians wanted to look like Denise, the girl from the provinces. Paul Poiret, whose surname had become his trademark, promised pompously that every lady "who dimly felt the slavery of her unfashionable clothes ... will today shout with delight and relief ... that she can cover her beauty and at the same time reveal it in the new and attractive gowns Poiret has given her." To make women look younger and more daring, Poiret not only replaced the corset with elastic bras and light suspenders; he also used strong colors and bold patterns instead of washed-out pastel shades and festoons. Furthermore, he rejected black stockings and gave women – and men – the illusion of bare legs by wrapping them in skin-colored silk.

However, what started off as so brilliantly simple soon got out of hand. Poiret constantly raised the waistline and with it the bust; the décolletage got lower and the skirts tighter. In 1910 he invented the hobble skirt, which tapered to such a tight hemline that it forced its wearer to take the tiny steps of a geisha. Poiret found this very amusing: "I have liberated their upper body, but I'm tying their feet." But he was wrong. This time women did not follow him.

His hobble skirt, the *jupe entravée*, did not catch on.

That did not much bother the fashion dictator. For a long time he had seen himself as the sultan who dressed his harem in the most magnificent Oriental designs. He forced his slaves to wear caftans, kimonos, pantaloons, tunics, veils, and turbans – and they all obeyed with delight. At last there was pure luxury again: colorful embroidery, lace interwoven with gold and silver, splendid brocades, fringed borders, pearls, and rare feathers. The crucial thing was to be exotic. Everyone was obsessed with the Orient, especially since the first successful performance of the Ballets Russes in Paris in 1909. Diaghilev's impressive, baroque production of *Scheherazade* and *Le Dieu Bleu* influenced the arts and fashion, in fact the whole lifestyle of the decade.

Poiret proudly claimed that he had discovered the magic of the East long before, at a carpet exhibition in the store Le Bon Marché. But he took the excesses of the Orient to the extreme only after the Ballets Russes had prepared the ground. In 1911 he held one of the most legendary fancy-dress balls of the century, "The Thousand and Second Night." The divide between dress and fancy dress was blurred. Flamboyant, extravagant Poiret tried to stage life as one great festivity. He traveled all over the world with his troupe of mannequins: London, Berlin, Vienna, Brussels, Moscow, St. Petersburg, and finally New York. He was inspired by everything he saw. Following the example of the Vienna Workshops, he founded a decorative arts school for the design of furniture, fabrics, and decorative objects.

He became the first couturier to develop his own perfume, ten years before Chanel. In 1911 he succeeded in creating one more scandal and good publicity with his pantaloon gown. Even Pope Pius X took the trouble to condemn this immoral Parisian by the name of Poiret. In the same year he opened his decorative arts school, where Raoul Dufy's artistic designs were printed straight onto the finest silk. This represented a revolution in the textile industry, which up until then had been capable of printing only the simplest patterns on the cheapest fabrics. And having seen on his travels how replicas were being made everywhere, Poiret advocated the foundation of the Syndicat de Défense de la Grande Couture Française in order to protect independent creations.

Poiret could no longer be called simply a couturier. He became the first real designer of the 20th century, who left his aesthetic mark on everything around him and on everything he could sell, from accessories to interior design. It would be another 80 years before this concept

In 1910, when Poiret had only just liberated women from the corset, he confined their legs in the notorious hobble skirt, forcing them to walk in short, rapid steps.

Opposite:
American millionaire and art-patron Peggy Guggenheim in an Oriental Poiret gown made of gold lamé sewn with colored beads, photographed by Man Ray. The background is a floral pattern designed by E. A. Seguy, from his *Floréal, Dessins et Coloris Nouveaux*, and shows his light touch.

Right:
Robe de soirée de Poiret, drawn by Georges Lepape, shows Paul Poiret's typical lampshade tunic over a long, narrow skirt.

Opposite, top left and right:
Paul Poiret's Oriental costume designs for actress Sarah Bernhardt (left) and for the play *Le Minaret* (right).

Opposite, bottom left and right:
John Galliano is an enthusiastic follower of Poiret's splendor, as shown by these two designs from his 1998 collection for Dior.

Paul Poiret

The Maison Rosine de Poiret,
Paul Poiret's boutique, where
his perfumes and accessories
were also sold.

was taken up again by designers: in the 1990s Ralph Lauren, Donna Karan, Calvin Klein, Gucci, and others presented everything from home collections to scented candles, just as Poiret did at his Oriental balls.

Nevertheless, Poiret was no visionary. He lived totally in his own time, a time before World War I when life still seemed to be all right. Then he was called up, and when he returned from the battlefront four years later, he found that everything had changed – especially women. "They are hives without bees," he complained, dismissing his new competitor Coco Chanel as an "inventor of luxurious wretchedness."

With such utterances he exposed his own inadequacy. Having considered himself the liberator of women, he could not understand that the war had done more for women's independence than fashion could ever do. He still believed that women were waiting for the master to force them into his amazing designs. "First they grumble, then they obey, finally they applaud." Now they only laughed and did what they wanted.

Poiret believed that he could win back his old clientele with a few brilliantly staged balls. The more he saw his hopes dashed, the more generous his invitations became. He laid everything on, including champagne and oysters – pearl necklaces included! – and appearances by great artists such as Isadora Duncan, Pierre Brasseur, and Yvette Guibert. Six months later he had accrued debts of half a million francs.

He found financiers who profited from his genius, but who also wanted to submit it to market forces. Poiret felt humiliated and waited for the first best opportunity to reestablish himself as king of the couturiers in one fell swoop. He thought that the moment had come with the international Art Deco fair held in Paris in 1925. Poiret fitted out three Seine boats with his designs. One served as a luxury restaurant, another as a couture salon, and the third as a boutique for perfumes, accessories, and furniture. As usual the décor was magnificent but the cost enormous. His financiers refused to pay. Poiret was bankrupt but continued to live in great style. He was bitter that other couturiers were now successful with his ideas: those who are ahead of their time are punished by fashion. When Denise left him, he sulkily withdrew to paint in Provence. He died poor and forgotten in 1944. But his work contributed to keeping fashion alive.

Opposite:
Paul Poiret loved fancy-dress balls, and every year, on the feast day of St. Catherine, the Paris fashion houses organized one for unmarried needlewomen over 25. Josephine Baker, Poiret's prominent client, is at the center of the front row. Poiret, in wig, with mustache, and holding a bowler, is unmistakable, standing among his employees.

This shoe is decorated with a 17th-century motif. The material was woven specially for Paul Poiret in the famous tapestry works of Aubusson.

These floral-pattern gloves were made by promising young designers at the Martine art school, which Paul Poiret founded.

Above: Colette (*center*) proved to be Poiret's most loyal friend. When he was impoverished, she gave him a chance in the theater. On the left in this 1927 photograph is the model Renée.

Right:
In 1926 Paul Poiret was once
again far ahead of his time
with this costume consisting
of a backless halter-neck top
and harem pantaloons.

Below:
This narrow paletot over a
long dress and high collar
also has an Oriental touch.

Poiret's love of the Orient can be seen in many of his designs, such as this silk ensemble (*left*), which inspired Galliano in his 1997 collection for Dior (*above*).

Mariano Fortuny (1871–1949)

Although Mariano Fortuny was not a couturier, it was he who created the only dress to become immortal. The Delphos evening dress, a nothing of pleated satin that fits into the smallest box when rolled up in a bundle, is worn to this day by the world's most discriminating women – assuming that they manage to secure one of the rare originals at an auction. Mariano Fortuny's 1907 design never goes out of fashion, because it has never been in fashion. Experts realized immediately that it was a work of art: at last here was a dress that revealed nothing and hid nothing.

Like an ancient Greek chiton tunic, it hung straight from the shoulder to the floor without shape-enhancing seams, pads, or drapes. To women who did not need a corset it gave the freedom of movement that they had been craving. Delphos became the ultimate dress for the modern dancer, from Isadora Duncan to Martha Graham. Many designers followed Fortuny's stroke of genius: first his friend Paul Poiret, and later the American Mary McFadden and the Japanese Issey Miyake with his collection "pleats please."

Born in Granada into a family of Spanish painters, Fortuny saw himself exclusively as a painter. In fact he developed the most diverse talents. From the age of 17 he lived in Venice,

becoming an engineer, inventor, photographer, collector, and explorer. His artistic interest in textiles and colors made him experiment with velvet and silk, as well as new printing techniques. Shape, however, did not interest Fortuny.

That is how the Knossos scarf was created. A sari-like veil of printed silk became a diverse and much sought-after stage costume, worn by Mata Hari, among others. Fortuny developed the Delphos dress from one length of fabric after he had found a durable way of pleating silk, and the secret of that method has still not been fully revealed, just as it remains a mystery how he created the subtle shades of color. All this makes Fortuny designs valuable museum pieces.

Opposite:
Actress Lillian Gish in a Delphos dress.

Below and right:
Mariano Fortuny applied for a patent for his Delphos dress in 1909. He submitted these drawings to the patent office.

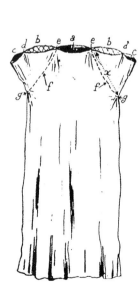

Jacques Doucet (1853–1929)

Born in the Rue de la Paix, where all the great couture houses were situated, and playmate of the Worth sons Gaston and Jean-Philippe, Jacques Doucet seemed predestined to become a couturier. As a young man he would have preferred to become a painter, but then he took over the fashion store which had been founded by his grandfather and which his parents had expanded in many different ways. He elevated it to the higher spheres of *haute couture* and soon became very successful. But the style, which he refined with such diligence that he is still considered one of the originators of the most lavish and sophisticated evening gowns of his time, was a discontinued design based on the elegant fashion of the 18th century.

The style of a grandly staged appearance was particularly popular with those ladies who wanted to draw the attention of prosperous gentlemen. "Doucet dressed us like good, respectable mothers," wrote Liane de Pougy, one of the most famous demimondaines, "or like colonels' wives." He continued to do this when respectable wives and mothers had long gone over to wanting to look like demimondaines.

Deep down Doucet was less interested in fashion than in luxury, and that is why he continued to adorn his pastel-colored dresses with lace, embroidery and appliqué, even though elegant Paris had long since decided on a new simplicity.

Nevertheless, it was Jacques Doucet who opened a way into the world of couture for the trailblazers of the fashion revolution. With his infallible eye for talent he discovered both Paul Poiret and Madeleine Vionnet, who probably did most to liberate the female body. Feeling that he was out of touch with his time, Doucet finally parted with his much praised collection of 18th-century paintings in 1912, and soon became one of the greatest patrons of Impressionism.

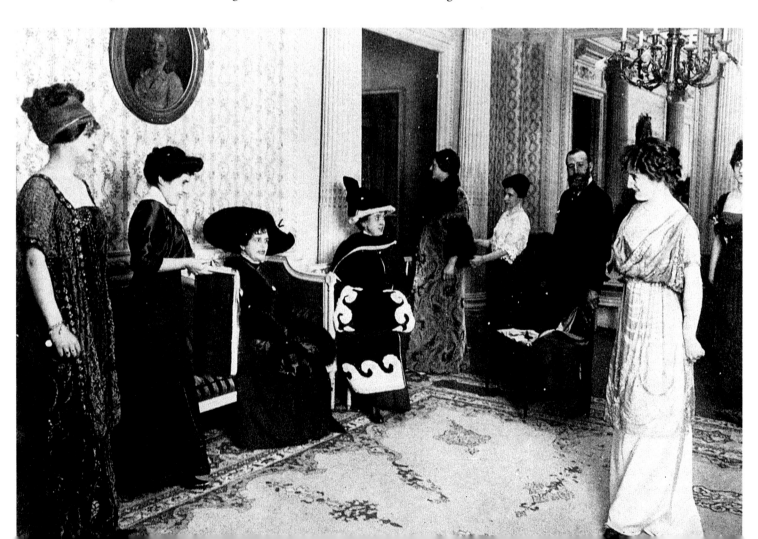

Jeanne Lanvin (1867–1946)

Jeanne Lanvin was 30 when she had her first child, and that was the beginning of her couture career. By then she had already been working in fashion for more than half of her life. The eldest of 11 children, at the age of 13 she began as a messenger girl, became a seamstress, and then a milliner. She was only 18 when she set up on her own as a milliner. The long hours of solitary work made her taciturn. To many she appeared cold but at the same time distinguished. In 1895 she married the Italian aristocrat Emilio di Pietro. Eight years later they divorced. At that time their daughter Marguerite was six years old.

"Ririte," Lanvin's pretty and musically gifted daughter, who would one day play a leading part in Paris society as Marie-Blanche de Polignac, gave her mother a new lease of life and a new direction to her work. Lanvin designed delicate, colorful dresses out of love for her little girl. They

were quite different from the usual children's clothes of that time, which were really no more than miniature versions of adult clothes. In this way she developed the first children's collection and laid the foundations for her couture house.

Soon afterward she added a line for young girls and women and so became the first designer to cater for all age groups. But more than that, she introduced youthfulness into fashion. Simple, innocent cuts and fresh colors, and most importantly the now famous Lanvin blue, made women of all ages seem feminine and romantic, but never sexy or fanciful. Her ankle-length dresses made in softly flowing fabrics have entered fashion history as *robes de style*.

From 1926 onward Jeanne also created men's fashion, which made Lanvin the first house to dress the whole family. It is also the only couture house which is still family-owned over 100 years after its foundation.

Jeanne Lanvin's most successful designs were the so-called *robes de style*, loosely cut dresses with a low waistline and an almost ankle-length skirt. Here (*left and center*) are two designs from 1923 and 1924. Warm wraps (*right*) – usually a compromise between a cape and a coat – complemented these light silk dresses.

The black and white gown (*left*) which Jeanne Lanvin designed in 1926 for theater director Jane Renouante was called La Nuit de Paris. John Galliano, who loves dipping into fashion history, slightly changed Lanvin's design for his 1998 collection for Dior (*above*). What was really new was the fashionable gray.

Unmistakably Lanvin: a 1924 dinner dress made of ivory silk satin with red silk appliqué.

Jeanne Paquin (1869–1936)

Many people suspect a man behind the name Paquin. In fact, Isidore Paquin (1862–1907) was greatly involved in the success of the fashion house as a financier, and more importantly as a skillful and charming manager. He knew how to pay court to his international clients, who were mainly aristocrats, actresses, and famous mistresses. But unlike its competitors Worth and Poiret, the woman at Maison Paquin was not the muse but the creator. She had learned her trade in the renowned Maison Rouff and said of herself, "I did not invent anything, I only left things out."

In 1906 Paquin introduced Empire-line dresses – one year before Poiret made his name with this design – and she was also a year ahead of him with a kimono coat. In 1900 she was the first woman to be elected president of the fashion section of the World Fair, and in 1913 she was the first female couturier to be awarded the cross of the Legion of Honor. Jeanne Paquin was also the first to set up branches in London, New York, Madrid, and Buenos Aires. It was her idea to have models parading her latest creations at glamorous opera premières and race meetings. In 1914 she organized the first true fashion show in London – a musical show that took place in the Palace Theatre. The designs she showed were called tango dresses and were no less sensational than the dance as she anticipated the spirit of postwar fashion.

Nevertheless, Paquin is not considered an innovator, as she retained the S-line for too long and introduced changes only slowly and discreetly. As a modest wife she somehow always stayed in the background, whereas her male colleagues showed no inhibitions at being celebrated as stars. She is remembered for her fur trimming and her romantic evening dresses in the 18th-century style. She looked so good in them that she was regarded as the best Paquin model. The death of her beloved husband at the end of World War I prompted her to pass the business side on to her brother-in-law and the design side on to Mademoiselle Madeleine. The couture salon of Paquin continued in existence until 1956.

LA JOUEUSE DE THÉORBE

Manteau du soir de Paquin

A magnificent evening cloak with kimono sleeves and long tails worn over a dress with train.

Mlle GABY DESLYS.

Costume by: PAQUIN.

Left:
The Parisian cabaret artiste Gaby Deslys wearing a dress by Jeanne Paquin. Note the emphasized derrière and ornate feather headdress.

Below:
This 1912 dress designed by Paquin and drawn by Paul Iribe makes a looser and more modest impression. It has a raised waist inspired by the Empire style.

Jeanne Paquin

The look of the decade

Apart from the hairstyle, round childlike eyes were the most important ingredient of the innocent look.

In the typical hairstyle of the time, called Gainsborough, the hair was worn pinned up, with added false hairpieces.

A translucent, soft complexion and a delicate waist were the most important facets of turn-of-the-century beauty, whatever the health risks. Murderously tight corsets deformed inner organs and caused indigestion problems, illness, and sometimes even death. The application of bleaching agents containing lead and arsenic could be just as fatal. But who cares about physical death when social death is at stake?

The woman chosen to be a man's wife was supposed to look harmless and natural, and so artificial aids such as make-up or dyed hair were scorned, at least officially. At the same time the skin was not to be suntanned or, even worse, ruddy, which made her look working-class. A woman's skin had to be as white as snow, at least when she was wearing an evening dress, and so liquid creams and white rice powder were indispensable. Little bluish violet veins at the temples, neck, and décolletage were touched up in order to enhance the impression of delicate sensitivity.

Nobody objected to white hair – in fact it was said to look young. Straight hair, on the other hand, suggested obstinacy and was scorned. Wavy hair, loosely put up, made a more agreeable impression, and in order to achieve this all available aids – curling irons, perms, and false braids – were condoned.

The appropriate scent for this pale, pastel-clad adorable beauty was lavender – so clean, fresh, and calming. Fingernails were made to shine with polishing paste but otherwise left untouched.

There is just one small thing that does not fit this picture of a neat, bourgeois way of life. Quite a number of these innocent, natural beauties wore rings in their nipples – known today as piercing – in order to raise the bust line. What sounds like further torture resulted in an appealing frictional effect, which distracted the corseted body from its agonies. Pain and pleasure were intimately linked.

Strangely, it was the feminists who made make-up socially acceptable. Their fight for the recognition of women's moral superiority and natural beauty made the first suffragettes ensure that they were exceptionally well groomed, neatly dressed, and carefully made up. This was a way of proving their point, and the more prominent and independent women were quick to emulate them. Actresses were used to wearing dramatic make-up on stage, and they soon adopted it in their daily lives. As these idols grew in status, middle-class women also dared to apply rouge, mascara, and eyeliner or have their hair hennaed in the latest Paris style.

The Gibson girl

One of the most influential women of the decade was not made of flesh and blood but came to life as a pen drawing created by the illustrator Charles Dana Gibson. Between 1890 and 1910 he regularly caricatured bourgeois reaction to female emancipation in the magazine *Colliers*. It always centered on the figure of a sporty, intelligent, beautiful, and stylishly self-assured young woman, who as the Gibson girl soon became the ideal of all American and British women and men. She was so popular that she was even available as wallpaper intended for the rooms of lonely bachelors. In fact, she was the predecessor of the pin-up girls who were later to adorn many a soldier's locker.

The Gibson girl, with her lightly waved, pinned-up hair, wore long-sleeved embroidered blouses with high, choking collars and flaring gored skirts. She usually lowered her eyes, as befitted young ladies of the time. Perhaps that was why many people failed to notice how much fuel for conflict the drawing held. The Gibson girl inspired her own sex to toughen their bodies with sports such as tennis, swimming, and riding, as well as to taking the steering wheel of the new automobiles. With wit and modesty she also pointed out to her gentle readers the problems of women of lower social status.

SARAH BERNHARDT

ISADORA DUNCAN

MATA HARI

ELEONORA DUSE

CLAIRE WALDOFF

ELSIE DE WOLFE

Idols of the decade

The fashionable models of this time were actresses, and the most obvious setting for *haute couture* was the theater, where it was presented in perfect lighting. This applied not only to the stage but also to all the box seats. In Paris it was usual for the lights in the auditorium to be left on throughout the performance. That way high society women and demimondaines could show their best side. It was, of course, the done thing never to be seen in the same design twice.

The best couture clients, however, were the actresses. Not only did they have the most lavish stage costumes designed for themselves, they also displayed amazing glamour in their private lives, which anyway tended to be more or less public. At the forefront was **Sarah Bernhardt** (1844–1923), who was the biggest star and unforgettable in her roles as Tosca, Joan of Arc, and Phaedra. In 1900 the young Paul Poiret designed the costume for her first breeches part in *L'Aiglon*. The youthful daredevil made a few disparaging remarks about the celebrated actress, who was then in her mid-50s and more fashion-conscious than ever. Poiret paid for it by losing his assistant position with star couturier Jacques Doucet. For Sarah Bernhardt the part was another resounding success. Even after having a leg amputated she remained the favorite client of the big fashion houses – despite her habit of having exclusive designs altered by her maid to suit her own taste.

The other great tragedienne of the age, **Eleonora Duse** (1859–1924), showed unquestioning loyalty. She always wore Worth, and when once his design was not to her taste, she wrote a long letter of apology for rejecting the robe, using the word "unfortunately" at least 50 times.

Fashion played a prominent part in the theater not only in Paris but in many other world metropolises. When in 1900 *Harper's Bazaar* nominated **Elsie de Wolfe** (1865–1950) the best-dressed woman on the American stage, many derided the fact that it was only her extravagant clothes that made her poor acting just about bearable. On stage, as in life, she was only ever seen in the latest designs by Doucet, Worth, or Paquin, and she soon realized where her real talents lay. She switched to interior design and with her love of light colors and everything practical she revolutionized the stuffy furnishings of the Victorian era. She was considered a guru of good taste on both sides of the Atlantic.

In Berlin an actress stood no chance of procuring an engagement unless she possessed countless dresses, because as part of her duties she was responsible for her own stage costumes. Just as everywhere else, Berliners most wanted to see the designs of the great Parisian couturiers, and so an actress had no choice but to run up debts and look out for extra sources of income. Not surprisingly, the profession soon fell into disrepute. It was only when a new theater bill was passed in 1919 that actresses were liberated from their couture obligations. From then on theater managers had to supply stage costumes. The public still expected to see stars in all their glory offstage, however, and favorite stars such as Fritzi Massari, **Claire Waldoff** (1884–1957), and Asta Nielsen obliged.

Dancers also had great influence on women's clothes and appearance, and it was due to them that fashion really changed. **Isadora Duncan** (1878–1927) and **Mata Hari** (1876–1917) were among the first who were brave enough to appear on stage almost naked, wrapped only in a veil. Couturiers such as Paul Poiret encouraged these appearances, which certainly liberated the body from the corset.

Isadora Duncan dared to give such public performances and dance unlaced and barefoot long before anyone else. The Americans regarded this as scandalous. She made her name only when she toured Europe with the troupe of the great American dancer Lois Fuller. Her solo performances began in Budapest, but it was in Berlin that she was most successful. After triumphant tours around the world and many passionate love affairs "Isadorable," as she was known, was dealt some hard blows by fate. Both her children drowned in the Seine, a third was stillborn, and her rich partner and lover left her. Her death is also legendary: on a drive through Nice in 1927 Isadora's long fringed shawl was caught in the spoked wheel of a Bugatti convertible and the great dancer's neck was broken.

Two women – one love

Edith Wharton (1862–1937) might be called a quiet revolutionary. The beautiful daughter of a prominent New York family had the courage to write books. This was simply not done in the circles in which she moved, and yet she did it successfully. She was the first woman to win the Pulitzer Prize, for her novel *The Age of Innocence*, which Martin Scorsese made into a film in 1993. Her sensitive description of the sheltered, circumscribed life of rich women around the turn of the century inspired her readers to break out and be themselves – and here too Edith Wharton advised them. She is considered to be the inventor of interior design, a sphere which was later taken up by many women, including Elsie de Wolfe. Wharton's book *The Decoration of Houses*, first published in 1897, is still constantly being reprinted.

Rita de Acosta Lydig (1879–1929) recognized the importance of a woman's home, designed according to her own personal taste. The Spaniard born in New York was one of the most beautiful and elegant women of her time and a much sought-after hostess.

The paths of the capricious Rita and the intellectual Edith first crossed in New York, and after 1908 in Paris, where both had moved. For some time they shared the favors of the diplomat and aesthete Walter Berry, who had been Edith's love for two decades. It was even more painful to Edith that Rita tried to compete with her as a writer. Rita's book *Tragic Mansions* was published in 1927, at a time when her glamorous life had turned into tragedy. Ill, abandoned by all her great lovers, and financially ruined, beautiful Rita – who had loved nothing more than the shoes she had made to measure (now in the Museum of Modern Art, New York) – devoted her remaining years to charity and the suffragettes' fight for emancipation.

Edith Wharton (*above*) remained successful throughout her life. She lived in various houses, finally on the Côte d'Azur surrounded by good friends. She is buried in a cemetery near Versailles next to her lifelong friend Walter Berry.

1910–1919

The liberated body

1910–1919

Nothing was quite the same after the first performance of the Ballets Russes in Paris. Subdued colors and delicate pastel shades, ladylike reserve and youthful modesty were gone for ever, swept away by a whirlwind of movement, color, and intoxicating splendor. Dancers such as Isadora Duncan, Mata Hari, Lois Fuller, Ida Rubinstein, and Cléo de Mérode had of course fired their audiences with enthusiasm and influenced couturiers, in particular Paul Poiret, before. But how could their scarcely veiled nudity stand comparison with the fantastic costumes of the Ballets Russes?

Fashion and society photographer Cecil Beaton, who was still a child when the Ballets Russes toured Europe in triumph in 1910, always remembered the explosion of color that he saw on the Paris stage. "A new world opened up for me," he said. "I had never seen anything as exciting as that before."

Previous page:
This suit with wide pleated pant legs offered unlimited freedom. A clever touch, the legs could be unbuttoned.

Opposite:
A poster advertising the ballet *Sheherazade*, with Vera Fokina and Michail Fokine. With its opulent costumes and magnificent sets, the Ballets Russes shaped the taste of the whole decade.

Right:
Cosmetics queen Helena Rubinstein never forgot the lesson she learned from performances of the Ballets Russes: more is more, even when it involves real jewelry. Within a few years she had established a worldwide beauty empire which not only sold make-up and cosmetics, but also offered customers beauty treatments in its own salons. This was an innovation; up until then professional hair and nail care had been the preserve of experts.

Helena Rubinstein, founder of the first international cosmetics company, was so electrified by the rich purple and gold tones that she changed all her furnishings. As soon as she got home, she ripped the white brocade curtains off her drawing-room windows and ordered new ones "in those brilliant colors with which I had just fallen in love."

All Paris fell under the spell of this visual display of pyrotechnics. It seemed as if the brilliant impresario Sergei Diaghilev was not only in charge of the décor and costumes of the Russian ballet, but also of fashion and make-up – in fact of the whole lifestyle of a decadent Parisian society. "Étonnez-moi," (Surprise me)

he demanded of his colleagues, and like him the whole of Paris was astounded by the sets and costumes created by artists such as Léon Bakst and Alexander Benoits.

Innovative music and dancers such as Anna Pavlova and Vaslav Nijinsky did, of course, contribute to the overwhelming success of the Ballets Russes. But it was the whole exotic-baroque work of art that cast a spell on the European élite and made fashionable society turn to the fine arts. Women, in particular, became infected by this Oriental fever. Now that women had been liberated from the corset, it was as if just one spark of color was needed to free them from restricting conventions too. Total liberation released itself in opulence and luxury. Fashion had only just said good-bye to the ornate style of the *belle époque* and advertised a new simplicity, yet now it offered

seductive, exotic glamour. Paul Poiret still set the tone, and his influence dominated until World War I. He dictated that plumed and beaded turbans go with pantaloons and fur-trimmed tunics. Even though his harem ladies went barefoot, they still had their underwear trimmed with fur; that much they owed to their spiritual homeland, Russia.

Isadora Duncan, whose loose, flowing robes had inspired Poiret to his revolutionary La Vague line, now privately wanted to wrap herself in rich, colorful Poiret designs too. She aimed to surprise and seduce the unique Nijinsky at Poiret's famous "Thousand and Second Night" ball. The much sought-after genius failed even to turn up, however, and so her ambitious plan to create a new divine dancer failed.

There was a great sense of freedom and liberation in artistic and creative circles. The décolletage had

Above:
Golf and archery were among the first sports to be taken up by women. This was perhaps because they could be played in demure long skirts and allowed sports enthusiasts to remain neat and tidy.

Right:
Elegant ladies at a race meeting in Auteuil, looking noticeably more relaxed than they had a decade earlier and obviously not wearing tight, restricting corsets.

replaced the high, stiff collar, even during the day. Although it was no more than a modest V-neck, it was deep enough for the Church to send out warnings of a devastating decline in moral standards. Indeed, daring ladies went as far as to put on so much make-up that they looked like courtesans. In fact it was considered chic to mix with the elegant demimonde. Anyway, what was the difference between an unrestrained dancer, a kept woman, and a spoilt wife? In truth the last could learn a lot from the others in matters of seduction – and she certainly did. As a result, one could no longer definitely say which social class a person belonged to. An addiction to pleasure linked everyone together.

While the Eastern trend flourished in the hothouse climate of sensuously perfumed boudoirs, a new fashion was developing in the fresh air of smart spas, and this took women further than merely to the next bazaar. It took account of women's growing enthusiasm for sport. How could women cycle, play golf or tennis, or go riding in restricting suits with narrow-cut jackets and tight ankle-length skirts? Culottes and women's pants did already exist, but were considered inappropriate and so were hidden under large skirts. They were also usually made of rough fabrics. Then a modest milliner who knew that a free spirit could develop only in a free body came up with the brilliantly simple idea of using soft, smooth materials for her clothes. Gabrielle Chanel introduced her jersey sportswear in Deauville in 1913. Her designs were cut wider and looser than suits of the time, and soft material allowed greater freedom of movement. Before then jersey

had been used only for underwear. Chanel had the courage to base her whole couture career on this nondescript fabric.

At the same time another woman developed a fashion style that allowed the body to move freely. In contrast to Chanel, however, who was more of a practical thinker, Madeleine Vionnet's greatest concern was beauty. Had the ancient Greeks not known that a noble body looked best when draped in noble garments? Well, surely the generation of women who, thanks to sports and gymnastics, could do without the corset, deserved to be lifted into the realms of classical beauty? To achieve this, Vionnet developed cutting techniques which today are still regarded as the highest art form. When she opened her own fashion house in 1912, women had not yet come to appreciate the ingenuity of her simple designs. It was the war that opened their eyes.

A jersey sports suit designed by Gabrielle Chanel. Its elasticity made it ideal for ice-skating.

World War I

The war diverted most women's thoughts from fashion, forcing them into working clothes, uniforms, and mourning. In England people remembered a day in 1910 which went down in the annals as "black Ascot." In memory of Edward VII, who had just died and certainly would not have wanted the races canceled, all visitors to the course appeared in elegant black. It was the fashion event of the decade. Bearing this example in mind, widowed ladies of society tried to do justice to the demands of mourning during wartime. Fashion magazines such as *Le Style parisien* carried designs for appropriate widow's clothes: always high at the neck, black, and loose, with full skirts and veiled hats. The longer the war went on and the more victims it claimed, however, the more clothing rules were relaxed. Only a few women wore black for a whole year or limited their jewelry to black jet. Gray and even mauve were soon considered just as proper, and widows began to wear diamonds and pearls when they went out.

Dress code at the theater became much more relaxed. Elegant evening dresses were still allowed but were no longer "recommended." Unfortunately there were not many performances to draw audiences into the theater. One of the few exceptions was Diaghilev's ballet *Parade*, for which Picasso designed the costumes and sets. It was thought so scandalous that Parisians flocked back to the Ballets Russes. Of course most people had other worries and were scarcely attracted to the theater by the slogan advertising a "break from the war."

While men were at the front, women did many of their jobs. They went into farming and building, worked in munitions factories, became drivers and conductresses on buses and trains, and even ran many businesses. They also went into military service, some being sent to the front, and not only as nurses. Women gradually became accustomed to wearing uniform.

The austere military style was soon reflected in fashion. Whereas before the war coats had normally been shorter than skirts and gave a glimpse of the seductive clothes beneath, they now resembled uniforms and covered everything. Sumptuous shawl collars with flattering fur trimming gave way to severe lapels. Clothes simply became more functional. The narrow, straight skirt was replaced by a calf-length pleated skirt. Hats became smaller and were worn with no decoration. Jewelry was more or less taboo.

In Britain a "dress for all occasions" was launched. This could supposedly be worn indoors and out, from morning till evening, and even in bed at night. Loosely cut and made of cheap, washable material, it was fastened with buckles and had no hooks and eyes. It failed to catch on even in Britain, let alone anywhere else. Clothes did become simpler, not as a result of

War jewelry: a bird brooch of black jet beads.

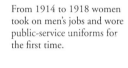

From 1914 to 1918 women took on men's jobs and wore public-service uniforms for the first time.

Opposite:
"Black day" at Ascot. Following the death of Edward VII, a great racing enthusiast, all visitors wore black in his memory. This made it a fashion event of great significance.

Left to right:
A Berlin postwoman and rail conductress, and an English postwoman. All three photographs date from World War I. The German uniforms appear much stricter than their English counterparts, and all three required the appropriate headgear.

any decree but because working women found that uniforms and working clothes were practical and had a certain appeal: they made women look competent and serious.

Fashionable clothes were still created and sold, but it did not seem right to appear in them on the street. A skirt and pullover seemed more appropriate. There was a certain nostalgia for wide skirts, which reminded wearers of the "good old days." People did not specially economize on textile materials during the war, but concessions had to be made with regard to quality.

In 1915 there was a short period of frivolity, when the so-called war crinoline was introduced. This was a mid-calf skirt made of abundant material and worn over several petticoats, reminiscent of the 19th-century crinoline. The new version was ridiculed in the same way as the outdated hooped skirt, and two years later it vanished from the scene. The length was retained for practical reasons, but the shape of skirts became straight again.

Many couture houses, including Poiret and Vionnet, closed during the war. Chanel, on the other hand, did very well with her jersey suits, which suited the times perfectly. After Deauville she opened a boutique in Biarritz, and refugees

from Paris, who arrived at the seaside resorts "with nothing," queued for the modest new outfits, which were worn without any jewelry or decoration.

For the first time German fashion had to get by without Paris models, and it stood up quite well. Berlin clothing manufacturers and dressmakers gained in skill and confidence. In 1916 they founded the Association of the German Fashion Industry, which was concerned with the creative rather than the commercial aspects of fashion. Their aim was to compete with Paris as the fashion capital of the world. This even led to a boycott of French fashion goods in 1923. Just a year later, however, Berlin fashion designers were returning to Paris in search of inspiration.

Above and far right:
Two illustrations from around 1915 documenting the existence of the so-called war crinoline. It was a preposterous waste of material during wartime.

An invitation to Chanel's first fashion show in the Rue Cambon, in Paris.

After the war

Many women did not want to give up the freedoms which the war had forced on them. Morals had changed, and so had clothes: both had become looser. The shorter dress that now revealed the ankles was more popular than pants, which reminded wearers of hard work and privations. Women wanted to enjoy themselves. They wanted to dance, and they could move best in the simplest dress, cut straight from top to bottom like a tube. This design also had the advantage of being something that every woman could copy and run up on her sewing machine at home.

The fashion industry needed new ideas and new customers. The nobility and upper middle class were on the decline. The nouveau riche and dollar-laden Americans ruled the Paris scene, together with actors, artists, writers, and the demimonde, who had also ridden on the fashion merry-go-round. These colorful people demanded fashions that picked up the rhythm of the approaching jazz age.

Three significant fashion houses were founded in 1919. Chanel set up in the Rue Cambon in Paris, where her empire is still to be found today. Edward Molyneux established himself in the Rue Royale, and his British understatement did well with the aristocracy and old-established families, especially during the forthcoming années folles (crazy years). Jean Patou, who had been active in various branches of the fashion industry since 1907, at last set up on his own. His comfortable sportswear bore the distinctive feature of his monogram and was particularly successful.

The first truly international artists' colony in Paris was formed in Montparnasse after the war. This picture was taken during the first exhibition of a center for Scandinavian art set up by Lena Börjeson (*on the right*).

Milestones in fashion:
Pants

Opposite:
Young women displaying their backless beach outfits on the promenade at Thorpe Bay, on the southeastern coast of England. They attracted all the attention with their comfortable, wide pants, which were much more suitable for the seaside than other day-trippers' outfits.

Below, left to right:
Amelia Bloomer wearing the bloomers, or Turkish pants, which she introduced in 1851; they were worn underneath a skirt.
A slightly modernized version of bloomers, which proved ideal for cycling.
The first appearance of a daring young Parisian in a pantsuit – what a scandal!

At the beginning of the 20th century attempts had been made to make it acceptable for women to wear pants, and these were not confined to sporty bloomers for cyclists. From 1900 onward a few adventurous young women dared to be seen on the boulevard in pantsuits, though they were frequently mocked and rejected by their own sex.

During World War I it became a matter of course for women to wear pants, as otherwise they could hardly have fulfilled their new tasks. This was not really a question of fashion. Nevertheless, quite a few women realized that they could look fetching in pants. Overalls were particularly popular, especially as they were reminiscent of the admired pilots' uniform. Women's pants were fine for work, but they remained taboo on festive occasions. The progress of pants kept pace with that of women's emancipation: whenever pants were acceptable for women great progress was made, but when a new period of femininity was celebrated everything slowed down.

Immediately after World War I the time had come to embrace the tuxedo as an acceptable form of evening wear for women. Yet in 1966 Yves Saint Laurent caused a scandal with his famous new version of a lady's tuxedo. His rich clients were barred from the best restaurants and hotels, unless they took their pants off and kept their jackets on – the shortest minis were preferable to long pants! In 1931 the mayor of Paris asked Marlene Dietrich to leave the city because she dared to wear a man's suit in public. By then loosely cut pants had already caused a stir both as leisurewear and as evening pyjama suits. But many more years passed before pants became socially acceptable. It was the end of the 20th century before it became acceptable for women of all social classes to wear pantsuits.

Riding breeches worn confidently by actress Anita Page, 1936.

Wide English riding breeches, 1919.

When jogging was still called running: a shorts suit for the sporty woman, 1925.

Playful starlet Joan Blondell in a beach suit, 1925.

Today this would be a town suit: an elegant beach costume, 1939.

Leisurewear with culottes for sunny days at the seaside, 1926.

Loose pajama outfit by Poiret for a cozy evening in, 1925.

Ready for the hunt in a sporty costume with a divided skirt, c. 1920s.

Aristocrats also wear rolled-up jeans: Princess Alexandra of Kent, 1954.

Neat and practical in 1950s leisurewear: shorts.

Bermuda shorts, 1965, for boyish figures only.

The successful singing duo, Sonny and Cher, in hippie times.

The pantsuit became socially acceptable in the 1930s.

Hot pants and platform soles – 1970s kitsch.

Knickerbockers for the landed gentry – for him and for her, 1901.

Shorts instead of bloomers – now cycling is real fun, 1947.

All in check – young and confident in trousers with flaired legs, 1975.

Pantsuit with flared pants in matching Charlie Chaplin print, 1972.

Comeback: knickerbockers in the city, 1980.

Off on vacation: neatly dressed and easygoing, 1945.

Baby-doll conquers Paris and shows her legs, 1968.

Space age with daisies: with love from flower power, 1967.

Frivolous instead of casual: short harem pants with high heels and black tights, 1978.

Jeans outfit with flaired legs and buttons all the way up to the thighs, 1971.

Edward Molyneux (1891–1974)

Opposite:
Typical Molyneux: a narrow evening sheath dress which gently accentuates the figure, complemented by a bolero cut as correctly as a jacket.

Below:
Molyneux showed British understatement in his fashions. Even his jaunty flapper dresses had a distinguished look. The material was somewhat firmer, the cut rather more demure and the pattern stronger than in most similar fashions of the time.

Captain Molyneux, as he was known to everyone, may have been the only Irishman among the couturiers. Originally he had wanted to become a painter, but Lucile – Lady Duff Gordon, a successful fashion designer of the *belle époque* – discovered his talent for clothes and sent him to New York to work as a designer in her American branch. She later moved him to her branch in Paris. Molyneux set up on his own at the end of World War I. A single commission made him famous overnight: Princess Marina of Greece ordered a bridal gown and fashion trousseau for her marriage to the Duke of Kent. This sent Europe's top nobility streaming into his salon, and Molyneux knew how to dress his customers in an aristocratic manner. He offered romantic evening gowns with high waists in delicate materials and colors, reminiscent of the Empire style as well as conservative day outfits in the English style of tailored suits.

Molyneux was praised for his perfect cut and good taste. Even his most lavish evening dresses had a certain severity and simplicity which made them appear up to date. His day outfits were held in even higher regard. He often complemented them with a three-quarter-length coat, which was an innovation. Those who traveled a great deal, such as aristocrats and movie stars, were especially keen to be dressed by the Captain, since he knew how to put together a versatile, practical, yet extremely elegant wardrobe.

Molyneux also designed lingerie, hats, and perfumes, including a fragrance called Numéro Cinq in 1926, even though Chanel No. 5 was already in existence. In the 1920s he opened several branches in the south of France, as well as one in London, and he was also involved in two nightclubs together with Elsa Maxwell, the most famous gossip of the day.

Captain Molyneux returned to London in 1939, but went back to Paris after World War II. He closed his couture house in 1950.

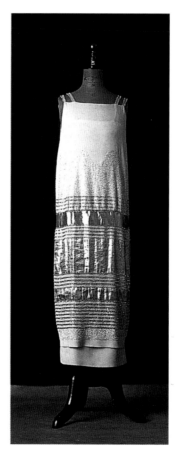

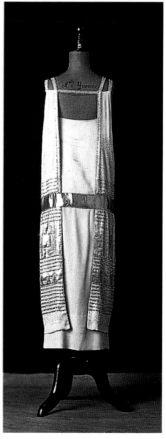

Jean Patou (1880–1936)

After working in various branches of the fashion industry since 1907, Jean Patou set up on his own at the end of World War I. He was successful with folkloric embroideries, Art Nouveau designs in strong colors, and above all with the sporty outfits that bore his monogram.

He became famous for the clothes he made for the tennis idol Suzanne Lenglen. For her he designed pleated skirts of white silk and straight white cardigans, as well as the famous headband, which became an inimitable part of the fashionable world of tennis.

Patou certainly did not succeed at the first attempt. In the end two trends in art – Art Deco and Cubism – led him to his own style, which incorporated their strong lines, clear colors, and geometric shapes. Most particularly it was the discovery of beige as a basic color which gave his collection its character. His strong patterns, colorful embroidery, and elegant monogram were all important. In addition he brought in a new fashionable color every season, such as "Patou blue" or "dark dahlia."

Patou worked closely with textile manufacturer Bianchini-Férier in order to create his own patterned materials. He was also very concerned about the way in which the material fell, since he wanted to produce simple, softly flowing garments, with nothing heavy or elaborate about them. This concern predestined him to become the first real designer of sportswear, for which he combined an austere silhouette and comfortable cut.

Below left:
French tennis champion Suzanne Lenglen played her first match in the United States on October 6, 1926. The greatest woman player of her time always wore Patou designs.

Below right:
Jean Patou, the master of fashionable sportswear, at a tennis tournament in 1926.

Opposite:
Two light creations of organza with lace and velvet ribbons, by Jean Patou. On the right, by contrast, is a severe design with pleated insets and matching shoes by Jacques Doucet. All three have a low waist, as was fashionable in 1924. This illustration by Christopher Demiston was for the lifestyle magazine *Art, Goût, Beauté.*

FRAICHEUR. — *Robe d'organdi blanc garni de rubans bleu et bouquet multicolore.*

Création Jean Patou

Robe d'organdi rose garni de rubans de velours du même ton.

Création Jean Patou

Robe de crêpe de Chine rubis plissée garnie blanc.

Création Doucet

Madeleine Vionnet: mistress of the bias cut

Madeleine Vionnet's visions took as long to become accepted as did pants for women, yet they play an extremely important part in the history of fashion. Without those visions there would have been no Hollywood glamour with off-the-shoulder dresses that swirled around the body as if they were made of flowing silk. Madeleine Vionnet invented the bias cut and elaborate draping. These remain unsurpassed to this day. Designer Azzedine Alaïa, himself an artistic dressmaker of the highest quality, took months to discover Vionnet's cutting secrets. He was the only one to succeed in deciphering an ivory-colored evening dress of 1935. Now one can admire the dress, wrapped around a dummy in the Museum of Fashion and Textiles in Paris. The perfect fit of this marvel was achieved by its having a single seam – the highest of all aims for Madeleine Vionnet. Her art has simply not been equaled to this day.

It must have been a love of geometry that enabled Vionnet to develop the most ingenious cuts from basic shapes such as triangles and rectangles. Having been born into impoverished circumstances in 1876, Vionnet had to leave school at the age of 12 – despite her talent for mathematics. She was apprenticed to a seamstress, worked for a time in Paris, and when she was 16 went to England. There she earned a living as a laundrywoman.

At the age of 20, after a brief marriage and the death of her small daughter, Vionnet managed the studio of London clothes manufacturer Kate O'Reilly. In 1900 she returned to Paris and started work for

Callot Sœurs, one of the most renowned couture houses. She became the right hand of Marie Callot Gerber, the oldest of the three sisters and artistic director of the business. Vionnet was eternally grateful to her teacher and mentor: "I learned from her how to make a Rolls-Royce; without her I would have produced Fords."

In 1907 Jacques Doucet entrusted her with the task of rejuvenating his couture. Vionnet did this by banning corsets and shortening hems. This was not to the liking of either the customers or the sales assistants, who rebelled against the new creative force. This meant that it was time for Vionnet to set up on her own, which she did in 1912. Her business closed during World War I, and it was only after 1918 that her inexorable rise began.

Madeleine Vionnet approached the female body like a doctor, always preserving its unscathed beauty. She sewed her ingenious seams like a surgeon, allowing the dress to follow the figure. This was a revolutionary idea, for up until then it had been the other way around: the body had to fit the current fashion. Vionnet worked like a sculptor in order to achieve her aims. Instead of drawing them, she created her designs on a miniature wooden model, which allowed

her to drape the material around the whole body and see how it best suited the body's curves. This helped her develop sinuous folds and the famous bias cut, which up to that time had been used for collars but never for a whole dress.

It was not easy, however, to put on a Vionnet dress. Her cut was so unusual that many customers found it very difficult to get into the dress and went to the designer to ask for instructions. This explains why many heiresses simply

Left:
Madeleine Vionnet, who developed all her designs on a wooden doll. As a mathematician she never forgot that a body has three dimensions and she never relied on paper.

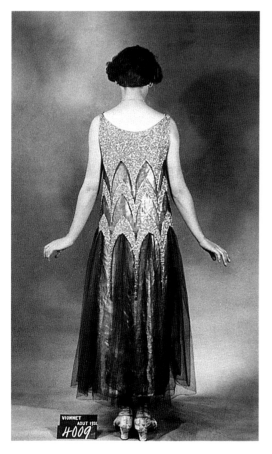

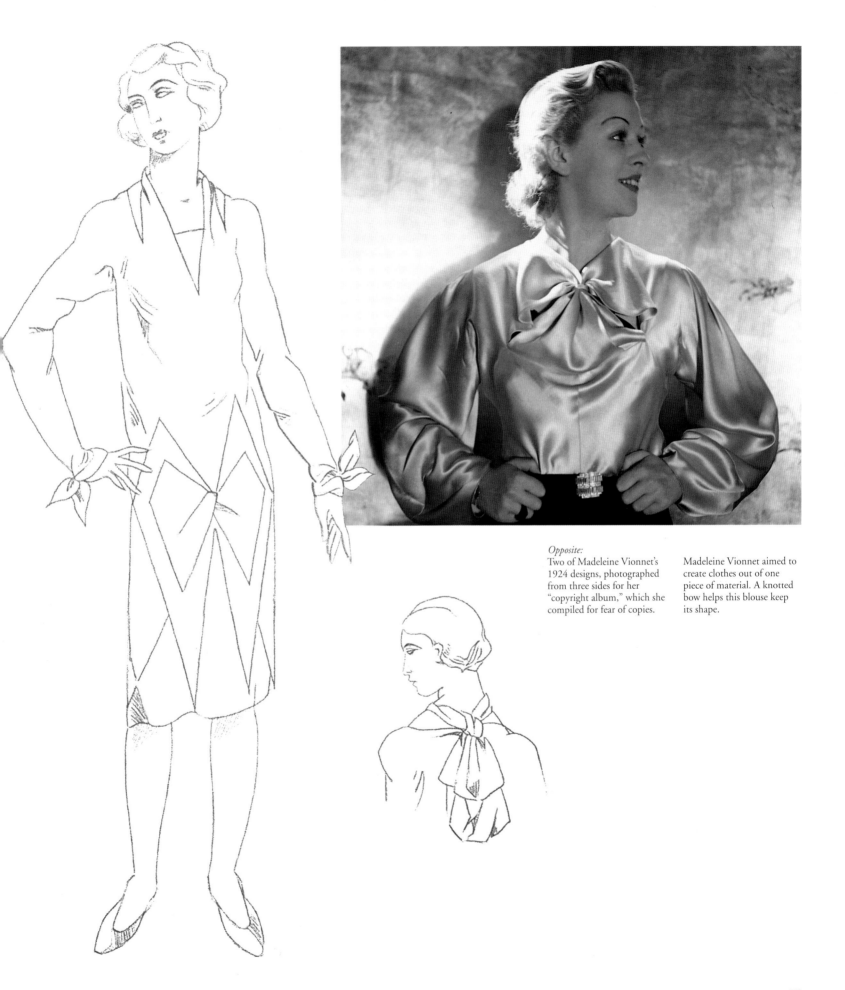

Opposite:
Two of Madeleine Vionnet's 1924 designs, photographed from three sides for her "copyright album," which she compiled for fear of copies.

Madeleine Vionnet aimed to create clothes out of one piece of material. A knotted bow helps this blouse keep its shape.

did not know what to do with Vionnet's expensive gowns.

The second important ingredient in Vionnet's marvelous creations was the material. Only soft materials could accommodate the body's movements, and so she exclusively used silk crêpe, mousseline, velvet, and satin. She had fabrics produced two yards wider than was usual, so that she could cut them on the bias. In 1918 Vionnet's suppliers, Bianchini-Férier, developed their own material specially for her. Rosalba crêpe, made of silk and acetate, was one of the first synthetic materials.

Vionnet was not greatly interested in color. She was happy with all the different shades of white, which was why her gowns were reminiscent of ancient Greek robes. She favored embroidery or stylized roses or knots as decoration. These decorative elements also served another purpose: they gathered the material at a strategically important point without requiring a seam. Vionnet was always careful to make sure that ornamentation did not weigh a dress down. Embroidery had to go with the grain of the material so that it could follow every movement of the body. Women who were keen to dance always wanted fringe trimming, and Vionnet was the first to apply each strand of the silk fringe individually, instead of applying the fringe by the yard, so as to preserve the elasticity of the material. Her designs were intended to be more than simple clothing: they were meant to be women's companions. "When a woman smiles, her dress should smile with her," she said.

Madeleine Vionnet knew that her technique was unique and she tried to protect her designs against copies. This was why she documented each of her designs with three photographs – taken from the front, the side, and behind – and put them in a "copyright album." She filled 75 albums, and these formed the basis of the collection of the Union Française des Arts du Costume.

Justice was more important to her than rights, however. She gave her employees the sort of social welfare benefits – short breaks, paid vacation, and allowances for sickness or in an emergency – that only much later came to be required by law. She set up a canteen, a dental practice, a sick bay, and even her own travel agency, which helped arrange vacations for almost 1,000 employees. Very little is known about her private life, however. She never understood how to market herself well and, once her fashion house closed in 1939, she was almost

completely forgotten. Yet until the end of her long life she continued to take an active interest in fashion. The Museum of Fashion and Textiles in Paris would never have been founded without her generous donation of the "copyright albums" and many of her original designs, even though it opened only in 1996, 20 years after her death. Then a wider public was able to discover what experts such as Dior, Alaïa, Miyake, and Yamamoto had always known: "The art of couture has never reached a higher standard."

Compared to Coco Chanel, Madeleine Vionnet is virtually an unknown today. Perhaps this is because she produced the Rolls-Royces of couture, whereas Chanel's designs succeeded in becoming the popular Fords of fashion.

A dress from the series known as "Greek vases." The long-legged, delicate horses augment the impression of tall elegance.

From 1928 Vionnet
had all her designs
photographed in front
of a three-part mirror,
so that they were
protected against
copies and kept in her
"copyright albums."

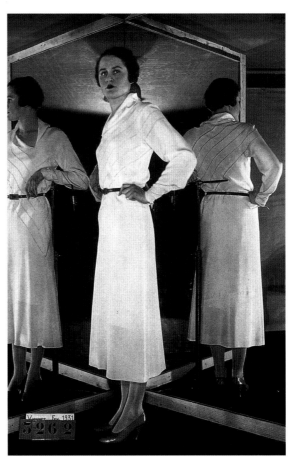

Madeleine Vionnet

No "copyright album" could stop John Galliano reviving Vionnet's ingenious bias cut. This design is from his 1998 collection for Dior.

The look of the decade

During the course of this decade women managed to personify three different ideal types: the little girl, the self-sacrificing Madonna, and the exotic vamp.

By 1910 make-up was already in general use, but the result was supposed to look as natural as possible. Helena Rubinstein's pink powder was a godsend, because it took the extreme artificiality away from faces which until then had been caked with white powder. Her competitor Elizabeth Arden opened her first salon at the same time. Soon the two queens of cosmetics were offering a growing list of new products to compete for the favors of their customers. They persuaded their high-society clientele to have regular facials. This treatment consisted of a pore-cleansing steambath, just as it does today.

During the war it was not the done thing to waste time and money on make-up. A touch of rouge on the lips, a speck of glistening Vaseline on the eyelids – that was all. Hair, which had previously been worn in pretty curls like Mary Pickford's, now had a severe parting. The men fighting at the front were supposed to know that their women had renounced all coquetry and were as modest and sensitive as Lillian Gish.

Selling beauty products to these self-sacrificing women was not easy. That is why most products suddenly claimed to be good for the user's health. Vaseline, for example, used to make eyelids and lips glisten, was called an ointment. Then as now, most people had no idea that it was a registered trademark. Because medicinal items could not be frivolous, women were more likely to decide on cosmetic surgery than on creams, lotions, and make-up. Paraffin injections for wrinkles were quite common.

After the war a line was drawn under virtue. Suddenly everyone wanted to look mysterious and dangerous. Hair was cut in a bob, eyes were rimmed with kohl, lips were painted a deep red, and accessories had to be as exotic as possible – just as Poiret had suggested with his Oriental look of 1910.

An illustration by Georges Lepape for Paul Poiret shows that the couturier anticipated the daring look of the 1920s at the beginning of the century: a bob, heavily rimmed black eyelids, sensuous red lips, and exotic accessories such as this turban. The complexion had to be even and matte; loose powder was one of the most important cosmetic products of the time.

Opposite:
Lillian Gish, the "sweet little girl," reflected the taste of the time. The silent movie star, who never really made it in talking pictures, made her stage debut at the age of five.

Idols of the decade

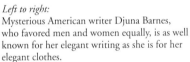

Left to right:
Mysterious American writer Djuna Barnes, who favored men and women equally, is as well known for her elegant writing as she is for her elegant clothes.
Theda Bara, an exotic, man-eating beauty with black-rimmed eyes, was the first screen star to be called a vamp.
Lillian Gish as a safe, sympathetic nurse on location for the moving melodrama *The Wind* (1928).

Opposite:
The American silent movie actress, Gloria Swanson, the pioneer of glamour.

Between 1914 and 1918 the self-sacrificing nurse was the ultimate ideal of all men and women. Red Cross nurses, in particular, were looked upon as saints. Their uniforms had been designed by the couturier Redfern. Admiration for self-denying service was so great that society women had themselves photographed in nurse's uniform or nun's habit and sent the pictures to their men at the front. Was this for reassurance, perhaps?

Stars of the silent movies came to prominence after the war. In America more than 5 million people went to the movies every day, and this love of the screen soon spread to Europe. National stage favorites were replaced by international screen idols. Loyal, self-sacrificing women such as **Lillian Gish**, portrayed in *Birth of a Nation* in 1915, gave way to the sort of self-confident man-eating vamps played by **Theda Bara**. The exotic beauty with a challenging look and small, heart-shaped mouth was regarded as the incarnation of sin. On screen, as Salomé, Madame Dubarry, and Cleopatra, she acted out all the suppressed fantasies of prudish Americans. In just five years Theda Bara played the cool sinner in 35 motion pictures, and then her time was past. Hollywood had invented a fairy-tale

past for Theda Bara, claiming that she was the child of a sheik and a princess. In reality, she was a dressmaker's daughter.

A new role model became popular – a woman who could be an angel and a devil at the same time. Her incarnation was **Gloria Swanson**, who behaved impeccably but who was not embarrassed to indulge in erotic fetishes such as satin lingerie, silk kimonos, and opulent furs. Her parts were daring and scandalous and dealt with subjects such as adultery, troilism, and the sexual liberation of women – and she played them all very elegantly.

Djuna Barnes also liked to shroud her origins and past in mystery. The gifted, good-looking American had her first poems published when she was only 18. She studied art, started a career as a journalist, and continued writing and drawing "serious" works. When she went to Paris in 1919, she was not unknown in intellectual circles. She became a friend of author James Joyce, wore the designer cast-offs of art-patron Peggy Guggenheim, and threw herself into love affairs with both men and women.

1920–1929

La garçonne

1920–1929

Jazz and the Charleston, bobbed haircuts and red lips, free love and cigarettes, birth control and short skirts, and, at the end of it all, the Great Depression. These are the things for which the Roaring Twenties are generally remembered. In reality the *années folles* (crazy years) lasted just five years, from 1924 to 1929, but perhaps people lived twice as fast in those years.

After experiencing the horrors of war, people wanted to enjoy themselves, and a need to make up for the missed years also made for undreamed-of possibilities. Technical advances such as the automobile, telephone, radio, phonograph, and various household gadgets made life easier and more pleasant. They created a belief in a better future, opening to women a multitude of new doors. Many women had stood in for their menfolk during the war, and now no one could expect them to be content to perform no more than menial tasks. They were soon doing jobs that conferred higher status and offered better pay than housework, and women decided for themselves how they wanted to spend the money they earned.

Women spent a great deal of their new money on their appearance. What was the point of it otherwise? They had just lived through a period when they knew that everything could disappear overnight, so the motto now was to "live for today" – so long as you were young and had some life in you.

The cult of youth was a 1920s invention, and the 1960s phenomenon was simply a revival. Those who wanted to belong had to be reckless and carefree. They lived life in the fast lane, leaving the old horse-drawn carriages behind. They used alcohol as fuel, deadening hunger pains and feelings of guilt with nicotine and opium, dancing until they dropped. There was no better way to slim, and the modern young woman of the 1920s had to be slim.

They were known as *garçonnes* (mannish girls), which came from the novel *La Garçonne* by Victor Margueritte, published in 1922. The book was censored as being

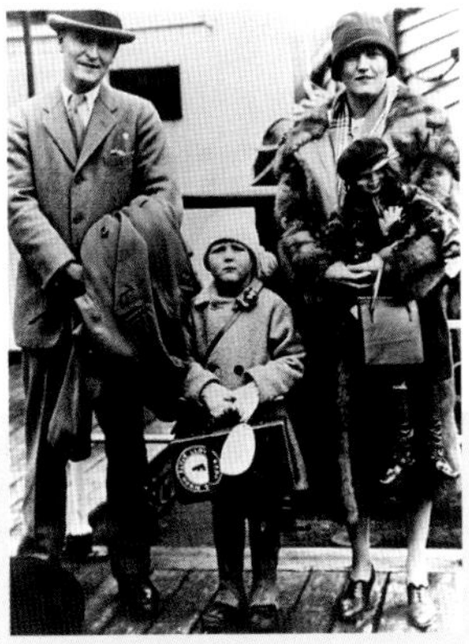

The Fitzgeralds
American novelist Francis Scott Fitzgerald was the great chronicler of the Roaring Twenties, and his novels, especially *The Great Gatsby*, published in 1925, immortalized the age. He is seen here with his wife Zelda, one of the most elegant women of her time, and their daughter. The movies made of Fitzgerald's books, with their detailed décor and contemporary costumes, offer a vivid impression of the age.

Previous page:
Hollywood star Gloria Swanson photographed by Edward Steichen, one of the greatest fashion and portrait photographers of his time.

Opposite:
The shadow of war had passed. It was time to dance, and the Charleston was the latest thing.

It became fashionable for women to apply lipstick in public, something which was unthinkable in earlier times. Cloche hats and strap shoes, to complement the bobbed haircut, deep red lips, and black-rimmed eyes, were considered chic.

Many working women looked as if they spent all day sitting at their make-up table. They invested their salaries in their appearance, in order to compete with others for that scarce commodity – men.

pornographic, since it described women who wore their hair short, made careers for themselves, wore men's clothes, and indulged in free love. It became an under-the-counter bestseller, however, and for many years the heroine served as a model of the androgynous young woman who made a principle of preferring to do things that were scandalous or forbidden.

If she had not lived like this, she would not have had fun. There were about three women to every man, and in some towns the ratio was as high as four to one. In this situation who could still afford to dream of being looked after as a devoted wife and mother? It was surely better to play the sort of man-eating vamp who was causing such a sensation in the movie theater. So young women started to make themselves up as if they were all stars of the silver screen.

The boyish young woman of the time had few clear sexual characteristics. Her hair had been cut short, but where had her bust, stomach, and bottom

disappeared to? Of course exercise, diets, and health cures were part of her routine, and the new elastic girdle flattened parts of the figure that the earlier corset had emphasized. Nevertheless, not every one of yesterday's matrons could become today's flapper. The solution to the puzzle is simple: age, along with inflation, starvation, unemployment, and political unrest, has been airbrushed out of the picture of the 1920s that has traditionally been handed down. What remains is the radiance of privileged youth, a class of young people who were able to turn a short age of economic and cultural wealth into an endless party.

There was a terrible sense of insecurity at the beginning of the 1920s, and this was the case in fashion too. For practical reasons skirts remained as short as they had been during the early years of the war. Then the couturiers had their say. They wanted to turn working girls into ladies again, and this

Opposite:
Hollywood star Joan Crawford modeling a typical flapper dress.

Boxing was a fashionable
sport and for women
fashion was sport. Boxing
matches became social
occasions to which women
wore the most elegant and
feminine of styles. This
contemporary illustration for
the then leading lifestyle
magazine *Art, Goût, Beauté*
shows designs by some of the
biggest names. Doeuillet's
love of pink shades can be
seen in his Phi-Phi dress
(*far left*) and in Mascotte, the
Oriental-looking three-piece
ensemble with matching
parasol (*fourth figure from
right*). Doucet is represented
three times, his loose dresses
printed with delicate
geometric designs are easy to
recognize (*second from left
and center background*).
Jeanne Hallée adorned her
olive-green dress with gold
lace (*third figure from right*)
and two navy blue outfits
with jaunty check peeping
through (*center foreground*).
Madeleine et Madeleine's
simple and uncluttered
design is in a harlequin style
(*far right*).

The short flapper dress demanded a boyish figure, helped by the appropriate underwear, such as the bandeau brassiere, which flattened the bust (*far right*). Low-cut backs led to the first backless brassieres (*above*).

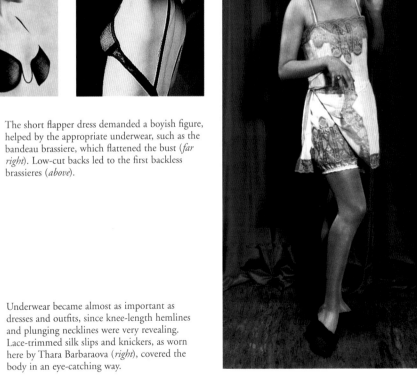

Underwear became almost as important as dresses and outfits, since knee-length hemlines and plunging necklines were very revealing. Lace-trimmed silk slips and knickers, as worn here by Thara Barbaraova (*right*), covered the body in an eye-catching way.

Opposite:
Light-colored silk stockings and strap shoes with solid baroque heels were essential accessories for dancing. They are modeled here by New York stage star Varda.

meant long skirts. Hemlines did not quite fall back to the floor, but down to the ankles. Shortly afterward they went up again, as calf-length, sack-like gowns came in. They had a belt or sash at the hips, and the top fell like a blouson over the low waist. This made for a dress that was comfortable but not very flattering. By 1925 the hem was just below the knee, and two years later it rose above the knee for the first time. This created the line that we normally associate with the 1920s: a simple top held up by two spaghetti straps, worn of course by a sweet young flapper.

For the first time in the history of fashion evening dresses were as short as daywear. It took a great deal of imagination to conjure a spectacular gown out of such a small amount of material. The answer was the same then as it is now: a suggestion of nudity. Transparent materials were used, trimmed at strategic points with glass beads or silk fringes, which emphasized what they concealed. Legs were

in light-colored stockings, which looked like a second skin, only prettier. The stockings were made of silk or rayon, as the newly developed artificial silk was called. There was a lot of bare skin to be seen, since necklines plunged almost to the waist both at the front and the back, to reveal – nothing at all.

One cannot help but wonder what was worn underneath. A product description of 1926 describes appropriate underwear as follows: "cream cotton combination of bust-flattener brassiere and corset with adjustable straps, back-stitched front panel, elasticized side and back panels, side fastenings with hooks and bars and four adjustable garters, along with a lace-trimmed crêpe-de-Chine slip."

Those without a large bust to flatten wore low-cut combinations made of silk or rayon. Stockings, blouses, and day dresses were all made of the new artificial silk, which was not expensive and made life easier by being washable.

Flappers could dance the night away without a care in the world: their complete evening outfit weighed practically nothing. It is impossible to gauge how much this liberation from heavy clothing contributed to the emancipation of women.

Because dresses were so flimsy, coats had to be all the more opulent to keep out the cold. They were draped around the body like a heavy kimono, and those with style held them closed with one hand, though coats usually had a single large button for this purpose. The shawl collar and wide cuffs, if not the whole coat, were often made of long-haired fur.

The upper classes mocked the fact that every little shop girl wore fur. Clearly they had not yet noticed that a salesclerk could have great career prospects. After all, she could become a Hollywood star, like Greta Garbo, or catch wealthy admirers, like Coco Chanel.

When it came to accessories, a shocking effect was more important than value. It was for this reason that long cigarette-holders were so popular: they could be held so provocatively and looked so lascivious. Strings of pearls were also still fashionable, and there was no need whatever for them to be genuine. Cigarette cases and powder compacts came in, both in the same style – extremely flat and with geometric designs. In the evening a feather boa or ostrich-plume fan added a coquettish touch.

The modern young woman needed just one eye to spy out worthwhile prey. Like any self-respecting buccaneer, she kept the other eye hidden. In the evening it might be covered by a headband, often of tulle, lavishly decorated and studded with beads. During the day the same purpose might be served by the tilted brim of a cloche hat. Small, tight-fitting hats came more and more into fashion now that hair was cut short.

Whether they were showing one eye or two, everyone wanted their eyes to be seen in the best possible light. It was the famous illustrator Erté, who had started out with Poiret, who first realized that a fine, thin arc would go best with the slim figure. He suggested that eyebrows should be carefully plucked, an idea which is regarded to this day as fundamental to any beauty treatment.

Shoes were designed for dancing. They were not cut too low and there was a buttoned strap across the instep, so that they stayed on even for the Charleston and the shimmy. The sturdy heels were slightly curved and not too high. The height of extravagance was to have dancing shoes made of the same material as one's dress.

The short, straight skirt lasted only for a few years. This was followed by flowing scarf drapes, tails, and trains, which were added to give an impression of height and elegance.

Opposite:
Warm coats, such as this luxurious design with a fur collar and embroidered sleeves, came into fashion out of necessity. Without them flappers in their flimsy dresses would have frozen to death. Poiret also designed a matching hat.

Above:
Actress Marjorie Brooks with typical 1920s accessories, a long cigarette-holder and an even longer string of pearls. Accessories were not always very practical, but all the more fashionable for that.

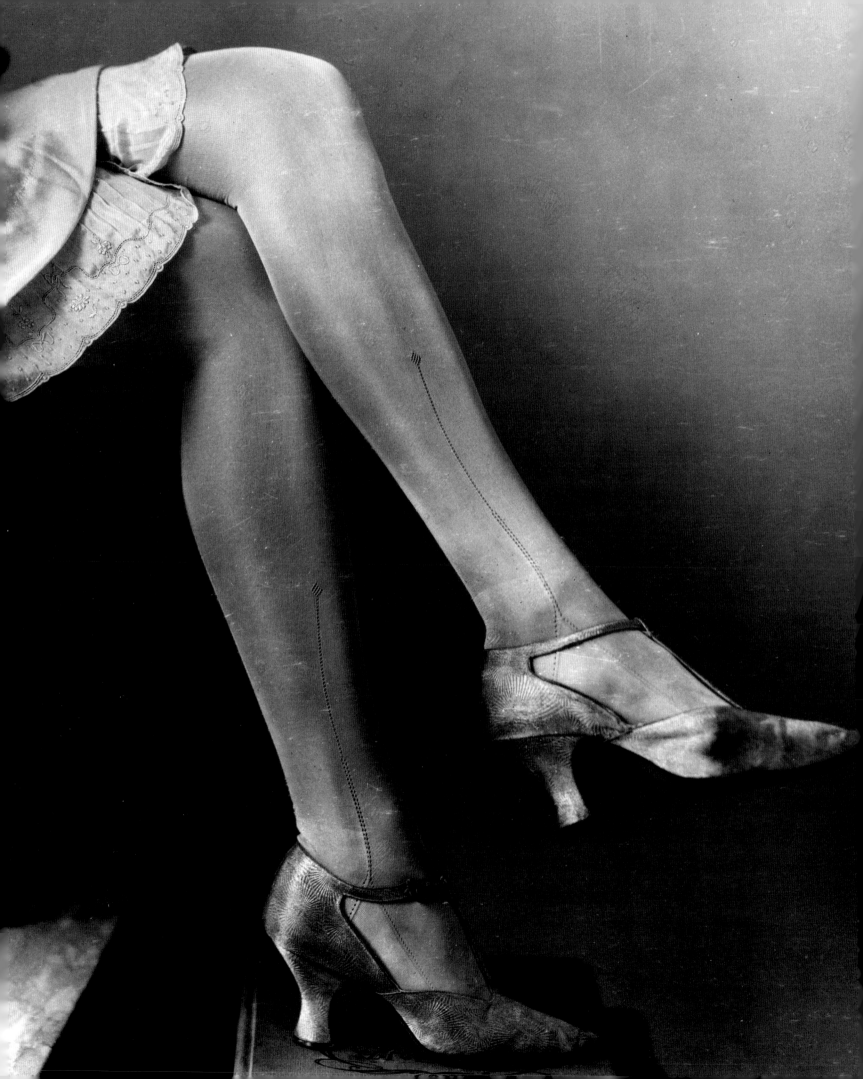

Ankle-strap shoes, Delman, 1920s.

This page and opposite:
These shoes were made for just one thing: dancing the night away. They were cut in such a way that they stayed on the feet easily. Ankle-strap shoes epitomized the Roaring Twenties, a time of wild parties and nonstop dancing.

Evening shoes, I. Miller, 1920.

Women who were or wanted to be neither flappers nor jazz babes preferred wearing longer dresses. More than anyone else, Jeanne Lanvin provided for the requirements of her couture clientele, and her *robes de style* (period dresses) were a long-running success. These dresses had a fitted top, a low waist and a bell-shaped, calf-length skirt. They were lavishly decorated, first with flowers and bows, and later they were influenced by Cubism and had geometric patterns.

Whereas evening wear was determined by a passion for dancing, day wear showed a great sporting influence. Skirts just covered the knee, and were either slightly flared or pleated. As well as light wool and cotton, jersey was used more and more. For tops, the first sweaters came into fashion.

Shirtwaist dresses, even though they were made of silk, were also part of the sporty wardrobe. In contrast to the straight flapper dress, they emphasized the waist, and women with a less boyish figure found them more flattering. Toward the end of the decade waistlines generally tended to have a more natural position, and skirts became longer. More serious times were on the way.

The Roaring Twenties ended with the terrible blow of the stock-market crash in October 1929. Money was suddenly worthless, so that the poor became even poorer and many rich people lost everything overnight.

Above:
Headgear was as narrow and elegant as the new figure and fashionable dresses. Two designs of 1925, by Jeanne Lanvin (*top*) and from the studio of Paul Poiret.

Left:
This typical flapper dress would have been worn as a slip a few years earlier. Accessories such as the fabric flower, string of pearls, and bracelets dissimulated the fact that so much bare skin was visible.

Mademoiselle Chanel

Margit J. Mayer

Coco Chanel realized that to win any war you needed a first-class uniform. She certainly wanted to win, more than anything else in the world. This will to win was shown in her exceptional face; the French writer Colette said she could see in it the determination of a little black bull from the Camargue. Chanel's war was fought for the liberation of women from their dependence on men, her chosen weapon was chic, and her strategy was pure witchcraft. She knew that you have to love a powerful adversary, even get under his skin, in order to defeat him.

Chanel liked men; her collections and numerous affairs are proof of this. She never forgot that it was men – or more precisely her first lovers – who had helped her financially to set up her first business; nor that it was men who had inspired her sensationally successful look with their wardrobes full of knits and tweed, the buttons and braiding of their uniforms, and their square perfume bottles. The jewelry she was given by men acted as a source of inspiration for her costume jewelry, and she adopted for herself the egocentric lifestyle which for ages led men to place liberty before love.

Quality, comfort, and the sort of proportions that accentuated the body's attractiveness without exposing it: these were the foundations of male elegance and Coco Chanel grasped them for herself and for all women who wanted to live like her. She instinctively understood one of the most important psychological principles of modern life: flexibility is power. She did not want to be the victim in elaborate silk flounces, but the perpetrator. She wanted clothes which fitted so well that one could forget all about them and concentrate on the world. It seems as if her jackets, whichever period they came from, found their proper purpose when they were worn unbuttoned or slung casually over the shoulder.

Chanel was not the greatest couturier of her age – this honor must surely be shared by Madeleine Vionnet and Cristobal Balenciaga; yet she was the greatest-ever creator of fashion, a small, wiry general who showed an army of designers what triumphs can be achieved with elegance that faces up to reality. Chanel's *œuvre* is her life in the form of clothes, vibrating with contradictions that were overcome by an obstinate energy. She combined masculine and feminine, toughness and charm, simplicity and luxury, dominance and submission into a paradoxical masterpiece from which modern woman smiles at us. Chanel herself was much too clever to admit this and insisted on calling her profession simply a "craft." But the truth is that Chanel was a great artist. Her best inventions – the little black dress, strings of pearls on plain knitwear, sling-backs with dark toecaps, and last but not least her own image – showed an alchemy of logic and beauty, an instantly plausible stylishness that transcended fashion.

A designer's look is always a way of exorcising impressions of childhood, a kind of creative revenge. The creations of Dior and Saint Laurent reveal the figure of a mother turned into a fairy-tale princess for one evening. In Chanel's case, cavalry officers and schoolfriends from wealthy families took on the role of the archetypal muse. What made Chanel different from the great homosexual designers and lent her style its modern sharpness was its primary drive: here was no longing for fusion with femininity, but full-blooded social climbing. One of her many witty sayings about love, life, and fashion, was: "If you were born without wings, then don't do anything to stop them growing." In her life she enjoyed the traveling rather than the arriving, and this determined the work of the girl who had no chance but still took it.

Gabrielle Chanel was born on August 19, 1883 in the small town of Saumur, in the Loire valley, the second child of an unmarried couple. Her father was a traveling street

Opposite:
Gabrielle "Coco" Chanel at work. She was rarely seen in glasses, but usually wore a lot of jewelry. Designs for the only wedding dress she ever made are pinned up in the background. Unlike other couturiers, Chanel did without the wedding dress as the highlight of every fashion show.

Mademoiselle Chanel in 1929, wearing one of her own hats. She started as a modest milliner, and became one of the greatest, most influential couturiers of the 20th century.

COSTUMES DE JERSEY

Three early designs by Gabrielle Chanel. The line is loose and clearly not supported by a corset. The skirts are so scandalously short for those days that the ankles can be seen!

vendor of somewhat dubious character. Her mother was a farmer's daughter from the Auvergne who died young, worn out by hard work and her partner's humiliating treatment. When she was 12, Gabrielle was put in an orphanage run by nuns, and at the age of 18 she was sent to a boarding school for young ladies. As a welfare case she slept in an unheated room and had to scrub the stairs after lessons. The unkindness she experienced in her deprived youth shaped her character for the rest of her life. It made her tough, and she became an expert in the art of survival. And she learned to sew.

She worked as a salesclerk in a drapers in the garrison town of Moulins, devouring cheap novels and dreaming of a career as a variety singer. Two of the childish chansons which she sang in the La Rotonde café – *Qui qu'a vu Coco* and *Ko-Ko-Ri* – were the source of the nickname she was given by the officers in the audience – Coco. At the age of 25 she met textile heir Étienne Balsan, and he invited her to become his mistress. Balsan owned a country estate near

Paris where he bred horses and entertained his aristocratic friends. Gabrielle certainly wanted to leave the provinces, and she had already learned that everything in life has its price.

She moved with Balsan to Royallieu and became an excellent horsewoman. She saw right through the song and dance caused by the male libido during the *belle époque*, which turned women into frilly pieces of candy with big bosoms and bottoms. Their status as objects was completed by their hats, which looked like vegetable stalls made of taffeta and gauze. Coco noticed that women always lost this dress-up game, and so she decided to sabotage it.

Photographs from that period show Chanel with her long hair pinned up, with bushy eyebrows, sometimes looking boyish in jodhpurs and a white blouse, at other times more like a governess in a cape and tie. Among the demimondaines in Balsan's circle of friends, who resemble puffed-up ornamental doves, she looks like a small falcon just waiting to pounce on its prey. The cleverer doves suspected that this

Chanel designed the costumes for *Le Train bleu*, produced by the great Russian impresario Diaghilev in 1924. She dressed the dancers in sporting outfits made of jersey and had them appear on stage with bare legs.

falcon was a sign of the future, and they wanted to know where Gabrielle bought her simple boaters and sporty jackets.

Chanel realized that she had something which could earn her money, something that would finish off the ponderous frou-frou elegance of the *belle époque*. This something was chic, the talent to make much out of very little. She persuaded Balsan to let her use his bachelor apartment in Paris, and she opened a hat studio. Balsan was replaced by Arthur "Boy" Capel, an English coal-mine heir and polo player, who according to Coco was the love of her life. Capel died in a car accident in 1919.

Capel had financed her move to the street in Paris which was to become associated with her name for the rest of the century: Rue Cambon. Little Gabrielle had become big businesswoman Chanel, and she never looked back. She kept just one thing from her past among doubtful women – the camellia, trademark flower of high-class tarts – and she turned it into a luxury accessory in white silk. In the summer of 1913 she opened

a boutique in Deauville, and two years later another in Biarritz. Her jersey tunics, flannel blazers, and straight skirts were the latest thing on the beach promenades. Her linen summer dresses and the first Chanel ensemble – ankle-length skirt, three-quarter-length jacket with a fabric belt, blouse teamed with the lining material – gave society women a new feeling that went straight to their heads like champagne: the feeling of youth.

It was not Chanel who liberated the female body from the whalebone cage of the corset. This had already been achieved by the artistic couturiers Mariano Fortuny and Paul Poiret, with their exotic tea gowns and tunic ensembles, beneath which the salon vamps of the time wore the new elastic girdles that made them feel like Isadora Duncan. Chanel had other plans. Her aim was to remove the corsets that were still in women's minds, the waiting for things to happen, the heaviness, the spiritual laziness which made them dependent on men. "Fashion is not something that only exists in clothes," she

Gabrielle Chanel in her youth. She already wears her hair short, and wears a relatively short skirt, as well as two-tone shoes, which became something of a trademark. This is how she must have looked when Russian Grand Duke Dimitri fell in love with her.

Above, left to right:
Designed by Chanel for
Madame Mansfield, this
beach outfit comprising of
bra top and wide-legged
trousers appears incredibly
modern.
Coco Chanel in 1930 at
her home in the south of
France, wearing her favorite
striped pullover and
comfortable jersey trousers.
Chanel made it socially
acceptable for women to
wear classic men's trousers
with waist pleats.

Opposite, far left:
Design for a check outfit,
1928.

*Opposite, clockwise from
top left:*
Chanel (*on the left*) in a
typical jersey suit.
The little jersey suit has
become narrower and
more chic, worn with a
blouse, belt, and jewelry.
Three-piece ensemble, 1935.
Dark blue suit with white
piping, 1938.

explained in one of her much-repeated sayings.
"Fashion is in the air. It has something to do with
ideas, with the way in which we live, with what
happens around us." In this way Chanel was a
designer in the modern sense, a precursor of
Calvin Klein and Ralph Lauren. She did not
simply want to sell her customers new lines, but
an awareness of life. Decades later this came to
be called "lifestyle" and made fashion in the sense
of "Which skirt length are we wearing this
season?" seem hopelessly old-fashioned.

In 1918 Chanel extended her Paris store. Her
look was no longer limited to the summer season
or to the wealthy patrons of bathing resorts. She
conquered the city with dress and coat ensembles
in beige jersey, which was then called "biscuit,"
as well as evening dresses in black lace and tulle
sewn with jet. The clothes appeared to be simple,
but they were marvels of the dressmaker's art.
Chanel's childhood experiences had taught her
that success never comes easily. If you want to
liberate the world, you must learn to suffer too.

Chanel carried the burden of her own
perfectionism with pride. Her cutters and
models, however, were less enthusiastic martyrs
to chic. The models would have to stand in front
of her for hours until an armhole or a collar

flounce was absolutely right and just the way she
wanted it.

Chanel would not allow anyone or anything
to put her off. She felt that time was on her side.
In 1926 she created the evening uniform for the
new woman who was slim, sporty, and boyish.
She had cut her hair short and liked to wear skirts
in which she could jump on a tram or dance the
Charleston. The new creation was a simple,
straight dress in black crêpe de Chine. American
Vogue called it the "Ford of fashion" for its
democratic functionality. This particular Ford is
still being driven today, with slight modifications
and updates, to cocktail and dinner parties all
over the world.

From the very beginning, the foundation of
the Chanel look was mobility, in both its literal
and figurative senses. Her designs followed the
body, and her collections followed the spirit of
the 1920s. Whether it was a rubberized raincoat
copied from her chauffeur, her *style russe* (Russian
style) with embroidery and fur trimming, or
geometric patterns in the blackest black, beige,
and red – Chanel's designs reacted to political
events such as World War I, which left servants
in short supply and forced society ladies to think
practically, and the revolution which caused a

Opposite:
Evening wear by Chanel.
The designer was her own
best model.

Left:
Chanel's discreet luxury was
evident when Karl Lagerfeld
revived this narrow-cut dress
of gold lace and tulle for
Chanel-Couture in 1996.
It took the embroiderers
of Lesage 1,280 hours to
complete the Hindu pattern
of the lace with multi-
colored beads.

Coco Chanel

Below left:
Behind the scenes, Mademoiselle Chanel at work with her models. She preferred young girls who came from good homes, such as the daughters of aristocratic émigré families. Since they had to change so quickly, the models wore dressing gowns.

Below right:
Coco Chanel in her studio in 1962 during the presentation of a collection.

wave of Russian aristocrats to flood Paris. Chanel also reacted to trends in avant-garde art. She counted the artist Picasso and Sergei Diaghilev, the formidable impresario of the Ballets Russes, among her friends; she slept with Igor Stravinsky; and she designed costumes for productions of Cocteau's plays *Antigone* and *Orpheus.*

Competitors such as Paul Poiret and later Elsa Schiaparelli were completely carried away by their inspirations, Poiret by the Orientalism of the Ballets Russes and Schiaparelli by the amusing shock of Surrealism. Chanel, however, always had things firmly under control and stuck to her belief that the primary purpose of fashion is to be of service to the wearer. She was never in the slightest bit interested in a hat in the shape of a telephone or a skirt in which the wearer could only mince along. "An elegant woman should be able to shop without being laughed at by housewives," she said. "Those who laugh are always right." It was this seemingly bourgeois, uncompromising adherence to the service aspect of fashion and renunciation of the visually extreme which led to what was later called the "timelessness" of the Chanel look.

She celebrated her 40th birthday with her first perfume, *Chanel Numéro 5.* Other fashion

designers sold their fragrances in opulent bottles with names such as *Nuit de Chine* or *Il pleut des Baisers,* but here too Chanel was true to her unsentimental self. Her name and a number – one assumes that it was the number of the test sample that she liked best, simply the fifth attempt – in a geometrically shaped glass bottle, that would have to do. She had learned from Boy Capel that to be really successful in business you had to make use of the latest developments in science and technology.

Chanel's perfumer Ernest Beaux experimented in his studio in Grasse with aldehydes and synthetic substances. Encouraged by Chanel, he mixed the first truly modern perfume in 1921. It contained more than 80 ingredients, including artificial jasmine in the form of benzyl acetate, which intensified the natural jasmine fragrance as well as making it last longer. "I don't want a smell of roses or lilies of the valley," Chanel declared. "I want a composed perfume. It's a paradox. Natural flower fragrances smell artificial on a woman. Perhaps a natural-smelling perfume has to be artificially created."

While competitors such as Madame Grès, Vionnet, and Lanvin made clothes for an exclusive circle, Chanel developed into a media personality. With her sure instinct for causing a

A classic. The plain shape of Chanel's first perfume bottle has an almost masculine feel. The fragrance itself stood out against the sweet, flowery scents of the time. Not least because of the convincingly modern yet timeless design of the bottle, Chanel N° 5 became the most famous perfume in the world.

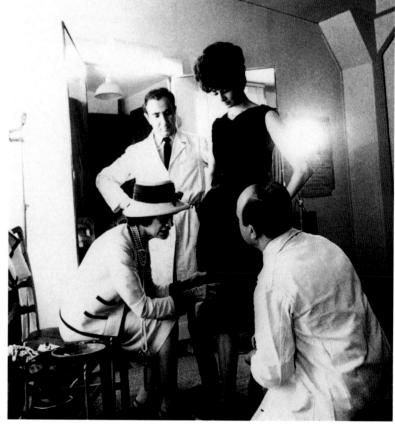

stir in public, she created her own legend and became someone with whom women in Europe and overseas could identify. Her career and private life merged into an attractive image spread by newspapers and fashion magazines, and this in turn pushed up sales of her perfume.

Coco Chanel's life in the 1920s and 1930s was a fascinating mixture of bohemia and bourgeoisie, glamour and hard work. She dined with artists in the fashionable restaurants of Paris, and though she told writer Djuna Barnes that nothing really amused her after midnight, in practice things seemed different. In any event, next morning she was in her studio discussing a plunging backline with her *première*, the dressmaker who ran the studio. She paid for Jean Cocteau's opium cure and went salmon fishing in Scotland with the richest man in England, the Duke of Westminster. One evening she was philosophizing with the poet Pierre Reverdy about the curse of human existence, while next evening she was playing cards with Winston Churchill.

The privations of her youth had given her an enormous appetite for traditional comfort and splendor, and now she could satisfy this appetite. Her apartment above the couture salon was decorated with Chinese coromandel screens, crystal chandeliers, and 18th-century furniture. The *pièce de résistance* was an enormous suede sofa, on which she held court like Cleopatra on her barge. La Pausa, her home on the French Riviera, was reminiscent of a movie star's Hollywood villa.

In 1931 Chanel made Hollywood producer Samuel Goldwyn an offer: she would clothe his stars, for the then unheard-of sum of $1 million a year. She could do with the money, since the Great Depression had caused her American couture customers to economize. She also saw this as an opportunity for international publicity. The venture was not a success, however. One can imagine what her clothes would have done for actresses with a Chanel personality such as Louise Brooks, Marlene Dietrich, or Barbara Stanwyck, but Goldwyn had thought of the aging diva Gloria Swanson, on whom Chanel's severe elegance had a banal effect. The fashion queen took revenge in her own way. She never looked more like a movie star than in the photographs taken shortly afterward for *Vogue* by George Hoyningen-Huene, Horst P. Horst, and Cecil Beaton. At the age of 53 she was more beautiful than she had been at 30. She had lost weight, she plucked her eyebrows, and her features had a melancholy tenderness reminiscent of Garbo in *Grand Hotel.*

Costume jewelry had existed long before Chanel's time, but she gave it soul. Her aim was never to try to deceive people by imitating real jewelry, but to create a purely aesthetic effect. Playing with luxury triumphed over financial reality, and the feminine principle triumphed over the masculine. She showed how rebellious she was by wearing the pearls and emerald necklaces that she had been given by lovers such as Grand Duke Dimitri and the Duke of Westminster together with her own exquisite imitations, which inevitably devalued the real jewels. You could seduce Chanel woman. You could give her presents. But you could not buy her. She had her own jewelry.

In the second half of the 1930s Chanel became tired, even bitter. The world economic crisis had reduced her income, and the political barometer in Europe was pointing toward a storm. Another great war was on its way. She felt that a world was coming to an end, and it was her world. In 1936 she was locked out of her own studio by striking workers. The peasant queen in her never got over such a humiliation. The previous summer her then lover, illustrator and art director Paul Iribe, had suffered a heart attack on her tennis court at La Pausa, and died shortly afterward. Feeling very much alone, she also felt betrayed by the press, which now favored the

In control. While guests watch her fashion parade, Mademoiselle stands in the background surveying the scene.

Opposite:
Chanel and her world.
White lilies – her favorite
flowers – in her apartment
in the Rue Cambon, Paris.

Left:
Cecil Beaton's Coco. The
great fashion photographer
captured Chanel on paper
for a change – standing in
front of the fireplace in her
apartment, where she was
often photographed.

Coco Chanel

Above:
The Sicilian Count of
Verdura designed some of
the most beautiful pieces
of jewelry for Chanel's
collections. She loved
wearing his wide, ivory-
colored enamel bracelets
decorated with colored
crystals.

eccentric look of Schiaparelli. When war broke
out in 1939, she closed her salon and laid off all
her staff.

She fled to Vichy, but soon came back to
Paris, which was then occupied by the Germans.
She began an affair with a German diplomat,
who helped gain the release of her nephew from
a prisoner-of-war camp and with whom she went
into exile in Switzerland after the war. When
accused of collaboration, she is said to have
replied: "A woman of my age cannot be expected
to ask to see the passport of a man who wants to
sleep with her."

From exile in Lausanne Chanel watched the
triumph of Christian Dior, who presented his New
Look in 1947. Wasp-waists, stiffened skirts and
jackets, women presented as pieces of
confectionery – the ghosts which Chanel had
driven out in the 1920s had returned to haunt her.
Fashion was again ruled by men. Men's desires
fixed a woman's shape, and this was what designers
such as Dior, Balenciaga and Fath delivered.

Pierre Wertheimer, who owned Chanel's
perfume licenses, informed Coco that sales of
Chanel N° 5 had dropped alarmingly, despite
Marilyn Monroe declaring that she would not
wear any other perfume in bed. Chanel was 70,
and she decided on a comeback.

French and English journalists called the
collection which Chanel presented on February 5,
1954 in her old salon in the Rue Cambon

"a melancholy retrospective" and "a fiasco." They
had seen the future, yet thought it was the past.
The 1960s would repeat the 1920s in many
ways, but in 1954 only Chanel knew that. The
American press was on her side, however, and
two seasons later she had also won this battle.
Her new tailored suit with its braid-trimmed
jacket and gilt buttons decorated with lion's
heads was the garment that every woman
wanted to have, in the original or as a copy. The
sling-back shoes with the contrasting toecap,
brooches made of colorful artificial gemstones,
and shoulder-chain purses were imitated all over
the world; at the end of the 20th century they
still defined the term "accessory."

Coco Chanel died on January 10, 1971, a
Sunday, in her suite in the Ritz Hotel in Paris.
Her last words, to her maid Céline, were:
"You see, this is how you die." *Time* magazine
estimated that her annual income was $160
million when she died. Yet the walls of her last
bedroom had no pictures; they were completely
white and bare, like the walls of a convent cell.

In the years after her comeback Coco Chanel
had completed her fashion arsenal. Later Karl
Lagerfeld took elements from this for the
Double C look of the 1980s, an ironic, over-the-
top satirical play on her drama. Even though the
designer was born into an industrialist family in
Hamburg, he is surprisingly similar in many
ways to the self-made French woman from a

Opposite:
At the age of 50 Chanel
was more beautiful than
ever, and she liked being
photographed by the
most famous photographers
of her time. She knew that
this was good publicity, an
idea that was taken up in
the 1980s by Jil Sander.
This profile by Man Ray
shows Chanel with the
inevitable cigarette and her
favorite jewelry.

Above:
Parading the Karl Lagerfeld
collection for Chanel in
the spring of 1998. The
couturier with the sunglasses
rejuvenated and updated
Mademoiselle's style. This
came as a shock to many at
the time, but proved to be
very successful.

humble background. This similarity runs from
private tragedy hidden behind a façade of
splendor – the love of Lagerfeld's life also died far
too young – and the amazing mania for work, to
the brilliant ease with which he incorporates
influences from his surroundings into his designs.

Lagerfeld treated Chanel's heritage with such
little respect that he succeeded in making it come
to life and regain its relevance. He seemed to
return to the roots of Chanel's style in his
collections at the end of the 1990s, with their
ingenious rusticity, the girlishness of their light
materials, and their elegant neatness. It was as if
her work had come full circle.

Coco Chanel was a conservative
revolutionary, a coquettish moralist, scheming
yet instinctive, feeling like a woman while living
like a man. She incorporated the paradox at the
core of the feminine condition in the 20th
century, right down to the detail of the cigarette
which was her constant companion –
dependence as a symbol of independence.

To the end she set great store by being
addressed as "Mademoiselle" rather than
"Madame," though in fact she was something of
a female gentleman. As such she always slightly
despised women as individuals. She accused
them of not knowing the meaning of honor. Yet
she gave a most valuable gift to women in
general: she created clothes which protected
them on their road to emancipation and made
them look as young, free, and capable of
surviving as they really would be when they
reached their goal at the end of the 20th century.
Coco Chanel did not merely look like a witch,
she really was a witch.

Opposite:
Chanel's heir. "Making a
better future from expanded
elements of the past": in a
kind of self-portrait Karl
Lagerfeld captured what it
means to take on Coco
Chanel's heritage.

The famous Chanel suit proves to be immortal. It survives every new fashion and skirt length. This is partly due to the wonderfully light tweed, which simply makes the wearer feel good, and also to the perfect finish, which guarantees that it will be reliable in any situation. Chanel's insignia are also immortal: the intertwined Cs, standing for Coco Chanel; the white camellia, here on a black silk-satin bow; the baroque costume jewelry with colored stones; and classic pumps with contrasting toecaps that make the feet look dainty.

The little black dress

Coco Chanel, at the height of her success in 1936.

Opposite:
Chanel's "little black dress" became a bestseller, and it will always be associated with her name. This is the original design, so simple and so perfect that American *Vogue* predicted "This is the Ford of dresses." The prediction was right: the Ford is still running today.

Anonymous beauty, 1924

Joan Bennett, 1928

1970s punk

Comme des Garçons, summer 1986

Marilyn Monroe, 1950s

Romy Schneider, 1962

Princess Diana

Judy Garland

Edith Piaf, 1959

Juliette Gréco, 1977

Martha Graham

Liza Minnelli

Opposite:
Top row: Since Chanel, the little
black dress has never left the
world of fashion. It was and still is
reliable in every situation, elegant
yet inconspicuous, and appears in
every designer collection.
Center row: A sad note added
by beautiful women whose lives
ended tragically.
Bottom row: Performers love the
mystic aura of black.

Right:
Audrey Hepburn wore the
ultimate little black dress in
Breakfast at Tiffany's, 1961.

Black is the beginning of everything, the number zero, the outline, [...] would seem to me that the other colors didn't exist. At the same time bl[...] different shades of black: the delicate black of translucence; the dull, dismal bl[...] taffeta; the strict black of silk; the flowing black of satin; the cheerful, forr[...] new materials seem fanciful when they are black.

I cannot relate to snow, I dislike milk, I prefer my brides to be colorful. O[...] And I roll around hypnotized in shades of gold and red. It is said that togetl[...] once wanted a totally red apartment in *Cries and Whispers*). One has to say tl[...] spoken about the subtle nuances of black (such as in a painting by Frans H[...] and variously faded by the sun – I would even say that black has a fragrar[...] and enthusiastic aficionados use poetic adjectives for their hides. In contrast[...] a small patch of black. It is hard to resist the gouache pressed from the tube, t[...] else splashing from the bottle. One wants to touch it, to spread it, with genero[...] it is light as much as shade (whose praises have been definitively sung by Barthe[...] is as irresistible as the night. Children should not be afraid of black, for ever[...]

tainer – then the contents. Without its shadow, its relief, and its support it

ne sum of all the colors. It is hesitant, variable, never the same. There are many

the mourning band; the deep, royal black of velvet; the overripe black of

ck of paint. Wool is reminiscent of coal, cotton has a rustic effect, and all

brilliant limewash of Mediterranean houses gives me an appetite for white.

h black they are the colors of madness (which is why director Ingmar Bergman

ck is a pillar of the south, a calming presence, something obvious: I have often

Velázquez), about the black fabrics worn by the Arlesians of my childhood

ich is given off by dyes in the sun. One could say the same about black bulls,

ite, black is penetrable. There is density, there is lust, a whole world even in

al-black acrylic overflowing from the can, or the ink from China or anywhere

ushstrokes or even with one's hands. Black is just as much matter as it is color,

s neither sad nor cheerful, but allure and elegance, perfect and necessary. It

mystery frightens them, it also contains the answer to its secrets.

Christian Lacroix

The look of the decade

The bobbed haircut gave the picture its character. Anyone who was not prepared to do away with her old plait no longer belonged. Since most men were against short hair, many women pretended that their hair had accidentally been burned by an oil lamp or a candle. Whatever the excuse, they seemed to think that the rigorous haircut had saved their lives. The writer Colette, who was ahead of her time in so many ways, had dared to take the step as early as 1903. But it was another 14 years before she was followed by the avant-garde, as poet Paul Morand wrote in his diary in May 1917: "Since three days ago it has been fashionable for women to wear their hair short. Everyone is joining in, led by Madame Letellier and Chanel …"

In the 1920s everyone started wearing their hair in a bob, with or without bangs, straight or wavy. The bob was complemented by dark-rimmed eyes and well defined, deep red lips. It was considered improper to make up or powder the complexion in public, and for this very reason tremendously chic. Women put on thick make-up, and the results could not be artificial enough. The *garçonne* complemented her revealed body with a dressed-up face.

The whole get-up was meant to provoke. Rouge was applied as a round patch; colored nail varnish was introduced in 1925, and this at last released nails from their natural look; eyebrows were rigorously plucked and penciled in as black lines with turned-down ends. Blondes preferred green or blue eye shadow, while brunettes chose brown and black. They all used kohl to make large almond-shaped eyes of unfathomable depth. Russian émigrées brought the secret of "beading" to Paris: a waxy substance was applied to every single eyelash so that it had a tiny "bead" at the tip. In comparison the application of false eyelashes, which were also already available, was child's play. The real advance, however, came with waterproof mascara. This was developed by Elizabeth Arden, who opened a beauty salon in Paris in 1921. Before then this American beautician had used natural pink shades, but she was very taken with the dark-rimmed eyes of the flappers in the jazz clubs of Paris. So much so that she experimented on a chambermaid until she had finally copied the sinful look to perfection

– whereupon the girl burst into tears and ruined the whole creation!

Helena Rubinstein, Arden's chief competitor, also claimed to have invented waterproof mascara. Whoever it was, it is undoubtedly true that the competition between the two giants of the cosmetics world contributed to the development of the beauty industry. The only other person who could keep up was Max Factor, a Pole who had worked as the first make-up artist in the theater of the Russian czar. Having fled to Hollywood in 1904, Max Factor helped create the image of screen greats such as Gloria Swanson, Pola Negri, Joan Crawford, and Greta Garbo. Before long he was selling his "make-up of the stars" all over the world.

Paris was the source of inspiration for all the new trends. It was there that aristocratic immigrants from eastern Europe met with black jazz musicians and literary giants from America, French intellectuals discussed life with Spanish iconoclasts, and rich heiresses got together with starving visionaries. This created a climate that made Paris the cultural capital of the world. After the international Art Deco fair took place in Paris in 1925, the American *Vogue* wrote: "The French have discovered the secrets of the force of attraction, and we should look upon our Parisian sisters as models of charm."

It was no wonder, therefore, that Coco Chanel's suntanned complexion was very quickly copied. In her unconventional way she got rid of the idea that "refined ladies" were as white as snow. In her opinion it was poor people, who worked day and night in closed rooms, who stayed pale. Those who could afford it went as often as possible to smart seaside resorts and came back with a suntan. Jean Patou certainly took the trend toward sunbathing into account when he launched the first suntan oil in 1924. Four years later Chanel followed up with a similar product.

It was Josephine Baker, however, who changed all previous ideas about beauty overnight. Suddenly black was beautiful, and the ideal of the lascivious lady of the harem gave way to the new idol of the explosive black woman. The whole world turned to Africa in the search for buried roots and new revelations.

Carla and Eleanor, the famous G Sisters from Berlin. In the 1920s make-up could never be striking enough.

Opposite:
This profile of the American silent movie star Constance Talmadge demonstrates how the bob showed earrings to their best advantage.

LOUISE BROOKS

CLARA BOW

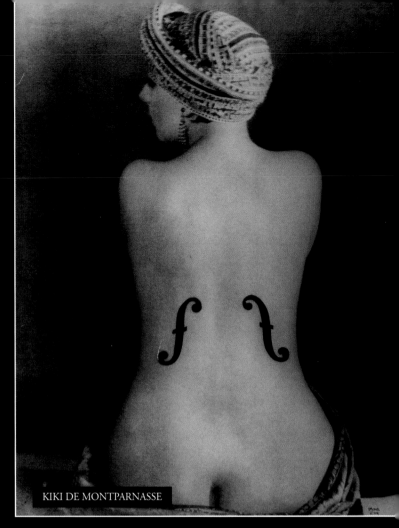

KIKI DE MONTPARNASSE

MARION MOREHOUSE

JOSEPHINE BAKER

NANCY CUNARD

Idols of the decade

The *garçonne* (mannish girl) was the stuff of which Hollywood stars were made. **Clara Bow** (1905–65), the little girl from the telephone exchange, was launched as "the hottest baby of the jazz age." Her greatest success was in the role of a salesclerk in the hit movie *It* in 1927. No one could explain what "it" was, but everyone sensed it when she lowered her eyes or glanced back over her shoulder. She looked like the nice Gibson girl of the previous decade, except that she had clearly lost her innocence at the same time as having her red hair cut. In its place she had gained "it," or sex appeal. Clara Bow's career lasted just eight years, but in this time she made 49 movies. Then the "jazz babe," who lived as fast as she worked, burned out.

Louise Brooks (1906–85) was considered to be the incarnation of the unrestrained, hedonistic flapper. In fact no one wore the pageboy cut and the short dancing dresses better than the photogenic revue girl who became a movie star. German director G.W. Pabst was convinced even more by her lively, erotic performances than he was by her flawless appearance. He took the girl from Kansas to Berlin and gave her the part of Lulu. After she starred in Pabst's *Pandora's Box* and *Diary of a Lost Girl*, Louise Brooks was spoiled for Hollywood. She refused most offered parts as being too superficial and soon went out of business. She had such charisma, however, that she is still considered to have been one of the icons of the 1920s.

Josephine Baker (1906–75) blew away all the Parisian idols like a whirlwind. How could Sarah Bernhardt and Mistinguett, or even the Russian ballet stars, compete with this 19-year-old who already had ten years' experience of singing in Harlem nightclubs? A feather and a few bananas were all she needed to take Paris by storm. The French capital was certainly well prepared, for African art and culture had more and more supporters, black musicians played in popular clubs such as Bal Nègre and Boule Noire, and even the most upright citizens danced the black bottom. It was as if the whole of Paris had simply been waiting for Josephine Baker. She became the darling of the nation as soon as she stepped onto the stage in the *Revue nègre* in 1926. Suddenly brown skin was fashionable, along with shaved armpits and hair gelled with egg-white. Josephine

Baker, the "natural phenomenon," became a model for all women who strove for authenticity. She was more influential than all the screen goddesses, because in the 1920s, if you were the star of Paris, you inspired the whole world.

If they were in the right place at the right time, women from all sorts of backgrounds could have great influence on the way in which others dressed, did their hair, and made up. Indeed, they could influence how they lived their lives. **Kiki de Montparnasse** (1901–53), for example, who struggled along as a painter, singer, writer, and movie actress, as well as being an artists' model,

Mother of the "forgotten generation"

All the artists, writers, and adventurers who had been turned into the "lost generation" by World War I met at Gertrude Stein's apartment in the Rue Fleurus in Montparnasse. From Picasso, Juan Gris, and Matisse to Man Ray, from Sherwood Anderson to Ernest Hemingway and F. Scott Fitzgerald, they all sat at the feet of the monumental writer, who had established her exceptional reputation with her 1,000-page work *The Making of Americans*.

Those who were not invited to Stein's salon counted for nothing in Parisian intellectual circles. The fact that she lived officially with her friend Alice B. Toklas, a former pianist, made it fashionable to belong to the lesbian circle, which included such elegant women as Djuna Barnes, Janet Flanner, and Natalie Clifford Barney. Gertrude Stein's apartment, with its early Picassos and other important Cubist works, was known as "the best art gallery in Europe."

made a deep impression on other women with her make-up skills. She would "put on three of four different shades of green, until her eye shadow went with her dress." She was also celebrated in certain circles for her daring use of eyeliner to improve her sparse pubic hair. She became Man Ray's lover and model in the 1920s, and he took famous photographs of her. For one shot he painted eyes on top of her eyelids, and there is the famous 1924 photograph of her as the *Violon d'Ingres*, meaning "hobby" or "passion" in the figurative sense. Above all, however, Kiki became the model of a "sincere, natural life without hypocrisy or prejudice."

Marion Morehouse gained respect and social recognition as the first mannequin. Tall, slim, and supple, she was the ideal type for flapper fashion. Star photographer Edward Steichen called her "the best model I have ever worked with" because "she changes each time into exactly the kind of woman who really would wear that dress." Other great photographers, such as Horst P. Horst and George Hoyningen-Huene, preferred Marion as a model because she looked elegant even in the most daring outfits. She married the poet E.E. Cummings, and later became a photographer herself, setting an example for many of today's models.

Nancy Cunard, heiress of the English shipping line, went to Paris as a poet and publisher. There she became one of the most striking figures of the city's café intelligentsia. She was much admired and photographed, and Man Ray was one of the photographers for whom she modeled. Nancy Cunard was as thin as a rake, wore more kohl around her eyes than anyone else, and loved to wear African ivory bracelets all the way up to her elbows. With her love of leopard-skin patterns, leather jackets, and pants suits, she would fit the picture of a fashionable city-dweller even today.

Coco Chanel certainly also belongs among the idols and models of the 1920s. More even than her fashion, her whole lifestyle was geared toward showing a new way to women striving for freedom.

1930–1939

The return of elegance

1930–1939

The Roaring Twenties, with their passionate desire for life, were followed by a decade of quiet elegance. Times were insecure, and the great stock-market crash of 1929 brought bankruptcies and mass unemployment. In 1932 14 million people had no food or wages in America; in Germany the figure was 6 million, and in England 3 million. In France many American couture clients stayed away, and the big American fashion houses which had bought the rights to produce a number of each season's designs in the United States now took up licenses for only one or two, which they copied endlessly instead. As a result there were as many as 10,000 unemployed in the French fashion industry alone.

Those who managed to rescue their fortune did not show it off, at least not publicly. They did not celebrate in bars or clubs, but arranged their celebrations in private houses: balls at Count Étienne de Beaumont's residence (he decided who belonged to the beau monde), dinners hosted by Viscountess Marie-Laure de Noailles (collector and patroness of the avant-garde), parties thrown by taste guru Lady Mendl (former actress Elsie de Wolfe). Everything from dress to interior design was of discriminating taste and value but, as society photographer Cecil Beaton noted, "No more showing off as in the 1920s, all that had been canceled."

This was not always due to the difficult times, but often simply a tribute to modern times: Art Deco and Cubism had fostered a preference for geometric lines, while revolutionary architects such as Le Corbusier and influential interior designers such as Jean-Michel Frank brought home décor up to date and awakened a sense for the functional. "Throw out and don't let anything stop you!" demanded Eugenia Errazuriz, a high-society lady who had come to Europe from South America. "Elegance means throwing out," she stressed and so led the way to a minimalism which

Previous page:
A great entrance for new elegance. The most stylish decade of the century announces itself with simple pathos. The 1930s remain to this day a source of inspiration for both fashion designers and interior designers.

Opposite:
As an actress Elsie de Wolfe was famous neither for her beauty nor for her talent, but for her taste. It was only when she made use of it professionally and became an interior designer that she became Lady Mendl and a much praised hostess.

It was Viscountess Marie-Laure de Noailles, influential patroness and collector of the avant-garde, who sent out the most sought-after invitations of her time. Here she is at a masked ball, flanked by painter Christian Bérard (*right*) and Boris Kochnow (*left*). Her place of residence, the Hotel Bischoffsheim, resembled a museum of modern art.

60 years later was to become a postmodernist cult. Chrome, mirrors, and glass determined the new lifestyle, which was a far cry from coziness. Skyscrapers such as the Rockefeller Center in New York and the Golden Gate Bridge in San Francisco were hailed as miracles of technology and promoted a belief in progress. Not everybody could put up with this strict modernity for long. After only a few months the socialite Charles de Beisteguis changed the much praised "machine for living" which Le Corbusier had created for him in the Champs-Elysées into a neobaroque fantasy construction. Horst P. Horst, one of the fixed stars in the firmament of fashion photography, found that, after a short apprenticeship with Le Corbusier, he could no longer get anything out of the pure doctrine of the modern movement either: "Everyone longs for beauty – why should working people live in prison cells?"

The majority of people, however poor they might be, wanted to maintain a certain standing. Appropriate clothing had never been more valued. Whereas the flappers of the 1920s had danced about in their fluttering little shifts day and night, the lady of the 1930s wore a long dress in the evening. And the dress had to be silk, because only the most expensive fabric of all could be cut on the bias to fall in its uniquely streamlined way and emphasize but not expose the figure.

By now everybody was copying Madeleine Vionnet's great invention of cutting across the weave of the fabric. The ingenious thing was that this cutting technique gave elasticity to the fabric long before Lycra was invented. And so bust, waist, and hips were again shown to their best advantage because bias-cut dresses hugged the figure and swirled around the hemline in natural folds. These glittering

The slim and slender silhouette, typical of the 1930s. This 1939 design by Edward Molyneux is unusual in that it has a high Empire waist and is embroidered with Napoleonic bees.

Waiting for the next dance. Elegant ladies in silk dresses with bare backs delighted their admirers.

Ginger Rogers and Fred Astaire were Hollywood's dream couple. But he hated her lavish dresses, which got in the way when they danced.

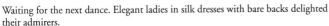

silk-satin evening gowns needed no fastenings: they could simply be pulled over the head or stepped into. The plunging neckline was, of course, a great help here. The very low-cut backs, in particular, knew no limit. This trend has often been attributed to prudish American movie censorship, which did not allow any cleavage to be shown. So Hollywood showed the bare back, which was then imitated everywhere. In fact, flappers had already drawn everybody's attention to the back, for the simple reason that when they indulged in the favorite pastime of their day – dancing – the back view made the greatest impact.

Dancing was still the main entertainment in the 1930s. Swing was in, and dancers moved to the sounds of a big band. The foxtrot and rumba were coming in, and the tango remained popular. Fred Astaire and Ginger Rogers were the top dancers of the movie world. Between 1934 and 1939 they made eight motion picture musicals, including *Swing Time*,

and showed that a couple only had to move in the right rhythm to be happy. Ginger Rogers designed many of her costumes herself, much to the annoyance of her partner, who was almost knocked out by her heavy, beaded sleeves. She also loved ostrich feathers, to which Fred Astaire was allergic.

Hollywood's exaggerations were not adopted by high-society dancers. Evening dresses showed a restrained elegance, stressing a slim, long silhouette yet flattering the female figure. The plunging low-cut back was often simply but effectively emphasized by a single string of pearls. By the end of the decade huge bows or even drapes reminiscent of turn-of-the-century bustles decorated the low-cut back. And the most unusual of all backless dresses, Vionnet's halter-neck, needed no jewelry at all, as this design caused enough amazement in itself.

The best companion for cold shoulders was of course fur, preferably silver fox. To wear two whole

The elegance and glamour of the decade were best expressed by long silk evening gowns. The style of elaborately gathered folds was taken up again by Lacroix in 1997 (*inset*).

A white fox with all the trimmings was regarded as the most flattering accessory of the decade. Eileen Lamb, one of the beauties of the age, wears a fur collar in which even the animal's head is used as decoration.

animals was considered especially chic. But nothing could rival the glamour of a cape made entirely of white fox. Those who could not manage that reached for a velvet cape or a brightly colored chiffon scarf. But what if one could not even afford silk? Coco Chanel showed some understanding for this kind of problem, taking the economic situation into account by adding cotton dresses to her evening collection.

Women knew how to make do in the years of the Great Depression. If they could not afford to buy new dresses, they simply lengthened their old ones, because even during the day short skirts were no longer worn. The hemline fluctuated around mid-calf, and shorter skirts were adjusted to the right length by the clever addition of ribbons, trimmings, insets,

and fur. Even the smallest piece of fur could be used to trim the neckline or sleeves. After all, fur meant luxury.

The rich wore furs during the day too. Persian lamb, karakul, beaver, and otter were made into three-quarter-length coats and worn over the obligatory princess-style dress. The princess line had no waist seam and was held together by a narrow belt. The result was a slim, sleek-fitting silhouette with soft flowing fabrics. The inset sleeves were long and narrow-cut, often with flared or ruffled cuffs. Sometimes skirts were made to look fashionably

Opposite:
Seductive interplay. Elegant jewelry emphasizes the backless dresses, but equally the intricately pinned-up hair and bare back set off the jewelry beautifully.

Hollywood star Jean Harlow in
1937, shown not as a man-eating
vamp for a change but as an
elegant young woman wearing
a straight skirt, waisted jacket,
and jabot blouse.

Below:
Tall and slim, the typical 1930s
silhouette. The narrow-cut dress
has wedge-shaped pleats so that
the wearer can move freely,
and the hemline is soft and
flowing. The stole is fur.

Opposite, above:
Imaginative little hats brightened
up the otherwise severe elegance.
As long as the face remained
uncovered, everything was
allowed. Designs by Caroline
Reboux from 1935 (*furthest left*)
and 1936 (*furthest right*), and
between them four hats from
1935 and 1937 by Jeanne Lanvin.

full by godets inserted below the hip-line. Freedom of movement was important, because even in the best circles it was now common for women to work outside the home, even if it was only for charitable causes.

Gloves and hat were an essential part of a ladylike outfit. To complement the sensible 1930s fashion, women went in for the most amazing headgear. At first hats were small and flat and had to be pinned into position on top of the hair. Then berets, caps, boaters, cloches, and pillbox hats came in, as well as all sorts of other fantastic shapes and constructions. The only thing all these hats had in common was that they had to be worn perched forward on the head. One of the most important milliners was Caroline Reboux, and among her many clients was actress Jacqueline Delubac, who was the wife of Sacha Guitry and for six decades one of the most elegant women in Paris. The most renowned creator of hats, however, was Elsa Schiaparelli, who, though trained neither as a milliner nor as a couturier, significantly shaped 1930s fashion.

The first of the famous Hermès squares. The silk scarves were such a success that since their launch up to 12 new designs have been brought out each year. These popular accessories have come to be seen as collectors' items too.

Suits had the same narrow cut as dresses, with a slim waist often accentuated by a belt. Lapels were wide and the neckline was very low, at least in summer. A blouse was worn underneath. Big bows and loosely tied scarves lent an impression of fullness to the top and made the waist look even slimmer. In 1933 Hermès launched the first of its famous silk squares, which are still sought-after presents and collector's items today. Contrasting colors were used: brown was combined with cream or navy blue, and white with black. Even shoes, which had solid high heels, came in two colors.

The preference for a very slim waist gave a new lease of life to corset manufacturers. They now used lightweight materials like lastex to make girdles that exercised gentle pressure – but only below the bosom, which was now held up again. The American firm Warner was the first to introduce brassieres with different cup sizes. Stockings were still made of flesh-colored real or artificial silk, and these were replaced by nylons only from 1939 on.

Above:
Two Parisians wearing narrow-cut suits by Jacques Heim, 1935. The basilica of Sacré-Cœur can be seen in the background.

Opposite:
The latest thing: in 1935 it was a handbag with a watch clasp.

Left:
With hat, gloves, and a small, flat envelope purse every suit became an elegant outfit, as shown here by actress Jacqueline Delubac, wife of Sacha Guitry and for over half a century one of France's most elegant women.

Elegantly dressed for the afternoon: designs by Edward Molyneux, 1936.

A dress designed for Macy's store, 1934.

Patterned dress with a print typical of the time, also designed in 1934 for Macy's.

Accessories were indispensable, especially since for many women these were the only things that they could afford to keep their clothes up to date. They carried clutch purses shaped like envelopes, small pouches with silver clasps, or – the very latest thing – bags with frames and clasps made of plastic. Costume jewelry was totally acceptable, thanks mainly to Chanel's daring move – the felicitous mix of precious stones and imitation gems. She and her new rival Schiaparelli employed outstanding craftsmen and artists, who created costume jewelry of unique quality. Paste necklaces were worn just as happily as real diamonds with a big evening gown. Paste gems, as well as metal and glass sequins, were also sewn onto expensive fabrics or used in embroidery.

Sunglasses were the latest thing. They were now seen as essential for the fashion-conscious, who devoted their spare time to sport, either actively or as spectators, as well as visiting seaside resorts and acquiring a suntan. In 1933 Alice Marble played tennis at Wimbledon in comfortable shorts, and soon shorts became popular even away from the playing fields. Chanel found them quite ridiculous, however, and rejected them. She wore her "slacks" – wide-legged long pants – at the beach too.

Smart city women could no longer imagine being without their long, baggy pants, especially their silk evening pajamas. Yet pants were still generally ignored and remained socially unacceptable, at least in public. Significantly, it was only in 1939 that *Vogue* showed women in pants and sweaters for the first time.

The 1930s were marked by political upheaval, and initially many people did not know quite where they stood. Idealistic intellectuals from various European countries and the United States regarded fascism in

Gloves were worn even with short-sleeved dresses. Some were quite flamboyant.

Cardigans also emphasized the slim line of 1930s fashion: outfit by Hermès, 1936.

Patterns were still inspired by Art Deco: sweater by Anny Blatt, 1937.

Europe as the greatest danger in world politics, and in 1936 they formed themselves into an international brigade which fought for the Republicans against the Nationalists in the Spanish Civil War. Others saw communism as the enemy, and this was cleverly used by Hitler when it suited him. The consequences of the economic crisis, with more than 6 million unemployed in Germany and a longing for order and stability, had helped Hitler to power. In Germany everybody wanted to believe Hitler's propaganda, that he would get rid of poverty and unemployment and lead the German people to new glory. His stand for conservative values, which put women back in the home and saw the family as the sanctuary of strength and happiness, was particularly popular with women, who realized that the liberalism of the 1920s had not brought them progress. Besides, Hitler's ideal of the German woman who neither smoked nor used make-

up, and who was clean, fit, and healthy, was not forced on people. Fashion magazines still showed the latest Paris designs, and so there was never the slightest suspicion that Germany was being isolated from the world. On the contrary, in 1936 the Nazis were delighted to be able to welcome all nations to the Olympic Games. They used the competition in Berlin, which was then the third-largest city in the world, for propaganda and a demonstration of power, and this impressed many people.

Sport united people over and above their political differences. Gymnastic clubs sprang up throughout Europe, nudist camps were set up, and the really rich and fashionable devoted themselves to motoring and aerial sports. Cycling, tennis, and golf remained favorite leisure activities. And at last bathing was fun for women too, thanks to the invention of tampons and new fabrics which made it possible to design

been given up for good. Day wear developed a more severe style, however. From as early as 1934 shoulders became broader, and four years later they were increased with extreme shoulder pads. These altered proportions in such a way that they looked good only with a shorter, fuller skirt. Then shoes also had to have more bulk: first came the wedge heel, followed by platform soles.

When World War II broke out in 1939, fashion seemed to have anticipated the catastrophe. Toward the end of the decade clothes took on the characteristics of a uniform, with angular shoulders, braided fastenings, tight skirts, feathered hats, gauntlet gloves, shoulder bags, and sturdy, flat shoes. The most important thing, however, was still an immaculate, well-groomed appearance, as if women had turned into eager recruits. During this period fashion was determined by perfection rather than creativity. That, however, certainly did not apply to the fashion of Elsa Schiaparelli.

tight-fitting bathing suits which did not lose their shape in the water. Despite or perhaps because of Hitler, it was the done thing to spend vacations in the German or Austrian Alps, skiing in the winter and hiking and climbing in the summer. Tyrolean peasant costumes were fashionable in the most elegant circles, and the dirndl was even copied by haute couture.

Germany remained in touch with fashion for some time, but politically the National Socialists became less and less acceptable. Slowly the Allies came to realize that Hitler's assurances of peace could not be trusted, and the threat of war loomed on the horizon. Resistance formed, and as always in dark times a yearning for opulence and beauty arose. In the early summer of 1938 the British royal couple visited France and inspired a neoromantic fashion revival. Even Chanel, the inventor of modern simplicity, suddenly designed evening dresses with very full, stiffened skirts and ornate trimmings, strongly reminiscent of the crinoline which one thought had

Opposite:
A lady with drive. Golf was considered a feminine sport and was particularly popular with women because they did not have to dress up for it. On the fairway they wore noticeably short skirts.

Shocking Elsa

Elsa Schiaparelli promised "bons vêtements de travail" – good work clothes – in her advertisements when she opened her salon in 1935, directly opposite the Ritz in the Place Vendôme. In fashion history she is remembered more for her daring and eccentric designs, though she actually started off with a very practical small sweater. This was different from others only in that it had a big white bow, which looked like a butterfly, knitted into the black background. Her first customer really was a working woman: Anita Loos, who had become famous with her novel *Gentlemen Prefer Blondes* and was a sought-after scriptwriter in Hollywood. The American store Strauss acted quickly when its buyers saw the flattering sweater and ordered 40 of them.

This order launched Elsa Schiaparelli's fashion career and also came to her rescue. She had only just arrived in Paris from the United States after a failed marriage; her daughter was ill and she had no idea how to support herself. She had not been brought up to be a career woman. She was born in 1890 in Rome, the second daughter of a well-off, cultured family. Although she had been allowed to go to school, which was unusual for a girl at that time, she had not been permitted to train for a profession. She was interested in music, the theater, and art, especially in radical futurism, but she did not take up any of them seriously. In the end she decided to study philosophy and secretly developed a passion for poetry. Her volume of poetry, *Arethsa*, was praised by the critics for its subliminal passion and condemned by her family for the same reason. It was time to get Elsa married. But whoever found favor in her family's eyes found none with Elsa, and vice versa. Highly educated, not pretty, but sensitive, gentle, and obstinate, she was 23 when she was sent to England to help a prosperous lady set up an orphanage on progressive lines.

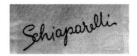

One afternoon she attended a theosophical lecture in London and was introduced to the speaker, Count William de Wendt de Kerlor. Next day she was engaged to him. Her aging parents – her father was over 70, her mother 60 – were alarmed and traveled to England, but they could do nothing to stop the wedding in early 1914.

Elsa had chosen a difficult partner. William, half Breton and half French-Swiss with Slav ancestors, was sure of only one thing – his amazing good looks. These, together with an inclination toward mysticism, made him irresistible to women. He exploited this whenever his self-confidence needed a boost, which was the case soon after the wedding. There was a war on, and in England there was no demand for philosophical lectures in French, so the young couple had to live off Elsa's dowry. In 1915 they moved to Nice, away from the war, which William had managed to avoid thanks to his Swiss origins. He could not enjoy the French Riviera, however, as unemployment had shattered his self-confidence. William left Elsa and went his own way.

There is a gap of almost four years in Elsa's history which she has never spoken or written about. It is impossible to know therefore why the Count and Countess de Kerlor arrived in New York in the spring of 1919. Only one thing is certain: William could not settle in America either and drifted away more and more. His only success were his private lectures on philosophy, which were enthusiastically attended by admiring female fans. He embarked on a passionate affair with dancer Isadora Duncan.

Elsa was 29 when, under difficult circumstances, she gave birth to her daughter Yvonne, nicknamed Gogo. A few months later she divorced William. She looked for work and came into contact with a group of artists that had formed around Alfred Stieglitz. In his gallery she met Marcel

Duchamp, the Baron de Meyer, and Man Ray. Elsa found it difficult to put down roots quickly but felt at home in these circles. Her search for knowledge and her wit were much appreciated. During her hard struggle for survival Elsa developed a very direct style of communication, which she adopted from American businesswomen.

After a short relationship with an Italian tenor, who died suddenly of meningitis, Elsa was on her own again with her daughter and her worries. In June 1922 a female friend helped her to go to Paris. There she quickly made friends with artists, some of whom she had already met in New York, such as Man Ray. They met up in Le Bœuf sur le Toit, then the place where all of Paris drank and danced: here were Cocteau, Picasso, Francis Picabia, André Gide, Igor Stravinsky, and of course Coco Chanel, who was already very successful.

Elsa's fashion career began when she met Paul Poiret. Her first encounter with the fashion czar has become legendary. Elsa accompanied a rich American woman to a fashion show, and afterward was seen by Poiret trying on a long black velvet coat with colorful stripes and bright blue silk lining. "Why don't you buy it?" the great man asked. Elsa admitted that she could not afford it, and anyway, when would there be an occasion to wear such a magnificent garment? "A woman like you," Poiret replied, "can wear everything anywhere. And don't worry about the money." The velvet coat was the first of many gifts from Poiret, who was always generous. But the greatest gift of all from their friendship was

that he recognized her creativity and encouraged her to produce her own designs.

"Pour le Sport," Elsa Schiaparelli wrote on the door of her first shop in the Rue de la Paix. She wanted to dress the modern woman as she had encountered her in the United States. The modern woman did not need intricate made-to-measure clothes, but functional separates, which could be mixed and matched to look different every time – the very concept that defines sportswear today. Elsa found an Armenian family who translated her original designs into perfect knitwear, and together they became rich and famous. These collections were the precursors of the ready-to-wear line, which did not really exist then. As expected, Elsa's sportswear sold particularly well in the United States. Among her Hollywood customers she soon counted Katharine Hepburn, Joan Crawford, and Greta Garbo, along with popular novelist and screenwriter Anita Loos.

What will be will be: at some point even the most practical woman wants to get out of her work clothes and into an evening dress. In 1933 Elsa designed her first long evening gown, a slim column of white crêpe de Chine, to be worn with a dress-coat with tails that crossed on the back. The design was a huge success and was copied worldwide. This was the beginning of Elsa's couture career.

The five years between opening her salon on the Place Vendôme and the outbreak of war were Elsa Schiaparelli's great time. Influential clients such as Nancy Cunard and Daisy Fellowes, both heiresses of considerable fortunes, deserted

La Schiap loved feathers
and a flamboyant appearance.
Artist and photographer
Man Ray, whom she met at
Alfred Stieglitz's avant-garde
gallery, photographed Elsa
in a white silk robe with an
accordion-pleated panel and
a feather cape.

Below:
Innocent cherubs have fun
with the sensuous lips of
Hollywood vamp Mae West.
This is how Schiaparelli
advertised her lipstick
Shocking Radiance.

Schiaparelli Red
"Shocking Radiance"
new accent for lovely lips

Elsa Schiaparelli

Right and opposite:
The harder the times, the
more frivolous the fashion:
shortly before the outbreak
of World War II the bustle
made a comeback and Elsa
Schiaparelli happily went
along to ruffle the *cul de
Paris* (the Parisian butt).
These four designs are all
from 1939.

Elsa Schiaparelli

Opposite:
Slim black dinner dress
from Schiaparelli's Circus
collection, looking as if it
was specially designed for
the Duchess of Windsor,
with a bolero sumptuously
embroidered in Studio
Lesage, 1938.

Chanel and Patou for Schiaparelli. The press hailed her creativity, courage, and uniqueness, and artists felt magically drawn to her. In her collections Elsa turned Surrealism into fashion by adopting its principle of taking ordinary objects out of their familiar setting and showing them in a completely different context. Everybody knew the shoe that became a hat, with its red sole cheekily turned up; the gloves adorned with gold fingernails; and the rag dress, that grand evening gown for very formal occasions with a pattern suggestive of much wear and tear. Its matching cape was decorated with real tears and thus caused a scandal – as punk fashion would do four decades later.

Salvador Dalí helped Elsa develop the torn fabrics, and he designed a black velvet purse in the shape of a telephone with an embroidered golden dial. He also painted the giant lobster motif which Schiap, as her friends now called her, used on a white evening dress. Her sense of Surrealist humor and her wish to shock made

Elsa an ideal partner for artists. Picasso inspired her to print fabrics with newsprint, and Jean Cocteau drew poetic embroidery patterns which were works of art in themselves. The firm of Lesage did full justice to Schiap's artistic knitwear requirements and produced articles that are still in great demand all over the world. Like her much admired mentor Poiret, Schiap knew how to win over to fashion the most exciting artists of her time. Painters Christian Bérard, Vertès, and Kees Van Dongen worked for her, as did the poet Louis Aragon and all-round talents such as Cecil Beaton and Man Ray. This creative atmosphere inspired Elsa to design the most daring collections. She called the first one Stop, Look and Listen, and this was followed by Music, Circus, Butterflies, Commedia del l'Arte, Astrology, and Cash and Carry. She seemed to surpass herself with each new collection, and this applied not only to the designs, but also to the presentation. She turned each show into a spectacle, as Kenzo, Gaultier, and Galliano did

Right:
Actress Hélène Perdrière on
the balcony of Schiaparelli's
boutique on the Place
Vendôme.

Butterflies fluttered through Schiaparelli's famous Music collection in 1937.

Schiaparelli had to persuade Jean Cocteau to draw designs for embroidery. One of the results was this famous evening outfit which had a jacket with the profile of a woman with golden hair.

Schiaparelli combined wool stockings and oversleeves – which again became the latest in winter-wear in 1999/2000 – with Bermuda shorts. And as if women were not wrapped up enough already, there was a cap for total disguise.

This is how a career woman went to the office: a "desk" suit with "drawers," some of which are false and some real pockets. The tailored suit was inspired by a drawing by Salvador Dalí.

The woman who lived in a shoe. The famous shoe hat designed by Dalí was inspired by his wife Gala. Schiaparelli had an evening outfit made to go with it. She was one of the few who dared wear the hat.

Opposite:
Hat designs for Schiaparelli's Music collection, 1937.

Elsa Schiaparelli

Above:
Gaultier adopted Schiaparelli's bust idea for his Jean Paul Gaultier fragrance for women in 1993.

Top:
The bottle for Shocking, Elsa Schiaparelli's first perfume, was modeled on Mae West's curves.

Left:
A sumptuously embroidered and artistically tied bow in Schiaparelli's favorite pink focuses attention on the derrière of this plain evening dress. This exceptional fashion shot is by the great photographer Horst P. Horst.

Opposite:
This audacious advertisement is by artist Vertès, who often worked with Schiaparelli.

Elsa Schiaparelli

Shocking de

Mae West and W.C. Fields during shooting of the movie *My Little Chickadee* in 1940. The similarity between the actress and the bottle for the perfume Shocking is unmistakable. Legend has it that, instead of going herself for fitting, Mae West sent a tailor's dummy made to her measurements to Schiaparelli's studio in Paris and the designer used the dummy for the bottle, which was a huge success.

Schiaparelli

Above:
Elsa Schiaparelli arrives in
London in 1935. "Pants for
women," she demanded,
taking up the famous slogan
of the suffragettes' fight for
the right to vote. She herself
is wearing a restrained
version, however: culottes
from her latest collection.

decades later. It is not surprising that Schiap became the darling of the press, much to Chanel's chagrin.

Countless publications declared that Schiap was an artist, but she refused to apply that concept to herself. "There are two words I don't allow – artistic and impossible," she said. For her the only artist among fashion designers was Poiret, whose courageous colors she adopted. Her claim to fame and her trademark was shocking pink, the brilliant color she used for everything from wrapping and lipsticks to sumptuously embroidered evening capes. She wanted to shock at all costs: her last collection in 1952 was called Shocking Elegance and her biography, published in 1954, *Shocking Life*. Her most successful perfume, launched in 1938, was of course called Shocking, and she promoted it with an anecdote: apparently artist Léonor Finio had used the tailor's dummy in Schiap's studio as a model for the female-shaped perfume bottle, and the dummy itself was modeled on the measurements of Mae West.

As far as Schiaparelli was concerned, nothing was impossible. Aspirins were strung into necklaces; plastic, beetles, and bees were used in costume jewelry; zippers decorated *haute couture* evening gowns; and she used the new synthetics to create dresses of cellophane and rhodophane. Schiap found buttons boring, so she made them into little models of crickets, circus ponies, trapeze artists, crowns, and sugar cubes. She was endlessly inventive, but her greatest achievement probably was that with no background knowledge "she revolutionized fashion between

1930 and 1940," as the actress Arletty (Arlette-Léonie Bathiat), who had once worked as a model for Schiap, wrote in her memoirs. Despite all the showy effects which attracted everybody's attention, Schiap's designs really were quite simple and very wearable. Her severe suits and pant outfits, often with buttonless, box-shaped jackets, were cut like a soldier's uniform but with rounded lines and a soft silhouette, and there was always that extra small detail. Her famous boleros were more than just a luxury item: they protected the breasts and shoulders, which according to Schiap were the most vulnerable parts of a woman's body.

At the outbreak of war Elsa Schiaparelli fled to the United States. In 1945 she returned to France. Not wanting to curb her imagination for economical reasons, she was increasingly plagued by financial problems. Her postwar designs no longer seemed to suit the times. Right up to her death in 1973, however, she was still receiving a good income from her perfumes, since she always retained the licenses. She retired as a fashion designer in 1954, the very year that Coco Chanel returned to Paris after 15 years away.

Opposite:
Typically "shocking Elsa."
If there was to be costume
jewelry – which had in fact
been made socially acceptable
by her greatest rival Chanel
– then it must be totally
different from real jewelry.
From a distance Schiaparelli's
famous insect necklace
creates the illusion of real
bugs crawling around the
wearer's neck.

MEMBERS OF THE ENSEMBLE OF *LE TRAIN BLEU* AFTER THE OPENING NIGHT IN LONDON

PICASSO

COLETTE

CECIL BEATON

LE CORBUSIER

COCO CHANEL (*extreme right*), IGOR STRAVINSKY (*third from right*), AND MARIE-LAURE DE NOAILLES (*center*), WITH FRIENDS

COCO CHANEL AND CHRISTIAN BÉRARD

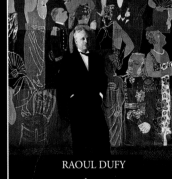
RAOUL DUFY

SCHIAPARELLI WITH DALÍ

COCO CHANEL AND SERGE LIFAR

SCHIAP, COCO, and others

There was always a great deal of speculation about the fact that Coco Chanel and Elsa Schiaparelli were supposed to be enemies. It was said that Chanel would never speak her rival's name, but referred to her as "that Italian who makes clothes." Chanel was even supposed to have maneuvered her competitor so close to a burning candelabrum at a masked ball that her costume caught fire. Conversely, it is said that Elsa always spoke of "that boring little bourgeois" and never missed an opportunity to demonstrate her intellectual superiority. The truth is that the two women moved in the same, best circles. This meant that both had achieved something that no couturier had done before, for dressmakers were seen as suppliers, however gifted or cultured they were, and suppliers were normally received at the tradesman's entrance. Chanel and Schiaparelli definitely entered the best houses through the front door, as welcome guests of the social élite.

Malicious gossip had it that Chanel achieved these heights only through her relationship with the richest man in England, the Duke of Westminster. Schiaparelli, on the other hand, on account of her background, education, and cosmopolitanism, belonged quite naturally to high society. Some of the designers' mutual friends used gibes to stir up jealousy between them for their own amusement, and both women found this useful. The blown-up competition between them pushed them to give of their very best. Both Chanel and Schiap orchestrated all their public appearances as media spectacles, and they were supported in this by top photographers and journalists. In this way they were their own best advertisers and they turned themselves into stars. This helped them reach beyond the exclusive couture clientele to a broader public which then wanted to buy their accessories and perfumes – and both women had come to realize that this was where big business lay.

Together Schiaparelli and Chanel changed the status of couturiers for ever, despite the fact that they could not have been more different. They may not have been the enemies that malicious Parisian pundits claimed them to be, but they certainly represented completely opposite positions. Chanel put forward simple, comfortable elegance, whereas Schiaparelli preached vibrant, colorful extravagance. One example underlines the difference: Chanel offered practical slacks, while Schiap designed capricious capri pants. On the other hand, Schiap offered severe modern plastic jewelry, while Chanel pinned shimmering baroque brooches to her simple jersey suits. Perhaps it is not so easy after all to draw the borderline between the two as far as style is concerned.

The artists and trendsetters of the time also found this difficult. Their circles of friends overlapped and for a time were almost identical. The whole of Paris, from Colette and Cocteau to Picasso and Dalí, in fact anyone who meant anything in 1930s Paris, found themselves drawn to the two giants of fashion.

Christian Bérard, the famous illustrator, painter, and stage designer, for example, designed costume jewelry for both Chanel and Schiaparelli. Cocteau, whom Chanel had helped with drug cures, accepted commissions from Schiap for embroidery patterns. On the other hand, he commissioned Coco to design costumes for all the plays and movies that he himself wrote or put on, which could not have been financially profitable for her. Furthermore, Chanel sponsored many artists of the time, including the Ballets Russes. After she had met the impresario Sergei Diaghilev in Venice, she offered to finance the revival of *The Rite of Spring*. Chanel also got to know Igor Stravinsky through the Ballets Russes, and he was captivated by her. The Russian composer was in financial difficulties, and Chanel is said to have supported him for years. Apart from the fact that Chanel was generous by nature, patronage also flattered her vanity and brought her recognition in society.

Schiap also helped many artists with commissions. For both designers, however, it was not merely a question of charity. They simply wanted to be surrounded by the most discussed artists of their age. Schiap had her new apartment decorated by Jean-Michel Frank, the most famous interior designer of the 1930s, with works by Dalí, Bérard, and Giacometti. She invited Chanel to the house-warming party, but Coco found the strictly modern ambiance "as cold as a graveyard."

Nina Ricci (1883–1970)

Italian dressmaker Nina Ricci, who opened her couture salon in Paris in 1932, developed and shaped her designs directly on a live model. In this way she was like Madeleine Vionnet, but this was probably the only similarity between the two designers. Nina Ricci had nothing in common with her fellow-countrywoman Schiaparelli either. She was neither provocative nor understated, and Chanel's modern simplicity meant nothing to her. Nina Ricci loved patterns and delicate colors. Flowers were an ever-recurring motif, and they were embroidered, printed, and appliquéd on her designs. Her clothes had to be romantic, feminine, and at the same time ladylike. They allowed the wearers, who came mostly from the upper middle class, to radiate discreet elegance, which was highly appropriate in the difficult political and economic climate of the 1930s. She gained a following that quickly grew. Having started with a staff of 40, Ricci was able to employ 450 women by 1939. She retired in the 1950s, and her son Robert, who had encouraged and helped her to expand the business, took over the running of it.

Opposite:
The evening gown Minuit by Nina Ricci.

Below:
This portrait of Nina Ricci, by Cireuse, dates from 1932, the year in which she opened her salon.

Alix Grès (1899–1993)

Chanel and Schiaparelli lent so much glamour to the profession of couturier that more and more talented people had the courage to set up on their own. The two giants outshone everyone else, however, and it might seem that it was due exclusively to them that 1930s fashion became the most copied of the century. It should be added that Vionnet's bias cut also continues to have a lasting influence.

Vionnet found a successor in Alix Grès, who worked with the same feel for material and movement. Alix, who traded under the name Madame Grès from 1942, had wanted to be a sculptor, but her family did not support her in this. She finally started to drape dresses directly on her customers, and like Nina Ricci she cut straight out from the material without making a pattern first. Her dresses were mostly white and their elaborate draping was reminiscent of Greek robes. They were presented without any decoration, embroidery, or accessories. This style made them classics in the truest sense of the word, and Madame Grès' 1930s designs do not seem old-fashioned even today. Alix opened her first fashion house in 1931, and right up to her death in 1993 she influenced whole generations of designers with her timeless ideal of beauty and her skill as a craftswoman. At the age of 81 she was daring and adventurous enough to launch a ready-to-wear range, for which she used mainly tweeds and soft woolen materials. As a doyenne of couture Madame Grès was chair of the Chambre Syndicale de la Couture for 20 years from 1972.

Opposite:
Presented like ancient Greek sculptures, two richly draped designs from 1935 (*right*) and 1939 (*left*). Alix Grès loved classical designs.

Right:
Madame Grès, as Alix Grès liked to call herself, fitting a dress. She often used up to 20 yards of material for a single design.

Maggy Rouff (1896–1971)

Maggy Rouff, who founded her own house in 1929, was one of the quiet fashion greats of the 1930s. As a girl Rouff wanted to become a surgeon, but she eventually went into the family-owned sportswear business in Vienna. Under her own name she developed an elegant, body-embracing line with drapes at the waist for day wear and uneven hems and ruches for the evening. She was seen as a cool intellectual, and in her designs even organdy, puff sleeves, and bows did not seem cute. Her early work in sportswear had taught her that even the most decorative elements had to be functional. Many of her early day dresses had scarves which could be tied in various ways as a collar. The house of Maggy Rouff was closed after her death in 1971.

Maggy Rouff presented her fashions without frills, just like modern designers. The coat (*below*) has a sculptural look; Rouff had a preference for sophisticated sleeves. Both designs date from 1934.

Marcel Rochas (1902–55)

It would be easy to think that all the leading fashion designers immediately before World War II were women. This was not the case, however. There was Marcel Rochas, for example, who opened his own fashion house and a few years later, in 1931, moved it to the Avenue Matignon. Rochas often came up with ideas that were as original as Schiaparelli's. There might be stuffed robins on the shoulders of a dress, or it might be printed with tiny books. Like Schiap he turned buttons into small works of art. He used transparent cellophane, phosphorescent lamé, and furs dyed in bright colors. In 1932 he also became the first to design a pantsuit in gray flannel that was intended for day wear; until then there had only been pants for leisure wear, or silk pajamas for intimate dinners.

Why just have feathers when you can have the whole bird? Marcel Rochas risked it in 1934. Alexander McQueen revived the idea for Givenchy in 1998/99 (*below*).

Mainbocher (1890–1976)

Opposite:
After 1939 Mainbocher also designed wide skirts, anticipating the postwar New Look.

Below:
Mainbocher, the first successful American couturier in Paris, was famous for his elegant style. The design with a summer pattern (*far right*) is not very typical.

Three influential designers each decided to combine their first and second names to form their trademark: Mainbocher, Louiseboulanger, and Augustabernard. The American Main Bocher resigned as editor-in-chief of French *Vogue* in 1929, and in the following year he opened a couture salon in Paris. In honor of Augustabernard and Louiseboulanger and in order to make his name sound more French, he called himself Mainbocher from then on. His elegant style soon brought him great success in Parisian circles. In the last season before the outbreak of war he created designs that were out of keeping with the current fashion, just as Molyneux and Chanel did. These designs, which had wasp waists and wide skirts, were precursors of the New Look which Dior would introduce almost ten years later to revive couture. Until then, however, outfits with a slight military feel, with wide shoulders and tight skirts, were popular with the few who could afford fashion in those days. For many people 1939 was the last opportunity for a long time to have clothes made to measure, and the threat of war caused all sales records to be broken by the collections of August 1939. Mainbocher left Paris in 1940 and opened a salon in New York, right next to Tiffany. From then until the 1960s he remained the undisputed leading couturier of the American upper classes.

Mainbocher believed that "wearability is half the secret of good clothes." He saw his customers as immaculate ladies whose appearance could allow no criticism. It was as if he was predestined to make clothes for a certain Wallis Simpson, who was well known for her pedantically neat and tidy appearance and who was to succeed in having the British king abdicate in order to marry her. Her wedding gown, a long, slim robe in a pale grayish blue, was of course by Mainbocher.

Duchesse de Windsor

Ensemble en imprimé et crêpe blanc. Long manteau cintré.

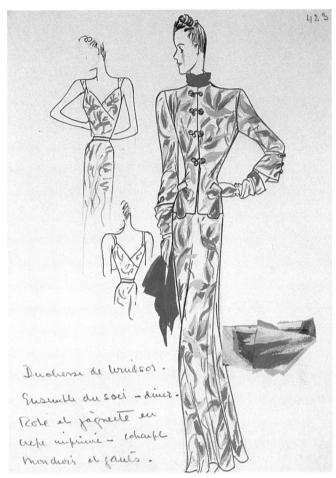

Duchesse de Windsor.
Ensemble du soir – dîner.
Robe et jaquette en crêpe imprimé – écharpe mouchoir et gants.

For many British people the world collapsed when the popular Prince of Wales, who had succeeded his father George V to become King Edward VIII, abdicated in December 1936 in order to marry the twice-divorced American, Mrs. Wallis Simpson. If at least she had been pretty! After all, the young king had earned a reputation as a playboy and trendsetter, and people had expected his reign to be a time of stylish amusement. And now he chose to go into exile in France, alone with this woman.

When England lost a king, however, the world of fashion won a queen. For Wallis Simpson, who became the Duchess of Windsor, knew: "I am not a beautiful woman. The only thing to do is to dress better than all the others." She achieved this remarkably quickly with the help of her friend Elsie de Wolfe, who introduced Mainbocher and Schiaparelli to her. The prudish elegance of her compatriot Mainbocher's designs especially matched the duchess's taste, and she was loyal to him for a long time. She patronized other couture houses too, such as Chanel. After all, she needed 100 new dresses a year.

The Duke of Windsor bought all his wife's matching jewelry, and it was important to him that they were always unique pieces. No other woman in the world should be able to compare herself to the queen of his heart. When the jewels were auctioned in 1987 after the death of the duchess, they fetched $50 million, which in accordance with her will was donated to AIDS research. Not bad for a woman who described herself in her autobiography as a simple housewife. In any event she ran her grand household strictly and with a fussy emphasis on order and neatness. She had the napkins changed twice at every dinner, and her hairdresser came three times a day to make sure that her hair was perfect. No wonder she became so famous in the world of fashion. After she had appeared on the list of the world's ten best-dressed women ten times in succession, the Duchess of Windsor was promoted to the fashion hall of fame. This meant that she had achieved her declared aim: her husband, who had given everything up for her, could be proud of her.

Above:
Mainbocher kept a separate design book for the Duchess of Windsor, who was his most important client. He had her exclusively in mind in all his designs, which consisted of long, slim dresses, never low-cut and usually with sleeves. The duchess did not like to reveal her boyish figure and so always remained elegant.

Opposite:
Mainbocher achieved worldwide fame with the wedding gown that he designed in 1937 for Wallis Simpson, the future Duchess of Windsor.

Augustabernard (1886–1946)

Augusta Bernard was the first to have the idea of combining her two names so that she could never be confused with anyone else. She set up on her own in 1919, and her unusual designs were attractive to confident women. The Marquise de Paris won the 1930 Concours d'élégance at St. Moritz in a silver lamé design by Augustabernard. For her evening gowns she often chose pale colors, perfect for a walk by moonlight and ideal for showing expensive jewelry to its best advantage. Her day dresses and suits were simple and practical, often worn with a scarf or a small V-necked blouse. Her favorite material for day wear was the sort of rough tweed that she probably grew up with in the provinces.

Right:
This flowing evening gown from the mid-1930s is typical of Augustabernard's creations.

Below:
Argentina in a simple outfit of grass-green serge by Augustabernard, with a collarless jacket, angled pockets, and a wide leather belt.

Louiseboulanger (1878–c. 1950)

Louiseboulanger's designs were considered young and daring. In 1927 she was the first to lengthen *garçonne* skirts by adding trains. After a short break she opened her own salon again in 1934 and surprised everyone with a modern form of bustle, which sat on the bottom like a pouffe. She was very imaginative in her use of her favorite materials, organdy and taffeta, which she used on the right and reverse sides in order to achieve different effects. In 1939 she gave up couture and in doing so took a sideswipe at her modern competitors: "When tennis came in, the demimondaine left the scene," she said. "Fashion went with her." This was far from the truth, for fashion was more diverse than ever, and only the war would stop new talent.

Left:
In contrast to Augustabernard, Louiseboulanger loved colors and patterns, as illustrated by this photograph by Man Ray.

Below:
Tulle dress by Louiseboulanger.

The look of the decade

Germaine Monteil, one of the greatest women in the world of cosmetics. In the 1930s she pointed out the importance of skincare, nutrition, and physical fitness to the complexion, in addition to good make-up.

Right:
The right perfume was essential to the elegant woman. Many fragrances were still heavy and sweet, but more modern, clear scents like Chanel N° 5 were catching on. Jean Patou was one of the first to launch successful perfumes, including Joy, which for a long time was the most expensive fragrance in the world.

Opposite:
Perfection was a question of make-up artistry. Plucked eyebrows were carefully drawn over; eye shadow and false eyelashes gave more depth to the eyes; a lip pencil was used to give the mouth a better shape, enhanced by lip rouge. All this created "natural" beauty.

In the 1930s the ideal of beauty was quite straightforward. A woman should be slim, but in a feminine rather than a boyish way. She should be sporty, suntanned, natural, and well groomed. The woman of the 1930s had realized that true beauty comes from within, and so she set great store by living close to nature, with healthy food and plenty of outdoor activity, if possible without any clothes on at all.

The heavily made-up mask of the 1920s was now seen as vulgar, and a so-called individual look was in demand. In order to achieve this, a woman needed the following: an eyebrow pencil to draw semicircles over the carefully plucked eyebrows; eye shadow in gold or silver, or possibly mixed with the usual blue, brown, or violet; mascara, or if necessary false eyelashes; Vaseline, to add sparkle to the eye make-up; and rouge for the cheeks, which was no longer put on as a blob but more evenly applied. She needed a lip pencil and a small brush for putting on lipstick. She had let her hair grow again and wore it at least to chin length, carefully waved and combed away from the forehead. The preferred color was blonde, best of all platinum blonde, which reflected light so well and went so beautifully with evening gowns in shimmering pearl and champagne. The matching complexion had to be flawless, like that of the screen goddesses, though of course Hollywood used all sorts of lighting and make-up tricks that were not available to ordinary women. It was a well-known fact that many a star achieved her "natural" complexion with the help of the Pan-Cake developed by Max Factor, and female fans made a fuss until compact make-up was made available to everyone in 1938.

"Beauty is not a gift but a habit," said Germaine Monteil, who founded her own cosmetics company in 1935 and drummed it into her customers that it was not simply a matter of putting on make-up. She introduced a care ritual of thorough cleaning, with one cream for the day and another for the night. Other companies brought out antiwrinkle creams enriched with estrogen or vitamins. It was expected of every woman that she made use of all these products, and in addition that she kept her body in perfect trim by practicing various sports. This all sounds so modern that it could easily refer to the 1990s.

Then as now people believed in the achievement principle, suggesting that beauty is always attainable. Hollywood delivered the best examples of this, by turning provincial actresses into immaculate stars overnight. Make-up artists were magicians who could fit every woman's face to the Greek ideal of a gentle oval which could be divided vertically into three equal parts and horizontally into five. Since practically no one came up to this standard, the make-up artists had a major job to do. They knew how to work with light and shadow so that every face looked like a classical sculpture under the studio lights. The woman in the street tried her best to come close to this ideal, to the joy of the cosmetics industry. There was much talk about personality, but in the end everything individual, including couture, was only for a small élite. The masses took their lead from the movies and tried to copy the total look developed by the studios, from the top of their head to the tips of their toes.

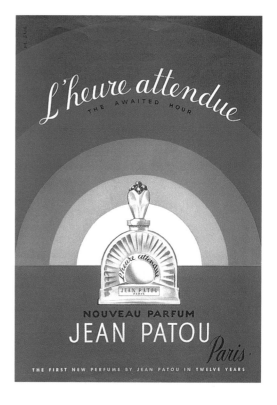

AMELIA EARHART

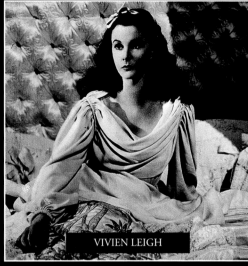

VIVIEN LEIGH

LENI RIEFENSTAHL

LEE MILLER

GRETA GARBO

MARLENE DIETRICH

JEAN HARLOW

Idols of the decade

Nothing could compare with the influence which the movies had on the general public. Nevertheless, one woman succeeded in becoming a worldwide idol without the help of Hollywood. **Amelia Earhart** (1898–1937) was the first woman to fly solo across the Atlantic. Her androgynous look – created by her pants, shirt, and necktie, and particularly her leather jacket – started a trend in fashion. The fact that her plane mysteriously disappeared over the Pacific on an attempted flight around the world contributed to her becoming a romantic role model to modern women.

The artistic circles of Paris had always chosen their own idols, and in the 1930s it was a young American woman who drew the most admiration: **Lee Miller** (1907–77) had been a top model in New York, and in 1929 she came to Paris to become a photographer herself. She chose Man Ray as her teacher, and she soon moved in with him. This relationship did not stop her from having affairs with other men, which in those days was the done thing in Montparnasse. Man Ray immortalized her lips in his famous photograph *Hour of the Weather Station: the Lovers*. Lee Miller was the favorite model of many other photographers, such as George Hoyningen-Huene and Horst P. Horst. At the same time she herself developed into an excellent photographer, and at the end of the war she became famous for her photographs documenting the horrors of the Nazi concentration camps. Their publication in *Vogue* caused great uproar.

Amazingly, it was a British actress who won the role coveted by every Hollywood beauty: **Vivien Leigh** (1913–67) was chosen to play Scarlett O'Hara in *Gone with the Wind* in 1939. Her passionate performance showed that the choice had been the right one, and it won her an Oscar. Some years later she won a second Oscar for another typically American role in *A Streetcar Named Desire*, and this secured her place in movie history. As well as being a great actress, she possessed a tender beauty that predestined her to become a star.

At any other time in history **Greta Garbo** (1905–90) would probably not even have been given the chance to become a screen idol. The Swedish former shopgirl was tall, broad-shouldered, flat-chested, and narrow-hipped, which meant that she was not exactly seen as star material when she arrived in Hollywood in the mid-1920s. However, the camera revealed hidden qualities in her symmetrical face, with enormous eyes that she mostly kept lowered and beautiful lips that she mostly kept closed. She possessed an unapproachable, alabaster beauty that implied that she knew all the secrets of love but kept them to herself. A screen goddess was born and set off a cult that was only furthered by her retirement from movies in 1941. Garbo remains unforgettable for her roles in *Anna Christie* (1930), *Queen Christina* (1933), *Anna Karenina* (1935), and *Ninotchka* (1939).

Marlene Dietrich (1901–92) was taken to Hollywood as the "second Garbo" after her sensational performance in *The Blue Angel* (1930). But she quickly showed that she was not a rehash of anyone else: she possessed her own unique charisma. Unlike Garbo, who showed no particular interest in clothes in her private life, Dietrich's liking for men's clothes made her a model for many women who did not want their taste in clothes or indeed their lifestyle dictated to them. Many of her movie costumes had a fetishistic character to them, from top hat and tails to feather boas and veils. In her later years Marlene Dietrich performed more as a singer and cabaret star, and in her sequined dresses she continued to demonstrate her inimitable feel for glamour.

Platinum blonde hair and white satin have been seen as symbols of the sinful female since the time of **Jean Harlow** (1911–37). The dentist's daughter from Kansas City started out as a little blonde angel. Hollywood then gave her an appearance that was so artificial that it looked almost cheap, but it was at least easy for her fans to copy. Her parts and dialogues, written by such intelligent scriptwriters as Anita Loos and Dorothy Parker, were much more natural, however. Her cheeky wisecracks were probably as attractive to men as the gaudy silk dresses beneath which she clearly wore absolutely nothing. Jean Harlow died of uremia at the age of 26. It may be that gentlemen prefer blondes, but blondes – artificial ones at least – seem destined to have a short life in Hollywood. Marilyn Monroe was another example in the 1960s.

The 1930s constituted a glorious yet fateful decade in the long life of **Leni Riefenstahl**, who was born in Berlin in 1902. Trained as a dancer, she starred in *Storms over Mont Blanc* (1930) and *The White Frenzy* (1931). She then directed and starred in *The Blue Light* (1932), which established her reputation as a movie genius. However, her success attracted a dangerous admirer in the form of Adolf Hitler. On the promise that she would have total control over her choice of material from then on, Leni Riefenstahl allowed herself to become involved in filming the 1934 Nazi rally at Nuremberg. Thanks to her talents, *Triumph of the Will* became a most influential propaganda movie. She was also criticized for being of service to the Nazis with her two-part *Olympia* (*Festival of Peoples* and *Festival of Beauty*), her record of the 1936 Olympic Games in Berlin. In this case, however, the International Olympic Committee was the client. In 1939 she received the IOC's gold medal for her work, which she richly deserved, for the documentary is a masterpiece of camerawork and editing. American director George Lucas expressed his admiration in 1992, when he called Riefenstahl "the most modern moviemaker of all." In Germany the general opinion of Riefenstahl is a negative one and her movies are seen as glorifying the Third Reich, since she has never distanced herself from her work in the 1930s and has never expressed a word of regret. No longer sought after as a moviemaker, Riefenstahl started a second career as a photographer, and once again her work was well received, at least outside Germany. Her books on the Nuba tribe of southern Sudan, published in 1973 and 1976, were praised, and the photographs were exhibited from New York to Tokyo. At the age of 70 she learned to dive and took up underwater photography, with inevitable success. With her unerring eye for beauty and its portrayal, Leni Riefenstahl deserves to be seen as one of the great talents of the 20th century.

The big white dress

Mistinguett (Jeanne Marie Bourgeois), here in a dress by Edward Molyneux, loved white. She felt that it helped make her look young, especially after the age of 60.

Opposite:
Innocent white looked decidedly sinful on Jean Harlow. Perhaps this inspired Courtney Love (*inset*) to wear this dress to the 69th Academy Awards ceremony in 1996.

Having established the "little black dress" as fashionable, in 1931 Coco Chanel conceived the idea of introducing a whole series of white evening gowns. Hollywood saw the potential of the "big white dress" at once and combined Chanel's idea with Madeleine Vionnet's artistic bias cut, which was always shown to best advantage in light-colored silk. This led to the development of that shimmering satin robe which became the quintessence of sex appeal. For a perfect skintight fit the dress was taped to the bare skin and could only be taken off with the help of an iron. In being taken up by the film industry, the dress lost both innocence and elegance but gained something that could only be found there: glamour. The "big white dress" has become an enduring image of Hollywood's stars. Its special quality is its ability to reflect studio lights, making it reliable for all the big entrances and performances, especially for blondes.

This beautifully draped, stylish dress (*right*), designed by Maggy Rouff in 1941, emphasized the figure. In 1994 Thierry Mugler revived this ingenious style (*above*).

Opposite:
This photograph of actress Carole Lombard in her house in Hollywood shows the sensual effect that can be produced from a combination of cut, material, and color.

Vionnet, *c.* 1935

Chanel, 1935

Lelong, 1933

Versace, 1995/96

Versace, spring 1995

Dior, summer 1997

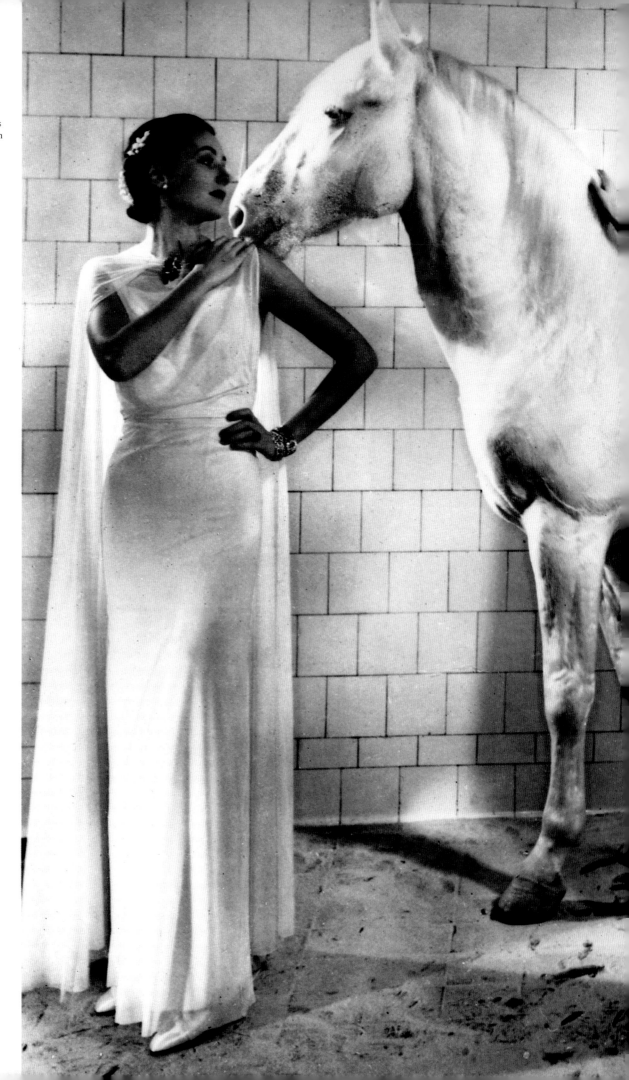

White heat. There is a great deal of subliminal eroticism in Edward Steichen's famous photograph of three ladies in white with a white stallion.

Fashion and the movies

Seductive, beautiful, and glamorous. Hollywood certainly knew how to dress its stars and it understood how the fashion industry could share in its success. Jean Harlow was the perfect example in *Dinner at Eight* (1933).

Movies changed everything, even fashion. *Vogue* rightly posed the question: "Which influences which?" Certainly each had a great effect on the other, and this helped to broaden fashion's influence enormously and made couturiers even more famous. Costume designers, on the other hand, were scarcely known outside the movie industry. Yet it was not as if they simply copied the great Parisian couturiers. The "big white dress," for example, was not merely taken over

from the couture salons but was transformed into a dress that seemed to fit and belong to a particular star like a second skin. In the movies it is fashion's job to serve. It had a supporting role.

No one understood this better than Gilbert Adrian, who adapted the "big white dress" for Jean Harlow and literally taped it to her body. The director George Cukor, who made many of the glamorous movies of the time, said of Adrian's work: "If an actress had a poor figure, it was best to cover it up, but if she had a great figure, then Adrian made sure that all her assets were shown to the best effect."

Clearly Adrian discovered assets where others saw none. He developed a style for Joan Crawford, for example, which strongly emphasized her shoulders. Initiates believed that he wanted to create a balance for Crawford's broad hips, but in reality he was impressed by her unusual physique. "You've got shoulders like Johnny Weissmüller," he told her in admiration, and dressed her up as if she really was the first Tarzan in movie history – only much more feminine. In 1932 he heaped ruche upon ruche on her shoulders for the movie *Letty Lynton*, and this puff-pastry construction made of white organza was so popular with the moviegoing public that Macy's store sold 500,000 copies at $20 each. The dress established Joan Crawford as a style-shaping movie star, and from then on her costumes were always mass-produced and sold all over the United States to wannabe career women. Adrian also invented the power suit for Crawford, and this came back in the 1980s. Most importantly, he realized something that others had missed: physical disadvantages can certainly be disguised by clothes, but they can also be emphasized so that they become something of a personal strength, maybe even setting a new trend. Adrian's wide-shouldered outfits sold so well in the 1930s and 1940s that he himself joked: "Who would have thought that my whole career would rest on Crawford's shoulders?"

Adrian achieved cult status with the 1939 movie *The Women*, in which he designed the clothes for Joan Crawford, Norma Shearer, Rosalind Russell, Joan Fontaine, Paulette Goddard, and Hedda Hopper. This wonderful comedy, directed by George Cukor, starred only

Opposite:
Adrian was a master at dressing stars in such a way that their figures looked perfect and they radiated brilliance.

Opposite:
Joan Crawford in one of her
famous dresses, half a million
copies of which were sold.

Right:
Not just fashion for the
movies, but a movie about
fashion: in the comedy
The Women "man-eating"
Joan Crawford showed a lot
of bare skin, Norma Shearer
was a good, honest wife all in
white, and Rosalind Russell
a silly gossip with a silly hat.
The costumes characterized
the roles.

Fashion and the movies

women and revolved around finding and acquiring the right clothes. It also set out the real importance of a woman's make-up: no woman can scratch another's eyes out without Jungle Red on her nails!

Adrian was born to parents in the fashion trade in Connecticut in 1903. After studying art he worked at first in the theater until he was discovered for the movies by the wife of silent movie star Rudolph Valentino. From 1928 to 1942 he worked for MGM and designed the look of all their great stars. He had the rare talent of being able to design historical costumes as well as fashionable clothes. Actresses often chose to wear his designs off the set too.

Adrian created a more moderate, much more successful style for Greta Garbo, who had not been shown to her best advantage in overblown Hollywood costumes. He created the famous slouch hat to go with her trench coat, and Garbo continued to wear this outfit even though she declared: "I never could stand his stuff." Others loved Adrian's clothes so much that he set up his own couture house in 1942. He died in 1959.

Travis Banton (1894–1958) was Adrian's counterpart at Paramount, being responsible for the image of the top stars. He dressed Marlene Dietrich from head to toe in expensive lace, exotic feathers, and magnificent furs. It was intended that her body remain a secret, like her accent. For comedienne Carole Lombard he created the bias-cut dresses that will for ever define the glamour of the 1930s. For Claudette Colbert he developed the "Colbert collar," which made the neck look longer and more beautiful. In *Love Me Tonight*, the most successful musical of the decade, Jeanette MacDonald and starlet Myrna Loy wore very little, but Banton used silk and lace with great imagination to create wonderful lingerie. Banton founded his own fashion business in 1938, but he went on working for various movie studios on a freelance basis. When Banton left Paramount, his place was taken by his assistant Edith Head (1898–1981), and she certainly made the best of this opportunity. With 35 Oscar nominations and eight Academy Awards, she became the most successful woman in the history of Hollywood.

Travis Banton, here with Claudette Colbert, created the image of Paramount stars. The secret of great costume designers is to let their talents serve the movie and to concentrate on the figure, role, and personality of the star in order to show her to her best possible advantage.

Opposite:
Marlene Dietrich, seen here in *Angel* (1937), was one of the great actresses for whom Travis Banton's designs became a trademark.

Below:
Costume designer Edith Head in her studio. For her stars, who included Grace Kelly, she designed costumes which every woman would have liked to wear.

She earned her first plaudits in 1932 when Banton was away at the Paris couture collections and she designed the costumes for Mae West's new movie *She Done Him Wrong*. The voluptuous actress gave the newcomer important instructions: "My dresses must be loose enough to prove that I'm a lady and tight enough to show that I'm a woman." Edith Head clearly understood exactly what Mae West meant, and it is partly due to the costume designer that the movie broke all box-office records and saved Paramount from bankruptcy.

Edith Head was also very understanding about problems with Barbara Stanwyck's figure, which were holding her back from becoming a glamour goddess. Edith thought up a little trick to improve the actress's rear view. She draped her in gold lamé and covered her in paste gemstones. Hollywood had a new sex symbol and Edith had a new friend. Her greatest talent, however, was her discretion, which made her a close friend of the stars.

"Edith was more of a coordinator than a designer," said Loretta Young, with whom Edith worked on five movies. This agreed with Edith's own assessment. "I knew that I was no creative genius," she said. "I was better at diplomacy than I was at design." Her skills meant that she stayed with Paramount until 1967, and over a period of 30 years she worked with stars such as Elizabeth Taylor, Bette Davis, and Grace Kelly, whose styles were copied by entire generations. She made 11 movies with Alfred Hitchcock, who had complete faith in her. She had the ability to conceal the secret depths of his cool blondes in the most bourgeois clothes.

When the first Oscar for costume design was due to be awarded in 1948, Edith Head, who was then 50, was sure that she would receive it, if only for her "ability to survive," as she put it. She was absolutely stunned when the award went elsewhere. In later years she took the coveted prize several times, however, sometimes for movies to which other designers had applied the real gloss, such as *A Heart and a Crown* and *Sabrina*. Audrey Hepburn preferred the work of the gentleman couturier Hubert de Givenchy, who was far too refined to quibble over tiresome questions of copyright. Hollywood really only wanted to work with the great French couturiers, but the pragmatic American costume designers had a better understanding of the movie business. They placed their talents entirely at the service of the stars, whereas the couturiers wanted to be stars themselves. The couturiers had a few hundred customers a year at most,

Edith Head with Grace Kelly. She designed Kelly's costume for Hitchcock's *To Catch a Thief* (1955). Fashion manufacturers and home dressmakers all over the United States copied the dress. Many creations from the studios of the Hollywood dressmakers took a similar direction. It was the same with the ready-made version of the white chiffon dress that Elizabeth Taylor wore in *Cat on a Hot Tin Roof* (1958), which sold in huge quantities and launched the fashion career of costume designer Helen Rose. The success of costume designs with American women shows that the prudish USA has its own tradition of frivolous extravagance.

189

1

2

3

4

5

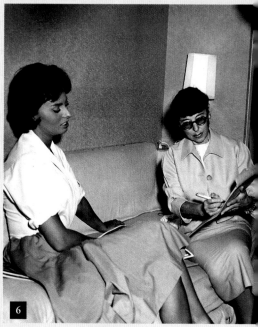

6

7

8

9

while the movies pulled in 90 million customers week after week, and most moviegoers could scarcely tell the difference between costumes and couture. Whatever a star wore was fashionable, both in the movies and in life. The stars attended the great Paris fashion shows and spent a large portion of their considerable income in the couture houses. Fashion and the movies flourished together in the heyday of the 1930s.

This was exactly what the big studio bosses had in mind, for most of them came from the clothing industry and had an interest in presenting and publicizing textiles and furs effectively. It is not surprising that fashion played a leading role in many early movies. At the same time, fashion designers had also discovered the importance of motion pictures early on. Soon after the first color movie came out in 1910, the *Kinemacolor Fashion Gazette* was published regularly in England, and Paul Poiret made a movie about his 1913 collection for the benefit of his American customers. However, when Poiret traveled to the United States, the movie was confiscated for its "pornographic content": it contained scenes of women wearing pant suits! In 1925 the Eastman Color Process made it possible to show natural skin tones and various shades of red, which made movies about fashion interesting and helped the success of the *McCall Fashion News*. The first movie in this series showed designs by Poiret, Worth, and Lanvin.

Changing fashions caused the moviemakers great difficulties. Just when they had finished making a movie with the latest, most expensive clothes, Paris would bring out a new line and make the movie look out of date before it even reached the theaters. This was one of the reasons why producer Samuel Goldwyn, who had previously been a glove manufacturer, wanted to have his costumes designed by Coco Chanel. She would surely know what Paris would be showing next; after all she was known as the great innovator. Chanel's simple black-and-white suits did not come across well in color movies, however, and her Hollywood connection was not a success. It is said that the stars boycotted Coco Chanel because the great lady of fashion did not look after them herself but had the work done by her deputy Jane Courtois, to which they took exception. Coco saw things differently and got on with her career without the movies.

Other Parisian couturiers, such as Molyneux, Patou, and Rochas, found it easier to deal with the pampered stars. The most successful of all was Schiaparelli, who worked first for English movies and then for Hollywood, where she designed costumes for sex symbols such as Zsa Zsa Gabor and Mae West. Katharine Hepburn, the nonconformist intellectual, would have suited her style better, and she found her way privately to Schiaparelli in 1933. Her look changed from careless to casual, and suddenly her boyish appearance was no longer ungainly but incredibly cool and turned her into a fashion idol. Schiaparelli's style also greatly influenced Joan Crawford, and we cannot be certain who introduced her famous shoulder pads – was it Schiaparelli, from whom Crawford bought couture, or Adrian, whose costumes made her a star?

During World War II Hollywood took over the definitive role in fashion. Most of the Paris couture houses closed, and the rest operated at a very low level. The movie studios also had to battle with restrictions such as tighter budgets, and some materials and luxury items such as lace, fur, and sequins were unobtainable. The 1943 movie *Casablanca* proved that it was possible to do without those things. It was an overwhelming success, even though Ingrid Bergman and Humphrey Bogart wore more or less realistic clothes. Bergman wore the severe outfits of the day, while Bogart had his crumpled raincoat, which up until then had been worn on screen only by gangsters.

Apart from this, realism was never in great demand, and attempts to use movies as propaganda rarely worked with the public. After all, people went to the movie theater to escape dreadful everyday reality and, if possible, to revisit the "good old days." The world seemed to be fine when women had laced-up wasp waists and wore skirts as wide as parachutes, even during times of civil war such as in *Gone with the Wind*. When they have been survived, wars are always victories, and moviegoers identified with Scarlett O'Hara when she took drapes down from the window to make herself a ball gown. Everyone had to take up their own needle and thread and make do with what they had. Old movie costumes were undone and altered for new parts. Gradually governments showed more understanding and gave the movie industry more material, so that moviemakers could create the dreams that make people happy.

Marlene Dietrich made a great impression with *The Flame of New Orleans* in 1941, in a dress of pure lace. Before the war the dress would have been copied a thousand times, but now that lace was unavailable it was simply a greatly admired, unique piece. Ginger Rogers' costume in *Lady in the Dark*, made of mink and sequins,

was seen as the height of extravagance. For her next movie, also made in 1944, she had to wear rayon instead of silk. Synthetic fibers were the savior of all festive occasions. For their daughters' final ball, thousands of American mothers tried to copy the white organdy dress worn by Deanna Durbin in *Nice Girl?*

In 1943 a movie came out that changed women's figures rather than fashion. It was the voluptuous Jane Russell who showed off her curvaceous figure in Howard Hughes' *The Outlaw*, replacing the androgynous type who had reigned supreme since the 1920s. Curves came into fashion, and if there were no curves, padding did the job. This prepared the ground for Christian Dior's New Look, which revived the hourglass silhouette of the turn of the century. The exclusive link between fashion and the movies ended with World War II. There would still be cooperation between the two fields, but their common influence on markets was broken. Couture and movies were never again as close as they had been during the time when silent movies became talkies and black-and-white tuned into color. Then fashion could still replace plot, and a talent for wearing beautiful clothes was more important than acting ability.

It was another 50 years before fashion and the movies found themselves together again, albeit in a different way. Designers grew tired of highly paid models simply posing in a meaningless way and began looking for expressive actresses to wear their creations, especially at important events such as the Academy Awards ceremony. This meant that couture and the movie world met up at least once a year, at the Oscars. This lucrative liaison began in 1990 with an article in *Women's Wear Daily*, the influential textile journal. The cover of one particular issue showed two stars: Kim Basinger was dolled up in a robe with a single long glove, while Michelle Pfeiffer was in a simple Armani suit. No words were needed to point out how modern glamour should look. Armani was flooded with requests from stars for the following year's Oscars. Five years later Uma Thurman appeared at the ceremony in a lavender gown and stole, catapulting herself onto magazine covers and bringing Prada to the attention of Hollywood. Since then the Academy Awards ceremony has become the most expensive fashion show in the world. By 1999 there was no longer a single star who did not appear in a designer outfit.

1940–1949

Fashion is indestructible

1940–1949

War and couture do not exactly go together, one might think. On the one hand the destruction of the world, on the other the creation of beauty. And yet it was in fashion, this frivolous nonentity, that French resistance found its natural expression. Despite the scarcity of material and strict emergency laws, French women lived up to their reputation of being the best-dressed women in the world, even during World War II. They showed their independence by overcoming all the problems of the time and developing a highly extravagant line. Everywhere else women saw it as their duty to dress modestly and unobtrusively, but French women kept the flag flying: blood-red lipstick as well as colorful clothes, preferably in blue, white and red, strengthened morale and the Résistance movement.

Nevertheless, compared with the natural elegance of the 1930s,

fashion did lose its lightness of touch during the German occupation. Many designs had an affected look: colorful silk scarves were turned into peasant dresses and turbans, or they were sewn onto outfits and pants as patches, not to cover up wear and tear but out of pure coquettishness. Hats and shoes got higher and higher. Women teetered on platform soles and wedge heels made of wood or cork. On their heads they balanced embellishments made of every conceivable material, from newspaper and veils to flowers, velvet, and feathers, for milliners were the only ones who did not suffer a shortage of materials.

Many women hit upon the idea of adding a real hat to this construction, if only to show the occupying power that they could do it. Despite the overornate headgear and clumsy footwear, the rest of the body was not shown to advantage, even if the short dresses were made of pure silk. This in itself was a scandal. "While we wear artificial silk," American *Vogue* complained, "French women

Previous page:
This photograph by Cecil Beaton is totally appropriate for the times. The model, wearing a suit by English designer Digby Morton, stands in front of a ruined building. British *Vogue* gave the image the caption, "Fashion is indestructible."

Opposite:
Fashion was in short supply, so women tried to divert attention from their clothes with daring headgear. Designs such as this one by Legroux were a source of stimulating ideas for women of few means.

Left:
A well-groomed appearance was good for morale, and so make-up had an important part to play, even in wartime.

are dressed in pure silk by the meter." The French lived by the motto, "All is fair in love and war," and gave free rein to their imagination. They were out to provoke, to show the boches, as they disparagingly called the Germans, that only Paris had a real flair for creative fashion. For the Nazis were said to want to move the home of *haute couture* to Berlin or Vienna.

Lucien Lelong, who was president of the Chambre Syndicale de la Haute Couture from 1936 to 1946, had to use all his powers of persuasion to save top fashion for Paris. He was undoubtedly helped by ordinary women on the street, who demonstrated every day that they could make more out of nothing than anyone else. They made it clear to the self-confident occupying forces that they could not simply transfer the spirit of a city to another location. Parisiennes made fun of German women by calling them *souris grises* (gray mice). Surely it was better to bring them to the city on the Seine for their clothes than move *haute couture* to the city on the Spree, where chic had been considered unseemly since Hitler came to power. Lelong succeeded in negotiating certain guarantees for

haute couture, which made it possible for couture houses such as Lanvin, Fath, and Rochas to survive.

This applied to his own business, too. Lucien Lelong (1889–1958) had founded his own fashion house in 1924 and soon became known for his reserved elegance. This was shown to its best advantage by his beautiful wife, Russian princess Natalie Paley, who was a successful model and the best ambassadress for her husband's creations.

Lelong was considered to be more of a good businessman than a great designer, and his most important work came during the war when he secured the survival of couture. First of all this meant looking after the wives of Nazi bigwigs, since customers could no longer come from other countries. Lelong thought up a way to reopen markets to *haute couture*, however: in 1942 the spring collections were shown in Lyons, which was in the free-trade zone where Swiss and Spanish buyers could complement the Germans and Italians. Of course materials were not unlimited, even though extra allocations were made, but the couturiers devoted all their energy to using up as much material as possible

Lucien Lelong (1889–1958)
Since his parents had a couture house in the heart of Paris, Lelong had little choice in his career. He was allowed to study economics and then joined the family business as a trainee. He created his first collection in 1907, and set up on his own in 1924. He showed a classical, very elegant line, having nothing to do with fashionable extravagance. In 1934 he introduced a less expensive line of ready-to-wear, sensing that hard times were ahead.

Above:
Creative minds thought up eccentric headgear. Women tried to make up for the scarcity of fashionable clothes with unusual hats created from the simplest materials with enormous imagination. The attractive results gave wearers cause to smile to themselves. Even newspaper came into play (*far right*).

Opposite:
Emergency rations. During the war small fashion shows were held in Lyons, since international visitors were still allowed to travel there.

1940–1949

so that there was nothing left over for the Germans. Their creations also involved a great deal of work, and the more hands that were needed to make them, the fewer workers were available for labor service.

This meant that Paris was reveling in extravagance at the same time that other countries were on short rations. In 1941 all the German fashion houses were put together in the Berlin Model Society, which was only allowed to produce goods for export. German women were still expected to look smart and tidy, as well as modest and conventional. They were supposed to wear no jewelry, furs, or lace, and certainly no make-up. German women were expected to have a single aim: presenting the Führer with as many children as possible.

In Britain rationing led to painstakingly precise regulations from 1941 onwards. Amount of material per garment, maximum length and width of skirts, maximum number of pleats, buttons, and accessories – all this was laid down in great detail. In order to save material, patch pockets, turned cuffs, and pants turnups were forbidden, as were pocket flaps and waist pleats. Ration coupons were needed for clothing, and workers had to give them to their employers as soon as they made a uniform available. Silk was absolutely taboo as far as civilians were concerned, as it was needed for parachutes. This made it seem wonderfully frivolous to make one's own underwear out of parachute silk – preferably recovered from shot-down enemy fighter pilots – even though it rustled and chafed.

Even the queen of England, who until that time had been dressed by Norman Hartnell in light blue, soft green, and pale violet tulle, now found it inappropriate to meet her suffering subjects in such showy dresses and chose more subdued colors. She

also commissioned Hartnell to design more functional clothes that would fit in with the "utility clothing scheme," in the hope that cheap-looking clothes would be more acceptable if they were promoted by the most famous couturier in Britain.

Charles Creed and Captain Molyneux, both of whom had learned their trade in Paris, returned to England at the outbreak of war. Together with Norman Hartnell they were commissioned to design uniforms for women in the army. Lady Edwina Mountbatten, a member of

Norman Hartnell (1901–79)
Tailor-made for the demands of his time, British couturier Norman Hartnell designed "utility clothes" during World War II, at the request of his government. He also designed uniforms for the Women's Royal Army Corps and the Red Cross. He was appointed dressmaker to the royal family in the 1930s, and later designed Queen Elizabeth II's wedding dress and coronation gown. He took most of his inspiration from painting.

one of the richest families in Britain, preferred to have her uniform made to measure by one of the famous Savile Row tailors, which meant it was a little shorter, fitted the figure a little better, and was much more stylish.

There was a total of 6½ million British women on active war service, of whom four succeeded in rising to the rank of general. In the United States there were 2 million voluntary women helpers in 1942, and soon afterward there were 4 million paid workers. From female telephone operators to engineers, the new "women power" was highly praised. It was only a decade since women had given up the independence that they had gained during World War I and had been reluctantly lured back into the home, but suddenly a readiness to work outside the home was seen again as a female virtue. The brave little soldier's wife was hardworking, thrifty, efficient, and imaginative. In the United States the restrictions were not as stringent as in England, but the moral pressure

on women was just as great. Even *Vogue*, which was normally totally in favor of luxury and the latest fashions, asked all its readers to "make do and mend."

The American government declared it a national duty to reduce the production of fabrics by 15 percent, and this meant a freeze on fashion. It was thought that if styles did not change, existing clothes would go on being worn. In reality there was a fundamental change in fashion between 1941 and 1945. Outfits became a little more military, skirts were shorter and tighter, and headgear became more and more unusual, until physical proportions were completely distorted. Even this had a special attraction, however, for the unusual get-up sharpened the appearance of a shapely figure and enhanced graceful movements.

This applied to working clothes, too. Marilyn Monroe recorded in her memoirs: "In the factory I wore overalls. I was surprised they insisted on that. Putting a girl in overalls is the same as letting her work in pantyhose, especially if a girl knows the right way to wear them." The same could be said of jeans, which were intended to be rough working pants and gradually developed into sexy fashionwear. Americans had always been ahead of everyone else in sportswear, and this trend continued during the war years. It started off with practical clothes for students, but soon everyone wanted the young college look with pleated skirts, sweaters, and little white socks. Even Elsa Schiaparelli, who was on a lecture tour of the United States, expressed her praise: "Amazing, the

Lady Edwina Mountbatten in her St. John's Ambulance uniform.

From the 1941 winter wardrobe. Fabrics had to be saved, so even coats were tightfitting.

Shoulders became broader as pinned-up hair made the slim wartime figure seem taller.

Protective clothing. What should the well-dressed woman wear during an air raid? Designers had ideas about that, too. Here is a hooded cape with comfortable pants by Robert Piguet. The gas mask makes a bizarre accessory.

Bunker outfit. Even Elsa Schiaparelli designed a special outfit for the dangerous trip into an air-raid shelter. It was very similar to a modern jumpsuit. It is doubtful that the shoulder bag was big enough to hold a gas mask.

inexpensive clothes on offer in America, especially sportswear – so tasteful."

Many people developed a feel for quality for the first time during the war. They learned to appreciate hard-wearing materials that also felt good next to the skin, such as cotton, wool, and linen. Suddenly the finish was also of great importance. Now that women made everything themselves, they could tell the difference between good and poor quality materials, and good and poor handiwork. There was practically nothing they did not try or turn their hands to: shoes made of cork, belts made out of pieces of wood, and even handbags made of carpet remnants.

Small envelope purses were replaced by roomy shoulder bags in which a woman could carry everything she needed. The shoulder strap meant it could easily be worn even on a bicycle, which was often the only available means of transport.

In all countries affected by the war women learned to make the best out of what was to hand, and women's magazines tried to help. "Make new out of old," was the motto, and magazines showed how to turn curtains into clothes, men's overcoats into women's coats, bedclothes into babywear, and net curtains into a wedding dress. There were instructions on how to turn collars, as well as on how to darn and

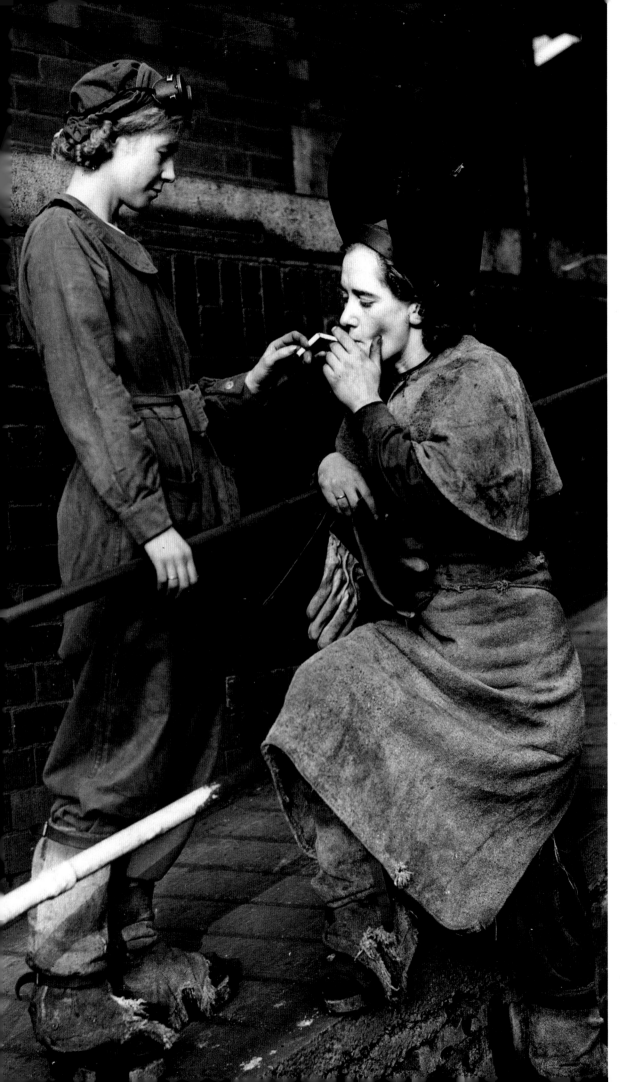

In the factory. Even rough working
clothes gave ideas for fashion, and
smoking became fashionable too.

Above:
Saving coupons. Everything was
rationed and could be bought only with
coupons. Women's journals gave tips
on how to save valuable coupons for
use on essentials; reworking old flannels
into baby clothes or children's shorts was
just one suggestion.

Cycling is fun. Parisian women were a shining example of how to cut a good figure on a bike. Skirts were shorter and turbans had to do for headgear, but even the war could not take away that certain *je ne sais quoi*.

mend. Knitting patterns were especially popular. Old pullovers were unpicked during long hours in the air-raid shelter, and the wool was used to knit new sweaters – preferably with a V-neck, for V stood for victory and that was what everyone was desperately wishing for.

After the war too many lives had been wrecked and people's memories were too somber for there to be any feelings of triumph. People soon had a desire to live again, however. There was an explosion of interest in the theater, movies, and music, especially in Germany where there was now an opportunity to discover the plays of Jean-Paul Sartre, Arthur Miller, Thornton Wilder, and Tennessee Williams, as well as the works of Bertholt Brecht that had been written in exile. In France cultural life had continued throughout the war: the first plays by Jean Anouilh had been successfully produced during the occupation, and Paul Claudel's *The Satin Slipper*, directed by Jean-Louis Barrault for the Comédie Française, was sold out night after night during wartime. The French were even more interested in movies, however. Altogether they produced 278 feature films during the war, including such individualistic works as Jean Cocteau's poetic fairytale *Beauty and the Beast*. Marcel Carné's *Les Enfants du Paradis* was an absolute masterpiece of the age and astonished the world when it was released in 1945.

The French love of movies led to the founding of the Cannes Film Festival in 1947, and to this day the movie world makes its way to the Côte d'Azur every

Made in the USA. Before the war Americans had admired immigrant designers such as Elsa Schiaparelli. After 1945 American college fashion and basketball shoes crossed the Atlantic to Europe, along with new dances such as the jitterbug.

May. Devotees of ballet, on the other hand, were drawn to London, which had always been a center of classical dance. After the war even more people found an interest in ballet, and the reopening of the Royal Opera House, Covent Garden, in February 1946 with a performance of *Sleeping Beauty* was a triumphant prelude to a whole series of brilliant productions. In 1948 the neoromantic movie *The Red Shoes* won many new friends for ballet. The young Moira Shearer made her movie debut in this wonderful production.

People's social lives did not get going again as quickly as culture. Something held people back from enjoying themselves "just like that." *Vogue*, for example, recommended that during the winter of 1945/46 evening dresses should be replaced by the more discreet *robe d'ambassade*, which took its name from receptions in various embassies. There, women appeared in pencil-slim dresses with long sleeves and a low square neckline. The skirt had to fall at least below the ankles. Jewelry and ornamentation were scorned, and at most a small amount of embroidery around the modest neckline was allowed. Such evening wear was also considered suitable for private dinners, and there were no great opportunities to dress up.

In 1945 *haute couture* reminded people of its existence with an unusual performance in Paris. The shortage of fabrics made it difficult to put on a big show, so the idea came about to present a "theater of fashion." The couturiers demonstrated their skills

In the mid-1940s fashion aimed high, with clumsy platform soles, high shoulder pads, and piled-up hair, as shown here by a design by Madeleine Vionnet. Some people liked the distorted proportions: Yves Saint Laurent, Wolfgang Joop with his "rubble women," and Jean-Paul Gaultier (*below and right*) reinterpreted a fashion that had been born of adversity – but with no great success with women.

The war-brides look inspired Christian Lacroix (*left*) and Givenchy (*below*) in 1998/99 to a high-necked, severe style with square shoulders and high, pinned-up hair. Since World War II platform soles and wedge heels (*bottom*) have repeatedly reappeared in summer fashions, even though they are very difficult to walk in because the foot cannot move naturally.

Opposite:
During and after World War II women did not want to let themselves go, and so a correct, somewhat angular suit was the most sought-after item, as shown here in a design by Rochas.

209

using tiny amounts of material on 200 small, wire-frame dummies with plaster heads and string hair. The dummies acted as the new ambassadors of fashion, and the brilliant allrounder Christian Bérard, a gifted painter, illustrator, and stage designer, created the perfect set for this original fashion spectacular. After a successful opening at the Musée des Arts Décoratifs in Paris the show went on tour right across the United States, winning old customers back to fashion and attracting new ones. It is interesting to note that the troupe of dummies were rediscovered 40 years later and were sent around the world again, to great acclaim.

Although in fashion terms the Americans had emancipated themselves during the war and were unbeatable in sporty everyday wear, they soon succumbed to the fascination of *haute couture*, which had nothing to do with practicality or value for

money but offered a feast for the senses. This fulfilled the expectations of the exclusive fashion magazine *Harper's Bazaar*, which looked at the postwar future with optimism and wrote: "We are expecting birds of paradise, not little brown chickens." They had to wait for their colorful feathers, however. It was as if designers' imaginations were curbed in some way. In the difficult postwar

Above:
Christian Bérard (1902–49) was an extremely talented painter, illustrator, and stage designer. His stylish, elegant designs reflected the spirit of the age. As a friend and colleague of many couturiers, Bérard had a lasting influence on the fashion of his time.

Right:
Théâtre de la mode. A small scene is enough to launch fashion in a big way, as shown in 1945 by an exhibition which presented *haute couture* on a series of dummies. For this Christian Bérard designed a stage set that showed Paris in its former splendor.

1940–1949

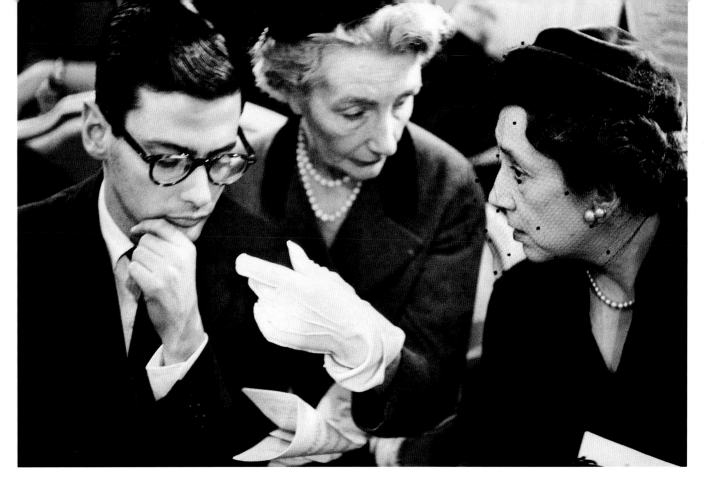

Above:
Feared critics, at a Paris fashion show in 1946/47. Carmel Snow (*center*),
legendary editor-in-chief of the American fashion magazine *Harper's Bazaar*,
with a young Richard Avedon (*left*), who went on to become one of the greatest
fashion photographers of all time, and Marie-Louise Bousquet (*right*), a French
colleague of Carmel Snow.

Opposite:
The New Look. It was Carmel Snow who called Dior's Corolle line a "new look,"
and the name undoubtedly contributed to its worldwide success. After the long,
meager years of the war, Christian Dior was the first to dare to put yards of
expensive material into wide skirts. This was just the kind of luxury that many
women had been yearning for.

period even the young couturiers seemed to feel
committed to reason and did not want to take any
extravagant risks.

The great breakthrough came in 1947. On
February 12 Christian Dior presented his first-ever
couture collection, and despite freezing conditions
outside, feelings inside the salon on the Avenue
Montaigne soon warmed up. People wondered when
they had last seen such gentle curves, narrow waists,
and extravagantly wide skirts. The answer, of course,
was in the *belle époque*. And yet this new line, two
world wars later, seemed provocatively new and
refreshingly feminine. It was Carmel Snow, editor-in-
chief of *Harper's Bazaar*, who gave this style the name
that it took into fashion history. "It's quite a
revolution, dear Christian," she told the shy
couturier. "Your dresses have such a new look."

So the Corolle line, as Dior had called it, became
the New Look that would define fashion for the
next decade. Overnight the previously unknown Dior
became the undisputed king of couture.

Cristóbal Balenciaga (1895–1972)

The whole world was talking about Dior and his New Look, but initiates knew that the real innovator was Cristóbal Balenciaga. Fashion photographer Cecil Beaton said of him: "He has established the future of fashion." Dior, the darling of the media, also showed Balenciaga unreserved admiration. When Balenciaga wanted to close his salon in 1948 because he was suffering from depression, Dior urged him to carry on.

Balenciaga could undoubtedly have turned his couture house into an international enterprise, similar to that of Dior's and others. But having been to the United States and seen the ready-to-wear clothes there, he was determined never to use machines. Individual items continued to be created by hand in the monastic isolation of his workshop. Balenciaga is regarded as an architect among couturiers. His stark designs are reminiscent of sculpture and his somber colors – preferably black, often combined with brown – remind one of paintings by Velázquez and Goya in the Prado in Madrid.

Balenciaga, the son of a Basque tailor, helped his mother with her work when he was very young. Sponsored by the Marquise de Casa-Torrès, he received a good education. At the early age of 24 he was able to open his own fashion house in San Sebastián, where he counted the royal family among his clients. He soon opened further salons in Madrid and Barcelona.

The Spanish Civil War forced him to give up his three establishments, but in 1937 he founded a couture house in Paris with the support of Spanish friends. He was immediately successful. All those on the list of best-dressed women, which came out once a year, became his customers: Mona von Bismarck, Barbara Hutton, Gloria Guinness, Pauline de Rothschild, the Duchess of Windsor, and of course actresses such as Marlene Dietrich and Ingrid Bergman. With a clientele like that, Balenciaga, reputedly the most expensive couturier, came through the war with no financial losses; in fact, he was able to reopen his Spanish shops.

Balenciaga's gowns were perfect for grand occasions as, with such dramatic detail as short capes, gigantic flounces, trains, and wrap-around effects, they literally created a frame for the wearer. His evening dresses were influenced by flamenco. Balenciaga invented collarless blouses, but also collars which elongated the neck. He created balloon, tunic, sack, and chemise dresses. From year to year his technique became more refined and his designs simpler. He worked with luxurious, often stiff fabrics which "stood up" in the silhouette he had designed. André Courrèges and Emanuel Ungaro learned their craft from him, and many other designers – most notably Hubert de Givenchy and Christian Dior – called him their master.

In 1968 Balenciaga closed the doors of his house, disappointed by trends in fashion which he felt had sold out to mass production and vulgarity. His customers mourned him. Mona von Bismarck withdrew to her bed and cried for three days, despairing of how she would be able to keep up her high standards.

Cristóbal Balenciaga treated fashion as art. "A couturier must be an architect for cut, a builder for form, a painter for color, a musician for harmony, and a philosopher for style."

Opposite:
Balenciaga not only designed but also cut and sewed at least one design in each of his collections. His skills can be seen in the detail of his designs, collars and sleeves, which are cut in such a way that movement does not hamper a perfect fit.

Cristóbal Balenciaga

Pierre Balmain (1914–82)

Below right:
Two elegant day suits which mirror Balmain's very own feminine style. Only the hats were slightly daring, as was usual in the 1940s. Balmain was against experimental fashion; he wanted to dress women to look pretty.

Below:
Pierre Balmain choosing a matching fabric for Maria Montez. His father owned the largest wholesale drapery in Provence, and from an early age he knew all about materials.

After training with Edward Molyneux, Pierre Balmain – who had broken off his architecture studies in favor of fashion – spent five years with Lucien Lelong, working side by side with Christian Dior. The two apprentices got along so well that they initially wanted to open their own house together, but when Dior hesitated for too long, Balmain set up on his own in 1945.

Balmain's first show was attended by Gertrude Stein, who came with her partner Alice B. Toklas and her poodle Basket. It was about that first night that the successful American author wrote her first and only fashion report for *Vogue* (see page 221).

Balmain's simple elegance, which was best exemplified in his 1952 collection "Jolie Madame", appealed most to the aristocracy. His most famous client was Queen Sirikit of Thailand. Later he also conquered North and South America with salons in New York and Caracas. Like Dior, Balmain quenched the postwar thirst for luxury and beauty with his lavish full skirts.

For some critics who were more interested in the avant-garde his fashion was too peaceful and safe. Balmain preferred gentle colors, such as pale gray, mauve, light yellow, and pistachio green and had his designs decorated with ornate embroidery. He also liked collars, cuffs, muffs, and belts trimmed with fur. Another reason for Balmain's popularity with his customers was the fact that he was a brilliant solo entertainer.

Opposite:
Grand entry. In the course of his career Balmain designed the costumes for numerous movies and many great actresses. Here Hollywood star Carroll Baker poses glamorously in a skintight sheer gown which Balmain designed for her in 1964.

Opposite, inset:
Wedding: *And God Created Woman*, and Balmain created an equally sensational dress for her. The movie, made in 1956, steered Brigitte Bardot toward becoming a screen goddess and sex symbol.

Stein on Balmain

They were depressing times when we got to know Pierre Balmain. We met his mother in Aix-les-Bains in '39 and she said she had a son in the army up in the snow-covered Savoy who read my books and would I sign one for him? Of course I was pleased, and then came '40 and the defeat and we asked after Pierre Balmain, whom we had never seen but who was up there in the snow, and then at last we heard that he was safe and then he was back and we met him.

He usually came to us on his bicycle, in fact we lived many miles away but that didn't bother anyone, and it was a cold winter and we were cold, and he made us beautiful, warm outfits and a wonderfully warm coat, and Alice Toklas insists that one of her outfits was just as beautiful as all those that he presented on his opening night, and why not indeed, for hadn't he designed it after all and didn't he come on his bicycle to supervise everything, and wasn't it simply like it always is in dark times, with the occasional bright spot.

We got to know him better and better, some children put on a few of my plays and he showed us the trick of how to make a tall girl even taller by standing her on a stool. Those were good days in those depressing times, and then Pierre usually went to Paris and brought back a breath of our beloved Paris as well as thread to darn our stockings and underwear, that was typical of Pierre, and then he moved around as young men had to in those days in order not to be sent to Germany, and then came the liberation and we were all in Paris, with Pierre full of a desire for action, and we were sure that he would make it, and he made it.

We were presumably the only ones at the opening night who had worn Pierre Balmain designs during all those long years, and we were proud of that. It is nice to know the young man simply as a young man and no one suspects anything, and now, well I suppose everyone will know soon. And we were so happy and proud. Yes, we were.

Genius and fashion. Gertrude Stein and her poodle Basket at Pierre Balmain's first fashion show. This led to the eccentric author writing her one and only piece about fashion for the December 1945 issue of American *Vogue* (reprinted above). Her companion Alice B. Toklas wrote an introduction to Balmain's collection in 1948: "Something beautiful at last, something that expresses tenderness, charm, and elegance in silk and wool, in lace, feathers, and flowers."

Jacques Fath (1912–54)

Below right:
Jacques Fath's favorite model was Bettina Graziani, who is seen here modeling for the artist Christian Bérard in a wedding dress. Fath, who never drew his designs but always draped them directly on the body, is watching with interest. The dress was designed for Rita Hayworth's marriage to Prince Ali Khan.

After training in business studies Jacques Fath devoted himself to designing hats. In 1937 he made his début as a couturier in a small apartment, and ten years later he became the first Frenchman to design a ready-to-wear collection for the American market. He was not worried by the Nazis either and expanded his business during the occupation.

He was simply everybody's darling – full of life, good-looking, and incredibly charming. His popularity, especially among the more colorful movie set, resulted in him long being thought a lightweight by the respectable fashion press. From the mid-1940s, however, he was increasingly appreciated, and today he is regarded as having been a great talent. He died of leukemia at the age of 42, and this early death meant that he perhaps never developed into a true master. His couture house survived for another three years, but had to be closed in 1957.

Fath's wife Geneviève Bouchet was a much sought-after model, and she played a large part in his success in fashion and society. With his feel for business and marketing, Fath was ahead of his time. He had no qualms about producing a reasonably priced ready-to-wear line, manufactured in France along with his couture clothes, or about selling his patterns for copying to *Vogue.* His accessories were available at affordable prices in his own boutique.

Rita Hayworth became his most famous client. He designed the wedding dress for her marriage to playboy and Ismaili prince Ali Khan. Ironically Jacques Fath, who always developed his designs directly on the body, draped this wedding dress on the model Bettina Graziani, who succeeded Rita Hayworth in winning Ali Khan's favor.

Below:
Jacques Fath was as much in demand as a socialite as he was as a couturier. Here his head seamstress is putting the finishing touches to an afternoon dress for Maria Martès.

Opposite:
Jacques Fath started his career as a milliner, and so no collection was complete without extravagant hats.

Jacques Fath's designs always had a little more flair than his colleagues' collections. That is why they were particularly popular with those who wanted to attract attention, especially people in show business. Among other innovations he launched bell-shaped coats with large collars (*right*). Notice the position of the model's feet, which is actually the fifth position in classical ballet. This makes the hips look slim and the legs seem longer, enhanced by the model's rotation, which shows the fabric in movement.

Jacques Fath

The look of the decade

In 1942 the manufacture of cosmetics was stopped for two months in the United States. That was enough to cause such an uproar that the country's intelligentsia had to debate the question of the importance of beauty care to the nation's survival. The answer was quite clear: cosmetics were classified as essential to life. "Cosmetics are to women what tobacco is to men," they said. Certainly both seemed indispensable when it came to keeping people happy in difficult times.

Cosmetics were raised to the level of a secret weapon. The nation whose women did not let themselves go, who looked after themselves, looked pretty as they did their war service, and presented a welcome sight to their men when they came home on leave – that nation would win the war. Women were supposed to be energetic and competent at work, feminine and loving in their private lives. The look that went with it was adult and sensuous, but never ever frivolous or provocative. British *Vogue* hit the nail on the head: "Beauty now is heartlifting not heartbreaking."

The eyebrows were slightly arched and carefully redrawn. Shaving and thick black lines were scorned, along with everything extreme. American women had it made: with their compact make-up, Pan-Cake by Max Factor, they could make their complexion look matte and hide blemishes at the same time, a luxury for which European women had to wait until the end of the war. They just had to make do with ordinary powder. The most important thing was lipstick; lips were fully colored, with a defined outline.

The quality of make-up products was poor, since they were lacking in basic ingredients such as glycerin and grease to make them light and smooth. This meant that powder and lipstick could not be applied evenly, resulting in uneven and crumbly layers of color. There was also a shortage of packing materials, such as metal tubes for lipsticks. In Europe some articles were not even available, despite government subsidies to the cosmetics industry. If in doubt, arms production, for which all factories had to work, came first. Necessity is the mother of invention, however: English women used black boot polish as mascara, shoe polish for redefining eyebrows,

and rose leaves and cotton soaked in red wine as rouge.

In the United States Elizabeth Arden introduced the Busy Woman's Beauty Box, which contained everything from a make-up mirror, cleansing cream, powder, and eye shadow to lipstick. This meant that the ever-growing army of working women could cope at all times with whatever was demanded. Despite the war, turnover in the cosmetics industry was constantly rising, because the many women who were earning their own money for the first time invested heavily in their looks. It was the done thing to stock up on cosmetics in order to be well equipped for the return of the men from the front.

This longing was expressed in the names of the most successful perfumes of the time. There was Attente (Expectation), En Attendant (Meanwhile), and Malgré Tout (Despite Everything). Parisian women queued on the Champs-Elysées to have their perfume bottles refilled at Guerlain or Caron.

In hairdressing salons hair was collected after cutting for use in the manufacture of thread. But not many women could afford a visit to the hairdressers. The bob had grown into long hair which was worn pinned up, high above the forehead. Those who could not afford a saucy hat twisted a scarf into a turban, which further elongated the silhouette. The turban suited many women; French writer and feminist Simone de Beauvoir, for example, continued wearing one until the end of her life. It also proved extremely useful, because in times of need untidy hair could simply be hidden beneath it.

Only movie people wore their hair loose. Starlet Veronica Lake became famous in America for her long, wavy mane of blonde hair. Long

Despite the war and the years of shortage that followed – or perhaps because of this – great store was set by looking after one's appearance, even though stocks of cosmetics were limited and the quality of products was poor. A discreet and sensuous look was desirable, as portrayed by actress Eleanor Parker (*top*). Hair was typically combed upward and pinned, mainly because nobody could afford a visit to the hairdressers. What remained of an old perm was just enough to be worn in a high curled fringe. In the mid-1940s there was an upswept hairstyle in which the hair was elegantly wound around the head and pinned in position (*bottom*).

hair gave women that touch of glamour which, for lack of jewelry and furs, they had come to do without. Not surprisingly, every woman whose hair was remotely suitable tried to copy Veronica Lake's Hollywood mane. This had disastrous results, with frequent accidents in munitions factories as women's hair got caught in the machines. Finally the United States War Department asked Veronica Lake to have her beautiful locks cut off in the interest of the nation. Shortly afterward another young actress with a similar hairstyle became world famous – Lauren Bacall.

But there was only one hairstyle that spelled real elegance, and that was a loosely coiled bun at the back of the head, which top hairdresser Guillaume designed in 1944 for Balenciaga and which became an international classic known as the *chignon*. It is in fact the traditional hairstyle of ballerinas. The hair is brushed out of the face, tied into a ponytail at the nape of

the neck, coiled into a figure eight, and then pinned down.

During the war women had no difficulty staying slim. Consequently the boyish look was no longer the ideal, and after the war everybody wanted to see female curves. A youthful make-up with natural and light shades became fashionable at the same time. Attention no longer centered on dark red lips but on more highly made-up, large eyes. This resulted in the combination of a child's face and a fully developed woman's body, a look that was encapsulated by Brigitte Bardot in the 1950s.

Color for the legs was even more important than lipstick or powder during the war. It was impossible to buy stockings, and as skirts got progressively shorter bare legs just did not look good. So women everywhere thought up all sorts of tricks. One of the easiest solutions to the problem was to draw seams with an eyebrow pencil, but a good eye and a steady hand were

Opposite:
The lack of stockings meant coming up with ideas for making legs look less bare, even if this meant no more than lines drawn with an eyebrow pencil to look like the nonexistent seams.

Below left:
Everything needed to conjure up a really natural-looking face is advertised here by Max Factor, who has added the magic word "Hollywood" to his name.

Below:
A 1939 advertisement for Shalimar perfume by Guerlain, a little sweet, very heavy, and certainly exotic.

needed to get a straight line. Before long there was a device which helped to move the pencil evenly along the leg.

Another possibility was leg make-up, but applying this was possibly even more tricky. Not only was it essential to be quick, in order for the color to be evenly distributed, but one also had to wait a long time until the legs were completely dry. Otherwise there was a risk of marking one's clothes, in which case one might as well stay at home. This meant that rainy days were fraught with danger. In the wet leg make-up became patchy and sometimes even washed off completely. So Elizabeth Arden's "Fin 200" tinting lotion came at just the right time; it was supposedly impervious to water, snow, or even mud.

Beauty salons specialized in giving working women a perfect morning leg make-up. Those who could not afford the products or professional help tried to tint the skin with chicory juice. Some found the whole thing much too difficult, gave up on it altogether, and wore short socks even with high-heeled court shoes. Others with GI friends had already heard about the gift which the United States had in store for Europe – nylons!

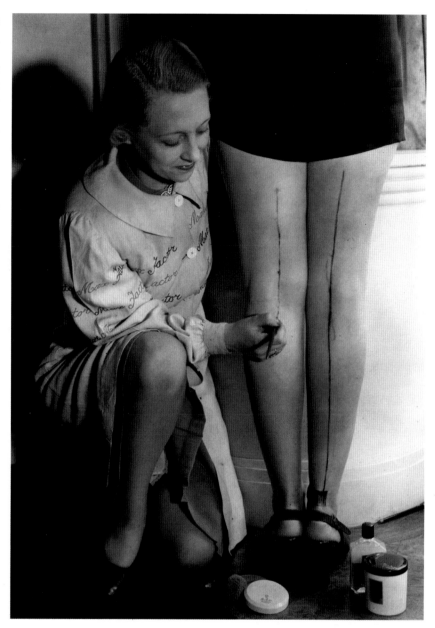

Hairstyles of the stars

Veronica Lake's dream hairstyle was really nothing more than the result of an old perm, which meant that it was almost straight until below the chin and was kept in shape by a few big waves. It was almost impossible to achieve this hairstyle, which Rita Hayworth also wore in *Gilda*, without natural waves or a perm. Best results were achieved if the hair was put in large curlers after washing; only then did one get evenly soft waves like those of Lauren Bacall, whose hair naturally had a lot of volume. After drying, usually under a hairdryer, dry ends were massaged with oil and then the hair was brushed over the back of the hand so that it curled under. Finally a side parting was made, and the hairline was smoothed with gel for extra hold. Sometimes a few curls and waves were needed over the forehead. As it was difficult to brush out long curly hair after a wash, it was also treated with conditioner. Those who could not afford professional help experimented with egg-yolk applications and vinegar or beer rinses to make their hair radiant and silky.

BETTE DAVIS

JOAN CRAWFORD

KATHARINE HEPBURN

INGRID BERGMAN

LAUREN BACALL

RITA HAYWORTH

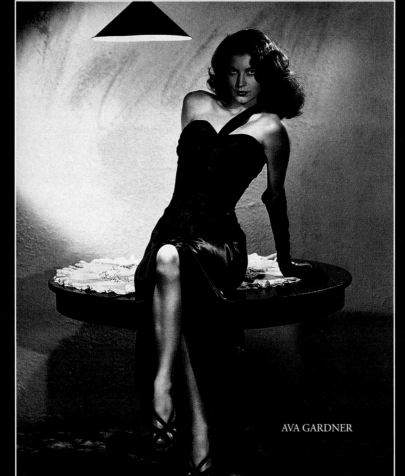

AVA GARDNER

LENA HORNE

Idols of the decade

The war consolidated Hollywood's position as the world's leading dream factory, where models were shaped for millions of people. There was no longer an international social, arts, and theater scene with a corresponding press. Cultural life lay in ruins everywhere, and when anything happened in an individual country, such as France for example, the rest of the world was excluded. Only movies could go on spreading ideals that went down well with the masses.

In the early 1940s **Ingrid Bergman** (1915–82) became the second Swedish actress after Greta Garbo to rise to screen stardom. No one could compare with her at putting across rich, deep emotions. This talent and her gentle natural beauty, which needed no special glamour treatment, made Bergman the ideal type for the war years. However, when she came down to earth from the realms of the noble, self-denying woman, such as she played in *Casablanca*, fell in love with Italian director Roberto Rossellini and had a child by him, she was dead as far as Hollywood was concerned. She later married Rossellini and won an Oscar for her performance in the American production of *Anastasia* in 1956, but she was never forgiven by the prudish American women's clubs.

In the 1930s **Bette Davis** (1908–89) was seen as a "cotton dress girl" and stood no chance against the sexy "satin sweethearts" such as Jean Harlow, but during the war she became an idol. She was quick-witted and independent, which was expected of women in those difficult years. So-called women's movies were no longer in demand after 1945, however, and her star waned. But in 1950 she made an unforgettable comeback in the role of sarcastic Margo Channing in *All About Eve*. Bette Davis was still gracing the screen when she was 80.

Joan Crawford (1904–77) already had several highs and lows behind her when she won an Oscar for *Mildred Pierce* in 1945 and established herself as the quintessential career woman. Her power suits became a uniform for every woman striving for success. Her characters became more wicked as she grew older, and this allowed Joan Crawford to remain a star for 50 years, just as Bette Davis did.

The third survivor among the strong Hollywood women who had minds of their own and yet also had longer careers than all the glamour girls, was **Katharine Hepburn** (b. 1907). She was so talented and so intelligent that for a long time her beauty was scarcely noticed. Today she is seen as the archetypal modern woman, and she is the only one whose style survived her long career – cool, clean, androgynous.

Lauren Bacall (b. 1924) is also famous for her style, though this was actually "borrowed" from Slim Keith, wife of director Howard Hawks. It was she who discovered the 19-year-old model in 1943 and recommended her to her husband as a partner for Humphrey Bogart in *To Have and Have Not*. A legendary couple was born, on screen as in real life. Bacall also created the "California girl" look that went down in fashion history – healthy, clean, sparkling, simply golden.

After the war no one was interested in the clean look any more. **Rita Hayworth** (1918–87) will always be remembered as Gilda, in an off-the-shoulder black evening gown, wearing long gloves and smoking a cigarette. In 1946 she became a symbol for everything that men had dreamed of during the long war years: silk sheets, alcohol, and sex, sex, sex. *Gilda* may have made her immortal, but it did not make her happy. After five marriages, including to Orson Welles and Prince Ali Khan, she lost her seductive self-confidence and appeared only in trivial movies.

The close-fitting, black silk-satin dress and long gloves also did the trick for **Ava Gardner** (1922–1990). Before 1946 she had to make do with minor roles, but then her appearance in *The Killers* turned her into Rita Hayworth's only serious rival. Together the two actresses founded the new age of the sex goddess.

The pinup girl

Pinup girls brought a touch of variety to the army locker. Betty Grable was the unbeatable pinup darling of American troops during World War II. This 1943 photograph of her in a bathing costume, casting an inviting glance over her shoulder, became the most sought-after image of the decade. This was apparently due to her shapely legs, which would be seen as too short for any self-respecting model today. In those days they were long enough to be insured with Lloyds of London for $1 million. Betty Grable's popularity as a pinup girl was greater than her screen career. Of all the movies in which she appeared, the only one worth remembering is *How to Marry a Millionaire*, released in 1953.

Lena Horne (b. 1917), the first black Hollywood star, has been almost forgotten. She was already a well-known jazz and blues singer when MGM put her under contract. Unfortunately Hollywood always chose to cast this extraordinarily beautiful, talented actress in a particular part in musicals and never gave her the opportunity to appear in a leading movie role.

In the 1940s the **sweater girl** had her own important position, with her own special image. Both the sweater and the wearer were always pretty, but harmless. It was only the fact that the sweater was actually too small or alternatively that the bust was too big that made the combination explosive. Whichever was the case, aircraft manufacturer Vought-Sikorsky sent 50 female workers home on the grounds that their tight pullovers presented a danger when working with machinery. It turned out to be more a question of moral danger. The sweater girls were allowed to lift soldiers' morale at the front, however, and those who did not appear in person to entertain the troops certainly appeared as photographs. Lana Turner was the first to offer the sort of sweater appeal that soon every shapely starlet wanted to parade before the GIs. Even Marilyn Monroe was a much sought-after sweater girl at the start of her career. Later, however, the GIs preferred to see her in a low-cut dress or a billowing skirt as in *The Seven Year Itch*. Or in the nude. An early calendar photograph of her was traded at black-market prices; after all, nude photographs were still taboo in those days.

1950–1959

New look – old ideas

1950–1959

The 1950s were the last great decade of *haute couture* before it took to its sickbed, where it remains to this day neither dead nor alive. There have never been so many independent couturiers, either before or since. They became so important that they were able to influence the worldwide fashion of the masses with their exclusive, extravagant ideas. Ahead of everyone was Christian Dior, who launched his New Look in 1947. He himself soon grew tired of this, which was why he brought out a new line every six months. However, the New Look had long since taken on a life of its own, without Dior, just as it would have been born without him, though perhaps quite a few years later.

The time was simply ripe for a dramatic change in fashion. After the meager clothing of wartime, women dreamed of soft lines and extravagant material, even if

reason spoke against this. Of course the critics were right when they said that it was quite unnecessary, disgraceful even, to produce a dress worth over 40,000 French Francs ($7,000) when most women could scarcely afford milk for their children. Feminists realized at once that the new line brought no progress. "The New Look is like keeping a bird in a golden cage," said Mabel Ridealgh, an English Member of Parliament.

After the horrors of war, that, however, was exactly what many women wanted: to be spoiled, to be looked after, to be responsible for nothing. That was why the New Look caught on, even if it signified an outburst of suppressed desires rather than an awakening to a better future. The New Look symbolized optimism as well as opulence, and what to many might have seemed cynical on its first appearance in 1947 appeared quite natural just a few years later. The economic miracle soon snuffed out any remaining doubts. This had

Previous page:
The quintessence of the 1950s look: the perfectly curved eye framed by a delicate, dark eyebrow, the blood-red lips, and the beauty spot on a pale, even skin. Model Jean Patchett in Erwin Blumenfeld's impressive photograph *Œil de biche* (Doe's Eye) of 1950.

Opposite:
This woman's attire says just one thing – expensive. She is simply demonstrating her husband's success with sophistication and luxury.

Left:
These two wonderfully opulent evening gowns, designed by Jacques Heim in 1953, were exotically named Fantasque (*left*) and Scarabee (*right*). Going out suddenly meant showing off splendid clothes again, having fun, and forgetting the difficult years.

been made possible by the Marshall Plan, which had been launched in the same year as the New Look and brought a general upturn. The New Look undoubtedly emphasized class differences, since it was only within the reach of the wealthy, but it was seen as a promise of prosperity, elegance, and zest for life, and served as an incentive to advancement for all strata of society. In this way it acted as the trigger for a completely new social group – the middle class. Any woman who had taken down her old blackout curtains and turned them into her first long, wide skirt in the new line could no longer be stopped in her search for beauty.

This new world really was beautiful. The stern face of modernity, in which form had to follow function, gave way to a pleasing design that was seductive in the same way as fashion. The hourglass shape of the New Look was also reflected in architecture and interior design, right down to the smallest practical object. Kidney-shaped tables, bucket chairs, tulip glasses, curved vases, as well as rounded glass ashtrays – everything reflected the sculptural lines of the New Look. The porcelain company Rosenthal

even used the name "New Look" for its "organic coffee service" in 1955. No wonder Christian Dior himself started to question reactions to his big trend-setting idea. "What have I done?" he asked. "What on earth have I done?"

What Dior did was to catch the spirit of the age, and the 1950s represented the first time that this spirit was not confined to a country or a stratum of society. What seemed to many like a revolution sprang merely from a global need for restoration. People wanted things to be as they were when the roles of men and women were clearly defined, except that now everyone wanted a share of the good life and the double standards of the propertied class. There was no rebellion in the 1950s; desire clearly took precedence. Department stores, synthetic fibers as well as ready-made clothes – all these made it possible for the broad masses to copy the style of the rich. In this way the ideas of *haute couture*

Opposite:
The consumer society supposedly makes for happiness. The economic miracle made it all possible – the house in the country and the perfect built-in kitchen with everything functional and effortlessly easy to maintain. This meant that the mother of the famly could look immaculate even when doing the housework (*above*), and in the evening she changed into a seductive woman of the world.

10 a.m.: a sporty twinset with obligatory pearls for morning coffee.

11 a.m.: a short raincoat and silk scarf offer protection against the wind and weather while shopping.

1 p.m.: a suit with a small hat, jewelry, and gloves for a lunch appointment.

2 p.m.: meeting a friend: who is wearing the more expensive outfit?

3 p.m.: relaxing at the hairdresser in more casual clothes.

4 p.m.: totally elegant for shopping in the city; fresh supplies needed!

5 p.m.: afternoon tea: black hat and gloves announce an alternative program.

6 p.m.: wearing a bell-shaped coat on the way to her first cocktail party.

7 p.m.: when the jacket is removed, the cocktail outfit turns into a short evening dress.

reached the high street. The whole lifestyle of the privileged seemed attainable to everyone: washing machines, refrigerators, automobiles, vacation trips, parties – ordinary people could afford at least a pale imitation of the big wide world.

This was something of a strain, however. The economic miracle had to be worked for, and it brought with it new duties to which many did not feel equal. Once you had jumped on to the consumer merry-go-round, you had to go faster and faster to keep up, you had constantly to have the latest thing and, even worse, you had to know exactly what was right when and where. The terrible tyranny of "good taste" caused many a sleepless night. Why were bungalows and kidney-shaped pools acceptable, but swinging garden hammocks and the new automobile with shark fins not? Social advancement did not mean the beginning of a classless society; on the contrary, it simply meant that the differences between social classes were defined more precisely and yet more harshly. A strong moral code was supposed to be helpful against this insecurity: "the done thing" soon became the unshakable rule for all social climbers.

Of course the rule applied primarily to women. In the 1950s they were put back in a tight corset both in the literal as well as figurative senses. After holding their own during the war, women now wanted to be more female again. Without realizing it, as a consequence they gave up some of the ground that they had gained in order to return to the home. It was all very

Not without my girdle

Anne Fogarty was a successful fashion designer, and she had even more success with a book which told women that there was nothing more important than their role as a wife. In *Wife-Dressing* she recommended that women should never wear jeans, even when doing the housework, but should always be dressed in feminine clothes – with a girdle underneath, for the posture.

Opposite:
In the 1950s women liked to show off what they had. Women who changed several times a day so as to be suitably dressed for the particular occasion were their husband's pride and joy. By changing their outfit several times a day women also showed that they were well organized and disciplined, for it was not so easy to be perfectly styled at every hour of the day.

tempting: husband as absolute ruler and provider, wife as custodian of the house in the country, furnished in a modern, functional way, with bright colors, easy to look after, comfortable, with all modern conveniences. Loyalty and honor were surely not too much to ask for in return, and it was also reasonable that any wife presented herself immaculately from morning until night in the same way as the people portrayed in illustrated magazines or in the movies. It first sounded like a fair exchange, but women undoubtedly had the worst of the bargain.

"Never forget that first and foremost you are a wife," wrote American fashion designer Anne Fogarty in her book *Wife-Dressing*, which came out in 1959. She considered it essential that a woman always wear a girdle everywhere, whether she was doing the vacuuming or attending endless cocktail parties. Fogarty laced herself up so tightly that she could not even sit down. Apparently this form of bondage gave her great satisfaction because it forced her to have perfect posture.

French feminist Simone de Beauvoir, who herself was always elegant and stylish, exposed the new female cult: elegance as chains. She recognized that women were simply acting as advertisements for the success of their husbands, laced up in new corsets and old conventions. Most women were not aware of this, however. Even if they aspired to their own career, like Anne Fogarty, or simply had to go out to work in order to keep up or even improve on their new lifestyle, they still complied with the rules laid down for female propriety. This manifested itself most obviously in clothes. One never went out without hat and gloves, one's purse matched one's shoes, one chose the same colors for accessories and eye make-up, one always wore high heels and nylon stockings except for sport, one only wore a low neckline in the evening and chose materials that were appropriate to the time of day. This for example meant no brocade before 6 p.m.! It was also not the done thing for a society woman to buy herself flowers or perfume – she expected to receive these things as a gift from her husband, probably as a reward for always making herself look smart for him. A woman with social duties – by his side – had to get changed up to six or seven times a day, as well as changing her accessories and matching her make-up and hairstyle.

Women's magazines claimed to make their readers' lives easier by helping them choose the correct clothes for every occasion. For lunch at home, it might be a velour dress with a slender skirt and matching stockings and suede shoes. If the lunch were elsewhere, however, it had to be a gray flannel dress with matching jacket, a small hat, gray suede gloves (a quick tip – keep these on when greeting people!), a gray patent-leather purse, and a slender gray umbrella. Suggestions such as these, which were really more like regulations, went on until the evening, with a description of the smallest details, from the right collar to the appropriate jewelry or perfume. They were accompanied by the required rules of behavior and manners, and the lists got longer and longer ...

This new kind of housewife would by no means have appeared before the mailman without make-up, let alone before her husband. She preferred to get up an hour before him in order to put on her mask, and to curl, backcomb, and spray her hair, until she was unrecognizable. Many a husband is supposed never to have got to see his wife's real face, since she took off her make-up only once he was safely asleep, or she carefully removed her day make-up and immediately applied her own night make-up for the

intimate hours alone together. It goes without saying that her fingernails and toenails were always perfectly groomed and varnished, and her clothes were always smart, attractive, and fashionable, even for housework.

Only the rich could cope with a life such as this without a great deal of stress, for they did not have to bother with children, cooking, washing and ironing, shopping, or cleaning. They also made fun of the social climbers' perfectionism. As always when people started to copy the customs of the ruling class, the upper echelons quickly set up new standards. The careful matching of colors and accessories, which had certainly been taken to excess, was suddenly seen as dreadfully bourgeois, and anyway it was much more fun to relax all the rules. Good taste was for ordinary people; those at the top now enjoyed breaking the rules of style.

They did this with a great display of splendor. In the 1950s glittering parties were the order of the day. The most experienced host was undoubtedly Count Étienne de Beaumont, who had always surrounded himself with artists, writers, and couturiers. His Kings' and Queens' Ball was the first of a whole series of lavish fancy-dress balls. His guest of honor, Christian Dior, appeared as the king of the desert in a lion costume designed by his former colleague Pierre Cardin, who had just set up on his own. Jacques Fath was seen as the most talented party host, and his Pirates, Gipsies, and Texas parties, with guests such as Rita Hayworth and Prince Ali Khan, went down in the annals of fancy-dress parties. The greatest and most photographed masked ball of the century was held at Carlos de Beistegui's Palazzo Labiain in Venice in 1951. This

Opposite:
9 p.m.: the later the hour, the more lavish the clothes. A silk evening gown with a mink-trimmed kimono by Horn. 1950s woman was certainly allowed to stand out in the evening, but she never revealed herself. Necklines were never too low, skirts never too short, and materials never transparent.

party caused all the couture houses to be booked for months. Among others Dior designed the costume for Singer Sewing Machines heiress Daisy Fellowes, who went as America 1750, as well as Salvador Dalí and his wife Gala, whose piled-up hair and hats increased their height to an amazing 8 feet. The host himself changed costume three times during the festivities, and his appearance in a ceremonial doge's robe and white, powdered wig represented the high spot of the evening.

The reporting of this unique occasion, which was later portrayed by Alfred Hitchcock in *To Catch a Thief*, acted as an advertising campaign for *haute couture*. Many a new customer, especially from the United States, piled into the fashion salons. Screen goddesses and real queens made for Dior, the king of couture. Rita Hayworth, Ava Gardner, Marlene Dietrich, Ingrid Bergman, and Lauren Bacall sat closely packed in the first row or even on the famous stairs, along with Queen Soraya and her successor Farah Diba, the Duchess of Windsor, and Barbara Hutton. Every single time they got to see an amazing spectacle, for Dior did everything to ensure that people's interest in fashion never tired. Over 11 years of his reign he introduced 22 different lines, he raised and lowered the hemline (but only between the knee and the ankle), shaped the female figure into an 8, or a letter H, A, or Y, and finally hid it in a sack. And women followed his ideas; not only his clients but all women.

The system of licensed sales that had been introduced in the 1930s made this possible. Buyers, who came primarily from the United States, had to pay a deposit in order to attend the presentation of a new collection. The amount was deducted from the price of subsequent purchases. These could take two forms: they could either buy a finished design or a pattern with exact instructions on the fabric that was to be used. Either way, copies were then made, sometimes so-called "original copies," which could be very expensive because they were made in very small numbers. Designs were normally reproduced in their thousands, however, and this meant that a Dior dress could be bought for $80, whereas the original might cost $950. Since there was so much copying, not to say theft, in fashion, most couturiers preferred to go in for lucrative licenses, although couture lost something of its exclusivity this way. In the 1950s, however, people wanted to show off their new wealth, and there were plenty of private customers who had one-off dresses designed individually, which gave couturiers ample opportunity to indulge their creative genius. Dior loved to be copied, even if this brought no money into his overflowing tills. He simply liked the fact that women all over the world were wearing his look.

They did not really have much choice, for, although there were so many different couturiers, the line was amazingly uniform. Dior set the tone, and the others happily followed. Even the new French prêt-à-porter range introduced by Lempereur and Weill, which was based on the American ready-to-wear model, took on the particular season's current trend without hesitation. The brisk exchange of trade and ideas across the Atlantic helped to democratize and internationalize fashion. For the first time women of all nations were willingly united by the dictates of fashion.

The New Look and the lines that developed out of it were characterized by soft, sloping shoulders, round hips, and extremely narrow waists. On informal occasions women wore shirt-waist dresses

Previous pages:
Think pink. During the economic miracle of the 1950s the whole world seemed to be pink. Actress Joan Collins, already perfect in the role of the seductress, poses with a pink poodle on her king-size bed.

Opposite:
Fashion designer Jacques Fath, the charming host of numerous fancy-dress balls, pays court to an opulently dressed Ursula Bagge.

Ricci revived early teenage chic in spring/summer 1996. Stylist Myriam Schaefer used gingham, once made popular by Brigitte Bardot, in the retro New Look with a wasp-waist and a full skirt. The tight-fitting jacket was correct and demure, as in the 1950s.

Freedom must be boundless on the other side of the Atlantic. Every European girl dreamed of America, the land of unlimited opportunites, chewing gum, jeans, and T-shirts. The plain little girl gradually turned into the stylish young woman.

and twin sets with pleated skirts and pearls. Otherwise a suit with a jacket fitted at the waist was appropriate for day wear, either with a pencil skirt or a full skirt with a petticoat. Toward the end of the decade geometric shapes reminiscent of the 1920s came in again, and hems rose up to just below the knee. This new slender silhouette was called "French bean" by the press, after the green bean used in *haute cuisine*.

1950s shoes were narrow, with tapering toes and medium or preferably very high heels, which became increasingly slender until they turned into the notorious stiletto heels. A variation were shoes that ended in a more or less broad square chisel toe. In the evening one wore peep-toe high-heeled sandals made of silk or brocade, sometimes decorated with jewelry such as paste clasps. The most sought-after shoe designer was Roger Vivier, who provided the footwear for all Dior's collections. For Queen Elizabeth II's coronation in 1953 he designed gold leather shoes with heels studdied with rubies. In 1955 he introduced the "choc" heel, which was so

While some young women were still playing the role of good little debutantes, others were staying up all night, smoking, discussing existentialism, and listening to "Negro music" in jazz cellars (*right*). Or they threw themselves about dancing to rock 'n' roll (*below right*).

Below:
Debutantes. Daughters were introduced into society dressed up like little ladies, in hat and gloves, ballerina skirt, petticoat and corset – exactly as their mothers had been.

Some of those who did not stick to the dress code of the time became style icons. Good examples were rebellious young men such as Marlon Brando (*above left*), James Dean (*above right*), and Bill Haley (*right*, in the light raincoat). With their leather jackets, jeans, and T-shirts, as well as their music and attitude, these were the real role models in fashion and they influenced subsequent generations.

1950–1959

curved that it looked as if it would snap at any moment, an unpleasant surprise that many wearers of high heels had already experienced.

Hats usually had a small flat crown, even if the brim was broad. These developed more and more into small decorative affairs that surrounded the hair, which had been carefully pinned up or set, with coquettish flowers, veils, or feathers. Sometimes the hat was replaced by a broad silk hairband. In the evening this could be decorated with a long feather that reached forward, keeping other people at a polite distance.

Leisure time became so important in the prosperous 1950s that a fashion was created for the purpose. The pastimes were simply too chic for people to think of simply donning comfortable old clothes. One went to garden and cocktail parties, played tennis and golf, and as soon as one could afford it, one drove to the Riviera or Capri, or one sailed to Jamaica. For all these activities people wore youthful, colorful clothes.

As a reaction to the dreary war years, there was an explosion of color in the 1950s. Dior's optimistic red became famous, and this was subdued compared to the multicolored "blot designs" that textile manufacturers took over from modern art. The biggest star and hero of the art scene was action painter Jackson Pollock. "Jack the Dripper," as he was called, sprayed, splashed, and dribbled paint over huge canvases laid out on the floor to create seemingly arbitrary designs. His fast, wild life, which tragically ended in a car crash in 1959, made Pollock into a cult figure just like James Dean, who died in 1955 at the wheel of his Porsche at the age of 24, and Jack Kerouac, who lived and wrote *On the Road* (1957).

Young people were fascinated by these tragic heroes from the United States. In Europe it was the theater of the absurd of Samuel Beckett and Eugene Ionesco and the existentialism of Jean-Paul Sartre and Albert Camus that acted as counterweight to the

Cult object. To teenagers the Vespa epitomized freedom and mobility even more than fashion, music, or movies. The Italian motor scooter with the New Look lines was very elegant, as shown by Audrey Hepburn in *Roman Holiday*.

dreary picture of the beaming nice guys of the 1950s. Young intellectuals demonstrated their contempt for the world by adopting the black clothes of existentialists and beatniks, whose muse Juliette Greco set a fashion example.

Nobody had any idea that Marlon Brando's T-shirted performance in *A Streetcar Named Desire* could set off a wave that would sweep away the old social order a decade later. But the white T-shirts, black leather jackets, and blue jeans worn by Brando in *The Wild One* (1954) and by James Dean in *Rebel Without a Cause* (1955) became a uniform which expressed an attitude of dissatisfaction and emptiness. This was also shown in the German movie *Die*

Halbstarken (meaning rowdy or teddy boy) with Karin Baal and Horst Buchholz. The seemingly limitless opportunity to consume could not cure the ills of youth for good.

Rock 'n' roll, which was sent around the world first by Bill Haley and then by Elvis Presley, was also an omen of things to come. So long as young people were still romping about on the dance floor, however, everything was right in the world. It was all just a fashion phenomenon; it only turned into a revolt ten years later. The new class of teenagers was lulled to sleep by consumerism and intimidated by the Cold War, which was as much a part of this contradictory decade as the belief in unlimited growth. They showed themselves to be fashionably elegant, and above all respectable. Petticoats and petting led as quickly as possible to the highest aim of all females: marriage. The youngest prominent bride of the age was Ira von Fürstenberg, who married Prince Alfonso zu Hohenlohe in Venice at the age of 15. Such dream weddings cherished romantic passions. In 1953 Jacqueline Bouvier, who as Jackie was later to become one of the fashion icons of the 20th century, married the then senator and later president of the United States, John F. Kennedy. In 1956 Hollywood star Grace Kelly became a fairy-tale princess by marrying Prince Rainier of Monaco. The shy Spaniard Fabiola was beautifully dressed by Balenciaga for her marriage to King Baudouin of Belgium. And the unusual half-German, half-Persian Soraya rose to the rank of queen through her marriage to the Shah of Persia.

Everything seemed possible. Everything was possible when girls from the most humble backgrounds became top models, as happened to Dovima, the Polish policeman's daughter who became the epitome of the majestic, immaculate, well-brought-up 1950s lady. Dovima played herself in the movie *Funny Face*, starring Audrey Hepburn, and she could not have been given a better part, for as a top model she had already achieved all her wishes. All that was missing was the right husband, but this was no real problem for models – they more or less had a free choice. Eliette became Frau Karajan, and her friend Simone Boucheron married Curd Jürgens. Fiona Campbell-Walter married Baron Heinrich von Thyssen-Bornemisza, Anne Gunning became Lady Nutting, Anne Cumming became Duchess of Rutland, and Balmain's star model Bronwen Pugh married Lord Astor.

Jean-Paul Sartre (1905–80)
Sartre's philosophical thoughts became fashionable: his huge community of fans took up all his ideas with great enthusiasm. His existentialism, however, which demanded self-responsibility, was by no means easy to translate into reality. Many simply emulated the fashionable side of the new philosophy, therefore wearing black clothes and hanging around Paris cafés and jazz clubs.

Opposite:
Rita Hayworth, in a bridal gown by Jacques Fath, and Prince Ali Khan on the way to their wedding. This was one of the dream weddings of the 1950s. Their marriage turned out to be rather less of a dream, however, and they were soon divorced. The successor to the red-headed movie star was the red-headed top model Bettina Graziani. Ironically, Jacques Fath, who always developed his designs directly on the body, had draped Rita Hayworth's wedding dress on the model Bettina Graziani.

Dior – the gentle dictator

Who was the man who revolutionized fashion by restoring turn-of-the-century virtues? Scarcely anyone knew him when on February 12, 1947 he caused a sensation with his Corolle line, which turned him into the undisputed king of couture until his death ten years later. When fashion enthusiasts pushed their way behind the scenes after the show they discovered a short, bald man of 42 with a sad smile, "rather like a rural administrator made of pink marzipan," as one of his friends said.

The shy, reserved Frenchman was very touched to receive so much praise from all quarters. An American fan described him as "a Napoleon, an Alexander the Great, a Caesar of couture!" Carmel Snow, who gave Dior's first collection the name of "New Look" to stand for a new development in *haute couture*, said: "Dior saved Paris as Paris was saved in the battle of the Marne." Thanks to Dior, couture, which had been in decline during the war, flourished again. There was such great demand for his dresses that for some time the salon on the Avenue Montaigne stayed open long after midnight.

The winter collection which Dior presented in August that year was equally well received. It showed dresses with huge skirts that had a circumference of over 40 yards (36 meters). Dior possessed the amazing ability to engender ecstatic enthusiasm twice a year for a whole decade. In 1949, 75 percent of all French fashion exports carried his name, and a Gallup opinion poll, carried out in the same year, showed him to be one of the five best-known men in the world.

How had the shy Frenchman managed all this? His abilities were certainly no greater than those of his colleagues. Cristóbal Balenciaga, who was regarded as the absolute master of his time, tended to keep his views on colleagues to himself, but he admitted that he found the way Dior handled fabrics dreadful – this lining with layers of drill, buckram, or tulle instead of "letting the fabric speak for itself," which was Cristobal Balenciaga's own credo. But the fiercest criticism came from Chanel: "Dior? He doesn't dress women, he upholsters them."

The truth is that the term "New Look" is the biggest misunderstanding in the history of fashion. What was new about dressing women up as sex objects and status symbols for men? What was new about women having to be helped into a taxi, needing huge suitcases to accommodate their clothes on journeys, and not even being able to get dressed without the help of a servant? In Dior's first collection there were clothes weighing 8 lb and evening robes of 60 lb, which were too heavy for the wearer to dance in. How could such nonsense be accepted by women who had already fought for the abolition of the corset at the beginning of the century, who had shown their fit figures in the androgynous flapper look of the 1920s, and who had felt good in Chanel's casual suits?

The New Look was a counterrevolution which took women straight back to the *belle époque*; it sprang from Dior's wish to revive "the tradition of great luxury" in French fashion. And exactly that was the secret of his success. Dior himself explained it somewhat flippantly: "Europe had had enough of bombs dropping, now it wanted to let off fireworks." With his return to a safe past, when enjoyment without regret was still possible, Dior satisfied the yearning of his contemporaries, who were more than ready for his reassuring message.

Besides, he was a brilliant marketer and introduced a new form of presentation into *haute couture*, which had nothing in common with the more formal, quiet performance of the prewar years. Dior's models made theatrical appearances; they majestically swirled past the audience, provocatively whirling their full skirts. As they came out one after the other, and all at the same exciting tempo, the imaginative name of each model was announced: "Number one, Verdi! ... Number two, Pergolesi! ... Number three, Wagner!" This spectacle might go on for up to two hours without ever getting boring. Dior's idea of creating a new trend every six months made quite sure of that. He was the first designer to change the hemline or even the whole line radically from one collection to the next. By ensuring that his fashion soon went out of fashion he made headlines and stimulated sales.

Dior needed masses of material simply for the foundations of his lavish dresses (*left*). The wide petticoats, tightfitting bodice with built-in bra, and stiffened hips gave the evening dress the required support. Despite its delicate appearance, a Dior original often weighed many pounds and was a heavy garment to wear (*opposite*). Thanks to modern textiles, the new version by Galliano for Dior (*inset*) is as light as a feather by comparison.

Christian Dior was born on January 21, 1905 in Granville, Normandy, one of five children of Maurice Dior, a well-known manufacturer of fertilizers. "It still smells of Dior," the villagers often commented. Even as a child Dior was always interested in fashion, and he loved and admired his extremely elegant mother. At first he wanted to become an artist, but his father was strongly against this and so Christian started studying political science, supposedly in order to become a diplomat. In return his father set up a small gallery for him, so that Christian would be able to indulge in his passion for modern art in his spare time. But as a result of the stock market crash and some bad investments Monsieur Dior lost everything and Christian had to support himself. He was forced to give up the gallery and worked for a short time as a freelance illustrator, before finding permanent employment as a dress designer with Robert Piquet.

In 1939 he had to interrupt his career and go to war, but he was discharged only a year later. He joined his father and sister in the south of France, where he worked as a farmer. In 1941 he returned to Paris and was lucky enough to be employed as a designer by Lucien Lelong. Within a few years Christian Dior had rejuvenated Lelong's line so radically that an American journalist inquired who the young man behind the scenes actually was. He managed to arouse the interest of cotton magnate Marcel Boussac, who obviously liked Dior's idea of designs that required extravagant

The final parade of every fashion show is headed by the wedding dress, which forms the climax of the occasion. Evening dresses are shown again behind the wedding dress. Daywear and outfits form the beginning of every show.

Opposite:
Even celebrities such as Marlene Dietrich (*second from right*) had to sit modestly at the foot of the famous stairs as Dior's latest creations were presented.

Above:
Christian Dior at work in his studio. Like a schoolmaster he used his stick to point out where alterations were needed.

Below:
Stars idolized the dictator of fashion: Lauren Bacall and Humphrey Bogart at a Dior show.

Right:
Dior decided on the outcome of the war of the hemlines for himself. Here he demonstrates the desired length.

Far right:
Fitting Madame Lazareff, founding editor of *Elle*.

Below right:
Dior loved and pampered his models; he referred to them as "mes filles" (my girls).

1951/52 – Ligne Longue

1952 – Ligne Sinueuse

1952/53 – Ligne Profilée

1953 – Ligne Tulipe

1953/54 – Ligne Vivante

1954 – Ligne Muguet

1954/55 – Ligne H

1955 – Ligne A

1955/56 – Ligne Y

1956 – Ligne Flèche

Opposite:
Birth of the New Look. This outfit, Bar, was the "mother" of the style which caused such a sensation. But what was so sensational about this design? The narrow shoulders, nipped waist, rounded hips, and especially the length and flare of the skirt – all these elements together created the hourglass figure. Compared with its predecessor – the angular, broad-shouldered wartime outfit with its short skirt – Dior's New Look displayed unaccustomed elegance.

use of material, and so the house of Dior was founded at 30 Avenue Montaigne, where it has remained ever since.

Insiders believe that Dior's mother, who had died long before, influenced his fashion most. Apparently, he never forgot the memory of her majestic beauty, coming to kiss him goodnight in her rustling skirts before going off to a ball.

Dior was a mother's boy, gentle, softhearted, anxious as well as dreamy. Everyone who worked with him described him as modest and extremely polite. He would bow at the lowest trainee and step aside to allow her into the lift first. The attention he paid to all of his many hundreds of employees was remarkable: he spent months choosing the right Christmas present for every single one.

Dior loved elaborate meals and he hated being on his own. He was always surrounded by a small circle of intimate friends, among them Jean Cocteau, Christian Bérard, composers Georges Auric and Francis Poulenc, and his directrice Raymonde Zehnacker. His great weakness was his superstition. He never made a single decision without having consulted his fortuneteller, Madame Delahaye. She was the one who had advised him to accept Boussac's offer jointly to set up the couture house of Dior, and Christian Dior took her advice on

everything, including the fresh flowers that always decorated his rooms.

Twice a year, before each collection, Dior regularly became deeply depressed. During the first day of his depression he locked himself in the study of one of his country houses near Fontainebleau or in Provence and refused to see anybody, except for a servant who was allowed to bring his meals on a tray. Sitting at his desk, Dior made provisional sketches on a large pad, lost himself in imaginary hieroglyphs and meaningless doodles, until the moment of sudden inspiration hit him and he clearly visualized the line of his new collection. During these anxious and stressful days half a dozen of his assistants would be in the house, waiting nervously for his appearance. When Dior finally surfaced, holding hundreds of sheets in his hand, they cheered and then devoted themselves to diligently drawing up his sketches.

Dior's gentle, soft-hearted personality, so obviously tortured by artistic anxiety, obscured the fact that he was also a shrewd businessman. He had already realized on his first visit to the United States, in 1947 to receive a design award at the invitation of the Texan store Neiman Marcus, that this market offered undreamed-of opportunities. "We are selling ideas," he said, by which he meant that a creation could not be

Above:
In order to keep interest in fashion alive, Dior introduced two new lines a year. Whatever the shape of the silhouette, whether slender or New Look, the hemline always remained demurely below the knee.

Y-line suit from 1955, similar in silhouette to the tulip shape of 1953. This line featured narrow, slender skirts with generous tops or dresses with wide V-necked collars.

"Talon boule": this 1955/56 skirt billows around its wearer, who looks as if she is about to fly away.

The A-line of 1955. The silhouette is narrow at the shoulders and flares slightly all the way down.

Sinuous-line suit from 1950. The S shape is suggested by the three-quarter-length jacket.

With the pleated skirt and gathered tops of his lily of the valley line (Ligne Muguet), Dior created a new variant of his successful New Look.

In his last collection before he died in 1957 Dior created a new line of straight outfits, with narrow skirts and rectangular tops.

Vertical-line suit from 1950. The jackets were generally narrowly cut and often had a horseshoe collar.

The "profiled line" of autumn 1952: the waist is narrow, with bust and hips emphasized as in the original hourglass look.

released for copying for one single payment. In other words, he invented the license fee. From 1949 onward Dior received a percentage share in the profits of each copy of his designs. This made the introduction of accessories and perfumes extremely lucrative. The first perfume, launched as early as 1947, was called Miss Dior, and Diorama and Diorissimo followed soon afterward. Jean Cocteau was proved right with his early interpretation of his friend's name: for Cocteau "Dior" was made up of "Dieu" (God) and "or" (gold).

Every great couturier is tortured by perfectionism – after all, fraction of inches can determine success or failure – but in addition Dior burdened himself with international business. This meant that he developed his own designs for his salons in London, New York, and Caracas, taking into account the special requirements of each country and adjusting to the physical proportions of his clients there. This added up to Dior having to supply about 1000 designs per year.

This production plan must have been particularly stressful for a designer such as Dior, whose ambition was to create a totally new look each season. His health suffered, partly because of the pressure he had placed on himself. In the mid-1950s he showed clear signs of stress. The army of servants who were looking after his various houses had to wear felt slippers so that Dior would never be disturbed. Sometimes he suffered from such nervous strain that his fortuneteller and his chauffeur Perrotino, a lover from his youth, had to drive him around the block a number of times before he felt strong enough to enter his salon on the Avenue Montaigne. His directrice, Madame Raymonde, was often woken up in the middle of the night by a telephone call from her master, who would then cry like a child.

Outsiders hardly noticed any change in Dior, except for his waistline, which was steadily increasing. Only Perrotino knew Dior's darkest secret: he had already had two heart attacks. And then there was another secret: Dior had been unhappy in love for years. Countless attractive young men had refused to be more than just friends with him. In 1956, however, Dior's affection was finally reciprocated by Jacques Benita, a good-looking young man of North-African descent. Genteel, conservative Dior, who cherished his good reputation, was so much in love that he was seen holding hands with his new friend in public. Wanting to make himself more attractive, Dior decided to go on a slimming diet in Montecatini in the late summer of 1957.

In mid-September Madame Delahaye saw bad omens in his cards and begged him to change his travel arrangements. For the first time he failed to listen to her. Dior took his chauffeur, directrice and goddaughter with him to the health resort in Italy. During the evening of the tenth day of his stay, on October 23, 1957, Dior collapsed shortly after finishing a game of canasta. At the age of just 52, one of the most influential couturiers of all time died of a cardiac arrest.

No seats to spare

Some celebrities and high-ranking guests, such as the Duchess of Windsor (*second from right*), were fortunate enough to be seated on one of the usual gold chairs. Others were happy to be allowed to squash on to the stairs to see the latest Dior collection being presented. Dior was used to dressing royalty, including Princess Margaret, Princess Soraya, the Princess of Yugoslavia, Princess Napoleon, the Duchess of Paris, and Princess Grace. No one could know that the great master's 1957 show would be his last.

Dior

René Gruau's brilliant
portrayal of Dior's love
of leopard skin was used
to advertise Miss Dior
perfume. This caused great
excitement among fans and
created many imitators
across the fashion scene.

Opposite:
Whether tiger stripes or
leopard spots, real or
artificial fur, the skin of the
world's big cats is constantly
worn in the world of
fashion. New interpretations
by Galliano for Dior at the
end of the 1990s (*above*);
fur parade 1969/70 (*below*).

What it looked like underneath ...

... was very important to women in the 1950s, because the New Look could not be created without the right foundation. Dior had claimed that, after the broad-shouldered "boxing outfits" of wartime, his line gave women back their feminine shape, but no one mentioned naturalness. Shoulder and hip pads created curves which made the laced-up waist seem even smaller. Dior himself created the appropriate "foundations" for his designs. They might be short taffeta slips, which with rosettes and ruches produced the necessary curves in the right places, or incorporated tulle and bone bustiers with padding at the bust and sturdy, corsetlike hooks.

Jacques Fath took out a patent on the *bustier corbeille* (basket bustier) which he incorporated into his plunging necklines. His cupped bra was also very successful and was a forerunner of the famous Wonderbra of the 1990s. The basis of the construction is always a semicircular wire frame, padded and backstitched, which sits beneath the breast as a supporting element. Depending on the strength of the pressure upward and toward the center, created by the shape of the cups, padding, and straps, the impression given is of a more or less ample bosom.

Marcel Rochas is said to have invented the *guêpière*, or waspie, an abbreviated corset which helped create the desired wasp waist. He is also credited with the corselette, the modern lighter version of the corset. Beneath their daywear, especially under a skirt and sweater, most women wore a bra and girdle. The bra had spiraling backstitched hems that made for a pointed shape, and the elastic girdle started above the waist and reached the top of the thighs, though it had the fatal tendency to roll both the top and the bottom. This could be stopped by wearing a tight belt at the top and attaching nylons at the bottom with strong garters.

In *haute couture* ingenious ways were found to stiffen skirts and create the desired "crease" in the waist, while ready-to-wear and ready-made clothes made do with petticoats made of nylon taffeta and tulle, or of cotton. Teenagers often wore up to four petticoats on top of each other which ensured that they revealed only frills and flounces when they threw themselves into rock 'n' roll dancing.

Opposite:
This was what lay beneath a Dior design. The whalebone strips supposedly forced the wearer to retain her posture as well as her composure, and the padded bra made a voluptuous impression.

Below, left to right:
What would have become of the petticoat without rock 'n' roll, and vice-versa? At last there was an opportunity to show what it looked like underneath, without of course actually revealing anything (*left*). Under closefitting dresses one-piece corselettes ensured the right shape, however slim the wearer and however uncomfortable and problematic the restriction (*center*).
The strapless bra was indispensable beneath an off-the-shoulder cocktail dress. In the 1950s women never went without a bra, even when it was not strictly necessary (*right*).

Every golden age has its tragedies

Jacques Fath died of leukemia in 1954, at the young age of 42. Three years later Christian Dior died of a heart attack, aged 52. Of course there were many other designers and successors to these two "golden boys." Nevertheless it was as if a shadow had fallen over couture, and it was certainly true that a golden age had come to an end. From the 1960s onward rebellious youth and its street fashion would run the show. Never again would anyone dare say, as Dior did: "I liberate women from nature." Nor would they declare, like Fath: "Women make poor fashion designers. The only job they should have in fashion is to wear it."

Coco Chanel was by then an old lady living in exile in Switzerland, but she was outraged by these words. A few months later, after a break of 15 years, she was back in Paris to present a new collection, but the provocative Jacques Fath was already dead. The belief that women were better fashion dummies than designers was still alive, however, and Chanel's first collection after return to France was not well received. Simple, practical, wearable, and elegant – only a woman could think that way, while male designers were wallowing in extravagance.

Women such as Vionnet, Chanel, and Schiaparelli had been leading figures in the meager years before the war, but now men ruled, and they had turned fashion into big business. At the turn of the century Jeanne Lanvin had started her salon with 300 French Francs ($50), but no one from the new guard was prepared to waste their time for minuscule sums. Indeed, textile manufacturer Marcel Boussac invested $500,000 in the house of Dior when it was founded.

Women won back their position as fashion designers, however, and Coco Chanel was ahead of them all. Already in her 70s, she created the garment that will forever carry her name, something that no other couturier has managed before or since. The "Chanel" is a simple suit made of light tweed, braid-trimmed with the skirt covering the knees, and to this day it still stands as a symbol of true elegance. Millions of copies are still to be found in stores all over the world, from New York to Tokyo.

This photograph by Robert Doisneau shows split images of grande dame Coco Chanel in front of the mirrored wall on the stairs between her private and business apartments in Paris. From there she could see everything without being seen herself, which satisfied her well-known need for control. The photograph did not turn out to be symbolic, however, for Chanel successfully proved to the world of fashion that she still knew best of all what women wanted to wear.

Hubert de Givenchy

Hubert de Givenchy was just 25 years old when he opened his own salon in 1952. He was the youngest of all the *haute couture* designers. Previously he had been responsible for four years for Schiaparelli's boutique line, for which he developed simple, versatile separates in a young style which he then carried over to *haute couture*. His first collection, which included a modest white cotton blouse with amazing black and white flounces on the sleeves, created as much attention in the press as Christian Dior did with his New Look. With his imaginative patterns and fresh colors, Givenchy seemed to revive couture, but he did not see himself as a revolutionary: all he was doing was striving for perfection. He chose Cristóbal Balenciaga as his mentor and master, and soon Givenchy was also seen as a guardian of classic *haute couture*, which raised cutting technique and finish to the level of art.

In 1957 Givenchy followed Balenciaga when the Spaniard decided no longer to allow the press into his shows. Journalists would only get to see the new collection eight weeks after the buyers, when their opinions would no longer have such an influence.

Naturally, as a consequence the press called for a boycott, but after the death of Dior Balenciaga was seen as the most important couturier and the press could not afford to ignore him. Givenchy profited from being mentioned in the same breath as his friend and patron. He was anyway assured of media attention since he had been designing for the latest Hollywood star Audrey Hepburn, both for the screen and privately. This developed into a lifelong friendship that influenced style.

The last of the gentlemen. Hubert de Givenchy's aristocratic background may never have been fully clarified, but he certainly had a noble manner. This made his farewell appearance even more moving, when at the wish of the new financial backers of his house he had to step down and make way for younger, less discreet designers, first John Galliano and then Alexander McQueen.
The dress interwoven with white linen with matching bolero in black jersey (*far right*) was designed by Givenchy in the 1950s. The closefitting animal-print design (*right*) is by Galliano from the autumn/winter collection of 1996/97.

Opposite:
Capucine was considered one of the most beautiful models of her time and was promptly signed up for the movies, including *What's New Pussycat?*

Louis Féraud

Opposite:
This gabardine coat from 1966 has a young and playful yet elegant look, in keeping with the decade of Swinging London.

Outsider Louis Féraud showed his first couture collection in 1955. Before that he had run a successful boutique in Cannes with his first wife. The new collection was full of strong colors, typical of his Mediterranean background as well as his love of all things Spanish and Native American. Some may have looked down their noses at the designs, but his frilly, low-cut dresses and loud, flowery patterns went down well with his new couture clientele, just as they did previously with movie stars and starlets on the Côte d'Azur, where Brigitte Bardot was his most important customer. Every dress she bought from him was ordered hundredfold. Many Hollywood stars who went to Cannes for the film festival, such as Ingrid Bergman, Elizabeth Taylor, Kim Novak, and Grace Kelly, also bought his designs. His popularity with actresses led to him making the costumes for about 20 movies, including *En Cas de Malheur* with Brigitte Bardot and Jean Gabin in 1958.

By chance Féraud's first collection in Paris was seen by Oleg Cassini, who was to become famous as a designer for Jackie Kennedy. He liked Féraud's carefree designs, which seemed so full of youth compared to the usual Paris couture, and he immediately entered into a contract which opened the American market to Féraud. This brought the Japanese on to the scene, and they also put him under contract. Féraud was soon selling his designs all over the world. Success came almost too quickly. Féraud went on long journeys in search of the new and the unseen. Finally he bought a property on the border between Paraguay and Brazil, where he produced the majority of his collections.

Exotic impressions from his journeys influence Féraud's work. He specialized in sumptuous, colorful patterns, which he designed in his own studio. The designs looked particularly good on black women, and Féraud became the first to employ black models. This caused a stir and was soon copied by many others.

Féraud's zest for life and his love of bright colors made him the darling of the stars on the Côte d'Azur. One of his most famous customers was Brigitte Bardot (*right*), seen here in a sexy slip dress in 1959. After his move to Paris, Féraud's designs became more severe. In 1960s style, his pantsuit (*far right*) had cutouts in the legs.

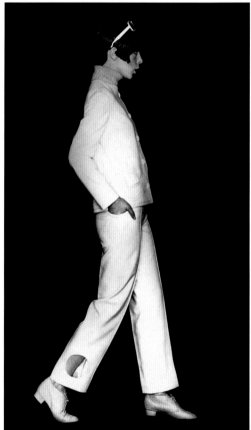

Valentino

Opposite:
This evening ensemble is from Valentino's spring/summer 1968 collection. The hand-decorated silk cape is worn over wide silk-crêpe pants. Whether by chance or on purpose, this design was photographed with the model in the same pose as in Valentino's preliminary drawing.

Below:
Extreme elegance. Valentino Clemente Ludovico Garavani, to give Valentino his full name, has always remained committed to elegance, even when his colleagues made concessions to the youth cult. Here are three coat lengths: maxi, midi, and mini.

Everyone who wants to be something in the fashion world goes to Paris, for anyone who makes it there belongs to the couture élite. In the 1950s in particular couture was still a closed circle, and it guarded against all intruders. The Italian Valentino Clemente Ludovico Garavani, later famous as Valentino, succeeded in entering the circle because he was clever enough to go to Paris to study in 1950. He took courses at the Chambre Syndicale de la Couture, as well as taking dancing lessons and showing an interest in the theater. The ultimate decision to go into fashion came about when he won a competition sponsored by the International Wool Secretariat, the same way that Karl Lagerfeld and Yves Saint Laurent were also to begin their careers. Valentino received an offer from Jean Dessès, where he worked for five years before following Guy Laroche, who founded his own house in 1957.

Valentino had only just become known as a couturier of lavish elegance when in 1968 he presented a surprisingly young, modern "white collection." This is seen as a high point in his 40 years of creative work. Based on this collection, he then designed the wedding dress in which Jackie Kennedy married Aristotle Onassis. A bright orange-red became Valentino's trademark, however, and he repeatedly used this color in his simple yet exciting evening dresses.

Valentino opened his own boutique in Paris in 1968, and since 1975 he has shown his ready-to-wear collections there.

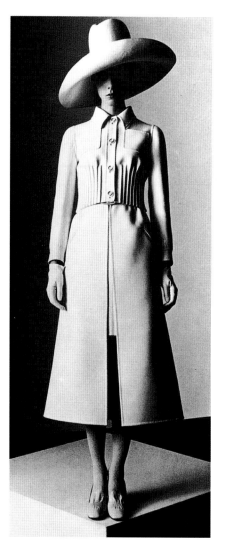

These drawings demonstrate that Valentino was also a talented fashion artist. They show a selection of his work.

Opposite:
Valentino's spring/summer 1969 collection was playfully romantic. The detail (*left*) is of flower patterns on a bolero lavishly decorated with paste beads – handmade of course. The classic evening gown from the autumn/winter 1989/90 collection (*right*) features geometric Art Deco patterns.

Milestones in fashion:
The cocktail dress

The cocktail dress was launched by Dior in 1948, and it proved to be a stroke of genius. With its plunging neckline or off-the-shoulder bustier in the style of an evening gown and the modest length of an afternoon dress, the cocktail dress was simply ideal for all early festivities. It could also be worn to the theater, to tea, or even to a summer ball. It had an informal look, but at the same time offered the opportunity to wear plenty of jewelry in the afternoon. It was often complemented by a bolero jacket, which later in the evening could be discarded to reveal the full effect. Women loved wearing a short evening dress because it made them look younger; teenage girls wore it because it made them look ten years older!

The cocktail dress was often off-the-shoulder, or sometimes had a heart-shaped neckline, as in this design by John Cavenagh. Whichever shape, the neckline gave the cocktail dress the elegance of an evening gown. For going out in the evening, it was often complemented by a jacket or coat (*right*). A hat could be worn with it to a garden party, but indoors hats were taboo. Gloves, however, were an essential accessory.

Whether a cocktail dress was
closefitting, as in the Fath design
from 1956 (*above left*) with the
extravagant cape, or a wider shape,
the hemline was always just below
the knee. The black design (*above
right*) dates from 1955; its creator
rounded it off with a broad-
brimmed, black velvet hat.

The look of the decade

The range of make-up colors changed as often as fashion – that is, twice a year. Ingenious combinations were created, such as ice-green eye shadow with moss-green eyeliner and copper-colored mascara, or silver-blue eye shadow with midnight-blue eyeliner and violet mascara. Turquoise eyelids and orange lips were another very successful combination. The important thing was that the look was color-coordinated to the latest fashion. In the 1950s it was much more important that eye shadow should match the purse than that it suit the wearer particularly well. This meant that women often looked as if they had fallen into the paint pot. But that did not matter so long as everyone could see that their make-up went with their gloves and hat.

In those days make-up products were not meant to beautify women in an invisible way. Their consistency was too heavy for that, and they had to be applied too thickly. Foundation lay on the skin like a damp mask and its color was usually much too light to look like a natural skin tone, at least on more elegant women. The fake tan of those who could not afford constant vacations in the sun was even worse. The caricature of 1950s beauty consists of an artificial brown foundation, with glittering silver eye shadow and bright orange lips. It is easy to mock today, as make-up products have become so much more sophisticated and can be applied so lightly. In the 1950s, however, the artificial look was what was required, matching the New Look in its revival of the *belle époque*, when women were like delicate flowers constantly waiting for a man to call. "Don't touch me" was written in invisible ink over every female apparition in the 1950s. Fashion was like sculpture, and make-up fitted it like a graphic. This was perfectly expressed in Erwin Blumenfeld's famous 1950 photograph *Œil de biche* (Doe's Eye): model Jean Patchetti reduced to a perfectly curved doe's eye, emphasized by the symmetrical arch of a dark eyebrow, above clearly defined red lips and a distinct beauty spot; the even, pale skin serves as a canvas for the paint, which has been applied with a sure hand.

Now that teenagers received reasonable pocket money, they too had become a target group, and cosmetics aimed at this younger market were soon produced. For teenagers the eyebrows were somewhat lighter in color and wider, and the lips were not as strongly outlined but were softer; Brigitte Bardot's pouting mouth was thought ideal. Her high blond ponytail was also adopted by countless teenagers, especially after Picasso immortalized the young model Sylvette with exactly this hairstyle.

Those teenagers who did not want to look sexy but preferred a more serious effect renounced colors altogether. Everything they wore was black, from their hair to their clothes and including black eyeliner. They wore their hair long or short, but it was usually straggly, with bangs.

Older women, on the other hand, changed the style and color of their hair as frequently as their clothes and make-up. Sometimes they wore it straight, then wavy, sometimes short, then chin- or shoulder-length or put up. The favorite color was still blonde, however, and if a woman's real hair could not be altered to suit the latest trend easily enough, she turned to hairpieces. Whether it was fashionable bangs or a classic chignon style, everything could be put on and pinned up. But nothing worked without hair spray, especially toward the end of the decade when the hair was backcombed and lacquered until it looked like candyfloss.

Ears had to be decorated, too. Thick, round clip-ons or large gold creoles were the favorite earrings. Sets of matching earrings, necklace, and bracelet were also popular. Gold chains and decorative brooches were put on as individual pieces. Of course the pearl necklace was an

Helena Rubinstein Announces Sensational Silken Lipstick!

New formula with atomized silk enriches color and gives your lips the look of living satin!

Above:
Cosmetics queen Helena Rubinstein's "silken" lipstick was a huge success – soft, smooth lips at last!

Opposite:
Light blonde hair, sparkling eyes, and a translucent complexion represented the ideal for the decent, respectable woman. Many men had no idea that this look required such an amount of artificial assistance, since 1950s woman was so adept at always appearing immaculately made up.

The new decorative arts

The perfectionism of the 1950s meant that making up became a true art. Beauty salons began to devote their attention less to caring for their customers' skin and more to instructing them on the correct application of the huge number of sophisticated cosmetic products. In 1954, to add to its popular Cream Puff compact powder, advertised by Ava Gardner, Max Factor introduced a new product that could be used to cover up dark rings under the eyes; it was called Erase.

The big question was, which comes first – covering up or making up? Professionals advised that blemishes such as rings under the eyes or pimples should first be covered up, and then make-up or powder applied to even out the complexion and give a matte finish. Rouge could be applied very finely on top so that the transition was not too harsh. Such care was not normally taken with the neck, however, and there was sometimes a visible line where the make-up ended; this was unfortunate, but the clean white collar was even more important than perfect make-up.

The Kelly bag was soon almost as famous and sought-after as its celebrity owner and namesake. This kind of leather bag had been developed in the 1930s, but in 1956 it acquired its new name from Grace Kelly, who in that year married Prince Rainier III of Monaco and retired from the screen.

absolute must for every woman. Pearls were worn in a modest single string with a twinset, or sometimes in several rows tied with a clasp. Dior brought in paste necklaces and smoky gray, brown-faceted glass beads which looked so wonderful that it would not have occurred to ask if they were genuine. One thing was for sure: a lady did not leave the house without jewelry.

She certainly never left without a hat either. As hairstyles became more lavish, however, hats became smaller. Ultimately all that was left was a kind of barette, before the time when hats disappeared altogether.

Headscarves were very important to women who rode in open-top cars, as well as to those who wanted to look as if they did. A square silk scarf was folded into a triangle and put over the hair to protect it. The ends passed under the chin and were tied at the back over the apex of the triangle, forming a kind of hood.

Gloves were also a must, though their use fell away during the course of the decade. At the beginning of the 1950s white gloves were worn even with a twinset. Medium-length gloves were worn with a suit, and long, elegant gloves with an evening dress. They were often made of the same material as the dress, as was the matching purse. Thanks to Grace Kelly, who was seen with it in many press photographs, a particular

Hermès bag acquired cult status. It had a leather handle and a combination-lock fastening, and soon came to be known as the Kelly bag.

Wide belts were the most important accessory of the decade. They were used to pull in the waist or, if this was unnecessary, to emphasize that fortunate fact.

Shoes were delicate, with pointed toes and a small, curved Sabrina heel, so called after the hit movie in which Audrey Hepburn starred. Hepburn and French star Brigitte Bardot, both former ballet dancers, also helped to make flat ballet-shoe pumps widely popular, especially among teenagers who found them perfect for their favorite pastime, rock 'n' roll dancing. Soon stiletto heels came in, however, and from then on women of all ages wanted to climb to new dizzy heights.

"La belle de jour" — Women simply did not appear without make-up and jewelry, even if it was only well-made costume jewelry such as this design for Dior from 1957 (*opposite*). Many cosmetics companies sought to attract customers in the same way as Elizabeth Arden (*above center*). A small, closefitting hat was used to cover the hair and show the face to great advantage (*above right*).

Italian shoe designer Salvatore Ferragamo, who made shoes for Hollywood stars, invented the stiletto heel in 1955. Hidden steel pins made it possible to construct high, narrow heels that were strong enough to hold a woman's weight, though not every floor surface was robust enough to take them. There were frequent complaints about ruined parquet and linoleum floors, but women loved the new high heels and stayed faithful to them.

Opposite page:
Salvatore Ferragamo with some of his most prominent clients' lasts. His shoes were always handmade to measure.

BRIGITTE BARDOT

ANITA EKBERG

GRACE KELLY

EVITA PERÓN

SOPHIA LOREN

GINA LOLLOBRIGIDA

MARILYN MONROE

AUDREY HEPBURN

LIZ TAYLOR

dols of the decade

No one embodied the 1950s ideal of immaculate perfection more than **Grace Kelly** (1928–82). Her manner and appearance were aristocratic long before her marriage to Prince Rainier of Monaco made her a princess. Director Alfred Hitchcock, who led her to stardom with *Dial M for Murder*, *Rear Window*, and *To Catch a Thief*, saw her as one of the most desirable of women – "a lady in the living room and a whore in the bedroom." As far as fashion was concerned, she was known for her "nice girl" look, with twinset and string of pearls complemented by sparkling white, short gloves, and of course the Kelly bag.

Audrey Hepburn (1929–93) symbolized the decade's respectable teenager: innocent, doe-eyed, fanatical about dancing. *Roman Holiday*, *Sabrina*, and above all *Funny Face* made her a fashionable role model for the young generation. *Funny Face* perfectly caught the 1950s obsession with fashion, with its teenage dream of an ugly duckling rising to become a top model and with a romatic wedding at its climax. Hepburn's bangs and thick eyebrows, and her black polo-neck, capri pants, and ballerina skirts were copied in their millions.

Marilyn Monroe (1926–62) combined innocent charisma with bombshell looks, and this made her the idol of all those who could not decide between the nice girl next door and the exciting vamp. She worked her way to the top of the American acting tree with *Gentlemen Prefer Blondes*, *How to Marry a Millionaire*, and above all *The Seven Year Itch*. Her carefully set, platinum-blonde hair, her "veiled" look (helped by false eyelashes in the outer corners of her eyes), her moist lips that were always half open, and her tiny beauty spot – all made for an appearance that was copied for many years.

Elizabeth Taylor (b. 1932) was also in a class of her own. First she was a child star, and then overnight she seemed to explode with feminity. She had all the physical requirements of a sex symbol, but her extraordinarily beautiful face was able to show real passion, and that was more than America and its movie industry could cope with. Nevertheless, in the 1950s she succeeded in making some movies that corresponded to her type and temperament, including *A Place in the Sun*, *Giant*, *Raintree County*, and *Cat on a Hot Tin Roof*. These were followed by countless roles, but she drew greater attention with her changing husbands, who number eight to date.

Brigitte Bardot (b. 1934) was an explosive mixture of childlike innocence and depravity. Delicate yet curvaceous, naive yet sophisticated, she embodied everything that people call "typically French." Like Audrey Hepburn she had been a ballet student, and the fact that she looked younger than other stars meant that she was greatly imitated by teenagers. After her 1956 worldwide hit *And God Created Woman*, her pout and bikini went down in history as symbols of seduction. Her style became fashionable too: ponytail, large hooped creole earrings, leotards, wide leather belts, fishnet stockings, and ballerina skirts. In 1956 Jacques Esterel designed a pink gingham wedding dress for her marriage to Jacques Charrier, which was much copied and brought gingham back into fashion.

Women who became sex symbols had the hourglass figure required by the New Look, and they also met the requirements of soldiers who after years of privation were looking for both a mother and a lover. The European answer to American bombshells such as Jane Russell, Marilyn Monroe, Jayne Mansfield, and Kim Novak were Italian actresses **Sophia Loren** (b. 1934) and **Gina Lollobrigida** (b. 1927). Swedish actress **Anita Ekberg** (b. 1931) made movie history with a single appearance – barefoot, in an off-the-shoulder evening dress in Rome's Trevi Fountain. This scene was the climax to Federico Fellini's *La Dolce Vita* (1960), which stood as a monument to the end of the decade.

When she was young, **Maria Eva Duarte** (1919–1952) a peasant's daughter, dreamed of becoming a famous actress, and her dream came true. But she gained much more fame as **Evita Perón**, wife of Argentinian president Juan Perón, at whose side La Presidenta (as Evita came to be known) did charitable work for the poor and campaigned for women's rights. Although she spent a forture on couture clothes, especially Dior, she was idolized as the "angel of the poor" since she had set up – supposedly as a "private" foundation – a welfare organization with many sanatoria, hospitals, and old peoples' and children's homes. In 1951 she was urged by the trade unions to run for the post of vice-president, but she had to give up this plan when she was diagnosed as having advanced anemia. Her death in July 1952 caused great grief, especially among the ordinary people of her country.

Bosom enemies

Sex symbols were very rarely seen together: the meetings would have been too explosive. Those who live by their bust measurement have to fight for every inch, and the stars did this with all the means at their disposal. It was not that the screen goddesses' breasts were not subject to the laws of gravity, but in those low-cut, strapless dresses they were given a little help by a simple trick – carpet tape! The double-sided adhesive tape was first used in Hollywood to provide guaranteed support at strategically important points. The removal of this secret weapon from the bare skin could be extremely painful, however, and the tape also ruined the lining of many an expensive evening gown. But necessity is the mother of invention, and new adhesive tapes and even adhesive cups were developed. These were much kinder to the skin and could even be hidden by body make-up and used in nude photographs. In the 1950s couturiers also took great trouble to build bust support into their creations. This was especially true of Jacques Fath, who designed for the curvaceous Rita Hayworth. And if it was a close-run thing in the bust stakes, the shoulders could always be pushed forward to give that little extra, as Sophia Loren demonstrates here to Gina Lollobrigida, her closest rival.

The wedding dress

The wedding of John F. Kennedy, later president of the United States, and Jacqueline Lee Bouvier in September 1953 (*above*) was celebrated in a similar royal fashion to the marriage of the future Queen Elizabeth II to Philip Mountbatten in November 1947 (*opposite*). Princess Elizabeth wore a satin gown designed by her royal dressmaker Norman Hartnell.

Where would couture be without weddings? The bridal gown forms the climax and conclusion of every fashion show and often represents the safest source of income for a couture house.

A single top-drawer wedding can ensure a studio work for an entire season. The bride's mother, bridesmaids, witnesses, aunts, sisters, and friends usually decide to buy their outfits from the house that has fitted the bride for the "most beautiful dress of her life." The 1950s saw some of the most brilliant weddings of the 20th century, and it was the couture dresses that

turned them into fairy tales. Wedding fever and the resulting competition for the most beautiful gowns broke out after Princess Elizabeth of Great Britain found her prince in Philip Mountbatten in 1947.

Money and power, nobility and fame, all had to come together to turn a marriage ceremony into a dream wedding which the masses would find even more moving than the most romantic happy ending at the movies.

Following page:
A dream come true. In 1956 Hollywood star Grace Kelly married Prince Rainier of Monaco to become a fairy-tale princess. The hopes and wishes of an entire generation of women were directed toward her.

Actress Linda Christian, who married actor
Tyrone Power in 1949.

Modeling a wedding dress by Carven, 1962.

The Shah of Persia and his bride Farah Diba,
1959.

Movie director Roman Polanski and actress
Sharon Tate, 1968.

Princess Elizabeth's wedding shoes of satin duchesse
with silver buckles set with pearls.

Senator John F. Kennedy and Jacqueline Lee
Bouvier, 1953.

Princess Margaret of Great Britain and
Antony Armstrong-Jones, 1960.

Desmond Fitzgerald and Louise de
la Falaise, 1966.

Lady Diana Spencer and Charles,
Prince of Wales, 1981

Yves Saint Laurent and Farah Diba's wedding dress, 1959.

Scherrer, 1994.

Gianni Versace, 1992.

Karl Lagerfeld with his models after the show for Chanel in 1995/96. *Left to right*: Nadja Auermann, Helena Christensen, Claudia Schiffer, the master, Shalom Harlow, Karen Mulder.

Chantal Thomas, 1995.

Callaghan, 1993.

Lolita Lempicka, 1997.

Pierre Cardin, 1989.

arven, 1992.

Paco Rabanne, 1995.

Christian Lacroix, 1990.

Christian Dior, 1995.

John Galliano, 1996.

Claude Montana, 1992.

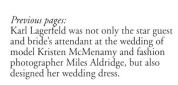

Previous pages:
Karl Lagerfeld was not only the star guest and bride's attendant at the wedding of model Kristen McMenamy and fashion photographer Miles Aldridge, but also designed her wedding dress.

ves Saint Laurent, 1996/97.

Torrente, 1992.

From first design
to finished article

Elke Reinhold. Photographs by Jacques Torregano

When asked how he created his exciting clothes, Yves Saint Laurent tersely replied: "I put my ideas down on paper, which are turned into samples and, if necessary, are revised by me." If it were as simple as that there would be thousands of designers. But there are only a few dozen who have really written fashion history, who have the ability to turn an idea, perhaps no more than a flash of inspiration, into a pioneering garment. *Haute couture* especially, which demands the highest cutting techniques, separates the wheat from the chaff. Despite all that fashion has produced in the course of the 20th century – high-tech fibers, computer-aided design, laser cutting, ready-made clothes in quantities of several hundred thousand – in many areas couture still follows the rules laid down by its founders. It still demands the craftsman's know-how and precision shown by Charles Frederick Worth and Paul Poiret when they were the best of their age. The path to the first design and from there to the finished article is almost exactly the same for the great couturiers at the start of the new millennium as it was for their predecessors around 1900.

How does a couture collection come about? Gianfranco Ferré, chief designer at Dior from 1989 to 1996, describes his collections as the child of his "momentary desire." At the moment at which one picks up paper and pencil, however, one might not necessarily have a clear idea of what one wants. One simply senses a need for something. For Ferré, for example, this might mean creating not just a garment but an entire movement. It could be that he was sitting in his archive a month before the presentation of a Dior couture collection, leafing through books, magazines, and old newspapers. Just then he received a phone call from François Lesage, the famous master of embroidery, who asked him "What do you fancy?", to which Ferré replied "The age of Empire." Immediately he remembered thousands of images from the time of Napoleon, the emperor's coat of arms, the image of a sensual woman such as Joséphine de Beauharnais. On another occasion they talked about Evita Perón, and Ferré designed his collection for a strong, determined woman.

The initial moment, the first idea for a collection, is a very individual thing among designers, now as then. Literature, movies, painting, a sculpture, a journey, foreign people and cultures, or any single event in his life can serve as inspiration for a fashion designer. Pierre Cardin was inspired to futuristic designs by the spectacular achievements of space travel in the 1960s, as well as his interest in microscopy, the computer, and geometric shapes. Christian Dior interpreted the female body in the form of letters, and when John Galliano created his first collection for Dior in 1997, he bowed to the great master with a variation on the theme of S. Yohji Yamamoto draws inspiration from old photographs with scenes of everyday life. Christian Lacroix is inspired by the Baroque period and its architecture, as well as by the south of France and bullfighting. Everyone has their own particular preferences.

Art is the one great passion that unites them all. Paul Poiret became a close friend of Raoul Dufy, who designed the most beautiful materials for him. Coco Chanel was mad about the Bauhaus and Picasso; Elsa Schiaparelli worshipped Francis Picabia, Jean Cocteau, and Salvador Dalí. Yves Saint Laurent, strongly influenced by his friend Andy Warhol, created a Pop Art collection in 1966, in which he used Tom Wesselmann's Great American Nudes series. In the 1980s Jean-Charles de Castelbajac had artists such as Hervé Di Rosa, Robert Coba, and Annette Messager use his finished clothes as canvases.

Just as art influences fashion designers and has a direct effect on their use of materials, so fashion designers are also often inspired by particular materials themselves. A style often takes as its starting point the technical possibilities of materials: in the early 1960s the development of Lycra inspired designers to figure-hugging pants and bodystockings; toward the end of the 1980s fibers such as polyurethane gave the idea of skintight leggings and cycle shorts. Particular

developments and inventions, many of which come from the research laboratories of NASA or the chemical giants Hoechst or Rhône-Poulenc, make particular new cuts and shapes possible.

Most designers, however, are more interested in the visual characteristics of modern textiles than in their practical qualities. When Azzedine Alaïa designed his collection in antistress fibers, he was more attracted to the special luster of the material than to its calming qualities.

Helmut Lang used thermofibers, which change color according to temperature due to their heat-sensitive mircocapsules. In this case, as in some others, the new material proved to be useless. Thermofibers in clothing obviously change color most in the areas where body temperature is highest, that is under the arms and in the crotch, and is thus only suitable for wearers who want to provoke.

For Sonia Delaunay (1884–1979), who was perhaps more famous as a textile designer than as an artist, the creation of materials and fashion were one and the same thing. In 1925 she gained a large audience through her presentation at the World Fair in Paris. Already twenty years earlier the Russian painter had begun experimenting with fabrics which, like her paintings, were made up of pure, luminous colors and geometric shapes. These made a vibrant overall impression which in her opinion fitted in with the modern street scene. Delaunay became the first artist to work as a textile and fashion designer. She also

did this to support her husband Robert, also an artist. Only followers of the avant-garde, like Hollywood star Gloria Swanson, were daring enough to wear Sonia Delaunay's works of art.

However great an inspirational effect materials can have on original designs, in *haute couture* they tend simply to inspire the creation of new fabrics. Christian Lacroix and his team, for example, arrive like a swarm of bees at the biannual Paris textile fair Première Vision, at which cloth manufacturers from all over the world present their latest creations. The top couturiers usually sign exclusive contracts with weavers in Lyons, Italy, Scotland, and Switzerland for their purchases. None of the designers simply buy the suggested fabrics from the manufacturers, however; they also develop their own materials in cooperation with the weavers.

Most couture houses select their materials a few months before a collection, in the same way as a sculptor selects his marble. First of all the designer produces sketches of his designs, up to 1000 per collection. Then he draws the most important details to emphasize the special features of each particular design. This drawing must be totally comprehensible to all those of his colleagues who will be involved in the realization of the design. This does not mean that the drawing must be perfect: Christian Lacroix, for example, who has ideas for many designs as he doodles while on the phone, knows that his

Above:
In her vibrant, "dancing" textiles, the artist Sonia Delaunay wanted to capture modern life with all its trappings, its new electric lights, its dancehalls and its women, freed of corsets and conventions. From 1930 on she worked on her "simultaneous" clothe which, just like her paintings featured identical geometric patterns and bright colors. With them she realized her dream of making "a walking piece of art." Even on the beach Delaunay and her clientele, which was mostly made up of her friends, attired themselves in art.

Opposite:
Final steps after months of creative work: designs for invitation cards to a *haute couture* show are colored with the help of polaroids.

A fitting in Jeanne Paquin's
studio in 1908. Many
couturiers, including
Coco Chanel and Jacques
Fath, never sketched their
ideas but draped and
perfected their designs
on living models or
dressmaker's dummies.

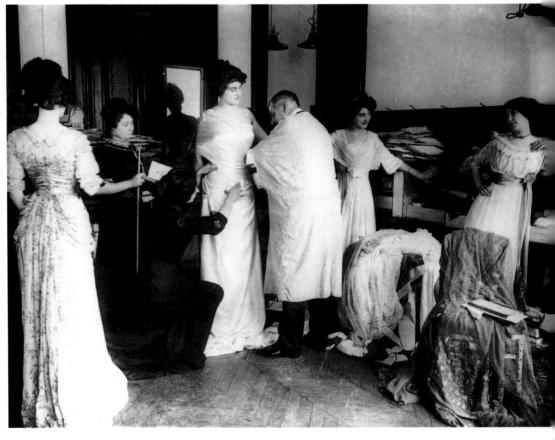

Below:
Dressmakers at Dior make
up *toiles*, or first samples
of a collection, out of cotton
cloth.

From first design to finished article

closest colleagues prefer his quick sketches because they present the basic essentials of his collection.

The production of the drawing is normally the only time when a designer works alone. This is not true of strange and beautiful creatures such as Paco Rabanne, however, who is famous for his metal creations which were borrowed from antique chain mail. He simply laid a woman on the table and cut and shaped the metal parts and foil directly on her body, which caused Coco Chanel to remark that he was not so much a couturier as a metalworker. As a rule the couturier makes use of his team once his sketches are finished. Until the early 1990s strict rules stipulated that, in order to belong to *haute couture*, designers in France had to have a studio with at least 20 dressmakers and produce a collection of at least 75 pieces. Today the number has been reduced to 50 "compulsory creations," and the rules are no longer as tough, with the result that designers such as Jean-Paul Gaultier, Thierry Mugler, and Josephus Melchior Thimister, who sometimes have fewer than half the number of many colleagues, were allowed to show their own *haute couture* fashion toward the end of the 1990s.

The most important position in the studio is held by the *première d'atelier*. She is the designer's right hand, and he explains all his ideas to her, leaving some room for interpretation. The head of the studio must assimilate the spirit of the collection. Designers such as Pierre Cardin, who can draw, cut, and sew, are rare. The *première* is therefore the main medium between the couturier and his studio. She is responsible for communicating ideas and assigning tasks to her colleagues through every single step of the design process. She also has to draw design models, bringing the garment to life with the help of the original sketches; she cuts cotton cloth for the first sample, tries it on the dummy, pins it, prepares the basic pattern and makes the prototype. She is often also responsible for the final selection of fabrics, buttons, and other details. Christian Dior entrusted all his sketches, which never contained details, to his *première d'atelier* Marguerite Carré, whom he affectionately called Dame Couture. She translated the sketches for everyone else working in the studio, and acted as Dior's memory as well as his hands. The master himself, who in his white shirt looked more like a surgeon than a fashion designer, never touched a pinned dress. Yet his eyes never missed a single tiny detail at a fitting. Many great couturiers, such as Madeleine Vionnet, Coco Chanel, Jacques Fath, and Madame Grès, never made drawings but created and draped their designs directly on a live model or dummy.

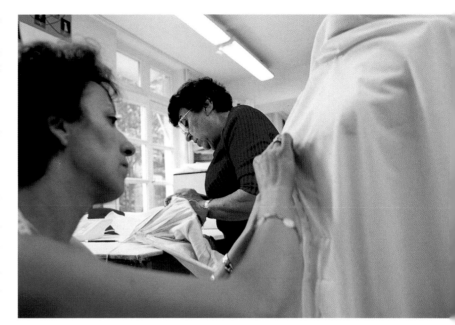

The dressmaker's dummy scarcely changed during the course of the century, apart from accommodating the current ideal of beauty. In Dior's day, for example, the waist shrank from 23 to 21 inches (58 to 53 cm). Although, at the end of the 20th century, *haute couture* has a worldwide clientele of only about 200 by contrast to 20,000 in 1943, some couture houses still possess dummies with the measurements of regular clients. They carry little labels with the name of the particular customer and save her the trouble of constantly appearing for fittings.

Once the design is ready, a model tries it on, bringing it to life with her movements and gestures as well as testing its wearability. At this

Above:
Jeanine Ouvrards with a prototype from the Lacroix collection for winter 2000. The head of the studio must be able to sense and interpret the designer's ideas more accurately than anyone else.

Top:
In Christian Lacroix's studio. His *première d'atelier* (forewoman), Jeanine Ouvrards, who started as chief dressmaker for Jacques Fath in the 1950s, makes and pins a sample design from Lacroix's sketches.

Silk printing for Christian Lacroix at Fabric Frontline in Zurich. Like most fashion designers, Lacroix does not simply choose from the fabrics that are presented at the international textile fairs, but has his own suppliers who create colors and patterns only for him.

From first design to finished article

Only a few factories still carry out silk-screen printing with up to 26 colors. In the studios of Fabric Frontline silk satins are created in an endless range of colors. These are finally printed, painted, embroidered, and finished for fashion houses such as Dior, Givenchy, Carven, and Lacroix.

Christian Lacroix's sewing studio. Every single design in his *haute couture* collection is first cut out from coarse cotton cloth and tried on the dummy.

stage things are perfected, added to, taken away again, replaced, shortened, or lengthened. This means that the garment continues to be worked on until it fulfills its purpose. Finally the *toile*, which is what the first finished garment in cotton cloth is called, is presented to the designer. This is the first time that he has the chance to look at a three-dimensional representation of his original design.

At this stage a prototype is made in the desired fabric, and once again this is tried on the model and corrected until it fits perfectly. In the meantime work is done by lace-makers and tulle-makers, embroiderers, pleaters, button-makers, and passementières, who are responsible for braiding and trimming. For lace, motifs from the designer's sketches or from archive patterns from the makers of the famous Calais lace are transferred on to graph paper. The course of every single thread is mathematically calculated, along with a code for the various colors; today computers are used to help with this. The embroiderer is given a colored drawing of the motif as well as a technical description of all the materials to be used such as pearls, sequins, beads, fabric flowers, gold and silver thread, silk thread, jade, paste, feathers, chenille, and appliqué.

The house of Lesage offers couturiers a collection of 250 to 300 samples each season. These samples are crucial to many designers for their own collection. "The day when Lesage reveals his collection to me," says Christian Lacroix, "is one of the high points of the season for me, a red-letter day, full of joy and excitement." Like most other designers, however, Lacroix also suggests certain themes to François Lesage for him to interpret.

The couturier's creations are still made entirely by hand, just as they were 100 years ago, and each one takes dozens to hundreds of hours. The record is held by Yves Saint Laurent, whose 1988 dresses Les Iris and Les Tournesols, both inspired by Van Gogh, each required 600 hours of embroidery work, and by Karl Lagerfeld, whose Atys for the 1997 Chanel summer collection kept the embroiderers busy for 1280 hours. Lesage uses over 650 lb (300 kg) of beads and 100 million sequins per year; a single article can require up to 100,000 stitches,

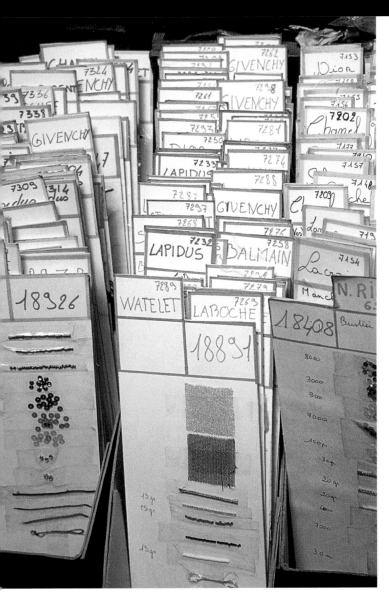

and a collection can take up to 25,000 hours of work.

The button-maker first produces prototypes for the buttons, which depending on the material are then cast, cut, or carved by hand. There are as many materials for buttons, which often carry the couturier's emblem, as there are threads for fabrics: mother-of-pearl, paste, wood, horn, plastic, marble, gold-plated, silver-plated, nickel-plated, copper-plated, engraved, or enameled. The braid-maker follows the designer's illustrations to make the trimming, edging, ribbons, fringes, and tassels which will be used to edge the fabric. Yves Saint Laurent is known to be one of the greatest admirers of passementerie, and since the 1970s he has not gone without it in a single one of his collections.

All those involved work hand in hand until the day of the show, when the designer presents the results of six months' creative work for the first time. While the models are getting changed behind the scenes, the designer is still probably making last-minute corrections, changing a seam here and adding a crease there. The bride is sent out on to the catwalk last, following a tradition set up in the 1930s by Paul Poiret. He was the first designer to include a wedding dress in his *haute couture* collection after it had become fashionable for whole wedding parties, from bridesmaids to bride, to buy their designs from one dressmaker. While the public admire the finished dress, for the designer a new season is already beginning. Lacroix once described this: "The bride is dressed. She is the last insect, actually still in her chrysalis. The others have already done their parage and played their part, with all the accessories that go with it. When the clothes come back behind the scenes from the catwalk, they no longer exist for me. They exist only for the time of that journey there and back."

NiVEAU 1
Bouquet Couleur
KE1.0001/2
KE1.0001/3

Embroidery by the traditional house of Lesage, which has worked with all the great couturiers of the century, from 1922 until today.

311

The house of Lesage, founded in 1922, specializes in high-quality embroidery. A family concern, it is already into its third generation of management. Lesage rarely produces embroidery according to predetermined designs, but rather sets the trends. Many designers, including Lacroix, visit Lesage for inspiration before they start on their own designs. Sometimes a couture collection is built around a Lesage motif or idea. The company's influence on couturiers is inestimable.

Embroidery by François Lesage. During perforation every single stitch is transferred through the parchment pattern to the fabric (*top left*). A single *haute couture* design might require up to 100,000 stitches (*top right*). Lesage embroidery stencils (*above left*). Working on a bodice by Christian Lacroix for Jean Patou (*above right*).

Opposite:
François Lesage designs all the embroidery himself. He specifies colors and materials on his design, and the detailed work is carried out by his colleagues. Shown here a tassel with glass beads for Olivier Lapidus.

More than 20 dressmakers work in Lacroix's studio on a new collection, embroidering, pinning, correcting, and modifying his designs.

Opposite and below:
The final tacking stitches are made to a prototype for the Lacroix collection.

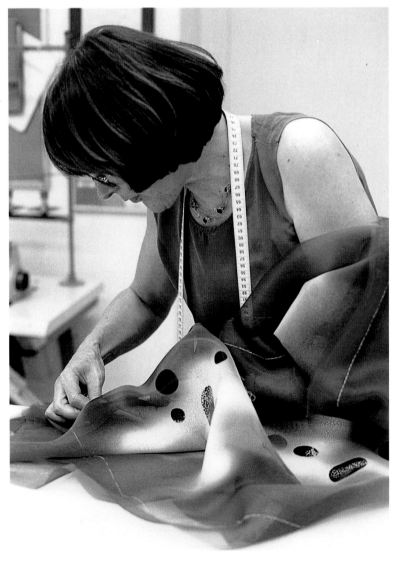

From first design to finished article

Several hundred hours' worth of embroidery and lavish passementerie go into a dress by Lacroix. The result is priceless.

Opposite:
Detail from Dior's spring/summer 1996 collection. A real butterfly could scarcely be more beautiful than this delicate version, made of glass beads and paste, that has settled on the strap of a dress. Paste gems playfully trickle down the strap like dewdrops.

From first design to finished article

The photographs on the following pages show preparations for the *haute couture* show of July 1999, at which Lacroix presented his personal millennium collection. At this stage everyone in the studio is always very nervous, and it is rare for a designer even to allow a photographer in.

From first design to finished article

Opposite:
Christian Lacroix and his wife and
muse Françoise Lacroix choose models
for the show.

Below:
A fitting in the studio. Only when the
model has been chosen can the really
detailed work begin. It may take many
days to apply the finishing touches.

Following pages:
Fitting. Lacroix is still missing a
top. He holds various possibilities,
including one that shows a hunting
scene. In his fitting room there are
all kinds of fabrics and accessories to
suit his ideas.

From first design to finished article

The designer works alone only when he is drawing his first designs. The rest of the process is teamwork, and much of it is done by trial and error. Lacroix is busy with detailed work in a large fitting room with a mirrored wall. As usual his *première* and his wife are there too. In the background is his "wall of inspiration," with a selection of

pieces of embroidery, feathers, accessories, color swatches, and so on. These are tried out on the model, who has to remain patient during hours of testing and examining, as one idea leads to another, and shortly before the end it all has to be done again from scratch. The creative process requires a great deal of time and a coordinated team.

From first design to finished article

A special material is prepared for this season's wedding dress: white color is applied directly on to the tulle. It takes many hours of concentrated work to achieve exactly the right effect.

Dress rehearsal in the rooms where the show is to take place. The wedding dress is put on layer by layer, and each one is full of complicated details. The slip must hang correctly (*below*); the decorated jacket must fit exactly over the waistband; and last but not least, the bride must be able to move elegantly with her train and feathers. All of this requires a large team of helpers.

Following pages:
The model who will wear the wedding dress concentrates her thoughts on her great entrance. The dress is covered in case of last-minute accidents, since there is no replacement.

From first design to finished article

As Lacroix's studio colleagues gradually complete their work, other workers appear on the scene: carpenters, painters, and paper-hangers finalize the stage, while electricians look after lighting and sound. Lacroix himself is highly concentrated in this situation.

He sits on one of the gold-plated couture-chairs for the press and for customers (*below*), listens again to the music that he has selected for the presentation, and goes through the individual steps of the choreography in his mind.

It is very important for Lacroix to become totally familiar with the catwalk itself, checking through the sequences of the individual models.

Lacroix takes the time to give an exclusive interview to Anna Piaggi, the famous Italian fashion journalist (*below*), before everyone has seen his new collection.

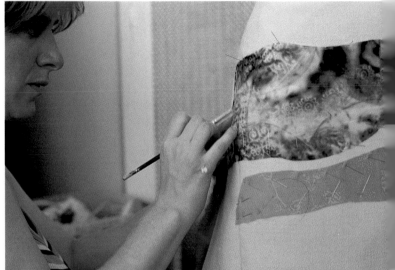

Behind the scenes each model has her own clothes-stand with the designs that she will wear, along with the relevant shoes and accessories. Surrounded by many helpers, she must be able to change in a matter of seconds, which is not always easy, especially when the pattern has to be stuck directly on to the material, as in this case (*top right*).

From first design to finished article

fter the climax of the show has been reached with the wedding dress, the master presents
mself to the audience (who hopefully are applauding wildly!). He gives a big kiss to his model
d thanks everyone for all those weeks of hard, concentrated work.

From first design to finished article

1960–1969

Sex, drugs & rock'n'roll for a better world

1960–1969

The Swinging Sixties were the most momentous decade of the century. This is demonstrated by the fact that opinions on this period continue to remain divided. For some, it was the golden age of a newfound freedom, while others see it as a murky decade which brought about the collapse of morality, respect for authority, and discipline. However, it is beyond dispute that whatever was put in motion during those years continues to have lasting social, political, and cultural consequences.

The change was stimulated by young people, who generally act as society's bearers of hope. The postwar baby boom meant that young people now made up a large proportion of the population, but above all they had more influence than ever before. Teenagers, discovered and wooed as consumers in the 1950s, grew up to become rebellious young adults who questioned every value their parents had ever held sacred. To some extent this was triggered by the economic miracle which had blossomed in the 1950s but which was only now bearing the fruit that could be enjoyed by the majority of people. However, many young people thought that the price for this abundance, in the shape of conformity, subordination, and self-denial, was too high. They rebelled against the authority of parents, church, and state, sought new values, and exposed the double standards which allowed people to do the exact opposite of what they preached in public.

In every period of history there have been clashes between generations. Now, however, young people were not merely revolting, they were devising a counter-culture of their own, and marketing this so fervently that it could never simmer away in secret but instead became omnipresent. At one point it even seemed as if the desire for a better world, with greater honesty and humanity, might be achievable. This was the objective which united young people, whether they were politically

Below:
The first German quality glossy magazine for young people: *twen* became the yardstick for magazines and advertising in the 1960s. The bubble translates "My girlfriend takes the pill. Am I more happy now?"

motivated, interested in popular culture, or naively dreaming of a life full of peace and love.

The stifling narrow-mindedness of bourgeois society, with its hollow rules of propriety and etiquette, provoked young people to rebel. Furthermore, the industrious generation that had brought about the economic miracle tried to spur its children on by pressurizing them to succeed: the wish "We want things to be better for you than they were for us" was combined with the ubiquitous threat "As long as you live under my roof you'll do as I say." This would frequently achieve the opposite effect to the one desired and induce in the young a reluctance to achieve and a rejection of the family and its trappings, including marriage, fidelity, and conventional gender roles. The root of all evil, it seemed, lay in duty. Young people asked what would happen if they refused to let people tell them what to do, if they were as relaxed and spontaneous in choosing their partners as in their choice of clothes – which should henceforth cease to act as status symbols. No sooner were these ideas formulated than they were realized: youth celebrated itself in heavenly freedom. Uschi Obermaier, "Germany's most beautiful communard," described it as follows: "Everything was brand new – fashion, music, philosophy. And of course, the lifestyle. We wanted our relationships to be different from those of our parents, and in communes we lived in a family which we had chosen ourselves. We lived by the

They sent the stones of rebellious youth rolling: without the contribution of the Beatles (*above*) and the Rolling Stones to the expression and shaping of the consciousness of Western youth, the 1960s could not have become the decade of subversion and uprising for an entire generation.

pleasure principle, tried everything."

Youthful experimentation was assisted by the contraceptive pill, which arrived on the market in 1961 and made simple and reliable prevention of pregnancy possible for the first time. Without this the sexual revolution would never have taken place. However, its contribution to the emancipation of women remains a matter of debate. Whereas men felt that they had been liberated from all responsibility, women soon found themselves pressured to be permanently ready for sex. There were few who could say of themselves, as Uschi Obermaier did: "I have always done exactly what I wanted, I have never seen myself as a feminist." Many women mounted the barricades of feminism as a direct result of the effects produced by the pill and the sexual revolution.

Furthermore, Uschi Obermaier's freedom was rooted in financial independence. As one of the top models of her time, she could afford whatever she liked. And she was not alone in acquiring wealth at an unusually early age. The economic miracle was still in full swing and young entrepreneurs with new businesses such as clubs, discotheques, sex shops, underground magazines, and boutiques, but especially those in the music business, profited from the boom. The youth market was supplied by young people who became rich by selling precisely what they

Opposite:
The 1960s were colorful – and expensive: this model is obviously very comfortable with the ubiquitous flokati rug and designer furniture; she wears a Bellissime velvet pantsuit by the now-defunct fashion house Ventrillon, 1967.

themselves liked best. These youngsters were not against consumerism as such, although they detested the adult world of impressive consumer goods. They merely spent their money on other things: fashion, travel, drugs, and rock'n'roll.

Music was the one element which united all Western youth and cut across boundaries of nationality, class, race, and gender. Bill Haley and Elvis Presley had been the forerunners; now it was the turn of the Beatles, followed by the Rolling Stones, The Who, The Kinks, Jimi Hendrix, and Eric Burdon.

Their music expressed everything that words could not – and young people would go to any lengths to be a part of it. High-class groupies were generally recruited from the pool of fashion models and beautiful heiresses who followed the wild musicians on tour and who contributed to the decade's lasting reputation for "Sex, Drugs & Rock'n'Roll." This image was not in the least dented by the fact that some rock'n'rollers took the "square" step of getting married, as Mick Jagger did with Bianca; just as long as it did not disrupt the libertine lifestyle.

Right:
"Beneath the paving stones, the beach!" was the students' battle cry during the May 1968 uprising. These were precisely the stones that they hurled at the Parisian police ... who responded with tear gas.

Opposite:
Love and peace in the days of flower power: a hippie couple after the 14-hour Technicolor Festival held in London in 1967 in support of the *International Times*.

Below:
"Make love not war": the protest against the Vietnam War spread to Europe in the 1960s and Joan Baez was one of its most celebrated voices. Actress Vanessa Redgrave is in the audience during this demonstration held in London in 1965.

Unlike the Rolling Stones, the Beatles did not content themselves with mere personal "satisfaction" but sought inner enlightenment. When in 1967 they pronounced Maharishi Mahesh Yogi as their guru, they became the outriders of a movement which sought insight from the East. And the Mods with their distinct dress and hairstyles followed new but recognizable fashion rules and were soon likened to the hippies, at least by the media, which liked to lump together anyone who wore their hair long. Young people themselves made strict distinctions between those who were "hip" (or "hot" or "in" or "cool") and real hippies, who were dropouts with little interest in anything besides marijuana and LSD. Nevertheless, the hippies' anti-plastic, pro-natural-materials stance was adopted by many who were far too active and committed ever to consider the option of dropping out.

Toward the end of the decade the plastic flower used by Mary Quant on her little-girl fashions had become a real flower symbolizing a plea for peace. The hippies' flower power movement appealed to the majority of young people and many adults. The flower was used in demonstrations against social class divisions, intolerance, racism, and war. The increased politicization of the young, whose initial aims had been merely to increase personal freedom, began in the United States with the black population's struggle against racial discrimination, and reached its zenith in the anti-Vietnam War demonstrations which students in Europe came to espouse. This included an ideological discussion with the established power structures. France and Germany in particular saw the development of an increasingly radical, student-led opposition movement which found its inspiration in the works of Karl Marx and Mao Zedong. The rejection of a political system which they considered

contemptible eventually culminated in the bloody student revolts of 1968 – the same year that, to global dismay, Russian tanks quashed the tender shoots of freedom in the streets of Prague.

In the United States, however, 1968 turned out to be another "summer of love," with open-air concerts lasting several days, echoing the famous "love-in" pop concerts of London and Los Angeles in 1967, being staged in San Francisco. The final occasion on which the youth movement demonstrated peaceful

unity was during the legendary open-air festival at Woodstock, New York, in August 1969, which attracted 1 million visitors and entered the history books as the greatest happening of all times. After this, flower power, pop, and rock seemed to lose their magic.

Subsequent concerts were marred by alcohol, drugs, and violence, and the disparate groups parted company; hippies retreated to communes or gravitated toward Oriental sects, homosexuals became active in the gay movement, women fought for feminism, some joined left-wing organizations and a few even turned to terrorism. The dream of love and peace, which had briefly seemed so tangible, burst like a soap bubble. Yet nothing was as it had been before.

Not even in the fashion world. For the first time in history, street fashion found entry to *haute couture*.

It is proof of Yves Saint Laurent's genius that he was the first to sense the dawn of a new era: in 1960 his shows featured black turtlenecks and leather jackets, thus making the statement that it was important to dress young Bikers and Beats in accordance with their standing. The international aristocracy of wealth and some of the press perceived this courageous step as an unforgivable break with the elegant tradition of the house of Dior, whose artistic direction had been entrusted to Saint Laurent two years previously. This avant-garde collection led to Saint Laurent's departure from Dior, and two years later he founded his own house.

Coco Chanel was unceremoniously dismissed when she offered free lessons in elegance to youth idol Brigitte Bardot. "That's for old people," was Bardot's comment and she stuck to her unconventional

Above:
Mini, march! Successful designer Mary Quant (*center foreground*), the mother of the miniskirt, presenting her shoes and tights, 1967.

Opposite:
1960s fashion is unimaginable without the uncomplicated, black-and-white graphic patterns which adorned simply cut minidresses.

1960–1969

Flower power in a miniskirt: with their
stylized hair and opaque tights – the
favored miniskirt accessory – these
women (*opposite*) seem like window
dummies. No floral pattern could be
complete without the daisy, flower
symbol of the decade (*below*).

Scandalous quartet: the British government came close to being toppled thanks to wholesome looking call girl Christine Keeler (*left*) and the Profumo affair; photographer David Bailey (*second from left*) ensured that his liberal lifestyle made for numerous scandals; top model Penelope Tree (*second from right*) replaced Jean Shrimpton in his affections as well as in front of his lens; and Marianne Faithful (*right*), singer and Rolling Stones groupie, was also no stranger to excess. The four pose for the launch of Bailey's visual chronicle of the 1960s, the book *Goodbye Baby & Amen*.

In the eye of the camera: the scandalous motion picture *Blow Up* by Italian director Michelangelo Antonioni, whose work set new cinematic standards, deals with the secrets of images and captures the degenerate morality of photographers and models in a world of luxury and drugs which even a murder fails to shake up. David Hemmings (*left*) is the photographer, a role closely modeled on David Bailey. Verushka, Countess Lehndorff (*right*) plays herself, an international top model.

boutique fashions. Elegance was the last thing young people wanted. That was what had been prescribed by their mothers in the 1950s, and it made every one look old. Now it was the turn of young people to set the trend and, this time, mothers followed their daughters – sometimes to the very limits of respectability.

We shall probably never know who really invented the miniskirt; was it Mary Quant or André Courrèges? A number of facts would indicate, however, that this revolutionary creation heralded from London, simply because this is the place where the 1960s youth movement was founded. Furthermore, plain little minidresses could be copied by any teenager at home and did not exactly look like a *dernier cri* of *haute couture*. They suited the lively boutiques of the Kings Road and Carnaby Street that were preferred by girls who did not want to look like their mothers. This was precisely the reason why Mary Quant opened a boutique there in 1955, selling

clothes that she had made herself. During an American tour ten years later, she hit all the world's headlines when she presented childlike models wearing miniskirts and dancing to pop music.

The real importance of the miniskirt sensation, which seemed as fresh and innocent as a child's pinafore, can only be appreciated by taking into account the fact that the 1950s were still defined by women with concrete atomic bosoms and teetering stiletto heels. Suddenly, here were little girls who seemed to be made entirely of huge eyes and long, slender legs and who innocently exhibited childlike bodies under transparent clothes.

The incarnation of this new ideal was Twiggy, the 16-year-old English girl who weighed a mere 90 lb but knew how to make a profit from every single ounce. At the age of 19, after three years in the modeling business, she had earned enough money to retire. Twiggy was the first model ever to have mass appeal; her appearances could draw crowds to compete with those attracted by the Beatles.

English girls were very much in demand: Sweet Jean Shrimpton and gawky Penelope Tree had successful modeling careers, which would once have seemed unlikely since neither conformed to conventional concepts of beauty. It was precisely this quality, however, that inspired photographers like David Bailey and Richard Avedon.

David Bailey, who was not really interested in clothes ("Clothes are just clothes"), likened every fashion shoot to a sexual act, with the camera as penis. Bailey was the model for the main character,

played by David Hemmings, in Michelangelo Antonioni's scandalous 1966 movie *Blow Up*, which features the German model Verushka von Lehndorff as herself. The movie is about a photographer who accidentally witnesses a murder and features space-age costumes and garish fantasy uniforms and was generally regarded as shamelessly exaggerated. However, documentary footage of London clubs of that era demonstrates that the fashionable reality of the time was even more outlandish. Small wonder then that Diana Vreeland, exalted editor-in-chief of American *Vogue*, was enthusiastic when David Bailey and his current favorite model Jean Shrimpton arrived in New York: "Stop – the English are here!" was her cry and it sounded as if she were trying to say: "Stop – from now on everything will be new!"

Blow Up featured a number of real models who were accustomed to moving in front of the camera. In the 1950s, models had been expected to pose regally, but for fashion shoots in the 1960s action became the order of the day.

And what about Paris? Naturally the fashion capital did not come to a dead halt while the rest of the world worshipped the cult of youth. *Haute couture* found a new icon: Jacqueline, the stylish wife of John F. Kennedy, who became president of the United States in 1960. She was no newcomer to Paris: she and her mother-in-law Rose Kennedy liked to attend the couture shows there each year, and rumor had it that the ladies would part with at least $30,000 each time – a matter which the Republicans elevated to the status of deadly sin during the election campaign. However, that did not prevent Kennedy from winning, a sure sign that the value of appearance could not be underestimated in an era of televised political debate. After grandfatherly Dwight D. Eisenhower and his Mamie, with her fussy charm, John and Jackie, as they were soon universally to be known, brought glamour and class to the White House – just when it looked as if the country would sink into a morass of prosperity and boredom. The charismatic young presidential couple awakened hope for an era of renewal. But the Cold War between East and West continued: in 1961 the Berlin Wall was erected and a year later the Soviet Union attempted to make Cuba its military base, causing the United States to react by initiating a blockade. The world seemed in imminent danger of nuclear war.

Fashion has the potential to be a matter of political importance. This was demonstrated when Jackie had to forswear the fashion houses of Paris and find herself an all-American designer. She opted

Their last appearance together: John F. Kennedy and his wife Jackie arrive in Dallas on November 22, 1963, the day this popular United States president was shot by Lee Harvey Oswald while on a procession through the center of Dallas in an open-top limousine with Jackie and the governor of Texas. The news of his death paralyzed the world. Kennedy's idealism won him much popularity in the USA and abroad.

Opposite:
In the hours that followed the assassination of her husband, Jackie Kennedy became the object of sympathy and respect. Could someone like Mamie Eisenhower and her characteristic floral frocks have radiated the same greatness as did Jackie in her bloodstained Chanel suit?

for Oleg Cassini, by no means a front runner in his chosen profession. However, he had once been engaged to Grace Kelly, one of America's most irreproachable style icons, and did not object to copying the great Parisian couturiers when Jackie so demanded. This is the legend. However, there have been claims that Jackie continued to wear French clothes, forcing New York fashion houses to order the clothes for her so that she would be seen officially to be buying "American." What can be said for certain is that she was wearing Givenchy again, as she had in the past, during the Kennedys' state visit to France in 1961, and that she appeared so majestic in the Élysée Palace that the press referred to her as "Her Elegance." This finally put a stop to the battles about Jackie's wardrobe. In the end it had turned out that Jackie's photogenic fashion consciousness was profitable not only to French couturiers but also to the American textile industry.

Jackie's heyday came to an abrupt end with Kennedy's assassination in November 1963. Even during this dark hour Jackie, who was still only 34 years old, demonstrated her composure and style in the blood-splattered Chanel suit which she refused to take off: "The whole world should see what they have done to Jack." Not until she married Greek shipping magnate Aristotle Onassis did Jackie's position in the popularity charts plummet from number one to number eight. Nevertheless, she continued

to exert her influence on fashion. In 1966 she wore a thigh-high skirt for the first time in public and the *New York Times* commented that, "the future of the miniskirt was now safe." Jackie's style probably had as much an effect on the rejuvenation of fashion as did the youth cult which emanated from London. A further factor was the conquest of space which after limitless growth promised a limitless future. As early as 1961, the Russian Yuri Gagarin had been the first person in space, but it was not until 1969, when the Americans Neil Armstrong and Edwin Aldrin succeeded in walking on the moon, that the new era really took off and influenced the way we dressed.

The first designer to present futuristic fashions was André Courrèges. Not only had he introduced the miniskirt to *haute couture* in 1961: in 1964 he created the space-age look, which broke with every tradition. His models walked briskly onto the catwalk, dressed in flat white boots and brilliant white or silver pants or suits of a severe geometric cut – looking for all the world as if they had been beamed to earth from outer space, truly beings from another planet.

Pierre Cardin was also fascinated by futuristic ideas and designed outfits which could have looked good on robots: sharply accentuated geometric cuts, preformed curvatures, and indentations. His short straight dresses bore fabric patterns and necklines which seemed to have been designed using a compass and ruler; black turtlenecks were worn underneath. Like

Outer space euphoria: for his winter 1968/69 collection, French fashion designer André Courrèges dressed his models as cosmonauts on a secret mission. He was the first designer to create truly futuristic fashions, which looked as if they had been conceived in a technical laboratory.

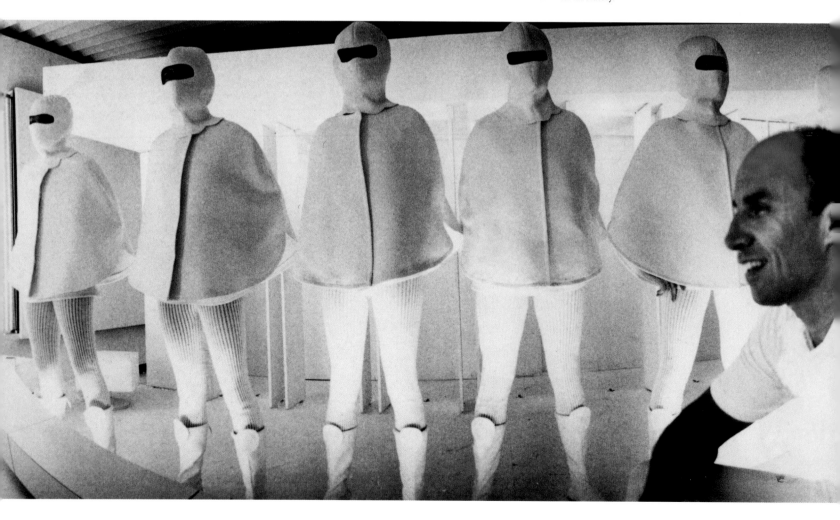

1960–1969

Courrèges, Cardin was fond of severe black-and-white patterns, but also used unusual color combinations.

The third important couturier in the trio of avant-gardists was Paco Rabanne. His "utopian" fashion made use of plastic and metal, and brought to mind astronautical equipment. He designed futuristic costumes for Jane Fonda in Barbarella, and his "chain-mail" outfits were featured in the movie *Who are you, Polly Magoo?*. However, his clothes did seem rather unsuitable for everyday wear.

Although he did not make women look like astronauts, the most modern fashion designer was Yves Saint Laurent. He found his source of inspiration in the street rather than in outer space and introduced to the catwalk something of the spirit of the times, subtly transforming it season after season by turning it into *haute couture*. He made bikers elegant, livened up the trend for unisex fashions with his introduction of tuxedos for women, and added elements taken from Op Art and Pop Art and also from the hippie trend and its Eastern influences. He recognized that young women, regardless of how much money they had at their disposal, preferred to buy clothes in boutiques rather than couture salons. In 1968 he launched his Rive Gauche range, named after the left bank of the Seine in Paris, favorite haunt of students, intellectuals and existentialists.

Generations of children have believed in the Man in the Moon, but until the spectacular moon landing on July 20, 1969, few people thought humans would ever set foot on the moon. Neil Armstrong, commander of the Apollo 11 lunar mission, spoke these famous words as he began his moonwalk: "That's one small step for man, one giant leap for all mankind." There seemed no obstacles to the conquest of space – a popular certainty at the time.

Ready-to-wear and boutique fashion was the most important innovation of the decade and all the couturiers contributed to it with their creation of secondary and sometimes even tertiary lines, each one progressively cheaper and aimed at a younger market than were the *haute couture* collections. On the other hand, boutique owners like Mary Quant in England, Jil Sander in Germany, and Dorothée Bis in France became respected fashion designers. This contributed to the blurring of class distinctions in fashion as well as society and, toward the end of the decade, absolute freedom reigned: minis coexisted with maxis, pants with skirts, futuristic shapes and patterns with folklore and psychedelia. Many saw this as an end to fashion which, in their opinion, could not survive without the kind of absolute dictate that Dior had practiced in the 1950s. Nevertheless the revolution did not come about; couture and society survived the earthquake triggered by youth but couture did change as new ideas were gradually absorbed.

Cristobal Balenciaga, the strictest proponent of couture, turned away in horror. "Fashion has become vulgar" was his response to ready-to-wear designs and boutique clothes, a reaction he followed with the closure of his French and Spanish salons. Clients like Mona von Bismarck did not know where to turn. Since then, fashion has never tired in its search for a new Balenciaga.

Genius of the century: Yves Saint Laurent

No career has been the cause of so many tears as that of Yves Saint Laurent (b. 1936), the talented and imperilled successor to Christian Dior. As the *New York Herald Tribune* observed, his very first collection led to "the emotional fashion binge of all time." This was on January 30, 1958, three months after Dior's death. Filled with apprehensive expectations, the international fashion community made its pilgrimage to 30 Avenue Montaigne in order to experience either the end or the future of *haute couture*. Would "this 21-year-old youth" be able to preserve the glamour and eminence of the century's most famous couture salon and thus save the French economy?

He would and more. He was received with even greater enthusiasm than that which greeted Dior's New Look. Saint Laurent's Trapeze line enriched the deceased king of fashion's opulence and clever cutting technique with a youthful lightness of touch. But his appearance probably contributed as much to the world's apparent desire to take him in its arms: he was so tall, so skinny, so young, so shy, and so helpless.

In any case, the Parisian press was exultant: "Dior's great tradition continues to be cultivated." Soon, however, major differences became apparent between Dior's ideas and those of his heir. Dior had always had in mind a feminine and mature woman whose appeal lay in her timeless elegance. His aim had been to preserve in *haute couture* the tradition and luxury of an epoch which had passed, and it was his greatest dream to "save women from nature."

In contrast, the young Saint Laurent wished not only to respect women's nature, he wanted them to be at the center of the turbulent, anarchic life of the 1960s. "Dauphin Yves" as the French liked to call him, rapidly began to breathe fresh air into couture. "Down with the Ritz, long live the street" was his credo and, accordingly, he rejuvenated fashion by adopting elements of youth culture. During his third year on the Dior throne, he consciously offended traditional followers with the Beat Look, which looked as if it had been plucked straight from the tumult of the street and deposited in the discreet salon: black leather jackets, turtlenecks, and short skirts as worn by impudent students on the left bank of the Seine. This was more than his employer could take. Boussac, the textile magnate whose riches had funded the Dior empire, parted with Saint Laurent and replaced him with the less daring Marc Bohan.

Despite Dior's inclination toward the past and Saint Laurent's preference for storming ahead, they were bound by a certain congeniality of temperament. Both grew up in wealthy, upper-middle-class families, both became aware of their homosexuality at an early age, both worshipped their elegant mothers. Both were great readers, tended toward intellectualism, and were very knowledgeable on the subject of art, and both were painfully shy. Both men showed early signs of an extraordinary talent for designing clothes: When 18, Saint Laurent won joint first prize with Karl Lagerfeld in an International Wool Secretariat competition and was subsequently hired to assist Dior, a sublime draftsman himself.

Unlike Dior, Saint Laurent has been lucky in love. A few days after his first triumph with the Trapeze line he met the highly educated and astute businessman Pierre Bergé, with whom he built a fashion business which eventually surpassed the house of Dior. Bergé, his senior by six years, acted as a protective buffer for his fragile friend. Saint

Opposite:
Yves Saint Laurent posed naked before Jeanloup Sieff's camera to advertise his first fragrance for men. The picture was seen as outrageous and set new standards in advertising. Thereafter other designers started to endorse their products personally, though Saint Laurent remained the only one to take his clothes off.

Left:
The artist as a very young man: the 21-year-old Yves Saint Laurent sketching on the blackboard in the Dior studio.

Above, left to right:
Robin Hood as rock 'n' roll hero. Bikers were the inspiration for Yves Saint Laurent's Robin des Bois collection: a rainproof black waxed cloth over a shirt of black deerskin, crocodile skin boots, and a leather hood made for a modern and very classy highway robber – a scandal! The safari jacket as worn by big-game hunters became a fashion classic in Saint Laurent's hands and has reappeared in his day wear and evening wear collections ever since. Celebrity model Veruschka von Lehndorff poses in 1968 wearing the original beige cotton bush-shirt with laced front and bronze chain belt. Raffia and linen, wooden and glass beads: do cheap materials have a place in *haute couture*? They do for Saint Laurent. His Bambara dresses in the Africaine collection of 1967 convinced both press and clients.

Laurent, who had already found disfavor as Dior's successor, was called up to serve in the army in 1960, where he was subjected to vicious harassment, resulting in a complete mental and physical breakdown within a few weeks of his arrival. The medical treatment he was given – electric shock therapy and tranquilizers – was primitive. His weight rapidly plummeted to a mere 80 lb and he became almost unable to speak. Pierre Bergé, with his acumen, energy, and dedication, succeeded in having his protégé discharged, nursed him back to health and finally found American financial backers for Saint Laurent's own couture house.

This opened in January 1962, and the crowds and expectations were as inflamed as they had been for Dior's first collection and Saint Laurent's first fashion show for Dior. The human throng which hurled itself at him with tearful enthusiasm was so frightening to Saint Laurent that he was forced to seek shelter in a cupboard. From then on the double-edged sword of the kind of mass appeal that is usually the preserve of sports personalities, movie stars, or rock singers would cause him great discomfort. He once referred to this sudden fame as "the trap of my life."

Dior had started the trend for presenting completely new collections each season, and Saint Laurent added yet another burden to this pressure. Convinced that *haute couture*, which

he thought unbefitting to the times, was nearing its end – "I am only keeping the salon going because I cannot ethically justify putting 150 people out of work" – he launched his relatively cheap ready-to-wear range. This meant that he had to design not just two but four collections each year, and it frequently drove the sensitive and easily stressed perfectionist to the brink of total exhaustion. He was also in constant fear of the public, whose reaction to his dizzyingly fast style changes could vary widely. While responses to Dior's luxuriously tasteful designs had been unwaveringly enthusiastic, Saint Laurent's experiments frequently overstretched the public's tolerance. Like Schiaparelli, whom he frequently cites as having been a great influence on his work, Saint Laurent repeatedly attempted to stretch, or even cross, the boundaries of fashion. In the 1960s he introduced new elements to women's wear which have since become staples: pants suits, safari jackets, transparent dresses, but above all the tuxedo, an item of clothing which will be linked to his name for eternity. Like Chanel, whom he admired for her practical ideas, he adopted many items from men's clothing while ensuring at all times that the masculine look also exuded eroticism.

This was best described by his friend and muse Catherine Deneuve: "Saint Laurent designs for women with a double life. His

Opposite:
Two masters, one immortal work: the perfection of Saint Laurent's cut for women's pants suits has yet to be surpassed, and Helmut Newton's suggestively erotic photograph captures this essence like no other. The gray pinstripe suit and pearl-gray blouse are part of Saint Laurent's 1975 collection.

NUIT DE GRENADE

The bright Babushka peasant costumes inspired Saint Laurent's spectacularly successful Russian collection for the winter 1976/77 season. Starting from the rustic basis of the wide skirt, Saint Laurent enriched it by adding a hefty element of Ballets Russes-Opéra, thus creating sumptuous gowns featuring embroidery, gold piping, braiding, trimmings, voluminous sleeves, and highly decorated boleros.

Opposite:
In 1969, Saint Laurent transformed the flower children's flea market look, with its patchwork and mix of patterns, into romantic outfits of silk and organdy for sophisticated hippies.

clothes for day wear help women to enter a world full of strangers. They enable her to go wherever she wants without arousing unwelcome attention, thanks to their somehow masculine quality they give her a certain power, arm her for encounters which may lead to disputes. However, for the evening, when she may chose her company, he makes her seductive."

For evening wear, Saint Laurent reveled in the retro and ethnic looks so beloved of hippies, except that he made them respectable. He admitted that, "for me, the evening is the time for folklore." He led his couture clients on successive voyages, from ancient China, Peru, Morocco, and central Africa to the aristocratic Venice of Casanova's time. His 1976 revival of the czarist Russian theme with a collection inspired by the Ballets Russes was celebrated as a sensation: "A revolution," the *New York Times* prophesied. Others were less enthusiastic about Saint Laurent's "Russian Revolution," which turned out to be the most expensive couture show ever staged: "too nostalgic," "more fancy dress than fashion" were the criticisms. Saint Laurent himself did not think of it as necessarily his best but definitely his most beautiful collection. His Russian peasant costumes confirmed his standing as the couturier with the century's best color sense. His subsequent Chinese collection, which featured even greater theatrical luxury, served

only to corroborate this. No other would have dared to combine yellow with purple or orange with pink and red, since Saint Laurent was the only one with sufficient talent to hit upon the right combination of colors.

Saint Laurent did not merely "scavenge" in student quarters (bomber jackets with chiffon skirts!) or distant countries and historic periods (Greek togas with a bare breast for evening wear), he was also influenced by the art of Matisse, Picasso, Mondrian, Tom Wesselman, and his close friend Andy Warhol: all have been represented in Saint Laurent's designs. However, not one of them could ever complain of exploitation; Saint Laurent's designs always took the form of independent homages to the respective artist. To Saint Laurent it seemed only natural that one might wish to dress as a living Op Art icon one day and a Chinese mandarin the next, and women agreed with him. It is thanks to him that they feel as comfortable wearing mini as midi dresses, that they are as happy to wear a 1940s-style retro jacket as an embroidered Mongolian blouse. Only the critics did not spare the malicious spite.

Even a less sensitive talent would have suffered under the alternating showers of gushing acclaim and devastating opprobrium. Saint Laurent, who never fully recovered from the breakdown he suffered during his military service, fought his depressions and suicidal tendencies by resorting to alcohol and drugs,

Following pages:
Art and the street provided Saint Laurent with most of the inspiration for his creations; one synthesis of this was the Pop Art collection of 1966 with which he enraptured Swinging London.

Left:
The celebrated Mondrian
dress introduced Saint Laurent's
interpretation of modern art into
haute couture.

Opposite:
Constant variety: red and pink
are two colors which frequently recu
in Saint Laurent's designs
and which he knows how to
combine as no other can.
Top left: a cheeky advance on the
transparent look, 1991/92.
Top right: the bow as focal point,
1983/84.
Bottom left: ensemble, 1998/99.
Bottom right: from the Russian
collection, 1976/77.

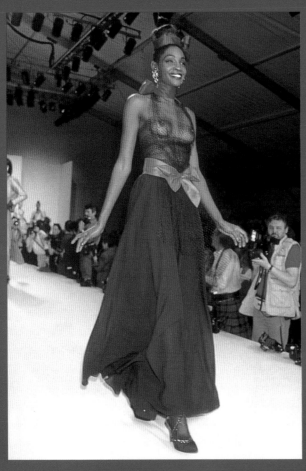

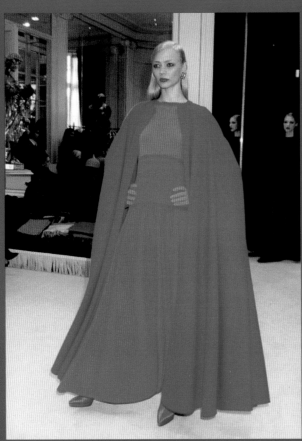

which rapidly led to ever greater dependence. He could not take a single step on his own and was constantly surrounded by his entourage of rich hippies. This group of reckless people, who liked to spend their time in Saint Laurent and Pierre Bergé's holiday palace in Marrakech, included Talitha, the beautiful wife of John Paul Getty Jr. who died from an overdose of heroin. Loulou de la Falaise, one of the world's best-dressed women and Saint Laurent's muse and right-hand woman, had to give up alcohol following a stomach operation.

Saint Laurent himself has spoken openly in several interviews of his alcoholism and drug addiction. In the mid-1970s he was admitted for the first time to the American Hospital in Paris for detoxification, and he has been back many times since. Neither his public admissions nor his unforgettable appearances when the once-beautiful young man was seen bloated, swaying and babbling incomprehensibly, could dent his image. Especially in France, where the romantic idea of fragile genius is nurtured, Saint Laurent is loved even more for his failings. In 1983/84 Yves Saint Laurent was the first-ever living designer to have a retrospective exhibition of his work shown at the Metropolitan Museum of Art in New York. Further exhibitions and distinctions followed; barely in his 50s Saint Laurent was elevated

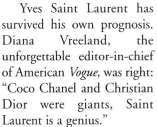

to Mount Olympus, as if he had ceased to dwell among the living. In fact, many people have been pronouncing his fashions dead for a long time. The truth is that he renounced "fashion which comes out of fashion" back in the mid-1980s and that he has since concentrated on the type of continuous development that had been the norm before the war, before Dior introduced the insane seasonal changes. The fact that this was yet another visionary decision was confirmed by the *New York Times* during the 1997 shows: "While the audience looks to other parts of the catwalk to discover something new, at Saint Laurent it can quietly see what will last."

There were tears in 1992, when a great gala was held to celebrate the 30th anniversary of the fashion house at the Paris Opéra and the master, teetering but happy, was seen to inspect the parade of tuxedos that he had designed. And tears were again evident when he handed over control of his innovation, the ready-to-wear line, to the Israeli-American Alber Elbaz. Since then Saint Laurent has devoted himself entirely to *haute couture*, about which he said, back in 1971: "it will stay for perhaps another five or ten years."

Yves Saint Laurent has survived his own prognosis. Diana Vreeland, the unforgettable editor-in-chief of American *Vogue*, was right: "Coco Chanel and Christian Dior were giants, Saint Laurent is a genius."

Quoi de plus beau

pour une femme

que

de nouer

autour

de

son cou

une passion

en

guise

de

Coeur

Yves Saint Laurent

The heart is Saint Laurent's favorite accessory: "What is there more beautiful for a woman than to wear her passion on her neck in the form of a heart." Movie star Laetitia Casta models the coveted jewel with a bridal outfit.

André Courrèges

The work of André Courrèges (b. 1923) produced the most accurate hit to the nerve center of the epoch. He and Coqueline Barrière (b. 1935), who was later to become his wife, opened their own couture house in 1961. They had both spent some years previously as assistants to Cristobal Balenciaga, where they had learnt to be sparing with decoration and instead to concentrate on the perfect cut. Courrèges, formerly a civil engineer and pilot, furnished his salon in the style of a modern laboratory, all white and sparkling chrome, with the constant accompaniment of progressive jazz. Here, without a glance back at fashion history and focusing on a future defined by technology, he and Coqueline developed the spring/summer collection of 1965 which was to become the epitome of modernity and would make fashion history.

This was the first occasion on which miniskirts appeared in a couture collection.

They were very straight and loose-fitting, adorned with piping and stripes, made of heavy materials, and structured in accordance with Bauhaus rules. Yet, thanks to the insertion of rounded forms, which were either stitched or ironed into the clothes, they did not appear hard or angular. The matching boots were made of white plastic and had square toes. Coqueline Courrèges remembers that "the models had to learn to walk all over again," and she herself took dancing lessons. The creator had to recalculate proportions. Hats, helmets, and wigs made of synthetic hair added elegance by elongating the new line.

The space-age look made Courrèges the most copied couturier of the decade; he blamed the press and so banished the media for two years while he continued to supply his clientele with Bermuda shorts and rompers to be worn under short dresses. This course of action earned him the wrath of Coco Chanel: "The man is intent on destroying woman, to demolish her shape in order to turn her into a little girl," the old lady fulminated. Courrèges coolly responded: "I have made women 20 years younger without the use of a scalpel."

Indeed, the key design device of allowing a gap of about 1 inch between dress and body brought about a freedom of movement which was more rejuvenating than any corset could ever hope to be. Couture Future, his secondary collection of 1969 introduced to ready-to-wear a second skin made of chunky knitwear – anticipating the advent of leggings and leotards. "I only ever wanted to design sportswear," says Courrèges, who was a keen mountaineer, light athlete, and rugby player. He eventually came to the conclusion that only pants could allow women unrestricted movement, thus making his famous miniskirt somewhat obsolete. However, this opinion did not prevent him from designing frilly dresses in 1972, which proved to be a flop.

Courrèges sold his business to the Japanese Itokin group in 1985 and since then he has devoted himself increasingly to painting and sculpture. His importance as the "Le Corbusier of fashion" has been rediscovered in recent years and his futuristic 1960s fashions are now finding new fans and imitators.

Pierre Cardin

Following Dior's triumphant success with the New Look which overnight reestablished Paris as the fashion capital of the world, the city was gripped by gold fever. In 1951 Pierre Cardin, who had previously worked for Paquin, Schiaparelli, and Dior as well as designing movie costumes for Cocteau, showed his first collection. Since he had little starting capital, the collection was restricted to 50 coats and suits. His designs were an overwhelming success precisely because Cardin had avoided any imitation of the two most influential fashion geniuses of the period, Dior and Balenciaga. Cardin, born in Venice in 1922, started out with 30 employees. A year later he was already employing 90. His prices exploded in like manner: he could demand up to 1,200,000 francs for a suit. With hindsight he remarked in an interview: "I would be ashamed to charge so much nowadays." And Cardin, who was a trained tailor by the time he was 14, proved to be not only a highly talented couturier but also quite a businessman. He was the first member of this exalted guild who did not think himself too good to design clothes for the Paris department store Au Printemps, and he was a pioneer of business links with Japan and China. Cardin, a marketing genius, is known as the fashion designer with the greatest number of licenses worldwide. Yet he is also one of the most innovative of couturiers. In 1958 he designed the first-ever unisex collection, which united men and women in a joint lifestyle statement.

However, Cardin's most revolutionary act was back in 1959, when he had the audacity to be the first couturier ever to produce a ready-made collection (for which there was no word in French). As a result he was expelled by the strict Chambre Syndicale. But even the latter soon had to accept that nothing would stop the American ready-to-wear concept from invading the motherland of fashion, and it was swiftly named prêt-à-porter, thus allowing couturiers to choose whether they wished to use this avenue to make money – and allowing Cardin to back into the fold.

Below, left to right:
Development: Cardin's first collection still conformed to the then dominant silhouette for women; his designs soon became less cluttered and more modern; finally his miniskirts and thigh boots proved him to be at the forefront of developments.

Sooner or later every idea is recycled. In 1969 Cardin compromised between the mini and the short-lived maxi by designing a partly see-through dress.

Left: circular or lozenge-shaped cutouts that created a three-dimensional effect were typical of Cardin.

Above: Paco Rabanne returned to the geometric cutouts of the 1960s for his 1999 collection.

Following pages:
Squaring the circle: the trend in the 1960s was the development of organic forms from geometric elements. Cardin's fashion and the architecture he influenced follow the same rules. The Palais Bulle (*left*) offers insights that are similar to Cardin's outfits of 1967 (*right*), which combined severity with rounded lines.

Paco Rabanne

Opposite:
Evening gown and cocktail dress made of matte, transparent rhodonite paillettes which fluoresce in various colors when subjected to artificial light.

With hooks and pliers: Paco Rabanne did not think much of soft femininity, and his seductresses belonged to a new era. Dressed in metal and plastic disks rather than laces and frills, they look sexy yet unapproachable in a cocktail dress and an evening gown from Paco Rabanne's first collection in 1966 (*below, left*). The classically cut evening dress (*below, right*) is fashioned from an unusual material: eau-de-Nil leather patches are secured with aluminum rivets.

"Don't seduce, shock" was the motto of fashion designer Paco Rabanne (b. 1934). Like André Courrèges, he radically broke with the past which Dior had so successfully revived. The future was the new buzzword and, for Rabanne, the future meant brand new materials.

The son of a chief seamstress at Balenciaga in Spain, Paco Rabanne distinguished himself as a student of architecture in Paris, but then redirected his activities to designing unusual accessories, trying his hand at everything from shoes to bags. He worked for Balenciaga, Cardin, and Givenchy, among others, and, for eight years, the house of Dior. He found his niche when he began designing plastic jewelry. His next step led to independence: in February 1966 Rabanne showed 12 "unwearable dresses" made of plastic disks, three months later he had the dancers at the Crazy Horse nightclub model his plastic beachwear, and in September he presented his first garments made of aluminum with leather and ostrich-feather trimming.

He had made it. In the 1960s his futuristic metal dresses became to show-business celebrities what white satin dresses had been to the Hollywood sirens of the 1930s. From the French pop idol Françoise Hardy to Audrey Hepburn via the James Bond girls, every modern heroine wore Paco Rabanne's chainmail, which was stitched not with thread and needle but with hooks, rivets, and pliers.

Paco Rabanne never gave up his experiments with unusual materials like Plexiglas, coated paper, or elastic bandages, and in the late 1990s he unexpectedly found himself the object of a revival, at the same time as his lifelong rival Courrèges. In the summer of 1999 he finally lost his faith in the future and announced his retirement from the world of fashion.

Left:
The future of sex: in 1967 Paco Rabanne and Jacques Fonteray anticipated the sexual emancipation of women with their costume for Jane Fonda in Barbarella. Reality lagged behind …

Opposite:
In 1998 Rabanne sent male and female protagonists wearing vaudeville costumes and ostrich feathers onto the catwalk: a Folies-Bergère for the new millennium?

Emanuel Ungaro

With the firm belief of a bright future, Emanuel Ungaro (b. 1933) began his career as an independent couturier. Based on the rigorous cutting technique that he learned during his six years with Balenciaga, and then applied during two subsequent years with Courrèges, his early collections featured severe combinations of blazer and shorts. Ungaro, whose forebears were Italian and who came from the south of France, soon developed his own style, which was based on a bold mix of colors and patterns. Flowers on checks, or stripes with large polka dots in bright colors are typical of Ungaro, who never succumbed to the pessimistic tendencies which took hold of some other designers. This, together with the elegant sexiness of his dresses and suits, won him a loyal clientele, particularly in the United States. Ungaro the couturier loves women privately as well as professionally. He started his salon with the Swiss artist Sonja Knapp. He had a well-publicized relationship with the beautiful actress Anouk Aimée, who remains a loyal client to this day. He married the Italian Laura Fanfani in 1989 and they have a daughter. Ungaro does not sketch his designs, but works directly with the fabric on the body of a model – for up to 12 hours a day, always with the inspiration of classical music. He is unusual in that he managed to remain independent for a long time. The Italian Ferragamo group took over the running of his business in 1996, while keeping Ungaro as the undisputed creative head of the organization. He returned to his beginnings for the 1999 *haute couture* show when he showed a modernized version of hippie fashion: long, frilly, floral skirts with cropped tops in matte mauve and beaded, chiffon pants worn with feather-light jackets or fur-trimmed stoles.

Opposite:
Bridal gown for a flower child: Emanuel Ungaro's 1969 wedding outfit was captured by Bert Stern, the photographer who shot the last pictures ever taken of Marilyn Monroe in 1962. That was the pinnacle of the career of the former art director who had been one the great stars of advertising.

Below:
The woman's friend: Ungaro is the *homme à femmes* whose fashions, even at the height of the cool space-age look, were more feminine than those of his colleagues Courrèges or Cardin, as illustrated by this outfit with cowboy accessories (*left*).

Karl Lagerfeld

The conclusions which Karl Lagerfeld (b. 1938) drew in the 1960s from the signs of the times were quite different from those drawn by Courrèges, Cardin, and others. While Lagerfeld's contemporaries saw the future in the space-age look, he put his money on the replacement of couture by ready-to-wear. And, instead of taking on the burden of his own couture house, he worked as a freelance designer. He thus went down the exact opposite path to that of Yves Saint Laurent, with whom he had shared first prize in the International Wool Secretariat competition in 1954, when both were still minors. Even without his own empire, Lagerfeld was soon known as Emperor Karl, ruler of numerous houses which blossomed and thrived under his creative direction. He first found fame, both personally and for his client, at Chloé, where he started work in 1963, remaining there for 20 years and, following a break of ten years, where he spent the years from 1993 to 1997 reviving his inimitable, young, and feminine flirt-look. In 1965, he began to design fur collections for the Fendi sisters in Rome, and today he is responsible for all their collections. However, his greatest coup has been the revitalization of the legendary Chanel style. At Lagerfeld's début in the Rue Cambon in 1983, nobody dared hope that he would bring Mademoiselle Chanel's spirit so congenially into the late 20th century. It is not surprising that clients, especially American women, are again flocking to Chanel, since Lagerfeld is a master at continually refreshing the look of the slim-line evening gown so much in demand at the end of the millennium – a distant reminder of Mademoiselle's 1930s cocktail dresses.

Below:
We seek him here, we seek him there ... Lagerfeld's genius is what might be called his split personality, which enables him to slip into a variety of roles. He occasionally neglects his own lines.
Left: a contemporary design from his 1997/98 collection which brought the Lagerfeld label back to the fore.
Center: an asymmetrical dress from 1999, simultaneously severe and playful, created by Lagerfeld for Chanel.
Right: an outfit from Lagerfeld's 1989 collection.

Opposite:
Crown princes: in 1954, the 17-year-old Lagerfeld (*left*) and 19-year-old Yves Saint Laurent (*center*) shared first prize in the International Wool Secretariat competition. These two rising designers would determine the face of fashion during the second half of the 20th century.

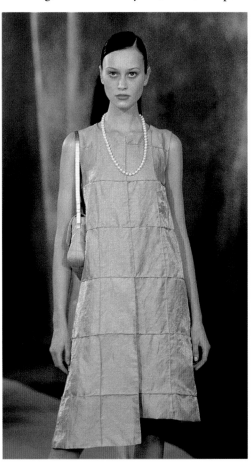

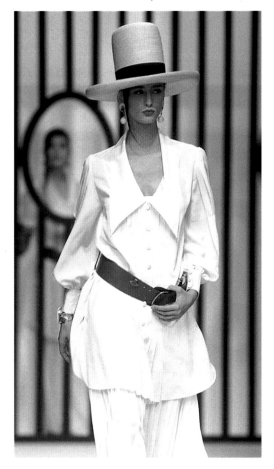

Marc Bohan

After Yves Saint Laurent's departure from Dior in 1960, Marc Bohan (b. 1926) took over as artistic director, which he remained until the fashion house passed to the Italian Gianfranco Ferré in 1989. During the course of three decades Bohan produced solid, traditionalist couture which he sensitively exposed to new influences. However, during an epoch when revolutionary ideas made fashion a subject for discussion and gossip, this shy and distinguished man who did not share other designers' talent for manipulating the media was easily overlooked. He ended his career, which had been dedicated entirely to the classical trade, in London, where he tried to breathe life into the honorable house of Norman Hartnell.

Opposite:
Elixir of youth: even the house of Dior could not remain unaffected by the youth revolution. Psychedelic patterns surfaced in the 1967 collection which Marc Bohan designed for Dior London.

The new look for 1960s couture clients, to whom Dior's New Look meant very little.

A modern lady of the harem: bouclé culottes-dress, 1967.

Guy Laroche

Guy Laroche (1923–89)

Guy Laroche, a milliner by trade, was another designer who found his entry to *haute couture* in a roundabout way. At the end of World War II he went to New York, where in 1949 he began to work in ready-to-wear. On his return to Paris in 1957, he made the transition to *haute couture*. His fashion is characterized by simple cuts and mostly delicate, though occasionally bold, colors. He was very popular in the 1960s, when he dressed many members of France's high society, including Madame Pompidou and author Françoise Sagan. Laroche has also designed menswear.

Below:
The colorful winter of 1971/72: short coats worn over pants or long, colorful pantyhose.

Following pages:
Guy Laroche's sketches for each collection would fill a notebook. This was his vision for 1960/61.

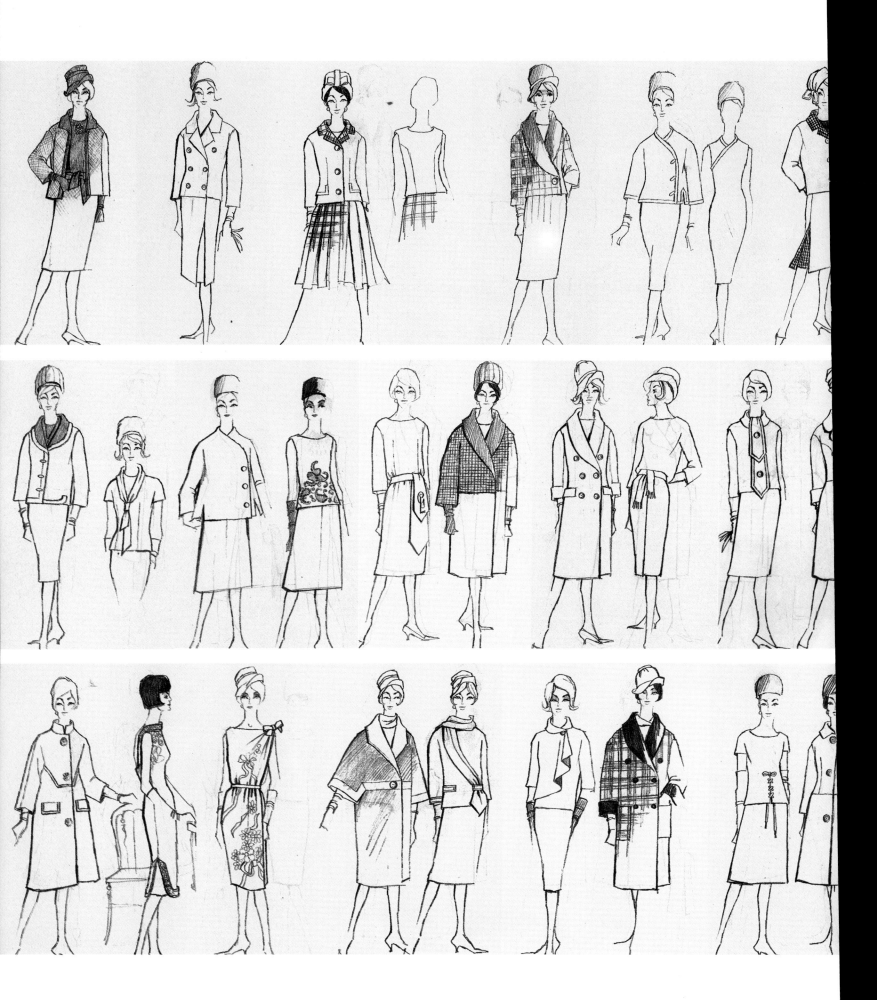

Sonia Rykiel

Opposite page:
Warm, comfortable, and chic: only a woman could come up with clothes like these two outfits of 1972, whose populist, antifashion statement influenced designer fashions.

Below:
Typical Sonia Rykiel garments are elegant yet easy-to-wear: narrow horizontal stripes in the 1997/98 fall/winter collection (*left*) and large checks in 1999/2000 (*right*).

In 1962, Sonia Rykiel (b. 1930) demonstrated "what you can do with a bit of yarn". Her career started when she was unable to find warm maternity wear in the right size, knitted her own and was so successful at it that other women began to ask for her clothes. Sonia then began to sell her designs in her husband's shop. As soon as the baby was born, the maternity garments gave way to figure-hugging knitwear items and she was soon designing complete knitwear outfits comprising jumpers, jackets, skirts, wide pants, scarves, and capes. They were always fluid but never baggy and thus popular with women who preferred to look slim and elegant even when wearing comfortable clothes. In 1968 Sonia Rykiel opened her own boutique in Paris, and five years later she was elected vice-president of the Chambre Syndicale du Prêt-à-Porter, a post she occupied for 20 years. The Americans christened her the Queen of Knitwear, a title which Sonia Rykiel deserves to this day, having become a designer of international renown without ever enlisting the help of *haute couture*. Her clothes are extremely suitable for leisurewear, although not in the American sense of sportswear but more in a typically French style which invites the wearer to indulge in an elegant form of idleness.

Mary Quant

Mary Quant (b. 1934) was at the heart of Swinging London. She gave us the mini, geometric haircuts, and brightly colored and patterned pantyhose. In 1955 she opened Bazaar, a small boutique in Kings Road where she sold simple garments made by herself. In the 1960s this grew to be a worldwide empire, for which Mary Quant designed young and uncomplicated clothes, accessories, and make-up. She was the first to use PVC for coats and boots and to design bags with long shoulder straps, and the first whose "look" – a new fashion term – was aimed principally at teenagers. In 1966 she was declared Woman of the Year in the United Kingdom. By the end of the 1970s she was almost forgotten. She sold her business and is now exclusively concerned with the make-up aspect, designing for other companies. Like Hardy Amies, Mary Quant is a fashion giant who earns a living from her fame in times past, especially in Japan, where her label is still a powerful seller.

The born Londoner studied fine art at Goldsmith's College before trying her hand at retail and design. Her inexpensive, extremely youthful clothes were an instant success: Quant's straight-lined, graphically simple garments could be worn both day and night. Although her clothes started off below knee level, her seams were hitched to shocking heights during the 1960s, thus giving birth to the miniskirt. For a glorious decade Mary Quant was in absolute harmony with her times. Pants suits, hot pants, colored panty hose, low-slung hip belts – whatever she launched hit the decade's nerve. The black daisy logo appeared on all her products, whether accessories, make-up, underwear, housewear, or furnishing textiles: this was the beginning of label-fetishism.

Opposite:
Mary Quant was not solely interested in pop culture: two models at Luton Airport, in Bedfordshire, show off her designs for new stewardess uniforms.

The pop designer and founder of boutique culture was even honored for her achievements in promoting British exports. She was 25 when she opened her first shop.

The look of the decade

The precise five-point cut favored by Mary Quant, queen of the miniskirt, in the early 1960s caused a wave of imitators such as had not been seen since Coco Chanel's avant-gardist bob of 1917. Every progressive-minded woman had to prove her independence by cutting her hair. Vidal Sassoon, Quant's "Figaro," based his asymmetrical cut on the Beatles' basin haircut, although endowing it with more fashionable sharpness. Taking the center of the top of the head as a starting point, the hair was cut sharply into five points, which allowed it to stay in place like a space-age helmet. This emphasis (or skillful illusion) on a round, radial head highlighted the daintiness and fragility of neck and body, and a further contribution to a childlike appearance was made by the eyes, which were enlarged by the use of every means available to the artistry of make-up. The decade's ideal type had no feminine attributes; instead she was a skinny nymphet, playfully experimenting with her sexuality. Vladimir Nabokov's novel *Lolita* appeared in 1959, thereby providing immature seductresses with an enduring epithet.

The corsets, suspenders, and stilettos of the 1950s were replaced by "no-bra" bras, woolen pantyhose, and flat boots. Heavily applied make-up gave way to a more natural look. "Old-style make-up is out!" Mary Quant declared, while simultaneously emphasizing that make-up was more important than ever – to ensure that the complexion appeared as perfect as baby skin. Under her tutelage, and not least with her products, young British girls learnt to apply make-up with such skill that they appeared not to be wearing any. Lip color was a no-no; a little gloss gave lips a suitably childish appearance. The eyes, however, had to be

quite different! In this area women were permitted to slap on so much color that the end effect was a naive overstatement which looked as if a child had been at work. A variety of eyeshadow colors, dark liner above and below the eye, several layers of mascara, and false eyelashes formed part of the standard equipment. Frequently, girls would seem to be having a joke, as for example when Penelope Tree, one of England's top three models, stuck the longer eyelashes to her lower lid, thus making her small, triangular face look as if it had been turned upside down. False eyebrows and stick-on or painted petals were not regarded as going too far.

Flowers stood for youth and naturalness, even if they were made of plastic like Mary Quant's trademark daisy (or marguerite – the shape is so abstract that botanists cannot agree) which was worn as costume jewelry. Plastic accessories and clothes suited the optimistic faith in the future and space-travel euphoria of the times. Even the colors of make-up and clothes seemed to have come straight from outer space. White and shimmering silver gave modern featherweights the appearance of weightlessness, all the way down to their flat boots which, in the form of ankle boots, could even be worn in the summer. The radial haircuts, geometric dress shapes, uncluttered Pop Art and Op Art patterns, and bright colors all contributed to a young, clean appearance which was represented most typically by Twiggy. She was the ultimate dolly bird, as the British liked to call these fragile fledglings.

The next underage model to make it to the top brought with her just the tiniest dose of depravity. Jean Shrimpton, known as The Shrimp, had dark shadows under her eyes which made her

look as if she needed to catch up on quite a few nights' sleep. She wore her hair long and straight, thus triggering the next hair trend. Again, the top of the head had to be round and full, and since most people's head shape did not quite fit the look, back-combing became all the rage. Alternatively, a hairpiece could be used. Hairpieces had been introduced earlier to enable women to copy Farah Diba, the Shah of Persia's new wife, who wore her hair voluminously pinned up, or Jackie Kennedy who wore her natural abundance of hair in a generously styled bob.

The 1960s were a "hairy" decade. Whereas some wore carefully arranged hairpieces on their heads with neat bows, others were growing their own hair and demonstrating against the establishment. Hippies set their wild manes against the fakeness of wigs as a symbol of a new sense of nature. And whereas, at the beginning of the decade, it had been difficult to distinguish between boys and girls because they wore their hair equally short, it was long hair that now provided the unisex look.

The cry of the wild brought everyone rushing back to nature. Real flowers, natural materials, and authentic clothes became the fashionable things to wear. Yesterday's new era of pageboy haircuts, short skirts, nylon stockings, and patent leather boots gave way to a return to paradise in bare feet and Jesus sandals, caftans and long hair. Jeans and other cotton garments, embroidered Afghan sheepskin coats, leather accessories inspired by American Indians, long scarves from India, and batik T-shirts were now *de rigueur* and were soon to be marketed in the most sophisticated boutiques, from Los Angeles to London and Paris. Hippies who took pride in their appearance searched through flea markets and secondhand shops for authentic clothes, but even the rare charm of worn velvet was soon copied by the fashion industry, which flooded the market with panne velvet flares and baggy dresses. The preference for naked skin expressed by flower children was also appropriated by *haute couture* in 1968, when designers suggested that see-through blouses be worn over bare breasts. Hippies painted psychedelic patterns all over their bodies, and fashion magazines like *Vogue* turned this into a trend. Veruschka von Lehndorff, Prussian aristocrat and model, whose perfect make-up was an important part of her trade, developed body painting until it reached the state of pure art and also became her new profession.

For those who preferred the well-groomed look to that of the alternative lifestyle, cosmetic queen Helena Rubinstein introduced the Day of Beauty in 1962. For $65 her customers would receive advice on dieting, a fitness hour, a massage, lunch, a facial, a shampoo and set, a manicure, a pedicure and, to round it all off, a perfectly made-up face. The whole process took six hours and was enthusiastically received by America's working women as the perfect way to prepare for the weekend.

Opposite:
Adorned with the decade's favorite flower, the daisy, a smart bow could be used to conceal the attachment of a hairpiece. Fine, blond hair in particular was often not thick enough to suit the requirements of the hairy decade.

Below:
Being young is never easy: even teenagers needed time and effort to achieve that young look of the 1960s. Eye make-up techniques became increasingly sophisticated and young skin needed to be looked after to safeguard a youthful future – or so the advertisements claimed.

The miniskirt

The miniskirt was the decade's most talked-about invention, but would it have had the same effect without the addition of pantyhose and boots? The combination of the three gave women the freedom of movement which was utterly to transform their attitudes. Mary Quant was probably the first proponent of the thigh-high skirt, but the combination of short skirt and boots was definitely André Courrèges' idea – the first time that an enduring fashion trend was born from the fusion of street fashion and *haute couture*.

Frank Sinatra's daughter Nancy released her only major hit, *These Boots are Made for Walking*, in 1966. Women everywhere were setting off on the long march of emancipation and Nancy's song provided the optimistic rhythm. Nevertheless Nancy's fashionable white boots had high heels! Just like Nancy,

many women fell into the trap of femininity and were intent on wearing spiky heels, stockings, and suspenders with their miniskirts. It was the persistent innovator Courrèges who explained to the world that: "Only by wearing boots with low heels is it possible to remain in contact with earth and reality." He was also enough of a realist to propose that woolen tights be worn with miniskirts in winter.

However, the most important innovation was the pantyhose, which made triumphant progress as the ideal accompaniment to the miniskirt. Pantyhose were available in all sorts of patterns and colors, to match Op Art and Pop Art and psychedelic hallucinations. Within the space of a decade they had pushed stockings out of the market. Years later, however, the latter became irresistible once more, as did suspenders and garters.

Above left:
Viva-Viva, a hand-knitted collection of clothes made by Mary Quant (*center*) from a new synthetic fiber, was presented in Milan in 1967.

Above right:
Miniskirts that did not come from the studios of fashion designers could be quite distinctively different. Only one thing was certain: the miniskirt had to be short.

Opposite:
Miniskirts and dresses designed in couture houses were sober, functional, and futuristic, like this short dress by Louis Féraud.

1929: British actress Annette Benson wears a saucy jersey minidress.

Buttoned and booted, 1967: minidress and leather thigh boots.

Another miniskirt combination: with strappy shoes and with knee-high socks.

Nancy Sinatra and her father Frank singing *These Boots are Made for Walking* in 1966.

An unusual slip-up during the elegant 1930s.

1968: but for the missing gun, this could almost be Faye Dunaway in *Bonnie and Clyde*.

1969: timid approaches toward unisex fashions. Naturally, the miniskirt is just for her.

Opposite:
Pop singer Cilla Black in graphic black and white. The pattern echoes Tintin's moon rocket.

1967: the addition of a wide-brimmed hat transforms the minidress into a respectable little black number.

A short version of Grace Kelly's pleated skirt and twin set.

Stations of an icon:

1) When she was no longer America's first lady, but had become instead the very private Mrs. Onassis, Jackie could frequently be seen wearing straight-legged pants teamed with a jumper or T-shirt. She always wore large sunglasses, and by the sea in Greece she protected her thick hair with a silk scarf, tied at the nape of the neck in the style of the 1950s.

2) The pillbox hat, a small round hat worn perched on the back of the head, was invented for Jackie.

3) At the time, this elegant, tailored coat seemed to reveal a shockingly large amount of the famous wearer's leg.

4) During a state visit to India, Jackie dabs color on President Nehru's forehead, in accordance with the host country's customs.

5) A young first lady in 1960: her distinctive personal style is yet to become apparent.

6) Jackie arriving in Rome in 1962 dressed in a leopard-skin coat. For her audience with the Pope she wore a more seemly outfit, which included a black lace mantilla to cover her hair.

7) Jackie in Mexico: her trademarks were pearls, gloves, and bow, this one attached to a narrow leather belt.

dols of the decade

acqueline Kennedy (1929–94) was 30 years old when she became America's first lady in 1960. She made her predecessors seem rather old by comparison, although this was not due solely to Jackie's youth. Where other ladies adorned themselves with furs, veiled hats, and jewels, she would wear a simple woolen coat and hat. Where others disappeared behind a cloud of frills, gathers, and tulle, Jackie accentuated her youth and good looks with a simple bow. She forswore patterns in favor of clear and usually pale colors. Her soft pink, which bore no relation to sickly-sweet baby pink, became the color of the year in 1962.

Jackie's style was young and uncluttered, and made her a typical representative of the 1960s as well as a herald of 1990s minimalism. The basic principle was to bring her personality to the fore. Her face was never overshadowed by hats or veils, and her hair, whether worn loose or pinned up, with bangs or without, always provided a strong, dark frame for her even face and widely spaced eyes.

The rules of etiquette often made hats a mandatory requirement of public appearance, so the pillbox hat, a small hat worn perched on the back of the head, and behind which it was impossible to hide, was developed especially for her. She also liked to expose other parts of her body. Her necklines were always generous and her collars designed to elongate the appearance of the neck, thus providing the perfect backdrop for jewelry: Jackie's triple row of pearls, worn on almost every occasion, became famous in their own right. Sleeves were three-quarter-length at most, a good length for showing off bracelets and rings, although Jackie generally preferred to wear medium-length gloves. Furthermore, some people thought that she bared rather too much leg; when she was no longer first lady, she even wore miniskirts. In the evening, long dresses were complemented by bare shoulders, which revealed an attractive, straight line. Her tops were always cut so that they gently hugged her boyish figure.

However, the ultimate Jackie outfit has to be the unadorned shift dress. Later, after Jackie had become Mrs. Onassis and was freed of all official duties, her clothes became even more youthful and simple: even with her striped T-shirts, narrow pants and sandals worn with large sunglasses and her hair in a ponytail, she continued to be a style icon. Jackie knew what was required to create an image: easily recognized elements used time and time again and reduced to symbols.

In the psychedelic Avalon Ballroom in 1966, a star was born whose style stood in the greatest possible contrast to the elegance of Jackie Kennedy: With her first public appearance, **Janis Joplin** (1943–70), wearing faded hippie garb of old velvet, instantly became established as "the world's best Blues singer." Her greatest success came three years later during the legendary Woodstock festival where she gave her best performances, frequently grasping a bottle of whisky. Her voice seemed to have no limits: she "screamed, roared, wheezed, rattled, breathed, and whispered with an almost frightening intensity as well as a concentrated musicality," observed critic Ulrich Olshausen. At an early age Janis Joplin fled the small-minded, small-town world of her family and found her home of choice in Haight-Ashbury, San Francisco's notorious hippie commune. She lived fast and played hard, hoping that she would not "be sitting in a damn chair in front of the TV when I'm 70." Her wish came true: at the age of 27 she died from a heroin overdose in a Hollywood hotel room. This sad end has added to her continued appeal as a legend. She was glamorized by the young, whose motto was "Hope I die before I get old," as in the prophetic song title of rock group The Who.

In 1960 **Joan Baez** (b. 1941) cut her first record and immediately had one of the greatest successes of any American female vocalist. She was 19 years old and had become a star overnight, and she used her fame to give weight to her political commitments. She supported Martin Luther King's civil rights movement, protested the Vietnam War and supported student uprisings. The ardent pacifist became one of the first fellow combatants of Amnesty International and Baez remains an active member of the peace movement to this day. Known as the "Joan of Arc of folk music," she was the heroine of the decade's idealistic youth movement.

France's youthful idol of song **Françoise Hardy** (b. 1944) came across as well-behaved but melancholy. In 1962 she sang the programmatic song *Je suis d'accord* (I agree) during an interval in a speech being made by President de Gaulle. The conventional French singer proved to be "in agreement" with the ruling or majority opinion throughout her career. Thanks to her fabulous looks she was nevertheless celebrated as a typical representative of the youth movement. Her long legs, boyish figure, mane of straight, brown hippie hair, and expressive eyes inspired leading couturiers like Courrèges and Rabanne to dress the cult singer in their futuristic designs. Her face fitted the times so well that in the mid-1960s she was even offered movie roles. However, after just a few movies Françoise Hardy returned to writing her sad love ballads.

In the title role of the 1967 movie *Barbarella*, **Jane Fonda** (b. 1937) was the incarnation of the space-age girl: sexy and chic in a black patent leather suit and boots and with a gun, she was earth-man's fantasy of woman in orbit. This was not surprising, since the film was directed by Roger Vadim, who ten years earlier had launched Brigitte Bardot with *And God Created Woman*, and whose aim it now was to shape the American actress into the sex symbol of the space age. However, Jane Fonda was not made of modeling clay, and she soon recognized that, however successful, *Barbarella* was not the prototype for a new woman. She left Vadim, returned to the United States, protested the Vietnam War, involved herself in environmental and women's rights campaigns, and thus became a real idol of the 1960s.

A single film established **Jean Seberg** (1938–79) as an eternal symbol of awakening youth: *Breathless*, Jean-Luc Godard's 1960 masterpiece, had the crop-haired girl portray an American student in Paris who is as timid as she is fierce, and whose fear of love causes her to become a traitor. Jean Seberg was never able to replicate this success. Her probable suicide in 1979 ended an unsettled, unhappy life, which had been additionally burdened by a slander campaign in the 1960s orchestrated by the CIA as a result of her commitment to the black civil rights movement.

Maria Callas (1923–77) earned the sobriquet "primadonna assoluta" as early as 1951, when she was engaged permanently by La Scala in Milan, and she remained an unchallenged star throughout the 1960s. Her unique voice, as well as her moods and the scandals, kept her name in the headlines. Many women saw in her a role model, because she had managed to transform herself from an overweight, ugly duckling into a beautiful, black swan and, as a reward, she had won shipping magnate Aristotle Onassis as her life companion. Yet, it was he whom she lost so publicly in 1968 when he suddenly married Kennedy's widow Jackie. That put an end to the Greek romance. Callas took her revenge by triumphing as an actress in her role as Medea in Pier Paolo Pasolini's film which hit the cinemas in 1970. Onassis left her a generous legacy in his will, but that was not enough to make her happy. She died aged 53 in Paris, reputedly from a broken heart.

In her role as a gangster's moll in the 1967 film *Bonnie and Clyde*, **Faye Dunaway** (b. 1941) caused a sensation and started a fashion trend. Her beret, neckerchief, tight jumpers, and particularly her way of chewing the end of a cigar while casually dangling a gun from her fingers impressed a young audience, whose lust for rebellion was equaled by a yearning for romance. As Bonnie, Faye Dunaway provided both. Although this was followed by some excellent performances, notably in *Chinatown*, *Network*, for which she was awarded an Oscar, and as Joan Crawford in *Mommie Dearest*, she will always be remembered as the cold-blooded, warm-hearted Bonnie.

English actress **Julie Christie** (b. 1941) became the darling of the fashion-frenzied 1960s when she starred in the movie of the same name, for which she was awarded an Oscar.

After that she held her own against the Beatles in the global popularity stakes. She was also the second Englishwoman, after Vivienne Leigh in *Gone with the Wind*, to be given a Hollywood role coveted by every actress in the world: Lara in *Doctor Zhivago*. She was beautiful, even without make-up, courageous yet vulnerable, and seemed unimpressed by the trappings of stardom. This helped to turn her into an idol for a generation of young people in the search for truth.

Below left:
Inspired by the "Bonnie and Clyde" look, several photographers chose to set their subjects in similar surroundings, as in this picture by F. C. Grundlach.

Below right:
Faye Dunaway in 1967 as the daredevil gangster's moll and romantic interest in the film *Bonnie and Clyde*. Her costumes, designed by Nino Cerruti, became all the rage.

FRANÇOISE HARDY

JOAN BAEZ

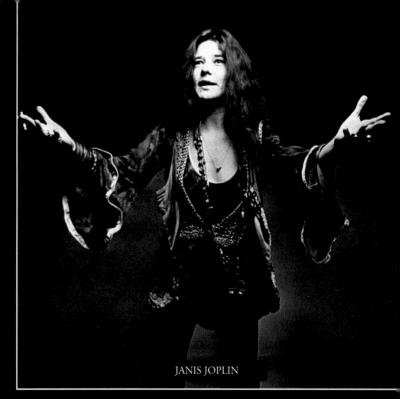

JANIS JOPLIN

MARIA CALLAS

JULIE CHRISTIE

JEAN SEBERG AND JEAN-PAUL BELMONDO

JANE FONDA

1970–1979

Anti-fashion – but with all the trimmings

1970-1979

With flowers in their hair, Jesus sandals on their feet, and a smile on their lips, the happy young idealists of the 1960s shambled into the century's seventh decade. Their utopia seemed to have materialized: the future belonged to young people (in Germany in 1970 they were given the right to vote at 18) and to their "love and peace" philosophy. The youth cult did indeed stay alive, but the young people who had brought it into being were getting older. Nature, at whose bosom they had sought fulfillment and enlightenment, turned against them. The gentle hippies with their beards and long hair aged quite rapidly and it was not long before the slogan "Never trust anyone over 30" appeared. The next wave of young people did not regard the lateness of their birth as a blessing; they suffered from unemployment, inflation, and boredom, and in no time at all the mere fact of youth could no longer automatically guarantee idealism and optimism.

The women's movement, which re-formed in the 1970s, labored

Simone de Beauvoir, France's leading feminist, viewed the resurgence of the women's movement with some skepticism. In her memoirs *All Said and Done,* published in 1972, she drew the conclusion that there was limited scope for new ideas to take hold after the protests of the 1960s.

under the same misapprehension. Feminists had to learn that feminity can no more guarantee a better world than can youth. Some "peaceful" women turned to violence to achieve their political objectives. One such was the journalist Ulrike Meinhof; as a leader of the Red Army Faction, she was responsible for bank robberies and bomb attacks in Germany. Women also strove for something that previously had been taboo: power. The first woman to take up the reins of a European government turned out to be a hawk rather than a dove: Margaret Thatcher won the 1979 British general election and, as prime minister, proved to be an iron lady. She did away with sloppy economics as well as with the "dissolute" youth who had made Britain the center of innovation for two decades.

Whereas the 1960s are remembered as the great period of youth revolts, the 1970s appear fragmented and lack a distinct profile. Nevertheless, they were anything but quiet. This was the time when

Opposite:
The hippie look became socially acceptable and flower children's getup was elevated to fashionable make-up. Even luxury-edition folklore rings were available, with real gemstones instead of colored glass.

Previous page:
Flared pants and platform shoes were part of 1970s chic, which people now prefer to call 1970s kitsch, although this is probably why it has offered such great potential for revival.

upheavals continued on a broad level. Sexual liberation, draft-dodging, experimentation with drugs, the demand for women's rights – none of these was now a minority issue, but they were taken up by and became the concern of the masses. The hippie's stoned love of peace was soon replaced by the belligerence, often intensified by hard drugs, of the political activist. In the United States it was the Black Panthers, in Germany the Red Army Faction, in Ireland the IRA (Irish Republican Army), in the Middle East the PLO (Palestine Liberation Army) who used any means to achieve their aims. Terrorism became a part of life. However, political groups were not alone in trying to push through their ideas. Individuals, mainly women, were also striving for self-realization, a search which had the power to destroy entire families. The old ways of life had been pronounced wrong and replacements had yet to be found. Consequently, many people felt vulnerable and therefore concentrated first and foremost on their own selves and lives. Tom Wolfe, the American author and journalist, aptly christened the 1970s the Me Decade.

At the same time as the Vietnam War was nearing its bitter end, the winter of 1972/73 brought the oil crisis and with it the debasement of the dollar. The economic euphoria which had begun in the 1950s was temporarily over, and the 1970s saw nothing but decline. Optimistic young people became pessimistic and exhibited their ugly side. The 1970s' reputation

Out of the attic, from flea markets, or copied: granny's dresses evoked granny's ideal of self-sufficient family life, but the dream soon froze to a pose.

as the decade of bad taste was well-earned. Platform shoes and hot pants, flared pants and polyester shirts, disco glitter, retro kitsch, and no-future punk, everything was tried, mixed, rejected, and then served up again. It is easy to dismiss it as mere protest, but here was at base a liberating, creative force which continues to make itself felt today. The 1970s saw the birth of postmodernism and eclecticism and thus the real fashion revolution.

It seemed so harmless when it began. It was the upright middle class, of all people, who warmed to the hippies' preferences and opted for natural materials like wool, cotton, and silk. "Noisy" psychedelic patterns and colors were replaced by a gentler palette of softer patterns and prints reminiscent of country and ethnic dress.

"Back to nature" appeared, and in 1973 the response was a "beige phase": neutral colors like khaki, sand, taupe, olive, and brick red always went together, making it easier to deal with the new way of dressing. Fashion, like life, no longer followed fixed rules, so that everyone had to choose what suited them best. Nowadays, putting together a wardrobe made up of individual items of clothing is a matter of course, but it is another legacy of the hippies, who first started this trend to demonstrate their individuality.

Opposite:
When antifashion becomes official fashion it loses its sting: this prettily embroidered crêpe georgette dress designed by Guy Laroche in 1971 would have made any hippie girl a welcome daughter-in-law, even in the best of families.

While the middle classes assiduously developed a new environmental awareness and tried in other ways to do everything "right" – thus preparing the ground for the "political correctness" of the 1990s – *haute couture* appropriately went for the hippie utopias. After all, isn't *haute couture* all about making dreams come true? The multicultural, harmonious, new, world of equal rights had not quite yet arrived, but at least it could be seen on catwalks. Saint Laurent was particularly adept at imparting the blessing of *haute couture* upon imaginative folklore outfits as well as on the black leather jackets of the antiestablishment, thereby making such outfits available to the super-rich who wished their image to be as "anti-establishment" as it was beautiful. Opium, the heavy, sweet perfume with which Saint Laurent crowned the decade, went very well with the shock fashions of the day, since both gave the wearer an exciting sense of worry-free youthfulness. Perhaps this display of Oriental splendor in the couture salon was a symbol of reverence to the petrodollar princesses who became the hungriest clients after the oil crisis, as well as angels of mercy. Without the beautiful women from the East and the growth in licensing for all kinds of accessories, many fashion houses might never have survived the recession of the 1970s.

Antifashion was the key concept. From cheap cotton garments to couture costumes, everything was allowed as long as it did not add up to an ordinary look. This made it more difficult to dress. It had been much easier when you just stepped into a ready-made dress or suit, rather than having to put together an entire outfit from different bits and bobs. But when in doubt, jeans would do. These had become the uniform of the nonconformists, and at the beginning

of the 1970s who didn't want to be counted as one of those? There was a good reason why, on the strength of its blue jeans, Levi Strauss won the American fashion industry's Coty Award in 1971. Denim jeans were worn by everyone, men and women, gays and lesbians, rich and poor. By then they were even permitted into universities and offices, although only if devoid of any of the embroidery and patches of the 1960s. Now they had to look faded, as if they had been worn for many years. In fact, many women who wore jeans looked as if they never changed their clothes. They demonstrated thereby that they really had no interest in fashion and that they had much more important things to think about. The trend for unisex did not lead to equal rights, but it did lead to a certain egalitarianism. He and she looked equally dreary and dismal; frivolity simply was not in it. Andy Warhol could make his cover design for the new Rolling Stones album *Sticky Fingers* as provocative as he liked, with the close-up of a jeans-clad man's crotch fitted with a real zip: since jeans had become mainstream they were simply dead.

Glam-rock brought some color back into the interplay between men and women, as well as some revolutionary potential into fashion. Gary Glitter, Marc Bolan, and most especially David Bowie used their extraordinary make-up and glittering elegance to protest against sloppiness in general and to plead for the aesthetically pleasing appearance. They proved that unisex did not have to mean that every woman became colorless. It could also mean that men revealed their true colors. The options available to men increased if they question their masculinity, or so went the message: bisexuals simply have more options, including more choice in fashion. This seemed to make sense to both male and female fans and London was soon awash with Ziggy Stardust clones.

American fashion was similarly influenced by black funk musicians. Emerging from the ghettos,

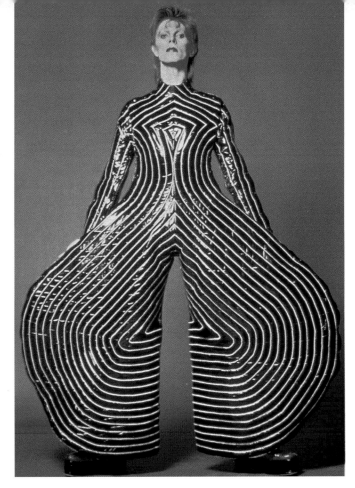

One of the most scintillating figures of the 1970s: pop star David Bowie wears heavy make-up, platform shoes, and a psychedelic glitter costume in his incarnation as Ziggy Stardust.

An agenda of pure provocation: glam rocker Gary Glitter in full stage gear is living proof that a glitter outfit will not make a softy out of a macho man.

they were not interested in old or worn-looking clothes; they wanted success and sought to anticipate this by dressing splendidly. They wore frilled shirts, tight-fitting Italian silk jersey pants, black turtlenecks, leather coats and, like the glam rockers, "lifting" boots. Platform soles could be up to 2½ inches (6 cm) high and heels could even reach 6 inches (15 cm). Choice of fabric was also determined by superlatives, multicolored, snakeskin patchwork being the tops for teetering funkers. The overall effect was certainly meant to be erotic: platform shoes and wide flares guided the eye upward to where the silk jersey really knew how to hug the body.

Such a glut of visually directed sex appeal gave designers the idea that even faded jeans could be enlived with a bit of glamour. They transformed raw

Opposite:
Disco glitter becomes gloss, provocation turns to wearable fashion: lustrous silver suit with the flared pants so typical of the 1970s. Photograph by F.C. Gundlach, 1971.

denim into fashionable bell-bottoms, hipsters, drainpipes, peg-tops, and even plus fours, had no hesitation in adding turnups or pencil creases, and used a wide spectrum of colors to complete the process of estrangement. Thus the classic workman's pants were turned into trendy lifestyle jeans which proudly bore the labels of designers like Fiorucci, Cardin, and Calvin Klein. These were not merely suitable for the office; a woman could promote her career with a pair as long as she wore the right blazer. The sloppy protest-look thus gradually became a distinguished uniform of success which demonstrated a woman's gravity in the workplace. Even Hollywood stars preferred to present themselves as competent rather than glamorous. From Candice Bergen, via Ali MacGraw to Meryl Streep, the publicity shots of leading ladies show them all wearing jeans and blazers. And Diane Keaton, Woody Allen's partner in several films, as well as in real life at the time, made

Glasses, a hat, a man's waistcoat over a white shirt, and baggy khaki pants created the enduring image of urban neurotic Annie Hall, alias Diane Keaton, in the mid-1970s.

A loose-fitting blouse, knee breeches, narrow boots with chunky heels, and a tasseled scarf tied around the hips – all that was needed for the unconventional city girl's Cossack outfit.

Return to the ladylike skirt: career women had to look young and feminine. Sunglasses were to be worn jauntily pushed back on the head, as shown by Dior in the spring of 1975.

her personal dress style in *Annie Hall* a model for millions: women could hide their figures and lack of confidence beneath white shirts, baggy pants, loose blazers, and a hat. Incidentally, the costumes for Annie Hall were designed by Ralph Lauren. However, an even greater furore was created by the below-the-knee, dark silk dress which, when worn with the obligatory blazer, could keep the working woman going from the office to evening reception. Women were learning to use clothes to advance their professional careers. Yet, as soon as they made it to the higher echelons, they became subject to a strict dress code. If women wanted to play with the boys they had to get out of pants and back into skirts. The successful woman wore a suit with a skirt, a silk blouse with bow collar instead of her man's shirt, skin-colored pantyhose, low-heeled shoes, and discreet gold jewelry. *Dress for Success*, the careerist's bible, was published in the late 1970s and in no time

at all the smart "preppy look," which prescribed every item of clothing, including leisurewear, from penny loafers to polo shirts, was widely adopted.

The excesses of the 1970s were permitted only in the evening, but then they were that much more extreme. Bored by the correct career outfits, designers and their clients sought to find solace in the disco of good taste. Polyester shirts in screeching colors, Lycra body stockings, silver lurex halter-tops worn with hot pants, old lace blouses with glitter jeans, synthetic silk 1940s summer dresses, 1950s cocktail dresses, granny's floor-length floral gowns, or modern evening gowns slit to the top of the thigh – everything was on show, including naked skin (if artfully painted, of course). The disco, originally conceived as a game reserved for gay men, became the stage where people who believed in Andy Warhol's credo that everyone could have five minutes of fame could exhibit themselves. The Pope of Pop and his Factory crowd

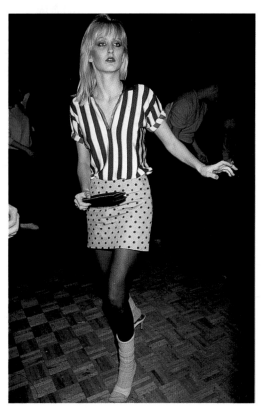

Pope of pop and disco king Andy Warhol wears jeans and white wig at the legendary New York nightclub Studio 54.

All in red in Studio 54, the lady of rock and fashion icon Bianca Jagger, ex-wife of Rolling Stones supremo Mick.

People who were not famous were occasionally permitted entry by the feared bouncers of Studio 54, provided they looked both attractive and unusual, like this blonde.

were at the center of Studio 54, the New York disco which became a legend despite being closed by the tax authorities after only two years. Its reputation came about thanks to the "beautiful people" who used the place to dance and consume vast amounts of cocaine. The disco craze was triggered and sustained by movies like *Saturday Night Fever*, *Grease*, and *Fame*. Even in the deepest countryside, former cowsheds were transformed overnight into glittering dance palaces. John Travolta and Olivia Newton-John were copied, Saturday night after Saturday night. As ever, people liked to dress up to go dancing. Dressing up, however, now meant something quite different. Distorted proportions and impossible color and fabric combinations were the big hits: "the best taste is bad taste."

Of all the 1970s fashion trends, it had to be the relatively minor, ironic, glitter kitsch of the disco movement which was briefly revived at the end of the

century, when a monument was erected to Studio 54 in the form of the motion picture *The Last Days of Disco*. The timing is unlikely to have been a complete coincidence. Then as now, general fashion was determined by minimalism and basics. Such simple, sensible clothes seem to provoke in people an uncontrollable desire for flamboyant excess. In those day the American designer Roy Halston was the first to create a cool and modern line of silk jersey tube dresses and jumpsuits, pantsuits, and cashmere twin sets with a reduced outline, using plain fabrics usually in white, beige, or pastels. Halston was a minimalist only when it came to his designs. His lifestyle was as excessive as could be expected of Studio 54's favorite dandy. In 1984 he was forced to declare bankruptcy, and he died from Aids in 1990. His label was revived in 1999 to coincide with the 1970s revival, but by then Tom Ford had already exploited Halston's legacy with his designs for figure-hugging hipster pants and

When punk became too "normal," many young people became new romantics. A perlon petticoat worn as a tutu over footless tights with leotard, high heels, and latex belt: another style inspired by Vivienne Westwood.

A punk couple in full costume pose for the cameras of shocked tourists and a sensation-hungry press. This provocative form of protest was soon to become a youth cult.

In 1994, Versace's use of safety pins, punk's outrageous jewelry, in *haute couture* helped the unknown starlet Elizabeth Hurley land a $1 million dollar contract with cosmetics giant Estée Lauder.

jersey tops, and only America's disco generation now remembers the 1970s designer Halston.

That was the generation which danced itself skinny during the 1970s, not only on Saturday nights, but also day after day in the fitness studio. The super-narrow, figure-hugging clothes first launched by Halston and then adoped by other designers, and which made use of fabrics that left little to the imagination, required the wearer's body to be extremely willowy. This resulted in a growing body culture which had the potential to degenerate into a manic dieting and fitness frenzy. In turn, this caused clothes to become even tighter. At the end of the decade women would lie flat on the floor to zip up their jeans. On the other hand, they wore shirts

Opposite page:
For the opening of their London boutique Sex, former teacher Vivienne Westwood (*right*), her partner Malcolm McLaren (*third from left*), and their employees strike rude poses to advertise their pornographic T-shirts. These were soon followed by torn garments and fetish and bondage outfits, which McLaren called "rubber gear for the office."

unbuttoned to the waist to demonstrate that they did not need to wear bras, thereby creating the first sporty, low-cut neck for day wear. Men's blazers became an exciting, feminine garment, especially when worn with nothing underneath. However, these little liberties seemed tiny compared to those taken by the punks! They covered their shaven, tattooed, and pierced bodies in whatever was deemed ugly by society: garbage bags, torn T-shirts, black fetish leather, glitter lurex, leopard-skin prints, army surplus uniforms, Doc Martens boots... In their targeted tastelessness they were not entirely dissimilar to the slightly older disco generation, but, whereas the 30-somethings in their laid-back maturity could declare the ugly and ridiculous to be amusing and charming, the punks acted in bitter provocation. They looked forward in anger, discovered "no future" and developed a hatred for the generation that preceded them, with its flower-power affectation and back-to-nature waffle. The punks replaced "love and peace" with "sex and violence," and all natural things with screaming artifice. Away with cotton, in with plastic! And only clashing things were put together: mohican haircuts died red and green atop the faces of pale children, toilet chains, tampons, and safety pins worn as jewelry, and leather jackets decorated with swastikas and skulls worn over lacy sex-shop underwear. The startling juxtaposition of "displaced" objects in these wild combinations frequently achieved a surrealist quality reminiscent of the Dada movement. This was true not only when the keen intelligence of Vivienne Westwood was responsible. The former teacher had a genius for turning punk into fashion, and she also knew when it was time to move on and start something new. In contrast to others, she was not involved in the punk revival of the 1990s which brought designers like Versace and Gaultier such unexpected fame. Punk girls of the 1970s would never have dreamed that their way of using safety pins would one day be adopted by *haute couture* – yet, the British actress Elizabeth Hurley, an unknown at the time, has her appearance in Versace's now famous "safety-pin dress" to thank for her lucrative Estée Lauder advertising contract and international celebrity status.

While Britain was inspired by the street, designers in France, Italy, and the United States increasingly established themselves with their own boutiques and lines. Stylists who used to work for the big fashion houses tried to lose their anonymity by becoming independent under their own names. Many of these names disappeared as quickly as they sprung up, but a few humble stylists made it to become great creators. In France this included Claude Montana,

Thierry Mugler, and Jean Paul Gaultier. In 1973, Yves Saint Laurent's partner Pierre Bergé and Jacques Mouclier, chairman of the guild of couturiers, successfully campaigned for a new rule to permit young designers to show their collections in public. Unlike *haute couture*, which is presented in January and July to a generally small and select circle in private salons, the designers were able from then on to show their prêt-à-porter ranges in March and October before a larger, though still select, audience which included the press, buyers, and celebrities. The first designers to turn their ready-to-wear shows into huge staged spectacles with audiences that were four times as large as those of the *haute couture* shows were Thierry Mugler and Kenzo.

In 1970 Kenzo was the first Japanese designer to establish himself in the French capital. He was followed by several of his compatriots who saw Paris as a springboard for the international market: the work of Hanae Mori, Junko Shimada, Issey Miyake, Rei Kawakubo, Yohji Yamamoto, and Junko Koshino has appeared on the catwalks of Paris ever since the 1970s and 1980s. However, quite a few of them continue to live and manufacture in Japan. In contrast to their Western colleagues' obsession with exposing the female form in ever tighter and more transparent designs, the Asians exhibited an aesthetic of concealment which borrowed heavily from the geometric forms of the kimono. While the West used new discoveries in nutrition and sports medicine to transform the body itself into a work of art, the Japanese in Paris were constantly developing new proportions which would change the body by alienating its form. Thus it was their garments which became works of art.

Following pages:
A completely new form of fashion photography was developed by Sarah Moon in the 1970s. Gentle, shadowy, located somewhere between dream and day, her pictures counterbalanced the hard and frequently lewd images produced by colleagues like Helmut Newton. The clothes are from Chloé's 1972 collection.

Opposite page:
Pleat sculptures: Japanese fashion designer Issey Miyake does not merely dress a woman's body, his creations transform it into a work of art.

Thierry Mugler

Woman as fetish: this concise label describes the fashion creations of Thierry Mugler (b. 1948). Like Montana, Mugler gave women padded shoulders and wasp waists when loose and natural clothes were still the order of the (feminist) day. However, he distinguished himself from his colleagues by accentuating the whole body with all its feminine curves. Thierry Mugler's aim is to make women to look like goddesses and heroines, or at least to resemble dominatrixes in their latex and vinyl "working clothes."

The question of whether ordinary women can, or would ever wish to, wear his sharp suits is of no concern to Mugler. He designs for the stars and aims for theatricality. He replaces the catwalk procession with expertly staged shows liberally peppered with celebrities who model his clothes. Jerry Hall, Veruschka, Lauren Hutton, Diana Ross, Ivana Trump, Tippi Hedren, and Sharon Stone, have all stepped on the catwalk for him. Mugler himself takes care of everything, from accessories, hair, and make-up to lighting and music.

Thierry Mugler began as a 14-year-old ballet dancer in his home town of Strasbourg. He is also a talented photographer who, like Karl Lagerfeld, produces his own advertising shots. In 1997, the self-taught man who came to fashion via drawing and window dressing, and who opened his own house in Paris in 1974, was invited by the strict guardians of couture to put on a couture show, and suddenly his theatrical designs, previously dismissed as fancy dress, became socially acceptable.

Yet confident and seductive women have always worn Mugler designs, even though, or perhaps because, his clothes have the power to unleash a minor scandal.

Shock-couture: a provocative suit from Thierry Mugler's 1999/2000 *haute couture* collection (*opposite*). The low cut, which exposes the top of the buttocks, is worn with a string of pearls (*left*). This creation was included in Mugler's 1995 ready-to-wear collection and must have impressed Alexander McQueen, whose own collection a year later featured pants worn so low that they were named "bumsters" because they were so revealing.

Jean-Charles de Castelbajac

Traditional costumes, sportswear, and art: Castelbajac's designs can absorb any number of influences, as in these jackets from his 1978/79 collection, reminiscent of large plaids and typical of his work in the late 1970s and early 1980s. Every season the couturier asks a different artist to decorate his famous "picture-garments" (*below right*).

Jean-Charles de Castelbajac (b. 1949) is a man with a mission. Maverick offspring of a conservative French aristocratic family, he allied himself with the Parisian student revolts of 1968 and has never ceased in his efforts to be a subversive force in fashion, of all fields.

With his first collection in 1970, he was the first designer with the temerity to upgrade sport and work clothing to the level of designer wear. His anoraks, parkas, and overalls all serve to carry the message into the world: "Saving the world is always in style." His environmental consciousness informs his use of such old-fashioned materials as felt and loden cloth, and he has even used timber and straw, or bandage gauze and fishing nets. However, he also works with nylon and modern art, and always with a sense of humor: a "raincoat for long journeys" is a laminated collage of postcards, and every fashion show ends with one of his "garment-pictures" by contemporary artists. Castelbajac's creations are rightly described as timeless since they do not follow particular trends yet they cannot be termed classical in the sense of being understated.

He has a childlike preference for primary colors and has even produced a jacket by sewing together teddy bears. However, this did not impede a commission in 1997 to create priestly vestments and pontificals for the Pope. Like most of today's designers, he also designs accessories and furnishings.

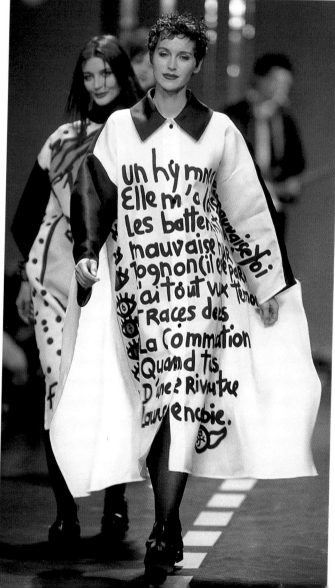

Claude Montana

In the early 1970s, influenced by punk rock and the fetish it made of uniforms and leather which he observed in London, Claude Montana (b. 1949) began to develop the aggressive power suit, a symbol of the 1980s.

Under his direction shoulders became broad, broad, broad, and waists very, very narrow. His jackets featured huge shawl collars, were fastened with a single button, were worn over short, tight skirts or tapered pants, and always teamed with high heels. Since everything was made of leather, originally in black with metal trimmings, Montana was accused of designing fascistic clothes. He subsequently began to use colors, particularly

plum, and his contribution to the 1980s' need for splendor was white leather decorated with gold embroidery.

Montana adores leather (he loves to wear it himself) and he is a master at working the material, learning his trade from the leather designer MacDouglas in Paris. He believes that leather demands a slightly aggressive, strongly structured form and that the soft material will always ensure that the outline is softened. The couture collections that he designed for Lanvin between 1989 and 1992 brought Montana recognition from quarters which had previously been unappreciative of his oversized leather creations. The house of Montana was founded in 1979 and went bankrupt in 1998.

Typically Montana: the finest leather is used to create luxurious fetishism in white, with gold embroidery and futuristic, oversized shoulders. This is a battle-dress for the war of the sexes (*below left*). This coat from his 1987/88 collection (*below right*) has a broad shawl collar which accentuates the shoulders, always a prime focus of Montana's designs.

Jean Paul Gaultier

Fashion knows no boundaries – or not if Jean Paul Gaultier (b. 1951) has anything to do with it. Since he does not think of himself as a designer, he travels more freely than others through time and space, grabbing hold of whatever takes his fancy, whether beautiful or not, and putting together various items to form new and surprising combinations. His first collection in 1977 brought him to the attention of the press, and he has kept his reputation as an *enfant terrible* ever since.

Gaultier, who is as committed to the rights of women as he is to gay issues, has neutralized the division between menswear and womenswear and prefers to show both collections together – with the result that one can never be sure who will be wearing the skirt and who smoking the cigar. His mixed doubles playfully swap roles or dresses and wear identical clothes as if they were twins. Furthermore, Gaultier was the first to use "real people," beautiful and ugly people, fat and slim, young and old on the catwalk.

He frequently demonstrates the attraction of "real clothes" by adopting various ethnic items, as in his Mongols, Fashionable Rabbis, and Grand Tour collections. He even transformed crude punk tattoos into poetic symbols for both skin and T-shirts. Gaultier has done more to extend the concept of beauty than many an artist, and has been a better spokesman for tolerance than most politicians. Naturally, this can only be achieved by occasionally causing offense. Madonna values Gaultier's talent for provocation, which is why the outrageous star had him design corsets with exaggerated conical breasts for her 1990 *Blond Ambition* tour – thereby liberating the corset from the myth of its being a tool for the subjugation of women. When Gaultier's eclectic outfits are relieved of their show accessories, what remains are witty, clever, and wearable garments. The Chambre Syndicale de la Couture invited the "young *créateur*" to show a couture collection in 1997, thus confirming his expertise and craftsmanship. Born near Paris, Gautier learned his trade at Cardin and Patou, and harbors a deep admiration for Yves Saint Laurent. As a new century begins, he is France's great hope for *haute couture*.

Fall/winter 1994/95

Spring/summer 1989

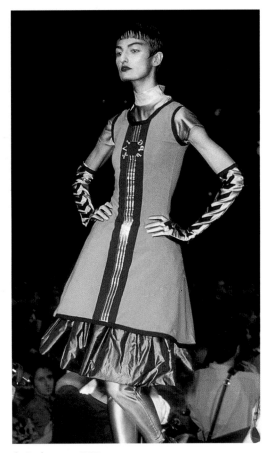

Spring/summer 1987

Fall/winter 1997/98

Spring/summer 1998

Spring/summer 1989

Previous page but one:
Just as Gaultier likes to be the
enfant terrible of the world of
fashion, so the fame of pop star
Madonna is based on a talent to
outrage. She asked the French
designer to create her wardrobe for
her *Blond Ambition* tour of 1990.

In 1998 Gaultier was inspired by
the dress style of Mexican artist
Frida Kahlo (*opposite, main picture*),
who was famous for her unusual,
folkloric clothes all of
40 years before this became a
mainstream fashion trend in
the 1970s.

Kenzo

Japanese designer Kenzo Takada (b. 1939), who in the world of fashion is known by his first name only, is unique in having brought a sense of fun to his refined versions of hippie garments.

In 1970 Kenzo was the first Japanese fashion designer to open a house under his own label in Paris, and his cheerful, unconventional ethnic garments quickly won over a globe-trotting young audience. From his mother country he brought the simple kimono cut, but combined it with South American, Oriental, and Scandinavian elements. This mixture of patterns and styles remains his special feature. Kenzo is regarded as the most European of all the Japanese who also settled in Paris. He is also one of the few stars of the 1970s whose style is still in vogue today. He designs menswear, children's fashions, and curtain and upholstery fabrics, as well as his women's ready-to-wear collections.

Below:
Colorful, young, and comfortable: baggy three-quarter slacks and striped blouses worn with dashing little berets.

Below:
In his 2000 collection, Kenzo returns to his Japanese roots with a new interpretation for the traditional kimono.

Hanae Mori

Hanae Mori (b. 1926) studied literature in Tokyo and brought up two children before she entered the fashion world. But this ambitious Japanese designer was aiming for Paris and *haute couture* – a decision that she had taken in 1962 after an encounter with Coco Chanel.

It took Hanae Mori 15 years to achieve her goal: in 1977 she opened a couture salon in the Avenue Montaigne in Paris, the first Japanese designer to achieve this. As a young wife she made her first fashion contacts through her father-in-law, a textile manufacturer, and she rapidly earned a reputation as a costume designer in Japan. From there, through hard work and determination, she gained the acceptance of the strict Parisian guild of couture, which led her first to open her own boutique in New York. Garments designed by the highly educated Hanae Mori tend to follow a Western line; they are very feminine and elegant, often of diaphanous silk and adorned with stylized Japanese flowers. In 1999, Hanae Mori handed over creative direction to her daughter-in-law Penelope Mori, a former Californian model, who combines cashmere jumpers with kimono dresses.

This cocktail dress (*below left*) betrays no trace of Japanese dress traditions and might equally well have been designed by a French couturier. The feminine elegance associated with Hanae Mori, the Japanese "grande dame," is further demonstrated by the wedding dress on which she is working (*below right*).

Issey Miyake

ISSEY MIYAKE

Opposite:
Lantern procession: every movement brings delicate animation to these cleverly pleated dresses from Issey Miyake's Flying Saucer collection of 1992, so reminiscent of childhood lanterns.

Accessories and costume jewelry have no place in Miyake's sculptural fashion cosmos, yet the master has a definite liking for hats, which he promptly turns into works of art, as demonstrated by these two examples from 1978 (*left*) and 1979/80 (*right*).

Issey Miyake (b. 1938) is regarded by many as a latter-day Fortuny, and not only because he re-created Fortuny's early 20th-century silk pleats in synthetic fibers and new colors. Like Fortuny, Issey Miyake has many talents and interests and he believes technology to be equal to craft and art: thus, like all Japanese people, he does not make a distinction between the fine and applied arts. For him there is no hierarchy of fabrics, and every fiber, whether synthetic or natural, can be worked with sophistication. This lack of prejudice grants him a huge amount of freedom in designing his garments, and he rejects the term "fashion." Together with Yohi Yamamoto and Rei Kawakubo, Miyake is one of the three great designers who revolutionized our ideas about bodies and clothes in the 1970s and 1980s.

Issey Miyake was born in Hiroshima. He trained as a graphic designer in Tokyo and subsequently went to Paris, where he studied couture and worked for Laroche and Givenchy. In New York he learned about ready-to-wear and showed his first collection in 1971. Since 1973, Miyake has presented his collections twice a year in Paris, yet his fabrics and garments continue to be manufactured in Japan. He has remained impervious to the Western mania for creating a "style": "My style emanates from life. And not from style." As a result he has developed light, washable, and transformable items which suit a modern, mobile lifestyle.

In Paris he remarked on another major difference between Western and Asian fashion design: "The cut of a Western garment is determined by the body, a Japanese one by the fabric." No wonder then that he has devoted so much attention to researching new fabrics; 100 Japanese factories work exclusively for him. Thus the link between technology and tradition has become Miyake's trademark.

His designs may place less emphasis on the body, but they certainly give it freedom. This was impressively demonstrated by the Frankfurt Ballet, which frequently performed in Miyake's pleats collection. His Pleats Please line has been in production for years, with continuous additions and developments, and has become something of a uniform for intellectuals and artists, with a cachet similar to that of Levi jeans. Individual, often startlingly colored garments are designed to be mixed and matched.

A further development is seen in Miyake's artist editions as well as his Twist series, where each garment is wrung and creased by hand. Like the other major Japanese fashion designers, Miyake experiments with the body's volume and continuously changes its dimensions. He has presented "wind coats" that look like parachutes, Plastic Bodies (premolded corsets), "suits of armor" made of black lacquered rattan and bamboo, and "blowup" clothes, but he has also shown artistically "tattooed" body stockings which fit like a second skin.

Miyake, who has worked with many artists and has installed several exhibitions in museums, is now widely regarded as an artist in his own right.

Opposite:
Miyake bustiers (*main picture*) have become a fashion milestone: the Plastic Body corsets of 1980/81 do not cling to the body but exist independently of it. As with all the Japanese couturiers, it is characteristic of Miyake that his garments neither follow the line of the body nor expose it.

This page:
A new development – Miyake first took motifs from the arts, then his creations became artworks themselves, like these dresses from his 1999/2000 collection, which with their winged sleeves are literally ready to take flight. He has now decided to concentrate solely on producing single artistic pieces. "Miyake making things."

1999/2000

1999/2000

1996/1997

1997/1998

1997

Fashion designer or artist? For Issey Miyake there is no boundary between the two, hence the title of his 1998/99 exhibition at the Cartier Foundation for Contemporary Art in Paris. *Issey Miyake Making Things* included his own creations as well as works by other artists made with his fabrics.

Issey Miyake

The look of the decade

What is beautiful? This question provoked serious discussion in the 1970s. Until then, certain ideals were more or less accepted by everybody. Suddenly the socio-psychological importance of appearance became a matter of interest to scholars. Whereas between 1920 and 1970 the number of worldwide publications on this subject was barely worthy of mention, the 1970s alone saw the publication of 47 scientific articles on the meaning of beauty. All agreed that good looks could help secure greater professional as well as romantic success. However, what exactly could be regarded as beautiful was a matter of great dispute. For some it was the hippie ideal of untouched nature, for others the glittering artifice of disco, and there were yet others who saw beauty in the aggressive posturing of warriors, revolutionaries, and social outsiders.

The "natural look" was adopted initially by working women who wanted to give the impression that work was more important to them than their appearance. However, they were very aware that they could secure their jobs only by providing something pretty for their male bosses and colleagues to look at, and so presented themselves as extremely well groomed, their hair always freshly washed, with blemish-free complexions and manicured hands. Bright colors were banished! Tinted moisturizers, skin-colored eye shadow, colorless lip-gloss and nail varnish, these were the career woman's secret weapons. A great deal of fuss was made about natural hairstyles. They were blow-dried or left to dry naturally, sophisticated layers and permanent waves provided the required volume, and newly invented streaks endowed highlights which only the sun could produce before. Because career women could not use anything else as bait, a head of thick, shiny

hair was a highly cherished physical attribute. This is the only possible explanation for *Charlie's Angels* actress Farrah Fawcett Major becoming world-famous solely thanks to her long, layered haircut: as sporty as it was sexy, her hairstyle was one of the most successful in the history of the movies and television.

Bodies were also expected to look naturally sporty and sexy. This required an all-year tan, to emulate the appearance of the rich and beautiful for whom life was a permanent holiday, or at least to give the impression of the kind of success which would permit exclusive holidays abroad. In the 1970s those in work liked to travel for their vacations. For those who had to stay at home, there were a number of self-tanning products which achieved increasingly "natural" results and brought rapidly growing profits.

A good, preferably superslim figure was either a gift of nature or was achieved through hard work. Healthy nutrition was a must, even for those with no need for diets – the business in slimming products was booming. Many women would regularly spend their vacations on health farms or in diet clinics and would be daily visitors to the fitness studio for the rest of the year. The extent of what could be achieved with a little discipline was demonstrated by Jane Fonda, who boasted a better figure at 50 than she had during her successful "Barbarella" years. Jane Fonda also showed that a fitness studio need not be the gloomy, sweaty gym of the past: her studio in Beverly Hills was bright, airy, trendy, and fitted with a Jacuzzi for later. Jane Fonda was so successful that her fitness program soon appeared in the form of books and videos.

For those who would never be converted to aerobics there was the daily jog, which soon became a national sport,

Above:
Grandmother's crochet shawl, a handmade ethnic belt and simple ethnic jewelry transform this simple, modern, black outfit into the garb of a well-groomed hippie.

Opposite:
Such fulsome "natural" beauty can be achieved only through a careful skincare routine and with sophisticated make-up techniques, but it can help find a partner for life as well as secure a successful career. A typical feature of the 1970s look: the crochet hat.

Left:
The sexy appearance of the three stalwart ladies from the television series *Charlie's Angels* proved to have a great influence on style generally. Farrah Fawcett Major's layered and blow-dried blond mane in particular caused hairdressers across the world to work up a sweat.

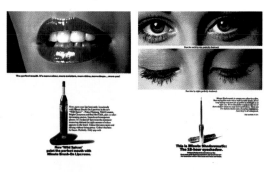

GREAT GLISSERS

Great new shine. Great new colours. Great new look for your lips.
Five new pots of pure colour. Bright. Clean. Transparent.
Loaded with moisturisers and sun screens to keep your lips
juicy and smooth. Dip in your finger and never stop glistening!
NATURAL WONDER BY REVLON

The healthy or natural look was the look adopted by women in the 1970s, especially working women who wanted to be taken seriously. Helena Rubinstein's make-up series "Beauty that works" reflected this.

Opposite:
The romantic look featuring ethnic clothes and jewelry was rooted in the dress style of the hippie movement yet, as a fashion entity, it is synonymous with the 1970s. For those whose hair was not naturally curly, hairstylists like those at Mod's Hair could help: in the 1970s perms became more popular than ever before.

although it was not without its dangers. Without proper preparation and professional instruction, jogging could kill by causing heart failure. Nevertheless, jogging has remained the cheapest and thus the most popular way of keeping fit.

The trend for all things natural finally brought about acceptance of the Afro hairstyle. Whereas previously black women had tried every means available to straighten their hair, they now wore the bushy halo with pride. This included political activist Angela Davies and fashion model Marsha Hunt, who became the mother of the first of Mick Jagger's seven children. Many white women tried to copy the Afro by perming their hair, but the results were almost always dismal.

Bushy eyebrows, as popularized by model Margaux Hemingway and child star Brooke Shields in the movie *Pretty Baby*, brought a touch of wildness to fashion. Margaux Hemingway, granddaughter of writer Ernest Hermingway and a natural beauty, was paid $1 million a year by Fabergé in one of the highest-paid advertising contracts ever. New antiwrinkle creams were popular, since they promised "eternal" youth and created a market-led response to the youth cult.

The same women who, during the day, appeared to allow nothing but water to touch their faces would, in the evening, delve deep into their make-up bags. Discos and clubs like Studio 54 in New York, Régine's and Les Bains Douches in Paris, and Annabelle's in London demanded glamour and glitter. Greater artifice meant greater esteem: eyebrows were pencil-thin; eyelids brightly colored and sparkling; lips ranged from deepest red to black; complexions were iridescent thanks to silver, gold, and fluorescent particles. Skintight Lycra and latex outfits were the nighttime replacements of the multilayered natural fiber garments of daywear.

Other options were provided by Roy Halston's minimalist designs and elegant 1930s fashion, which underwent a revival in the 1970s. Most importantly, women had to look feminine at night and be free to experiment with anything that contradicted the professional correctness of their day.

Then, the first generation of girls who had never worn anything other than pants came of age. Naturally, they also wished to define themselves by their choice of clothes, and the retro looks which the "old guard" had made use of were out of the question. They wanted to look like no woman before them, perhaps more

like soldiers. With camouflage outfits from army surplus stores and smeared make-up in dirty colors, they looked as if they had just emerged from the trenches, and proved their political awareness.

The most provocative critique of ideals of beauty was provided by the punk movement. With rings and needles in ears and noses, with tattoos, brightly colored Cherokee haircuts, or gelled devil's horns, and large quantities of black color on nails, lips, and eyes, anything that frightened the middle classes seemed beautiful to the punk rockers.

Yet it took very little time before law-abiding citizens came to adopt ideas from the underground. Toward the end of the decade the natural look had become insipid and was finally laid to rest, and blood-red lips against pale skin came into fashion, with deep shadows around the eyes. This artificial looking make-up harked back to the 1920s and heralded the beginning of women's new-found confidence.

Ecologically correct:

A woman revolutionizes the beauty business: in 1976 Anita Roddick, granddaughter of Italian immigrants, used a £4,000 ($6,400) loan to found her Body Shop in London. Her idea was to set the secret knowledge of the world's women against a giant industry devoted to chemical preparations. The idea worked. Within a few years, the Body Shop had become the symbol of natural, environmentally friendly cosmetics, produced by time-honored methods by women from every corner of the world. Shop after shop was opened, and Anita Roddick became a millionaire virtually overnight. Yet she never lost sight of her original concern: to manufacture honest cosmetics which both serve the needs of consumers and benefit manufacturers. She was also the first to ensure that make-up artists were awarded a kind of copyright for their creative designs. The big cosmetic companies have had to adopt some of the "small" Body Shop owner's philosophy and marketing strategy: we must thank Anita Roddick for the large choice of organic and natural cosmetic ranges now available.

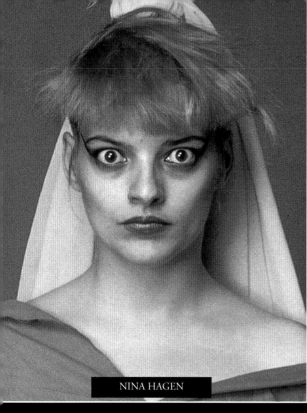

NINA HAGEN

ANGELA DAVIS

OLIVIA NEWTON-JOHN & JOHN TRAVOLTA

LAUREN HUTTON

PATTI SMITH

CATHERINE DENEUVE

CHARLOTTE RAMPLING

JANE BIRKIN

LIZA MINNELLI

BIANCA JAGGER

dols of the decade

Commitment, provocation, or enjoyment – these were the options in the 1970s, when people could become famous and admired just for being in the right place, at the right time, and wearing the right outfit, thus gaining entry to the select club of beautiful people whose stylish idleness filled the gossip columns of the glossy magazines. **Bianca Jagger** (b. 1950), the fiery Nicaraguan who became famous by marrying Mick Jagger in 1971, was one of them, and so was **Jerry Hall** (b. 1956), the blond model from Texas who replaced Bianca at Mick Jagger's side. Both were widely imitated.

It was also thanks to the dance craze that **Olivia Newton-John** (b. 1950) achieved her rapid albeit short-lived rise to fame. Her appearance alongside John Travolta in *Grease* turned her into a teenage idol.

Two movies brought the 1930s retro look to the attention of people who yearned for decadent elegance: *Cabaret* and *The Damned*. **Liza Minnelli** (b. 1946), with her large, childlike eyes and short, unruly hair above a full, feminine mouth and body, became a likable star through her role in *Cabaret*: strong yet vulnerable, sassy and affectionate, and beautiful in her own way, she was a model for many women who felt uncomfortable with the roles traditionally open to them.

Charlotte Rampling (b. 1945), however, was not a star with whom women found it easy to identify, although many would have given anything to acquire her mysterious and erotic allure. Her reserve, which seemed to conceal a dynamic force, the sensuous mouth, but mostly the intensity in the gaze of her heavy-lidded green eyes defined Charlotte Rampling's dangerous yet tempting appeal. Her role as a Jewish prisoner of the camps in Liliana Cavani's movie *The Night Watchman* of 1973, in which she appeared half-naked, with a Nazi cap on her head, caused a scandal yet it transformed her into an icon of desperate seduction (or seductive desperation) and certainly turned her into an icon for the future generations of punks.

American musician **Patti Smith** (b. 1946) similarly touched upon the darker aspects of eroticism. Another serious, dark woman, equally powerful and frail, she was a source of inspiration for Belgian designer Ann Demeulemeester who designed all her collections on Patti Smith, her ideal model since her youth.

British actress **Jane Birkin** (b. 1943) combined hippie nonchalance with French *savoir-faire*, which resulted in her becoming a sex symbol of innocent seductiveness, especially when she sang the duet *Je t'aime* with her partner Serge Gainsbourg. She was thought capable of emulating the erotic obsessions of Charlotte Rampling, but not the elegance with which she made everything even more "wicked." Jane Birkin stood for a vaguely sluttish natural look, her straggly mane of hair and torn jeans being copied by millions.

A "tidy" version of the natural look was presented by **Lauren Hutton** (b. 1943). Her refusal to have the gap between her teeth and her slightly crooked nose surgically corrected was precisely what helped her to become the most sought-after model of the decade. She was the first model to be awarded an exclusive contract guaranteeing her an annual income of $175,000 for 35 days' work. In return, she was forbidden to appear in advertisements for companies other than Revlon, although she was free to pursue her career as a model. Thanks to the unprecedented generosity of this deal, she became well-known enough to be offered movie roles. *American Gigolo* with Richard Gere was the high point of her otherwise average career. Nevertheless, she was in great demand again as a model in the 1990s, by which time she was over 50.

Catherine Deneuve (b. 1943) is the embodiment of everything cherished by the French: beauty, elegance, refinement, but also a hint of depravity. This was suggested in Luis Buñuel's movie *Belle de Jour*, in which she plays a respectable middle-class woman whose sexual fantasies drive her to becoming a prostitute in a daytime brothel. She was subsequently awarded a series of leading roles in the 1970s and became established as France's leading movie star, which she remains to this day.

Catherine Deneuve is regarded as the incarnation of the designs of Yves Saint Laurent, to whom she has remained faithful for three decades. Her status as a national deluxe article, comparable perhaps to that of Chanel No.5, often disguises the fact that she is an excellent actress as well as a woman who has succeeded in maintaining her independence despite being linked with the names of influential men such as photographer David Bailey, director Roger Vadim, and actor Marcello Mastroianni.

Black, female, and intellectual, **Angela Davies** (b. 1944) nevertheless became an idol, thanks, in part, to her good looks. She had the confidence to wear her hair frizzy, thereby starting the trend for the Afro hairstyle. Angela Davies, who studied literature in Paris and philosophy in Frankfurt, was an early convert to the black civil rights movement in America. A gun licensed in her name was used when her bodyguard kidnapped some hostages in an attempt to gain the release of black prisoners. As a result she was charged with murder and joined the list of the United States' ten most dangerous criminals. After 16 months as a remand prisoner, she was released in 1972.

By the 1970s feminists could no longer be dismissed as ugly suffragettes for the simple reason that so many members of their vanguard were extremely attractive. Out in front was **Gloria Steinem** (b. 1934), cofounder and editor-in-chief of the feminist magazine *Ms*.

The American **Shere Hite** (b. 1942) consciously presented herself as a sex symbol, flaunting her platinum locks, pale skin, and blood-red lips; she questioned 3000 women about their sexual preferences, habits, and fantasies and then published the shockingly explicit bestseller *Hite Report*.

Nancy Friday (b. 1937), who in *My Mother My Self* had the temerity to question the sacred mother–daughter relationship, was another photogenic feminist with whom other, less attractive combatants found it difficult to compete, at least in the male-dominated world of the media.

Nevertheless, astute women knew how much they owed to women like **Betty Friedan** (b. 1921), "mother of the movement," who became famous for her book *The Feminine Mystique*, and to **Alice Schwarzer** (b. 1942), the founder of *Emma*, the German feminist magazine. These women were elevated to the rank of idol.

British fashion

Katharina Hesedenz

London was pulsating – and designing fashions for the next millennium. St Martin's College of Art and Design was foremost among the talent factories, and it had already produced the successors to Galliano and his ilk. Wild young things like Antonio Berardi, Owen Gaster, and Tristan Weber were not entirely unjustified in hoping that British eccentricity would ease their entry to the club of super-designers. They were profiting from an ability to accept and analyze the banal realities of life and were commenting on them with their own personal fashion statements. Britain was building a new world of extravagance. Yet it all seemed so harmless when it started, and even up to the 1960s Britain's comfortable fashion designs were barely distinguishable from those on the Continent. It was only when young designers like Mary Quant began to find their inspiration in the street did British fashion develop its very own flair.

Norman Hartnell (1901–79)

Not just any old couturier, Sir Norman Hartnell was the British Royal Family's tailor. In the dressmaking shop of his Mayfair salon (*below left*), seamstresses work on the embroidery for Elizabeth II's coronation garments. The mannequin in the foreground is wearing the matching headdress.

Naturally, the robe designed by the couturier for Her Majesty's enthronement may only be modeled by the Queen herself (*opposite*).

Hartnell also created Elizabeth's wedding dress. The master presents his design in 1953 (*below right*).

The coronation of Elizabeth II in 1953 triggered a wave of enthusiasm for the monarchy and British fashion. The ceremony was broadcast on television, thus allowing people in 25 million homes to witness the radiant 28-year-old monarch in her satin Norman Hartnell gown: in this dress, which was encrusted with pearl and crystal embroideries of the emblems of the British Empire and Commonwealth, she embodied the youthfulness, optimism, and strength of an era.

As Elizabeth II's official tailor, as well as her mother's and occasionally her grandmother's, Sir Norman Hartnell (1901–79) dressed three generations of British royals and became one of the people responsible for the image of the British royal family. The theatrical flair of his well-cut day ensembles and extravagant *robes de style* was well-suited to official events.

In his youth Hartnell dreamed of an acting career. Instead, he worked for short periods for three different dressmaking establishments, including Lucile's salon, before opening his own house in Burton Street in 1923. That year his first evening gown, made of silver and gold tulle, caused an uproar. It was worn by Lord Weymouth's fiancée and some described it as "the eighth wonder of the world." In 1927 he designed an equally sensational wedding dress for Barbara Cartland, with a long waist and tiered, frilly skirt.

In *Silver and Gold*, his autobiography, published in 1955, the successful British designer describes his early difficulties in his own country, where success was not forthcoming until he opened a branch in Paris in 1927. In 1965 he introduced the special collection, a precursor of ready-to-wear clothing. In 1977 Norman Hartnell became the first couturier ever to be knighted, just two years before he died. His salon finally closed its doors in 1992.

Hardy Amies

In contrast to Sir Norman Hartnell's theatrical grandeur, Hardy Amies (b. 1909), his rival for the Queen's favor, based his career on elegant understatement. The son of a dressmaker, he spent 60 years consistently concentrating on suits, coats, and evening wear, paying no heed to short-lived trends and gags. His motto was: "The best-dressed women wear clothes which would not look absurd in the country."

Having spent several years in France and Germany, and after trying his hand at being an English teacher, a journalist, a traveling salesman, and a writer, the 21-year-old finally trained as a dressmaker at La Chasse, his mother's employers. He showed his first collection in 1946. Ingrid Bergman was the muse for the elegance of his feminine tweed suits with rounded shoulders and padded hips, and which became an instant success. In 1950

Amies opened a boutique in Savile Row and won the patronage of Princess Elizabeth, whom he continued to dress for four decades. Increasing criticism of the Queen's homey-looking wardrobe was of no concern whatsoever to either the wearer or the creator.

Amies was knighted in 1989 and, on the occasion of his 80th birthday, he passed on his duties as royal dress designer to Ken Fleetwood. After Fleetwood's death, this position was taken by Jon Moore. Amies's greatest commercial success were his distinguished menswear designs, although this sportswear aficionado demonstrated an unexpected propensity for extravagance in his designs for Stanley Kubrick's cult movie *2001: A Space Odyssey*. The 90-year-old designer would like his epitaph to read: "He was a court dressmaker with an elevated sense of humor."

Opposite:
Hardy Amies's 1968 collection was surprisingly fashionable. This was unusual for the traditionalist couturier.

Below left:
From Hardy Amies's 1955 collection: a gold lamé suit with a mink collar features the classic style that made the couturier so popular at court.

Below right:
Hardy Amies's vision of a grand wedding in 1960: large quantities of tulle gently flowing down the staircase, accessorized with long gloves and a sparkling tiara – a design fit for a queen.

Biba

In the early 1960s, following Mary Quant's example, fashion designers began producing ever-changing collections inspired by the street, transforming London's Kings Road and Carnaby Street into Meccas for fashion-hungry youngsters with small wallets.

Celebrities like Twiggy, Julie Christie, Mick Jagger, and Princess Anne, however, had the pleasure of shopping at Biba. The glamorous Kensington Church Street boutique was opened in 1963, and its low-priced romantic Hollywood 1930s styles triggered a global Biba-mania. The five-storey Art Deco palace also housed a restaurant, roof garden, and flamingo pools and it became the meeting place for the international jet set as well as the quintessential embodiment of a new lifestyle. Yet by 1976 it was all over. Biba's founder, Barbara Hulanicki (b. 1938) was unable to prevent its closure: she sold the rights to the name in 1970. She now lives in New York with her husband where her futuristic new label Fitz & Fitz can be seen in the Flat Iron district. Her autobiography, *From A to Biba*, was published in 1981.

Vivienne Westwood

The Beatles broke up in 1970, thereby finally sounding the death-knell for basin haircuts, the beatnik look, and *Avengers* chic. Flower power and hippies were the look of the early 1970s, but things had gone further in Britain, where the first punk rockers had already started to shamble along London's Kings Road: bands like the Sex Pistols, the Clash, and The Exploited provided the music for a revolutionary street style which aimed to create antifashion and come as a slap in the face to good taste.

Traditional features of feminine seduction such as netting, animal prints, and black leather were torn, cut, and adorned with safety pins. Vinyl, fetish, and bondage looks saw the light of day for the first time, and women discovered a new sense of freedom. Beyond the reach of society's rules and dress codes, female punks developed and redefined their roles, a new aesthetic, and a language free of inhibitions. Bondage pants were complemented by skintight T-shirts decorated with zip fasteners above each breast and erotic texts – such as "His hand cupped her breast as he pressed her against the wall ...": these were outrageous bestsellers at Sex, the West End boutique opened by Vivienne Westwood in 1970.

Designer Vivienne Westwood was born in 1941 in Glossop, Derbyshire, and had a much greater influence on fashion than most people would suspect. John Fairchild, media guru and publisher of the American *Womenswear Daily*, counts her among the six most creative talents of the century. Part of this must surely be her visionary ability to jettison a trend before it has become banal.

In the late 1970s, Vivienne Westwood dropped the safety pins and began to work on the archeology of historic silhouettes. Whether *fin-de-siècle* grandeur or rococo decadence, Westwood continues to combine traditional methods with modernity and undisguised irony. Each year, inventions like the collapsible crinoline, known as a Mini-Crini, the bottom cage, the fetish platform shoe, and the twin set and pearls for men, have caused fashion shock waves – only to reappear in a bowdlerized form in the collections of other designers.

An easy relationship to sex seems to run in the family: Joseph Corre, Westwood's son by musician Malcolm McLaren, owns the hottest lingerie shop in London: Agent Provocateur, in Soho's Broadwick Street. She is constantly threatened with financial ruin, but her creative reputation has gained her many honors, among them a guest professorship at Vienna's School of Applied Arts. "The Queen really did inspire me for a while" is how she explains her choice of an imperial orb as company logo.

Westwood was awarded the OBE in 1992. She attended the tea party at Buckingham Palace without a slip, like Sharon Stone in *Basic Instinct*. The Queen, head of a conservative fashion community, was "not amused."

Right:
Prêt-à-porter fall/winter
1995/96 collection.

Previous pages:
Fall/winter collections:
1996/97 (left) and 1995/96
(*right*).

ondon-born Naomi Campbell shows Westwood, fall/winter 995/96 collection.

The eccentric model Kirsten McMenany appears sweet and charming in this 1996 prêt-à-porter dress.

Platform soles 10 inches high: small wonder that even a professional like Naomi Campbell could not remain upright.

fall/winter 1995/96 collection: the main inspiration for this collection was baroque costume, men's as well as women's.

A last-minute adjustment before the 1997/98 show. The collar is reminiscent of priestly attire.

The show is over: Vivienne Westwood in person after the summer shows of 1999.

The designer re-created
historic paintings for her
Five Centuries Ago collection
of 1997/98.

Zandra Rhodes

Zandra Rhodes began by designing exotic and crinolined robes for her own wardrobe: they subsequently became highly sought after among artists and partygoers. Her designs are still very popular in Britain, Japan, and the United States, but less so in Paris and Rome, the centers of classic fashion.

Zandra Rhodes (b. 1940) has always been adept at defending her territory. In 1967, dissatisfied with the design and quality of conventional fabrics, this trained textiles designer and artist bought a share in the Fulham Clothes Shop, where she showed extravaganzas designed and printed by herself.

She set up on her own in 1970 after her caftans, organza jackets, house dresses, and silk scarves had been highly praised and her work subsequently published by leading fashion magazines. Major American department stores ordered her creations and this remains her main market. A smart businesswoman, she has always produced couture as well as ready-to-wear collections.

Zandra Rhodes's personal style has barely changed in decades: she likes to present herself as a happy fusion of Peter Pan and Ziggy Stardust, with overstated make-up, bejeweled face, and spacey hairstyles in luminous colors.

However, her delicate pastel-hued silk dresses eschew shocking effects and are – then as now – decorated with lively patterns, jagged and tasseled borders, appliquéd flowers, and beads.

Jasper Conran

The economic boom, combined with a strong dollar and the emergence of a neo-rich Arabic clientele, triggered an unexpected couture upswing in the 1980s. The ladies of the jet set traversed the world to the rhythm of sumptuous charity galas where they would be seen in made-to-measure chic.

London's exclusive fashion houses had hoped that Margaret Thatcher's election victory in 1979 would bring about a return to the lifestyle of the landed gentry and thus to their dress codes. In reality, however, they profited from the support of Lady Diana Spencer. The whole world was in love with the Princess of Wales and eager to see her fashion choices. Lady Di wore clothes by Jasper Conran, Rifat Ozbek, Anouska Hempel, Arabella Pollen, Bruce Oldfield, Amanda Wakely, and Catherine Walker. Yet only the first three were

able to capitalize on the fame that this brought them. Jasper Conran (b. 1959) is the son of British design czar Sir Terence Conran. Jasper studied at Parsons School of Art and Design in New York and subsequently worked for Fiorucci and Henri Bendel before showing the first collection under his own name in 1978. Jasper Conran rejects ostentation, abhors passing trends and cheap effects, and likes to reissue his bestsellers year after year with only a few subtle variations.

About his timeless cocktail dresses and figure-hugging jackets Mary Quant says: "Damn clever. He makes elegance seem just that little bit dangerous." In 1990 the society darling began designing theater and ballet costumes: "This keeps me earthed, I don't have to worry whether the designs sell or not, and I can develop freely."

Jasper Conran provides a contrasting program to the colorful opulence of Zandra Rhodes with his severe, figure-hugging creations, like these two coats from his fall/ winter 1997/98 collection (*below, left and center*). His most famous client was Princess Diana (*below right*).

Katherine Hamnet

Fashion with a message: political T-shirts – made from environmentally friendly materials – made Katherine Hamnet famous. Even Margaret Thatcher could not avoid taking notice of her (*opposite*). In 1989 the politicized designer presented her first collection in Paris, but in 1994 her show was in Milan.

Because of her radical political views and daring statements, Katherine Hamnet was an unsuitable protégée for Princess Diana. Born in 1948, this graduate of St Martin's School of Art and Design created her own publicity. A committed ecologist, she founded her own company in 1979 and is still its director today. She was the first to promote torn jeans and increased her notoriety with the political T-shirts of her 1984 "Choose Life" collection.

Widely talked-about slogans like "Stop Acid Rain" and "58% don't want Pershing" were reminiscent of fashion's potential for provocation, which had disappeared in the late 1970s. Margaret Thatcher complained that "We don't have Pershings, we have Cruise Missile," but Hamnet's reputation as a rebel was made. From then on her relaxed jeans style and sequined stretch evening dresses were taken as an expression of sex, rock, and opposition.

Rifat Ozbek

Rifat Ozbek was born in Istanbul in 1954. He too went on to study at St Martin's School of Art and Design in London. This self-declared anthropologist of fashion combined East and West in his début collection of 1984 – long before ethno-chic finally turned into a megatrend. Ozbek now shows his collections in Milan, where his new manufacturer Aeffe took him in 1991. He combines strong colors and patterns with inspirations from belly dancers, Russian military uniforms, Gypsy skirts, and Native American tribes. "I want to urbanize the ethnic," he says. "My clothes should take the wearer on a journey, open new horizons, and encourage new experiments. Above all, they should be sexy." Ozbek's most sensational collection was his least typical: his spring/summer 1990 collection was entirely white, and introduced an era of spiritual minimalism which is only now being fully felt and which many of his colleagues have imitated.

Opposite:
A combination of military uniform and cowboy boots: the mermaid's train directs the gaze to the legs.

Below left:
Despite the lace, frills and embroidery, Rifat Ozbek's designs are still modern and simple.

Below right:
Less ethnic, more futuristic: despite their mixture of materials and styles, Ozbek's creations are always harmonious.

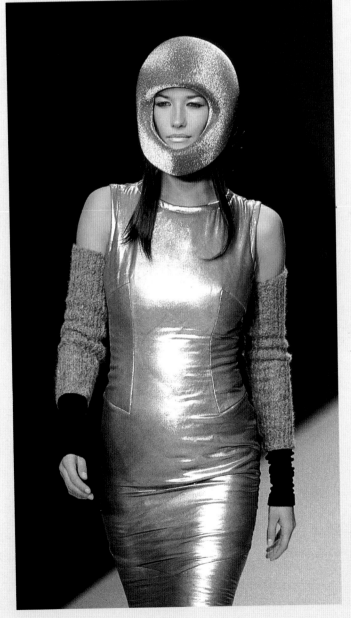

John Galliano

Below left:
Galliano likes to stage-manage everything, including his own appearances. Dressed in a Union Jack jacket, he wears a fur-lined hat from the workshop of his favorite supplier Philip Treacy.

Below center:
A classic suit with a pleated skirt à la Galliano, 1997/98.

Below right:
A friend, even in need: Kate Moss in a Galliano tutu from his 1996 collection.

Throughout the 1980s, fashion designers like Paul Smith, Bella Freud, Joseph Ettedgui, John Richmond, Helen Storey, and Red or Dead engaged in a guerrilla war against the regulating powers of good taste and defended Britain's creative status. Yet more and more companies were showing their creations in Milan and Paris, and enthusiasm for London's fashion shows reached an all-time low in the early 1990s.

The metropolis of Brit-chic has finally awoken from its trance. Hat designer Philip Treacy exhibits his head sculptures around the world. Handbag designer Lulu Guinness is unable to keep up with demand for her unique handcrafted bags. Patrick Cox wannabe loafers sell as well as Guccis. Even the restrained Burberry check suddenly developed character and cult star talent in the spring/summer 1999 season.

The city owes this boom to a quartet of designers who all studied at St Martin's School of Art and Design and have since conquered three of the most famous couture houses in Paris as well as an exclusive knitwear house in New York.

The most famous member of this quartet is undoubtedly John Galliano. His biography reads like a thriller. He was born in 1961, the son of an English plumber and an Andalusian mother, in Gibraltar, where he lived until he was six. His first collection, shown in 1984, was an overwhelming success which prompted the exclusive fashion store Browns to buy every single item. From day one, Galliano established himself as the declared darling of both fashion scene and press. In 1990, fashion's bird of paradise first showed his "new glamour" in Paris.

In 1991, not for the first time, financial ruin threatened, forcing Galliano to put in a "creative intermission." Once again, salvation came in the way of support from loyal fashion scene friends. Kate Moss, for instance, modeled

John Galliano for Dior,
1999.

Opposite page:
Dogs match the dress, a pageboy provides contrast: an elegant evening gown from Galliano's 1998 *haute couture* collection for Dior.

Above left:
John Galliano's Glamorous Designs, 1999.

Above right:
In 1998 Kate Moss presented the designer's bold mix of styles.

In 1997, exactly 50 years after Christian Dior's explosive couture première, John Galliano presented his first collection for Dior, whose chief designer he had become. This was not without paying homage to the early czar of fashion, as demonstrated, for instance, by the pink gown's exuberant fullness (*above right*). Also in the fall/winter 1999/2000 collection, Dior's echoes, here the slim line, are unmistakable (*above left*).

for him free of charge, and Parisian designer Faycal Amor produced his collections between 1992 and 1995. Since being appointed creative director of Givenchy (1995) and then Dior (1996), Galliano has indulged in luxury and the delights of costly femininity.

Galliano's historically inspired gowns, which Yves Saint Laurent dismissed as mere circus spectacle, transform women into fairy-tale princesses. Hidden beneath the effervescence of spectacular details like waterfall necklines, plaitwork, and lace cascades are unexpectedly wearable and exquisitely cut dresses. His shows for Dior have been set in a castle, a train entering a station, a garden in the open air. However presented, they are

always more extravagant than all the other fashion shows.

Since Galliano has ensured that the Dior label causes a stir, his gowns have gained star appeal and have been seen at Oscar award ceremonies, the Cannes Film Festival, and Venice Biennale. A welcome side-effect is the fact that his perfume and accessories are selling as never before.

Opposite:
Décolleté creations for Galliano's first ready-to-wear collection for Dior, fall/winter 1997/98.

John Galliano

Alexander McQueen

Alexander McQueen was born in the East End of London in 1969. At the age of 22, he presented one of the most innovative and original final-year collections at St Martin's College of Art and Design. This earned him an apprenticeship with Anderson & Sheppard in Savile Row and then employment with the theater costumiers Bermans & Nathans. He subsequently worked for Koji Tatsuno in Tokyo as well as Romeo Gigli in Milan.

For his first collection in 1996 McQueen featured low-riding "bumster" pants and declared the bottom to be the new décolleté. McQueen loathes clichés like "East End boy conquers Savile Row" but he loves spectacular fashion shows. In September 1997 he presented the most technically complex runway show in fashion history.

In October of the same year McQueen was nominated Designer of the Year, and a few days later he was appointed John Galliano's successor at Givenchy. The renowned fashion journalist Suzy Menkes attested that his first collection for Givenchy showed "creative substance" as well as "masterly technique, cut, and subtle decoration" – undoubtedly the most important requirements of the season.

Typical of McQueen are impeccably cut garments whose seriousness is belied by the addition of provocative and erotic elements. Richard Martin, costume curator of the Metropolitan Museum of Art in New York, noted admiringly: "Of all the contemporary designers, the disrespectful Alexander McQueen has the most highly developed sense of optical and emotional proportions."

Following pages:
With regard to hair ornaments and head coverings, McQueen is full of new ideas.

Below:
Alexander McQueen's first two collections for Givenchy demonstrate that this *agent provocateur* of fashion has thoroughly learned his trade with some of London's most prestigious tailors: they are perfectly cut and always very wearable. Women may opt to add either butterflies and pagodas, or pearls and an elegant hat if they so wish.

Stella McCartney

Although Stella McCartney (b. 1971) may have profited from her famous parents' name, it is her immense talent which has brought about her triumph. Her final-year show at college made the headlines. Ex-Beatle Paul and his wife, photographer Linda McCartney, sat in the first row while their daughter's friends Naomi Campbell and Kate Moss performed on the catwalk. However, even without her VIP support, the public would have been convinced by Stella's début outfits.

It should be borne in mind that the 23-year-old Stella McCartney had already had an eight-year career in fashion by then. She began at the age of 15 with work experience at Christian Lacroix's Première Couture collection. The following year she began to work for Betty Jackson and *Vogue* magazine. After graduating, she was trained by Savile Row tailor Edward Sexton and in 1995 she set up on her own.

Two collections later, in the fall of 1996, she was summoned to Chloé in Paris, where she was asked to replace Karl Lagerfeld, the old master who had spent two relatively long periods as director. There were some who, purporting to be in the know, spread a rumor that the decision had been name-led. Instead, the house got exactly what it had hoped for: a young designer with fresh, unstuffy ideas and new variations on classic themes.

McCartney is another designer who likes to reinterpret the past, yet her results are more in keeping with the times than, for example, Galliano's. In her first show for Chloé in March 1997 she presented a series of *belle époque* corsets, romantic and sensuous dresses, cleverly cut lace petticoats, and delicate camisoles, and updated versions of Mary Quant's pantsuit.

Stella McCartney mixes Portobello flair with gentle Parisian femininity, and achieves commercial success. Chloé's turnover and reputation have grown to an extent which the house would not have dared to hope for in 1996.

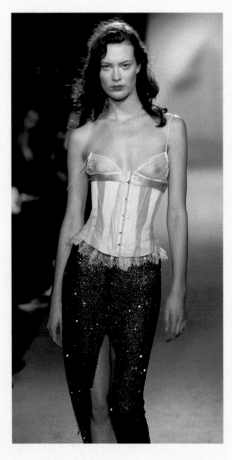

Hussein Chalayan

In its November 1997 issue the German magazine *Focus* had this to say about the most recent Paris fashion shows: "Although the French press derided McCartney's walking tablecloths, Galliano's prêt-à-ôter (un-dresses), and McQueen's look for 'Southfork ladies in sex bars,' the Voguettes' – jargon for *Vogue* girls – and other fashion victims' delight in the British trio was secure."

Soon afterward, the knitwear company TSE Cashmere called Hussein Chalayan to New York, where he received an enthusiastic welcome. Unlike the history-obsessed new Parisians, Hussein Chalayan has no interest in the past. Homages to past epochs or famous predecessors are not his style. "I do not concern myself with the history of fashion and am no fan of glossy magazines" is how Chalayan, who was born in Cyprus in 1970, apologizes for his blessed ignorance. "I reflect the body's function in the cultural context of architecture, science, or nature – and then attempt to translate my findings into clothing." Chalayan's working methods demand devotion to the cause: the models for his final-year show had to be injected against tetanus because the jackets, which had previously been buried, were covered with rust particles. His fall/winter 1997 collection dealt with the essentially British ritualizing of the weather. Then as now, his subtle allusions, for example glass bead embroidery to symbolize rain drops, have a tendency to reach the audience's subconscious. Furthermore, his globally valid fashion designs have a surprisingly intense visual power. In the spring of 1999, German *Vogue* celebrated Chalayan's floor-length mohair tube dresses for TSE, whose transparently woven giant turtlenecks can be draped liked veils. Only those who know that their designer counts in Turkish, thinks in English, and dreams in both languages, will understand the allusion to the yashmak of Islam – in the modern guise of figure-flatterers, they also directly confront the senses.

Simple and clear shapes are presented in Hussein Chalayan's fall/winter 1997/98 collection. His women may be completely covered or almost naked – either are possible with his collections: the Turkish-British couturier maintains that his work is the design of ideas, not fashion.

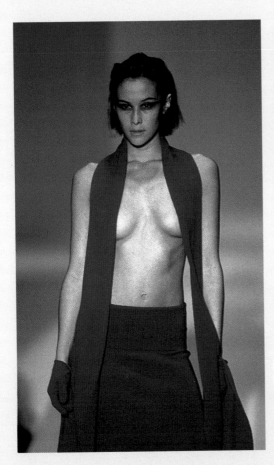

1980–1989

Dressed for success

1980–1989

How could it have been any different? After the Swinging Sixties and the wild 1970s, the 1980s lashed back: they retaliated against the hippies and their alternative lifestyles, against the refuseniks of wealth and power. At long last it had become hip to make money, dress well, and have no interest in politics.

The 1980s were a decade of contrasts. No decade had ever before witnessed such unscrupulous consumerism, while the gap between rich and poor grew ever wider. At last we were permitted openly to wallow in luxury: we had entered the "gimme decade," as Tom Wolfe so aptly baptized the 1980s. Ronald Reagan's election as president of the United States in 1979, followed in the same year by Margaret Thatcher taking power from the Labour Party in Great Britain, conclusively heralded change: the Western world had once again become conservative.

In fashion, everything seemed harmless at first. The wild period of punk became established, spiky hair

Neither power nor fashion could intimidate her: rubbing shoulders with the world's leaders, Europe's first woman head of government, Margaret Thatcher introduced the smart pinstripe suit of the career conscious woman to the international stage of politics.

and mohicans were absorbed by the general fashion repertoire, even the catwalk featured high-class punk fashions. However, back home in Britain, punks were back out of fashion. Most British women were already reveling in a fever of new romanticism: Vivienne Westwood's romantic pirate collection was highly successful, Boy George and Prince dressed in playful velvet outfits with ruffled shirts and fantasy suits. And in 1981, Lady Diana married her Prince Charles: her fairy-tale wedding gown was viewed and copied by millions, and women, whether young or old, dreamed of being just like Lady Di. Thanks to Diana, marital fidelity, considered bourgeois in the 1970s, was rehabilitated.

Yet, as the decade began to reveal its true colors, the romantic mood faded: the baby-boomers of the 1960s had grown up and wanted one thing above all else: to make money, as much money as possible, as quickly as possible and without considering others. Trade unions and

Opposite:
Nobody could surpass Grace Jones, the Jamaican model, singer, and actress, as a symbol of both 1970s disco-glamour and the power of 1980s woman. Yet she was an entirely artificial product. Jean-Paul Goude, the French image-maker, styled the athletic pop singer as an icon of aggressive female beauty; even her hairstyle and make-up were determined by him.

Previous page:
The décolleté is a sign: here comes a successful woman who can afford to wear an exclusive Saint Laurent couture garment, even during the day. There is no getting around the padded shoulders of the power-dressed woman in the 1980s!

Money, power, and sex: Like *Dallas*, *Dynasty* revolved around the three great themes of the 1980s. The outfits worn by "good" Krystle Carrington, with her blond, blow-dried hair, and by her no less attractive, albeit scheming, counterpart Alexis made both ladies world-famous and appealed to millions of television viewers, who saw it as the embodiment of luxury.

Yves Saint Laurent's sunflower jacket proves that 1980s fashion could be rich and sumptuous without degenerating into the glamorous style of the nouveaux riches. The embroidery, inspired by van Gogh's famous sunflower paintings, was produced by Lesage.

other mutual societies ceased to be of interest to anyone.

The watchword was "work hard and play hard," meaning that all the money was spent as quickly as it was earned. The real in-crowd worked a 12-hour day and partied through the night. A major element of the career ladder was appropriate clothing, "dress for success" being a mantra which Nancy Reagan and Margaret Thatcher taught the world.

The main symbol of the 1980s was the yuppie (young urban professional). Yuppies wore suits and ties without having to fear that they might look like their fathers. For many people this came as welcome liberation from the "casual terror" of the 1970s. Yuppies preferred to be single and childless, worked

on the stock exchange, or in law, or had media careers. The male yuppie dressed to conform with the so-called power look: double-breasted suits by Armani, Hugo Boss, or Ralph Lauren with heavy padding at the shoulders, as seen in the television series *Miami Vice*, were *de rigueur*. This uniform personified ambition and drive; to put it simply, it was the external manifestation of an inner attitude to life. Although designers like Armani gave the male silhouette greater masculinity by inserting shoulder pads, the same designers also ensured that men's fashion became more feminine overall. Soft, flowing fabrics, narrow leather ties, colorful shoes, all of these could now be worn by men. Incidentally, *Miami Vice* dished up everything the 1980s had to offer: sun and

Full steam ahead for confident women: the winter 1979/80 collection was both elegant and sophisticated. Long-sleeved, heavy woolen pullovers and cardigans over Yves Saint Laurent's asymmetric, slit skirt (*left*); Sonia Rykiel presented a knotted, wraparound skirt combined with a jacket and jumper (*right*).

sand, palm trees and pop music, cocktails and cocaine, designer suits, Ray-Bans, testosterone ... *Miami Vice* was unbelievably cool.

The female yuppie was as widespread as her male counterpart; for day, she wore highly tailored power suits with equally extreme shoulder padding, a short, tight skirt, and an elegant blouse. Alongside the basic power business suit, the pantsuit became a standard working outfit for female managers. The shoulder pads, borrowed from menswear, functioned to exude authority and power and to realize emancipatory ambitions: women were paid less than men, but slowly but surely they were beginning to play with the Old Boys, whether on the stock market or in any other business. On the music scene, singers like Grace

Jones and Annie Lennox, with their cropped hair, cold gaze, and angular bodies, showed men how to do it. Many women liked to balance this aggressive and masculine look with expensive underwear.

Evening wear also turned aggressive. Although it provided a total contrast to the muted colors of the office suit, the shoulders were again highly emphasized. Dresses came close to the hysterical: balloon skirts, puff sleeves, shiny fabrics in brash colors. Christian Lacroix was the decade's most desirable evening gown designer and widely regarded as the savior of *haute couture*. He wallowed in the neobaroque, and designed imaginative, scintillating gowns for career women who sought adventure after dark.

Television series like *Dallas* and *Dynasty* provided perfect objects for the study of 1980s fashion and lifestyle. J.R. Ewing, Bobby, Pamela and Sue Ellen

Collars tied with bows and high-heeled pumps add a feminine touch to Pierre Cardin's sporty, casual look of pants and blazer.

Taking his inspiration from ballerina skirts, Pierre Cardin created *haute couture* tutus for his 1988/89 collection.

Somewhere between a physician's sober white coat and futuristic astronaut: a coat-dress from the house of Balmain.

from *Dallas* showed just how nice it could be to have a lot of money and live on a luxurious ranch called Southfork. And yet, plagued by a series of vicissitudes, they also seemed to be sending out a message: money won't buy happiness, "It merely soothes the nerves," sang Rio Reiser, the German pop and rock star.

Yet in the 1980s this was not what yuppies wanted to hear. For them, problems of either a moral, ideological, or political nature just did not exist. And why should they? NATO had secured world peace in 1982. Glasnost and perestroika, the mid-1980s policies of Mikhail Gorbachev, the new people's hero, signaled the beginning of the end of the Cold War. The 1980s were a quiet period, not unlike the 1950s, and it was possible to concentrate on expanding the economy. A politically frustrated, aimless generation came of age, which in its youth had endured neither war, hunger, nor great parental repression. What could this generation possibly want to fight for, or – more importantly – against? So why not worship vile

Mammon? Harsh pragmatism became the order of the day and created severe pressure to succeed. After all, it is as easy to come down as it is to go up.

Yuppies lived life on expense accounts, with no sense of responsibility. Three-star restaurants, five-star hotels, flights to any destination became a habit – as long as it was expensive. Shopping replaced rest as a form of relaxation, and short-lived affairs and uninhibited sex replaced long-term relationships. Pop icon Madonna sang the 1980s hymn: "I am a material girl, and I am living in a material world."

Partying and working were not the only excesses. The fitness craze also continued to grow: body-building and aerobics were practically mandatory for both men and women, and again women tried to achieve as masculine a shape as possible, except with regard to bosoms, which were back in fashion. Calvin

Opposite:
Wicked, tough, and a woman to the core: this is how Madonna presented herself in her 1990 Blonde Ambition concerts. The bustier was specially created for the tour by Jean Paul Gaultier.

Klein crowned these ambitions by designing men's underpants for women. They were an instant bestseller.

What is masculine, what feminine? Pop stars like Prince, Michael Jackson, and Boy George exemplified the transformation of male gender identity during the 1980s. The feminine look of heavy make-up, sexy clothes, and long, perfectly groomed hair demonstrated that vanity was by no means the preserve of women. Men began to think about their appearance. Suddenly, even underwear became important. In the 1980s this had to take the form of boxer shorts, preferably brightly colored and featuring a Disney or other cartoon character – a development which must also partly be ascribed to the growing self-confidence of gay men.

Thanks to the aerobics craze, Lycra became a popular fabric, and had a major effect on fashion design: outfits now emphasized body contours like never before. 1980s woman would go out on the streets wearing nothing more than a body and leggings. Azzedine Alaïa, the King of Stretch, as the Tunisian star designer is often described, is inspired by Lycra and other stretchable fabrics. His garments cling to the body and emphasize curves in a way which is reminiscent of Madeleine Vionnet, although in her case it was the sophisticated cut that did the trick.

The 1980s were the fashion designer's decade *par excellence*. However, where creativity was once the main ingredient of fashion design, marketing would now guarantee a designer's success. American designers were eventually granted access to the fashion scene's Mount Olympus because they were the first to understand this fact: Calvin Klein and Ralph Lauren became giants of marketing and made immense profits. However, the Italians also learned a

Azzedine Alaïa is famous for the unmistakable way in which he shapes and emphasizes the female form – thanks to a perfect cutting technique and flexible fabrics. The King of Stretch poses between pop star Grace Jones and his "muse" Linda Spierings.

lesson: Milan now attracted more and more attention, not least thanks to its parties and freebies.

Jean Paul Gaultier and Vivienne Westwood abhorred the tasteful business style of such yuppie designers as Giorgio Armani, Ralph Lauren, Calvin Klein, Claude Montana, and also Donna Karan. They were in search of exuberance, eccentricity, and extravagance and wallowed in colors, shapes, and incongruities of style. Westwood put her models in mini-crinolines, Gaultier dressed his male models in skirts and adorned Madonna with cosmic conical breasts. And what would have become of the 1980s without Madonna? Each year she astounded her audience with a new image, and Madonna fans had difficulties in keeping up with her. There was a time when divas would cultivate a very particular, individual style, but Madonna demonstrated that styling alone sufficed. The popular culture of the

The large floral pattern is typically Kenzo. It looks as if a new generation of flower children has been born. This dress dates from 1987.

Kenzo 1985/86. The Japanese couturier repeatedly found inspiration in folk and national costume.

1980s was shaped by Madonna more than by anyone else, and no other has had such an intense relationship with fashion. She has artfully made the hottest fashion labels her own, including Dolce & Gabbana and Versace. She has an unerring nose for the season's trends, and seduces her audience of millions with every new identity. High-class prostitute, street girl, Marilyn Monroe diva-look, from whore to saint, Madonna has demonstrated that a woman can be every woman by utilizing the appropriate look.

During the course of the decade, the other megastar of the 1980s, Michael Jackson, ousted his greatest competitor, Prince – undoubtedly the better musician – and fled further and further into a world of fairy-tale fantasy. This also fits in well with the overall trend: *Star Wars* was a box office hit; adventure movies boomed, as did dance movies like *Flash Dance*, *Dirty Dancing*, and *Fame*. Problems had to be avoided at all costs, having fun was prime, and after us the deluge! This extreme escapism was partly a consequence of the exciting, taxing, thoroughly committed, political 1970s.

A major contrast to the Western fashion scene in the 1980s originated in the Far East. The most original and creative ideas hailed from Japan, from Yohji Yamamoto, Issey Miyake, and most notably Rei Kawakubo. These designers were like a cleansing

A creation which reveals its beauty not by accentuating the body but by the movement of the fabric: Issey Miyake 1983.

Rei Kawakubo's multilayered, sacklike garments provided a stark contrast to the Western tradition: Comme des Garçons 1984/85.

agent on the tastelessness and excesses of their British, American, French, and Italian counterparts. Their principles were asceticism and deconstructivism, with which they questioned every previously accepted norm. Japanese fashion was oversized and sacklike, consciously concealing the body instead of putting it center stage. This was unique, new, unheard of in the history of fashion. A fashion journalist consequently complained, "Why should we pour all our money into health and fitness if we end up looking like tramps?"

Rei Kawakubo of Comme des Garçons hid the female form under layers of fabric. Her geometric garments negated traditional Western ideas of fashion. They were not decorative and neither did

they flatter the female body. Her unspectacular and functional garments seemed shockingly radical. And yet this outsider managed to cause a real stir: she made fashion for the kind of woman who did not even exist ten years before – a woman who wanted to demonstrate her personal and financial independence.

Although Comme des Garçons' early fashion shows were heavily criticized, intellectuals, artists, and media types were rapidly won over. Another first: artists like Dennis Hopper, Robert Rauschenberg, and Francesco Clemente stepped on to the catwalk for Comme des Garçons; Comme des Garçons shops were designed to look like art galleries, and artists like Cindy Sherman used them as spaces to exhibit

Wir danken Fiore Crespi für ihren 10 jährigen Einsatz im Kampf gegen AIDS.

Photo: Platon   Art:Moschino

" Die Anzahl der mit HIV
infizierten Menschen in der
Welt steigt täglich.
Durch den Gebrauch eines
Präservatis wird eine
Infizierung verhindert. Noch
immer besteht die AIDS - Gefahr
darin, die Krankheit zu ignorieren. "

J.C. CHERMANN
Direktor der Forschung
Französisch Nationales Gesundheits-und
Medizinisches Forschungsinstitut.
Forschungseinheit für Retrovirus und
Assoziierte Krankheiten.

MOSCHINO

their work. Thus the old dream of every fashion designer finally came true: fashion and art entered into a real symbiosis.

If anyone thought that the yuppies and their money had been alone in shaping the 1980s, they would be mistaken. Once again youth culture bore a great deal of responsibility, except this time the youth culture was not white, but black. The black power movement's slogan of the 1960s had regained relevance: but in the apolitical decade of the 1980s, "black is beautiful" referred mainly to black music and fashion. The trend clearly manifested itself in 1981. The 1980s were going to be the

Run DMC only rapped in Adidas: thanks to them, the striped trainer experienced an unexpected global comeback in the mid-1980s. Young people's choice of consumer fetishes appeared indiscriminate, thereby giving rise to the trend scout.

decade of black electro-beat dance music: hip-hop, rap, and house music by black bands like Grandmaster Flash, Run DMC, and Public Enemy. In New York and Los Angeles, 1970s discos were where street fashion and street sounds as well as hip-hop developed. A new dance style emerged: break dancing. Skillful break-dancing required comfortable clothes: sportswear and, naturally, trainers. In the spirit of 1980s label fetishism, hip-hoppers had to have Reebok, Nike, and above all Adidas. Run DMC rapped in 1985: "My Adidas and me, close as can be, we make a mean team, my Adidas and me." When the audience at a Run DMC rap concert in Madison Square Garden were asked who among them was wearing Adidas trainers, 20,000 young fans waved their Adidas trainers in the air.

Opposite:
Sequins are replaced with red ribbons and condoms in every imaginable shape and color: Franco Moschino, who died of Aids in 1994, frequently used his designs as an antidote to silence and to warn against the dangers of the virus.

This meant salvation for the south German sportswear company. It is almost inconceivable now that Adidas came close to ruin and was saved by the fiendishly clever idea of marketing a basketball shoe as the number one trainer, and especially in the United States.

Break dancing conquered the world. Young people with ghetto blasters practiced acrobatic dance moves on the street, and there were national and international break dancing competitions. The angular sound and jerky hip-hop dance movements mirrored their aggressive, tough lifestyle, and the constraints and demands of black street life. The homeboy style of the black ghetto boys was made up of baggy pants, trainers, and baseball caps. These were worn with heavy necklaces and such emblematic pendants as Mercedes car badges. White youth quickly caught on to these outfits and tried to better the original. In 1984 this style found entry in the European fashion scene when Vivienne Westwood – who else? – designed her first trainer. Many of her colleagues would still be following her lead in the 1990s.

House music, another black music style which became established in the mid-1980s, was also rooted in 1970s disco music, while being equally influenced by jazz and Latin music. House artists liked to wear suits à la *Miami Vice*. Acid house, a British variation of house music, found its fashion expression in fluorescent tops made of a mix of fabrics and African prints, and Lycra sportswear which harked back to the 1960s. Although many of these fashion excesses never penetrated as far as *haute couture*, they, like the Japanese designers, had a lasting influence on fashion. The 1980s obsession with dance and sport and with their stars finally made the link between music and fashion closer than ever before.

By 1985, however, the party mood began to feel more muted. The World Health Organization officially declared Aids an epidemic. This was a rude awakening for many people, because sexual freedom, whether expressed in fashion, pop music, or society, had become a way of life. The gay movement had just achieved an unprecedented degree of self-confidence. Aids changed almost everything, and highlighted the limitations of 1980s hedonism. In some people this induced a sense of spiteful vindication. The megasuccess of *Fatal Attraction* demonstrated most impressively the American talent for using society's growing fear of Aids for the propaganda purposes of morally puritanical ideas. The movie grossed millions and transmitted the message: don't have affairs, be monogamous, and nothing bad will happen to you. A further global threat was literally brewing in the sky. In 1986 an accident took place at the nuclear reactor at Chernobyl, in Ukraine. This caused worldwide alarm because, for the first time, the dangers of governmental nuclear policies were unambiguously brought home. In addition to this, reports on the growing hole in the ozone layer seemed to be issued on a daily basis. Sensitive people began to develop a new environmental awareness, although in truth this was probably not unconnected to the narcissistic health mania and body cult of the 1980s.

However, this new awareness did have an effect on fashion: during the late 1980s, supermodels Naomi Campbell, Claudia Schiffer, and Christy Turlington, and other celebrities staged protests against the fur trade and refused to wear fur on the catwalk.

There were other areas where people's self-absorption seemed to be on the decrease. On July 7, 1985, pop star Bob Geldorf organized Live Aid, the largest pop and rock concert ever to be televised globally. The proceeds went to the starving in Ethiopia and in other needy African countries.

The collapse of the stock market in 1987 heralded the demise of the yuppie cult and the culture of luxury. American author Brett Easton provided a perverse interpretation of the hedonistic lifestyle of the 1980s in his book *American Psycho*: he postulated a world of labels and joyless luxury where a Wall Street stockbroker's isolation and spiritual sterility cause him to get his kicks from staging the killing and cruel butchering of people.

The end of the decade also brought political turbulence: in Germany, the Berlin Wall, powerful symbol of the Cold War between East and West, fell, and Soviet world power dissolved. At the end of the decade all doors seemed open, although it was not yet evident where they would be leading to.

Regina Schilling

Opposite:
No fur please. Like Cindy Crawford, many celebrity models supported animal protection campaigns. Their highly publicized refusal to wear fur on the catwalk had a major effect on changing public awareness.

Christian Lacroix

If there is one couturier who embodies the spirit of the 1980s, it must be Christian Lacroix (b. 1951). No other has drawn on such plentiful resources as he, artistically spreading out the full wealth of his baroque imagination in an orgy of color and pattern, velvet and silk, lace and embroidery, frills and drapes, decorations and jewels. Society journalist Julie Baumgold wrote after Lacroix's American début in 1987: "Garments of such brilliance and challenging luxury have probably not been worn since the 18th century when French aristocrats were taken on carts rattling across the paving stones to the guillotine." Lacroix did not escape punishment either. He was accused by many of manufacturing ostentatious kitsch, which was typical for the excesses of the decade.

His critics overlooked the fact that the highly trained Lacroix is a master of his trade. More importantly, he possesses wit and daring. Only conservative couture salons rely solely on opulence; in Lacroix one finds the impudence of the punk rocker. Like the artists of the street he mixes whatever catches his eye and pleases him. And since he sees more and knows more than the standard punk, his results are often shockingly sumptuous and colorful. But why should this be a sin? Fashion may as well be dead without lightness of touch. Indeed, *haute couture* already appeared to be dead by the early 1980s, when Lacroix breathed new life into it.

Lacroix was born in the south of France. His original aim had been to follow his fine art degree with a career as a curator, but when he met his wife Françoise, whom he still admires for her talent for fashionable improvisation, he realized that he had to follow another path. He trained with Hermès and at the imperial court in Tokyo. In 1981 he took over couture at the traditional house of Patou, where he caused astonishment and delight with his alarming colors, brash accessories and, naturally, the infamous pouf, the puffed-up short balloon skirt which gave not two hoots about wearability but did promise a great deal of fun.

In 1987, with the financial backing of the luxury goods group LVMH, Lacroix was able to open his own couture house, the first new couture house to open since Yves Saint Laurent's in 1962. Lacroix's first show was cheered like no other since Dior or Saint Laurent's a quarter of a century before. He was twice awarded the highly coveted Golden Thimble, once for a collection that he created for Patou, and the next for the second of his own collections. That same year, Lacroix went to New York a celebrated prince of fashion. However, the presentation of his luxurious collection coincided with the collapse of the stock market. This was an opportunity for many people to distance themselves from ostentatious displays of magnificence.

Lacroix presented his ready-to-wear collection in 1988, to which he added a sportswear line entitled Bazar in 1994. Yet the heart of his work remains as ever his lavish *haute couture*, about which *Detail* magazine wrote that it "brings a smile to all our faces."

Maestro and model in 1987 (*left*), studying *W* magazine on the front page of which is Marie, dressed in a Lacroix dress. The bodice and skirt of this dress (*right*) are reminiscent of the pouf, minus the necessary padding underneath.

Opposite:
The pouf, a thigh-high balloon skirt, caused a furore and catapulted Lacroix to international stardom. Here it is modeled by the designer's favorite model, Marie, in 1987.

"Down with the corset" was the protest slogan at the start of the 20th century. At its end, Lacroix sent it back to the *haute couture* catwalk in every variation and color imaginable. Yet it has now become an item of outerwear in its own right, to be combined with a wide range of skirts featuring the playful mix of styles and patterns for which the French designer is so well known.

Azzedine Alaïa

ALAÏA PARIS

Of the two slogans which governed '80s fashion, "dress for success" and "dress to kill," Christian Lacroix should be regarded as the leader of the first and Azzedine Alaïa (b. 1940) as the master of the second. Naturally such simplification fails to do justice to either of them, and it took a particularly long time for Alaïa's important contribution to couture to be recognized. His garments were far too sexy for anyone to be interested in their fabric or the technique of the cut. All eyes were on the woman who wore them. And she would have sensed with every step and move what Alaïa's clothes were doing for her. He developed the Lycra stretch which, acting as an allover body corset, shaped everything while allowing freedom of movement. However, the real secret lay in his cut, which has been thoroughly analyzed and boundlessly admired by experts like German designer Natalie Acatrini: "The man is a genius!" she recognized at a time when most people were underestimating the

diminutive Tunisian. His spiral seams shape and elongate the legs, lift the buttocks, hold the waist, and support the bosom. Alaïa, who had originally intended to become a sculptor, gained this mastery by taking apart old garments by Madeleine Vionnet and Balenciaga and then reconstructing them. Although he worked for Laroche for a while after arriving in Paris at the age of 17, most of what he knows he has taught himself. And he has always personally sewn garments for his private clients, among them Greta Garbo, Arletty, and poet Louise de Vilmorin. He did not show publicly until 1981. Alaïa does not obey the rules of prêt-à-porter, whereby a new collection is served up every six months; he stages his shows when he is ready, and his clients are happy to wait for him, since his garments, which he frequently still cuts and sews himself, make a goddess of any woman.

Tina Turner also knew how to use the couturier's cutting talent to her advantage and that of her 1980s comeback (*below left*).
A narrow waist and boyish hips are emphasized by the contrasting batwing sleeves (*below right*).

Romeo Gigli

Born in 1949, the Italian Romeo Gigli has always followed his instincts. As a poet of design, he sought the flower of romanticism while the rest of the world was busy pursuing "sex" and "success."

Over pencil-narrow pants or skirts, his placid women wear gold-threaded blouses with cup-like collars which perfectly frame their Madonna-like faces. Most beautiful of all, however, are his coats: protective mantles of sumptuous velvet, so richly embroidered that they look as if the treasure chests of ancient kingdoms had been plundered to make them. Gigli found inspiration for his collections, which frequently feature ethnic motifs, on his journeys to China, Egypt, and South America. He loves the muted but rich colors of old paintings and uses printed and processed velvet in a way which is reminiscent of Fortuny.

Severity is not his thing, as is amply demonstrated by these ready-to-wear examples. Romeo Gigli does not create for the powerful woman of the 1980s but for a forgotten romantic.

Opposite, main picture:
The skirt of this outfit folds itself around the body like a second shape, a cocoon – a silhouette which did not put the body on show and satisfied sensitive women's need for protection.

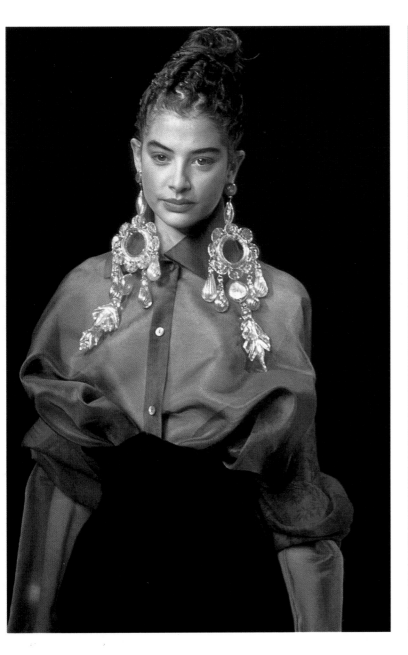

Rei Kawakubo

Opposite:
The only thing worth showing is what has never been seen before. This is Rei Kawakubo's philosophy, and why the Japanese designer's 1997 collection was fitted with "hunchbacks." We are now accustomed to such displaced proportions; new bag designs similarly distort the silhouette.

COMME des GARÇONS
HOMME PLUS

A shock to the wealthy 1980s was brought about by the emergence of Japanese designers whose garments appeared poor, formless, and even shabby. Rei Kawakubo (b. 1942), the real person behind the label Comme des Garçons, was slated by the press after her first Paris show in 1981: it was said that her cavalcade looked like a funeral procession after a nuclear attack. Western women found it difficult to understand Kawakubo's Asian sense of fashion. "I don't find revealing clothes sexy," she said and showed instead asymmetrical, loose, angular long robes in somber colors. With her clothes, she said, women did not need long hair and a large bosom to feel feminine.

Kawakubo was educated in Tokyo and follows a Japanese aesthetic which traditionally values unevenness and imperfection as signifiers of life. It was therefore a matter of course for her to present a tattered jumper as a "ace

pullover." This controversial piece now hangs in a museum in London, but initially Kawakubo had to explain that the art was inherent in teaching a machine, that would normally knit perfectly, that it should drop a stitch every now and then, exactly as human hands would.

Fashion journalist Suzy Menkes wrote after the Comme des Garçons show in 1983: "My head feels drawn toward the Japanese ... but the French can dress my body." In 1997 Kawakubo spectacularly questioned the body's proportions by padding it in "impossible" places, thus effecting a deformed appearance that seemed absurd and monstrous, as if the models were hunchbacked. Naturally the padding was removable and what remained were beautifully made garments, as always with Kawakubo – but there lingered a period of thinking about the body and how it should be presented.

Kawakubo's early collections featured the colors gray, beige, and mainly black. This example (*below left*) is from 1987.
When the designer, who wears only black herself, added the first touch of color to her 1989 collection there was quite a stir in the world of fashion (*below right*).

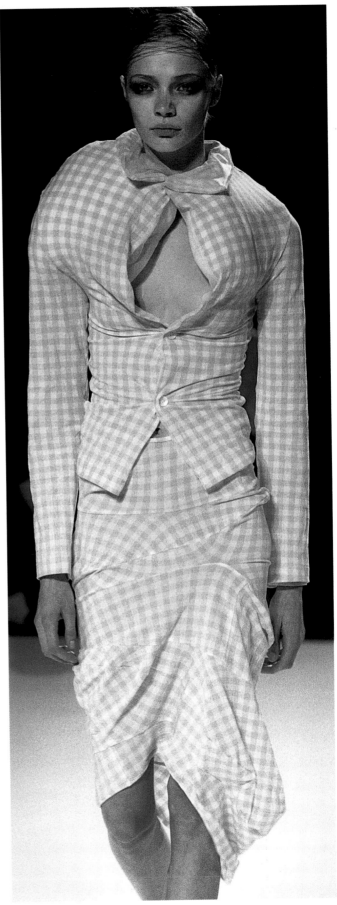

Yohji Yamamoto

Rei Kawakubo's compatriot Yohji Yamamoto (b. 1943) was a major contributor to the convulsions that shook Western fashion. The women he sent on to the catwalk, for the first time in 1981, all seemed to hail from a strange and very serious world: not Japanese, not European, perhaps poets from another star. Initially they wore several layers of loose, dark garments, as if to protect themselves from the cold wind which blew in from the fashion press. Yet within five years the critics finally understood that the Japanese had triggered a gentle revolution which offered an alternative to the body's exposure. The tirades of hate turned into songs of praise. And Yamamoto's garments became softer, even hinted at a waist sometimes, or featured a dash of color. Since then, the

qualified lawyer and fashion designer has become well established in both the West and the East, and he has been the recipient of many honors. In 1989 Wim Wenders made a movie about him entitled *Notebook on Cities and Clothes*, and he has worn nothing but Yamamoto ever since – as do Karl Lagerfeld, architect Jean Nouvel, and dancer Pina Bausch. Naturally they have all sworn an oath of allegiance to black, the antifashion color which the Japanese designers established during the brightly colored 1980s and which has not left fashion since, and neither has the influence of the Japanese been interrupted. In the meantime Yamamoto has achieved cult status. His once severe and somber designs are becoming ever more cheerful; his shows are turning into poetic dramas, the master's touch becoming lighter.

Opposite:
His clothes are not meant to provide a second skin; he aims to create more space for movement, and to achieve this Yohji Yamamoto likes to cut the material against the weave.

Below, left and right:
Yamamoto's silhouette is sometimes sculptural, other times flowing. For the Japanese designer who is regarded as a master of cutting, the character of the fabric is the determinant factor. Rigid material inspires him to angular designs, flowing fabric to round and softly falling forms.

The Antwerp Six

Below, left to right:
For his fall/winter 1996/97 collection, Walter van Beirendonck took himself on to the catwalk. The designer even presents his creations on the Internet (http://www.walt.de).

Dries van Noten incorporates the subtle colors of the Middle East, which he so loves into Western fashion.

Despite critical acclaim, Josephus Melchior Thimister has temporarily frozen his couture line and is instead designing ready-made garments for Genny.

Paris had barely learned to appreciate the Japanese fashion invasion when the next revolution announced itself from distant London in 1985: "The Antwerp Six" – Ann Demeulemeester, Dries van Noten, Martin Margiela, Josephus Melchior Thimister, Dirk Bikkemberg, and Walter van Beirendonck – jointly introduced their early designs and landed themselves a reputation as wild young things. With their aesthetic of the incomplete, they have taken the avant-garde scepter from the Japanese and carried it into the 1990s. Apart from the fact that they are all graduates of the demanding Antwerp Academy, they are connected only by their interest in individual pieces, with which people can do whatever they like: "We are not interested in creating an entire look," declares Dries van Noten (b. 1958), who was the first member of the gang to go it alone in Antwerp back in 1985. He loves both the Middle East and Far East – embroidery, scarves, wraparound skirts worn over pants, diaphanous sarongs and jackets. In 1985 Martin Margiela (b. 1957) went to Paris, where he spent three years as an assistant to Gaultier and subsequently started up on his own. The man who never gives interviews and who will not allow photographs of himself, whose label is a simple piece of white fabric, rapidly rose to the status of cult designer with his deconstructed garments whose lining and seams can be worn on the outside, or whose shoulders, waist, or armholes may be displaced. This radical avant-gardist was appointed by the traditional house of Hermès in 1997 to take care of their women's collection. By then his former fellow student Ann Demeulemeester had also reached cult status, and the rest of the gang had also established themselves with their own collections.

Opposite:
Drunk with color: Dries van Noten is inspired by Indian saris and Indonesian sarongs, which serve as the prototypes for his own fabric designs.

The look of the decade

The 1980s brought about an "extended" look which was no longer limited to make-up, hair, and the usual accessories. In order to belong – that is, be a successful Yuppie – outward demonstrations of hard-earned spending power were of major importance.

A well-rounded, perfectly toned, and correctly nourished body had become the basis for beauty in the late 1970s. Now anyone rich or successful had to have daily sessions with their personal trainer, who would know what exercises were required to shape the body to make it slimmer in one place while adding bulk in another. Body-styling became more important than fitness. If exercise alone did not bring the desired effect, there was plastic surgery, which increased by 65 percent in the United States alone. Breast enlargements were popular again: many supermodels, like Iman and Stefanie Seymour, whose boyish figures had catapulted them to fame, now presented well-filled décolletés. In contrast, waists, stomachs, and thighs were slimmed down overnight thanks to liposuction – and some of the excess fat could frequently find itself recycled to augment lips that were thought too thin. Furthermore, new antiaging products with liposomes, ceramides, or collagen worked expensive wonders. And AHA (alpha-hydroxy acids) creams, originally developed to fight acne, proved to be veritable rejuvenators which carried off damage caused by the sun, such as age spots and fine wrinkles, with the outer layer of skin. Cosmetics and medicine thus began to work in close collaboration, and dermatologists became women's closest allies in matters of beauty.

With so much professional care, make-up was no longer needed to conceal

blemishes. "Makeup no longer serves to improve or rejuvenate," said Serge Lutens, one of the world's most famous make-up artists, who had worked for Dior before moving to Japanese cosmetics giant Shiseido in 1980. "We are now dealing with design, with emphasizing the expression of a face." He had a preference for strong colors but conceded that most women would only want to wear these in the evenings.

Working women continued to use only natural, transparent shades which allowed well-cared-for complexions to shine through. Loose powder to provide a matte finish was a definite must. Blending was very important: various shades of eye shadow, blusher, and foundation had to be blended so that the transitions between each became invisible. No more marks between face and neck! Yet suntans, whether natural or fake, were out of fashion; well-informed women knew at last that the sun's rays have nothing but an aging effect on the skin. They were also taught how to apply their make-up by professional make-up artists, who were no longer exclusive to the stars and models, but who for a fee had become willing to advise and work on ordinary women. A lasting solution was provided by permanent make-up: eyebrows, eyeliner, and lip liner could be tattooed in the color and shape of the wearer's choice, thus enabling her to present an early morning face which was already "on." The plant-based pigment gradually breaks down over several years. This sounds practical, but has one major disadvantage: fashion changes too quickly. A permanent black eyeliner with bright red lip liner looked hopelessly out of date by 1988, when Revlon brought out The Naked, its new line of makeup.

1900 lipstick invented. Now lipstick reinvented.

Beauty through natural forces. Spring water, hydro-spas, and beauty farms promised 1980s woman a fresh, healthy appearance. Elizabeth Arden responded to this trend with Lip Spa, a particularly moist lipstick.

Opposite:
It was goodbye to the skinny children of the 1960s and emaciated disco queens of the 1970s: natural beauty and health were now in favor. Star model Rosemary McGrotha embodied the ideal type: tall, sportive, and with a sparkling zest for life.

Left:
Big hair was brushed away from the face, lips were full, and an ample bosom signaled vitality. Supermodel Iman bares her breasts, which have been enlarged by implants in a "wildcat" dress by Versace.

CINDY SHERMAN

FLORENCE GRIFFITH-JOYNER

ISABELLE ADJANI

GLORIA VON THURN UND TAXIS

CHER

IVANKA & IVANA TRUMP

MERYL STREEP

MADONNA

Idols of the decade

There was a time when describing **Gloria von Thurn und Taxis** as "the craziest princess in the world" would have been a gross understatement. The princess from Regensburg provided weekly headlines for *Bunte*, the German gossip magazine, and filled the gossip columns of the world's gutter press, from the British *Sun* to *Paris Match*. Her exalted look was published around the world, especially her constantly changing hair creations, for which she hired the services of such star hairdressers as Gerhard Meir of Munich. The wife of Johannes, Prince of Thurn und Taxis proved that one could feel as much at home in the nightclubs of New York, London, and Saint-Tropez as in the royal houses of Europe. Gloria the party girl danced through the night with Mick Jagger and Michael Jackson without ever forgetting her strict, devoutly Catholic principles, which put the family above all else.

Nobody will ever forget the pop diva of the race track, American sprinter **Florence Griffith Joyner** (1960–98): with her supertight, fluorescent leotards and matching nail varnish and lip color, she not only made sport history but also fashion history. "How does she do it?" the world asked when, with flowing curls, 6-inch-long long nails, and huge earrings, she won silver for the 200-meter sprint during the 1984 Olympics in Los Angeles. A star was born who perfectly symbolized the body cult of the 1980s. Following her double gold at the 1988 Olympics in Seoul, Flojo adorned the front page of the glossy magazines for months before retiring from the sport under suspicion of doping. The "black gazelle" from the ghettos of Los Angeles died of a stroke. She was only 38 years old, and yet she revolutionized the world of sport like no other and proved that biceps and beauty are not mutually exclusive.

Madonna, aka Madonna Louise Veronica Ciccone, was not just the idol of the 1980s – and the 1990s – she is also the author of one of the greatest success stories of the century. She was born in 1958, one of eight children of an Italian immigrant family in Detroit. Her extreme ambition and famous exhibitionism were already apparent by the time she was a teenager obsessed with rising above the seething masses. From high-school showgirl she rapidly developed into a singing, dancing, and acting all-rounder. In 1983 *Holiday* earned her her first number one hit. A year later she was already selling more records than any other singer on the globe. Millions of women copied her style of extremely short, lingerie-inspired skirts and corsets combined with religious jewelry and badly bleached, permed hair. Even people who do not like her music have to admire her for her intelligence and business acumen and the million-dollar empire that she built: an edifice whose foundations, structure, and roof are all made of the same material, namely consummate self-promotion.

If there is one person in the world who could hold a candle to Madonna, it has to be **Cher** (b. 1946): who would have thought that the Californian girl with a background even more modest than that of Ms Ciccone's could ever surpass her 1965 hit *I Got You Babe* and the subsequent hype surrounding the Sonny and Cher duet? She did it in the early 1980s, first with internationally acclaimed movie roles (*Silkwood, The Mask, The Witches of Eastwick, Suspect*), and then with her resurrection as a rock singer. Her new style, clothes made of netting and leather straps which just covered nipples and pubis and an allover tattoo, encouraged many women over 40 to adopt an aggressive and sexy dress style. Cher made tattoos socially acceptable and was the first to stimulate public discussion of cosmetic surgery without ever commenting directly on speculations surrounding her allegedly innumerable operations.

The third in the coven of self-promoters is photographer **Cindy Sherman**, who was born in 1954 in New York. Her work, in which she acts as model, costume designer, director, and photographer, pays tribute exclusively to herself, and hit the art world like a bomb in the early 1980s. Her self-portraits achieved horrifying prices and proved again that success is merely a question of self-marketing.

The rise of **Meryl Streep** (b. 1949) to become one of the century's busiest and most popular actresses began in 1978 with her role as Inga Helms in the television drama *Holocaust*. A year later, the then 30-year-old received an Oscar for her portrayal of a combative mother in *Kramer versus Kramer*. Following the death from cancer of her partner John Cazale, she devoted herself exclusively to movies for many years and produced one cinematic success after the other. Despite criticism that her perfectionism could override realism, the public saw in Meryl Streep the embodiment of a fusion of gentleness and toughness. As Karen Blixen in *Out of Africa*, Streep inspired fashion designers from Paris to New York to adopt the safari look, one of the biggest fashion trends of the 1980s. The wife and mother of four has succeeded like no other Hollywood icon in protecting her private life from the pressures of stardom.

Ivana Trump (b. 1949), ex-wife of American property tycoon Donald Trump, whose fortune was at one point estimated to be $5½ billion, was admired by women in the 1980s not so much for her beauty as her social status. The former Czech ski racer fed the society gossip columns for a decade. Her backcombed, blond hair caused outrage, and her insatiable appetite for furs, jewels, and other luxury goods to compensate for an unhappy marriage reflected the thoughts of many women.

In 1990 a panel of French movie experts nominated **Isabelle Adjani** (b. 1955) the Best Actress of the 1980s, a decade in which the beautiful French actress has known both high points and troughs. After years when her beauty and talent made her the darling of the press, she became the victim of a campaign of defamation in 1986, when she was reported to be dying of Aids. As usual, Adjani fought – and won. Her public denial of the story, which was broadcast live on television, followed by her excellent performance as sculptress Camille Claudel in the movie of the same name, reestablished her status as the top French star. Isabelle Adjani is probably the only actress to be granted entry to the Comédie Française, the oldest theater group in Europe, at the age of 17 and with no training. This natural talent, discovered by the cinema while she was still at school, does not make life easy either for herself or others. Moods have repeatedly jeopardized Adjani's career, although they also earn her the sympathy of many women who would dearly love to be as rebellious as she is.

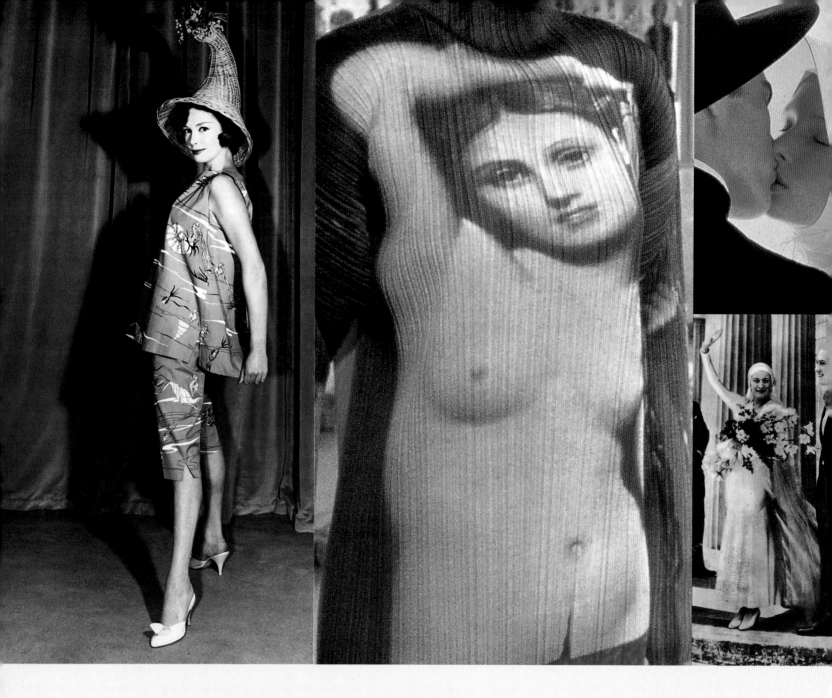

Italian fashion

Bonizza Giordani Aragno

During the immoderate 1980s, "Made in Italy" described a new, extravagant style linked primarily to the city of Milan. When, in the late 1970s, Italy's ready-to-wear proponents, the Alta Moda Pronta, decided to move to Milan, the northern Italian town grew immediately in international status to become the catalyst for fashionable trends and styles: tales are told of hordes of wealthy American ladies arriving from the United States with no luggage in order to stock up on clothes during their stay in Milan. Colorful and abundant luxury, entirely devoted to hedonism and featuring the consciously sensational, was once more the order of the day. Designers like Giorgio Armani, Gianni Versace, Gianfranco Ferré, Franco Moschino, and Dolce & Gabbana established

themselves on the international market and, together with known names like Krizia, Missoni, Fendi, Ferragamo, Biagiotti, and Valentino, they gave a boost to the Italian fashion industry.

The success of Italian designer fashions in the 1980s was due mainly to shrewd marketing strategies. One man in particular was responsible for Milan's victory over Rome, Italy's metropolis of *haute couture*, and Florence, where the Alta Moda Pronta houses had previously been at home: Beppe Modenese. In 1979, the successful Milanese businessman organized the first fashion show to be staged at Milan's exhibition center, featuring over 40 designers. The success story of Italian *haute couture*, or Alta Moda as it is patriotically

referred to, began in Rome after World War II. Thanks to its cosmopolitan atmosphere, the city was teeming with tourists; American cinema and fashion caused it to become a center of frenetic activity. Demand for quality products grew. Shoes by Salvatore Ferragamo – famous clients included Greta Garbo, Sophia Loren, and Audrey Hepburn – and leather goods by Gucci became fashionable, being regarded internationally as the embodiment of Italian elegance. Photographs of artists and movie stars arm in arm with Italian couturiers circulated in the international press.

Florence was the location for the first Alta Moda Pronta show, held in 1951. It was so successful that it soon had to be moved to the Palazzo Pitti, where it was staged from then on, being synchronized with the Parisian events calendar. It became the springboard for a new generation of fashion designers: among the ready-to-wear designs presented there in the 1950s were collections by Emilio Pucci, Krizia in 1964, and Missoni in 1966. In 1962, the Italians decided to follow the example of the Chambre Syndicale de la Haute Couture in Paris and founded the Camera Nazionale d'Alta Moda in Rome, with the aim of planning, coordinating, and distributing Alta Moda.

In the 1970s many of the established ateliers had been forced to close because they lacked marketing strategies: although their designs were conceptually very interesting, they were simply not fashionable. Ready-to-wear collections and the marketing of designer-label perfume, eyewear, leather goods, textiles, and furnishings gave a push to some of the economically deadbeat houses and helped them achieve international recognition in the 1980s. By the end of the 20th century, Italy had become established as a center of elegant high fashion. A new, young generation of designers would ensure the survival of the famous houses.

The design, elegance, and quality of Italian fashion have now completely displaced the old cliché that Italy was all about sun, pizza, and gigolo fashions.

Roberto Capucci

Roberto Capucci, who was born in Rome in 1930, was and remains in a class of his own. He regards himself as an artist who develops each garment like a sculpture in fabric – and sells the exclusive original without ever making any copies. In the late 1950s he became famous for the box line, which he continually developed and perfected. Capucci has never cared for trends and lines: like an artist, he pursues his ideas over decades. His garments could literally stand alone, and yet they are wearable. However, a woman wearing one of his dresses would need to have a strong personality as well as be rich enough to afford one, otherwise she might run the risk of being utterly dominated by his creation. Between 1962 and 1968 Capucci successfully served the fashion élite in Paris, but then he turned his back on commerce and returned to Rome. His first, albeit delayed, appearance was in 1951, on the occasion of the first fashion show to be held in Florence in the house of Marchese Gian Battista Giorgini. All the great fashion houses were represented, but Capucci was not wanted; he was thought too young. Yet the fashion artist did not have to forfeit his triumph. He showed his collection in the house of Giorgini on the day after the fashion show – and sold out completely.

Sorelle Fontana

The fashion house of the Fontana family was founded in 1907 in Parma, but the sisters Zoe (b. 1911), Micol (b. 1913), and Giovanna (b. 1915) moved it to Rome in the 1930s.

They won the custom of the Italian aristocracy and then, in the 1950s, of the cinema's international élite. When they made the dress for Linda Christian's wedding to Tyrone Power in 1949, the international news organizations declared them the first port of call for Hollywood stars. Elizabeth Taylor, Jane Mansfield, Ingrid Bergman, Joan Collins, Kim Novak, Ursula Andress, and Raquel Welch have all had the sisters in the Via Liguria dress them.

Nevertheless, their best client was Ava Gardner, who asked the house of Fontana to design not only her private wardrobe but also her movie costumes, the most famous being Sorelle Fontana's designs for *The Barefoot Princess*. Despite the Hollywood glamour, the Fontana sisters never lost sight of their connections to the discreet aristocracy, creating for instance Maria Pia von Savoyen's wedding gown.

In 1994, Micol, by then 80, described the house's unmistakable style as follows: "Our specialty is embroidery, the pattern of which we design ourselves. And we do not make fashion – we create elegance."

Ava Gardner at a fitting. Like this American actress, many celebrities had their clothes made by the Italian couture house of Fontana, including Margret Truman, daughter of United States president Harry S. Truman, who wore Fontana on her wedding day. One of the leading houses in the world of fashion in the 1950s, Fontana finally closed its doors in the 1980s.

Emilio Pucci (1914–92)

During the 1950s, a period when Italian fashion designers became known beyond their country's borders and were acknowledged as competitors of the French, Emilio Pucci was in the vanguard.

He is regarded as the inventor of the famous Capri pants which enjoyed a revival in the late 1990s. Without a pair of these, no fashion-conscious teenager in the 1950s would ever have considered going on the obligatory Italian vacation. Capri pants take their name from the fishermen of Capri, who used to roll up their trousers to avoid getting them wet.

Pucci, who founded his house in his family's Palazzo Pucci, initially found inspiration for his colorful designs in the ancient flags which he saw as a child at the annual Palio in Siena. In the 1960s Pucci dressed the international jet set in silk jersey dresses and pantsuits with psychedelic patterns in aggressive colors. His pajamas and housecoats were particularly popular among women who liked to wear them to casual parties.

His eccentricities had a revival in the late 1980s, when for a short while they became desirable collectors' items.

Opposite:
Psychedelic: silk jersey featuring colors and patterns that looked as if they had been designed during an LSD trip made Emilio Pucci one of the most desirable designers for the hippies deluxe of the 1960s. The ideas came from ancient flags.

Below:
The couturier's preference for color and unusual patterns was also reflected in his sport and leisurewear, with which Pucci was consistently successful. Here it is being shown in London, 1957.

Gucci (1881–1953)

Below right:
International celebrities were frequent visitors to the traditional design house of Gucci. The Italian couturier shakes hands with Princess Grace of Monaco and her husband Prince Rainier.

Below left and opposite:
Tom Ford's crazy young style helped Gucci achieve renewed success. Both designs also show the leather accessories which made the Italian company famous.

GUCCI Two of Italy's major fashion-in-the-1990s phenomena were the established fashion houses of Gucci and Prada. Gucci was founded in 1904 by saddler Guccio Gucci, who began by producing exclusive leather goods. The famous moccasin shoe followed, as did silk scarves, ties, eyewear, and of course bags and travel goods.

In 1994 and thanks to the support of American designer Tom Ford, the company rose phoenix-like from the ashes of near financial ruin in the late 1980s. Within a few years Tom Ford had managed to increase substantially the profits of the Gucci luxury label. His 1950s renaissance – using predominantly hightech fabrics, which he conceived not as mere imitation but rather as the reinterpretation of a direction in fashion in the spirit of the cool 1990s – was even well received in the cheapest mass-produced clothing circles. For example, it was thanks to him that the double-breasted Caban jacket of the 1960s came back into fashion. In the spring of 1999 he found his way back to Gucci's traditions: he presented leather, although somewhat unconventionally for the luxury label, in the form of peasant dirndls with provocative leather tops worn under fur coats.

Giorgio Armani

The 1980s was the decade of contrasts: an illusory world of the superfluous, but also an arena for a variety of new products and creative trends. A major contribution to the success of Italian designer fashion during this decade was provided by Giorgio Armani (b. 1934), who fascinates as much by his timeless style as by his excellent business sense. Since 1991, even Alitalia's stewardesses wear Armani.

After dropping out of medical school, Armani took on various temporary jobs and became a buyer and salesman for the department store La Rinascente in Milan. His early experiences in the field of fashion design came with Nino Cerruti for whom he eventually designed the Hitman collection. He set up his own company in 1970.

"Gorgeous George," as *Time* magazine called him, was the first to add new elements to menswear. It is impossible to conceive of leisurewear now without the pullovers with the typical eagle emblem, and the relaxed design of his leather jackets and jeans.

Armani's particular design trademark is the classic suit which has been equally influential on menswear and womenswear. It became the symbol of a relaxed, businesslike appearance for either sex. The determining factor was no longer the formal requirement of perfect fit, but the enjoyment inherent in wearing clothes that symbolize freedom.

For working women the pantsuit acquired a legendary character. Wearing Armani equaled the acceptance of a philosophy of life: "I wanted to tidy up, get all manner of things out of the way, I thought of the intelligent, adult woman in severe clothes. I like fashion that is invisible," is the master's comment on the matter.

When Richard Gere spread out his "working clothes" – Armani jackets, shirts, and ties – on the bed in the movie *American Gigolo*, Armani got the final push to success. Soon the label became a must for all who valued the idea of cool understatement.

With the establishment of Emporio Armani in 1981, Armani introduced a secondary line with its own chain of shops, which were soon supplemented with accessories and jeans. Because of his success with Emporio, the whole industry decided to bring out secondary collections: among them were Valentino with Miss V, Valentino Jeans, and Oliver; Krizia with Krizia Poi; Ferré with Oaks and Studio 0001; Missoni with Missoni sport; Coveri with You e Young; and Versace with Istante.

After a long period during which lingerie was damned by feminists, it finally began to reemerge: panties, bras, bodies, and slips were triumphant once more and came in brand new designs. Armani brought Armani Underwear on to the market, a sober, young line for both sexes. Gianni Versace's Anatomia was rather more luxurious and sexy. The art of seduction had reached a new phase: attractiveness had to be combined with comfort, and again, Armani made sure that his designs looked good and that the garments were of the best possible quality.

1980s fashion would be unthinkable without it: a woman's blazer styled like a man's suit jacket (*below left*). Comfortable yet perfectly cut and made of precious fabrics, the couturier endowed it with typical Armani elegance.

Opposite:
Giorgio Armani brought men's suits to womenswear. Simply and elegantly cut, he knew how to give them a feminine feel. As with these outfits from 1993, since he made no plans for anything to be worn underneath, he allowed space for precisely those undergarments which would become increasingly popular in the 1980s, particularly lacy lingerie.

Missoni

Knitwear and the erotic: there is not a trace of mutual exclusion at Missoni. Indeed, it is quite the reverse, as demonstrated by these designs from the 1997 and 1997/98 collections.

One of the greatest success stories of Italian fashion design is the career of husband-and-wife team Rosita (b. 1931) and Ottavio (b.1921) Missoni. They succeeded in liberating knitwear of its conservative image and in elevating it to the status of art: some of their designs have already been exhibited in the Metropolitan Museum of Art in New York. Stars like Tom Hanks and Luciano Pavarotti like to be photographed wearing Missoni.

Ottavio, a successful athlete in the 1950s, had already entered the fashion business by the time he met his wife: he and a friend designed the woolen tracksuits for the Italian national Olympic team of 1948.

In 1953 the newlywed creators opened a small knitwear workshop in the vicinity of Milan and began by working for the La Rinascente department store. They finally entered the market under their own name in 1966. Missoni's patterns are unmistakable, although the cut and color of each collection always conform to current fashion trends. Missoni's individual colors are obtained by careful blending. The exciting wave patterns, which are often inspired by African motifs and Op Art, are also created by the complex combination of a variety of colored yarns. Missoni's big fashion break came in 1969 when Diana Vreeland, the famous editor of American *Vogue*, was so enthused by the young and sportive collection presented to her by Rosita Missoni, that Missoni designs very quickly achieved cult status.

Rosita and Ottavio's daughter Angela took over as creative director of the house in 1997, since when it has also regained its cult status.

Gianfranco Ferré

When Gianfranco Ferré (b. 1944), whom some fashion writers describe as the master of form, was appointed artistic director of Dior in 1989, this was seen as quite a scandal, especially by the French fashion establishment. An Italian designing for Dior!

Despite the criticism, he has proved that his style's sober functionality and simple elegance can be combined with Dior's luxuriousness to form a successful symbiosis: the cones, cylinders, and pyramids which form the base of his designs are always transformed into unusual and elegant garments. His creations eventually earned him the Golden Thimble, the Oscar of French fashion.

In the late 1960s, Gianfranco Ferré crowned his architecture studies with a doctorate, yet began to make his name in a completely different field: having started working on jewelry and other accessories, he began in 1974 to design collections for Baila. In 1978 he introduced his own label and launched an Alta Moda Pronta collection which earned him international admiration. When, in 1986, he finally began to make advances on *haute couture*, his path to Paris had already been smoothed, and he stayed there until 1996. Ferré became famous as the "architect of the white blouse," a garment to which he was particularly devoted. However, these desirable blouses were difficult to transport as the stiffness of the fabric meant that they could barely be folded. These fabric sculptures also required a great deal of starching and ironing to bring them back into shape after laundering. With these sculptural masterworks, as with other items in his collections, color was secondary to form. Very occasionally, Ferré would add a colorful accent as a contrast.

The man who loves white blouses – and who designs ever new variations on the theme. Below are two examples from Gianfranco Ferré's fall/winter 1994/95 collection for Dior: with gigot sleeves worn by Nadja Auermann (*below left*) and with wide balloon sleeves (*below center*). For his own collections which he still presented annually during his time with the French fashion house, a favorite silhouette is provided by the tent line (*below right*).

Gianni Versace (1946–97)

Gianni Versace invented the supermodel phenomenon in the 1980s by contracting models to work exclusively for his house.

The international world of fashion lost one of its greatest creative forces in July 1997, when Gianni Versace was shot outside his home in Miami. Versace was born in Calabria, in southern Italy, and learned dressmaking in his mother's workshop. Early collections for Callaghan, Alma, Genny, and Complice followed soon after.

In 1978 Versace founded his own company and became one of the truly big names of the 1980s fashion scene. The uniqueness of his style was apparent in the free combination of the patterns and forms of disparate artistic styles and their patterns and forms, from antiquity to the Renaissance, from the Baroque to Futurism. His own comment was: "My inspiration is not scholarly, it is more instinctive, I always look ahead. The past is just an excuse for experiments. Classical means contemporary to me."

His work is further characterized by an excessive use of color: yellow, red, and purple recur time and again in combination. The master of neobaroque whose emblem was the golden head of Medusa was never afraid of any fabric combination: leather, so characteristic of his designs, was matched with silk, lace, or denim to create unusual and exciting combinations. For him fabric exists to shape the body, to drape it so that its pulsating vitality comes to the fore.

As well as extravagant, exuberantly colored and patterned garments, Versace produced another line of purer, reduced designs, as demonstrated by his elegant and timeless simple black evening gowns. Another determining factor in Versace's designs was the carefully staged eroticism of a garment. This applied to menswear as much as to his womenswear collections.

Another reason for Versace's success was his creation of the supermodel concept, that symbol of 1980s womanhood. These models were icons who dominated the press with their beauty, uncanny elegance, and scandals. Claudia Schiffer, Christy Turlington, Linda Evangelista, Cindy Crawford, Naomi Campbell, Carla Bruni, and Helena Christensen: all are Versace's creatures.

Versace was also interested in ballet, theater, and opera: he designed costumes for Maurice Béjart and Bob Wilson. His last major project on the subject of fashion and art was shown at the 1996 Biennale in Venice.

His sister Donatella, who had always acted as his muse, took over the creative direction of the house after his death. His brother Santo continues to run the business side of this family concern, which thrives on the name of the great designer although it is in fact a far-reaching family empire.

Claudia Schiffer, spring/summer 1995 collection.

Tina Turner in Versace during a concert in Paris.

Shalom in Versus, Versace's secondary line, New York 1996.

Kirsten McMenamy, spring/summer 1996 collection.

Claudia Schiffer, fall/winter 1994/95 collection.

Christy Turlington, fall/winter 1994/95 collection.

Gianni Versace

Fashion can be created even with very little material. Helena Christensen in a minidress from Versace's fall/winter 1993/94 collection.

Moschino (1950–94)

A wink at Sonia Delaunay's designs, in a patchworklike coat (*below left*). The skirt from Moschino's summer 1997 collection is made up of individual picture-patches (*below center*).

MOSCHINO JEANS

Garment-objects are designed down to the last detail: the Japanese lady's "bust" (*below right*) even includes her hairpins and, as with any bouquet, this bunch of fabric roses (*opposite*) is wrapped in cellophane.

As the mass media discovered the catwalk in the 1980s, every fashion show which they could turn into a spectacle was grist to their mill. Within the fashion industry this rapidly caused a sense of hysteria. Anyone with any self-respect wanted designer clothes. Soon there emerged the phenomenon of the fashion victim. This was exactly what Franco Moschino was trying to point out with his designs: he was interested in unmasking fashion and the cult of the label. However, he was so adept at this that his inversion of symbols, reminiscent of Dada and Surrealism, became precisely that which had the most effective advertising impact. For Moschino, questioning established fashion was the starting point for something new. He was not interested in creating cheap copies, he wanted to be provocative and perverse, and to make people smile, as demonstrated, for instance, by the T-shirt on which were printed the words "Chanel No 5." Chanel were not amused and sued. Or there was the advertisement for Moschino, the

perfume that he launched in 1990, which featured a woman in a golden corset sucking perfume out of the bottle with a straw. Emblazoned across the poster were the meaningful words "*Solo per uso esterno!*" (For external use only!).

Moschino initially studied at the renowned Brera Academy of Art in Milan. He subsequently worked as an illustrator for magazines like *Gap*, *Linea Italiana*, and *Harper's Bazaar*, later designing for Giggi Monte at Basile and working for Gianni Versace and Cadette until 1977. In 1983 he produced his Couture collection for Aeffe, and in 1988 Cheap & Chic and Moschino Jeans.

In his polemical way, he describes himself as an artist at the service of fashion. This is why his fashion shows could quite easily become happenings where the audience were allowed to pelt the outfits they did not like with tomatoes.

Moschino died of Aids in 1994. His work is continued by his colleagues.

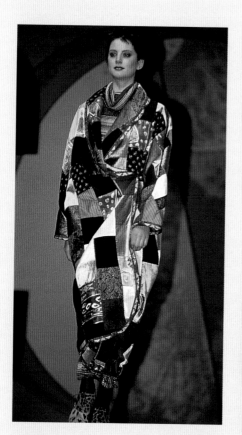

Dolce & Gabbana

This is another now firmly established Italian fashion giant who is closely linked to the name of pop icon Madonna. For her 1993 concert tour, Madonna wore Dolce & Gabbana, the design firm whose young designers like to use secondhand ideas in order to endow their collections with nostalgic flair.

Tailor Domenico Dolce (b. 1958) and graphic designer Stefano Gabbana (b. 1962) showed their first sultry chic collection to Milan in 1986. In 1989 they released their swimwear and lingerie collections and in 1993 their perfume Dolce & Gabbana came on to the market. This was followed by accessories, perfume for men, eyewear, and an equally flamboyant secondary collection for young people.

It is no great surprise that Madonna has been such an enthusiastic supporter of Dolce & Gabbana's designs: both men adore the eroticism of such curvaceous women as Anna Magnani and Sophia Loren. It is precisely for this sensual type of woman that they designed their collection of beaded corsets, black stockings and lace underwear as outerwear. Their garments combine eroticism and glamour "as an homage to the more sensual aspects of existence," as the German *Frankfurter Allgemeine Zeitung* put it.

Dolce & Gabbana's menswear is no less nostalgic: it echoes the gangsters and Mafiosi of neorealist Italian movies in the 1960s.

Opposite:
On the occasion of the 1997 première of the movie *101 Dalmatians*, a happening was staged at which every last accessory had to be right. Here Jerry Hall is Cruella de Vil, naturally dressed in a creation by the Italian design duo.

Dolce & Gabbana's designs always pay homage to the sensuality of women – Italian women – whether utterly concealing, as in this outfit from the 1993 collection modeled by Helena Christensen (*below left*), or in this crocheted creation (*below right*), which allows a glimpse of the black lace lingerie worn underneath.

Prada

"Shockingly ugly" was the first reaction to the creations which Miuccia Prada began to show in the mid-1990s. But the style of these simply cut, 1960s-style garments (*opposite*), as well as the taboo colors and patterns, are what catapulted her to fame. Her designs with cut seams (*bottom left*) and the romantic 1999 "forest fairy" collection (*bottom right*) were appreciated by a large audience. An absolute must for anyone in the know: the famous black nylon Prada bag (*bottom, far left*).

Prada was another highly traditional leather goods house until Miuccia Prada (b. 1950), the niece of Mario Prada, the man who founded the company in 1913, joined the business in the late 1970s. Following successful designs for backpacks and handbags, she had the temerity to bring out her first ready-to-wear collection in 1985 – although success evaded her on that occasion. Her big break did not come until 1995. In an interview, she had this to say on the matter: "I don't make elegant clothes anymore, but the opposite. I make ugly clothes from ugly materials; 'bad taste'." Her first clothing designs were inspired by plastic tablecloths and curtain patterns of the 1950s and 1960s, and proved very successful with younger women. Her 1999 shows featured forest-inspired creations: skirts covered in hallucinatory-colored leaves, dresses decorated with pebbles and reminiscent of suits of armor which seemed vaguely to bring to the minds of fashion critics the image of Robin Hood.

The supermodel phenomenon

Elke Reinhold

"Christy and I wouldn't get out of bed for less than $10,000 a day." Linda Evangelista's famous comment in 1991 marks both the high point of the supermodel era and its end: this arrogant statement by the 26-year-old triggered the backlash against the triumvirate, as the three top models Linda Evangelista, Naomi Campbell, and Christy Turlington were known on the fashion scene. The very scene that had helped them to join the world's most famous and highest-earning women now turned away in disgust. The supermodels had grown into monsters who overshadowed everything around them and who could say with ample justification that they were bigger than the product they were being used to sell.

The fall of the supermodels would take a few more years, but by the early 1990s the zenith of the phenomenon, which had been developing for decades, had already been and gone. In any case, it could not have grown any more. The products that they were supposed to advertise were not alone in becoming pale in their presence: their names were more famous than those of international society ladies or even Hollywood actresses. Not to mention their wealth which, for the most famous among them, was said to amount to tens of millions of dollars. These young women under 30 symbolized fame, wealth, power, and beauty; they were the embodiment of success. Every man desired them, every woman wanted to be like them.

Previous decades had also had their share of modeling stars – Veruschka, Twiggy, Jerry Hall – yet none of them achieved the status and wealth of the supermodels. Claudia Schiffer, Cindy Crawford, and the triumvirate were a creation of the designer decade and the idols of a period dominated by image, power, and glamour. The expression "supermodel" was not coined until the late 1980s, when the fashion industry and the luxury goods industry in general found itself in a severe slump. The supermodels helped to hide the fact that fashion was in crisis and kept glamour alive. It was not only the designers who supported them in this. Photographers like Steven Meisel and Peter Lindbergh, and the editors and stylists of international fashion magazines, contributed heavily to the transformation of models into icons of the outgoing millennium. Finally, even Hollywood actresses helped them on their meteoric rise: since they no longer desired to be divas and preferred to be anonymous, walking about like girls-next-door, people were hungry for alternative idols to admire and imitate.

In order to be "super," girls had to have more than just a pretty face: they needed the so-called x-factor. "She has 10,000 expressions and a real love affair with the camera," the enraptured Karl Lagerfeld once said of his muse Claudia Schiffer. Cindy Crawford, whom designer Isaac Mizrahi spoke of in the same breath as Andy Warhol, Judy Garland, Marilyn Monroe, and Jackie Kennedy, had the advantage of being an All-American Dreamgirl. With regard to Azzedine Alaïa, whose designs are aimed at glamorizing the female form, it was always said that the models used for his shows were the most beautiful: Naomi Campbell was a longtime favorite. Exclusive contracts tied models to designers so that they would represent that particular house's image. When Karl Lagerfeld became Chanel's designer in 1983 he chose the French Inès de la Fressange as his muse.

Gianni Versace took the exclusive modeling deal to extremes: he did not just want one girl, he wanted them all, and just for himself. If a model agreed to work exclusively for him during Milan fashion week, Versace would pay a bonus fee. Other designers would subsequently offer the same fees, but drop the exclusivity requirement. Soon one was outbidding the other, so that catwalk fees quickly reached $20,000 for a 30-minute show. Cosmetic companies imitated the designers: Paulina Porizkova became the face of Estée Lauder, Christy Turlington appeared in adverts for Calvin Klein's Eternity, Cindy Crawford in those for Revlon. The models achieved ultimate cult status when singer George Michael hired the triumvirate plus Tatjana Patitz for his 1990 *Freedom* music video. From this moment on, models became the rock stars, and their rock star boyfriends mere hangers-on: Guns'n'Roses singer Axl Rose with Stephanie Seymour, INXS singer Michael Hutchence with Helena Christensen, and so on. Wherever they went there were hordes of screaming teenagers and police protection.

The supermodels were seen as publicity magnets. Whoever succeeded in tempting them on to their catwalk could be assured of international front pages featuring their designs on the following day. The profitable goddesses resided in the largest suites of the best hotels, flew Concorde, went around with bodyguards in chauffeur-driven limousines, kept their own chefs, managers, assistants, and fan clubs, and socialized with kings and presidents. And even married them.

What was a most disreputable occupation at the turn of the century has become the career equivalent to an admission ticket to high society. It is also the only profession in which women earn more than men. Early models were not much more than live clothes racks. This changed with the introduction of fashion photography toward the end of the 19th century: the modeling career was invented. In the beginning it was mainly society ladies, dancers, or actresses who modeled clothes in the budding fashion magazines. In the couture houses things were a little different, with the sales girls generally modeling the maestro's creations for the clients. These early models were nameless creatures who usually came from the lower end of society – unless they were the wife of a fashion designer, like Marie Vernet, who started modeling garments designed by her husband Charles Frederick Worth as early as 1850. The first professional models were needed in 1894, when the catwalk was introduced. It was unthinkable for society ladies to exhibit themselves in such a fashion. The catwalk models had a more dubious reputation and were even compared to prostitutes. As late as the early 1950s, prostitutes in New York would assume a

Behind the scenes: until the 1970s, models did their own hair and applied their own make-up. Nowadays they are the victims of whole crews who put vast amounts of effort into styling them for the catwalk. Here, Naomi Campbell undergoes the treatment for Thierry Mugler's ready-to-wear show on March 16, 1995.

Three models from Patou's early period in 1927. Nowadays, it would not be acceptable for the size of models to vary so much; agencies demand a minimum height of 5 feet 7 inches.

In the 1940s, fashion was presented to clients in an unhurried way and at floor level. Nowadays music, theatrical effects and dance have important parts to play.

Lucky was one of the most desired models of the 1950s because she represented the era's ideal of aristocratic elegance.

disguise by carrying hat boxes. Models, who also had to carry hat boxes in those days, had to undergo the indignity of being spat upon in the street.

Jean Patou, the first European fashion designer to use professional models, caused a sensation in 1925 when he brought over to Paris six American models. In 1915 the world's first model agency was opened in New York by unemployed actor John Robert Powers. In 1946 Eileen Ford started her New York agency which, together with Elite, continues to be one of the largest model agencies in the world and the mother agency of numerous supermodels. Ford and her agency made a major contribution to raising the status of models. However, right up to the 1950s, only a small number of models became known by name; among them were Lisa Fonssagrives, who adorned the pages of all the major fashion magazines from the mid-1930s until the 1950s, and who is described as the first-ever supermodel. She paved the way for Jean Shrimpton and Twiggy, symbols of the 1960s, for Gunilla Lindblad, Jerry Hall, and Lauren Hutton, whose contract with Revlon in 1973 secured her a payment of $400,000, the

highest amount ever paid to a model at that time, and the start of the multimillion-dollar image-model business.

The booming advertising industry introduced models into every aspect of life. On billboards the size of houses and in television spots they sold fashion and cosmetics, but also lemonade, cars, and pocket calculators. The top models were omnipresent.

At the same time, the fashion world began to complain about the creatures that it had created. Photographers and editors fumed about the airs and graces of some of the girls: Naomi Campbell's bad moods and perpetual tardiness, for instance, caused her to be ejected from the model agency Elite. The agency proclaimed publicly that no money in the world was worth burdening colleagues and clients with her.

The designers became infuriated by the girls' exorbitant fees and the fact that nobody seemed interested in the designs any more. Until the late 1980s, press reports of their shows had been strict critiques of fabric and cut. Now journalists were more interested in Linda Evangelista's alleged pregnancy, Claudia Schiffer's engagement to David Copperfield, and Naomi's

affairs with boxer Mike Tyson and actor Robert de Niro. Speculations surrounding Cindy Crawford's alleged pseudo-marriage to Richard Gere went so far that the couple eventually paid £25,000 for a full-page announcement in *The Times* to attest to the sincerity of their love for each other.

The fall 1995 prêt-à-porter shows in Paris featured few supermodels because the designers decided to put a stop to constantly rising fees. For the 1996 shows, the supermodels were all replaced by new, young faces who had been selected with an eye to a new generation of consumers. Girls, like the little underfed Kate Moss, the aristocratic punk Stella Tenant, and the Asian Jenny Shimizu, a consciously aggressive, tattooed lesbian, characterized the new look for the children of the wealthy.

Above all however, it heralded the big time for the *jolie laide*, the beautiful yet ugly Kristen McMenamy, who was perfect for the ragged designs of grunge. The models were made to look like ordinary girls, were permitted to wear their hair unwashed and their lipstick smeared. The trend of unkempt kids culminated in the second half of the 1990s in the heroin look,

Delicate Kouka, with her big eyes, was the face of Dior in the 1960s.

The Texan Jerry Hall, now a mother of four, still takes to the catwalk for Thierry Mugler, Vivienne Westwood, and others. Occasionally she may even be working alongside her daughter.

Linda Evangelista, the personification of the supermodel, reinvents herself over and over again, sometimes just by changing her hair color.

which after some initial enthusiasm drowned in a storm of global indignation.

The fashion scene's fervor for these girls, of whom many were dependent on alcohol or heroin, and for their emaciated bodies, which could sometimes barely stagger on to the catwalk, lasted a very short time. Following the drug death of 20-year-old photographer Davide Sorrenti in 1997, the mood of the fashion scene turned: fashion magazines which printed half-dead bodies on their front pages received hate mail, advertisers canceled, and agents forced their models to undergo detoxification.

Only a few girls were able to survive the sudden death of this trend with a fresh face. Kate Moss, who by her own account had not stepped on to the catwalk for ten years without being "under the influence," and who consumed vast amounts of cannabis for most of her career, said goodbye to the lifestyle that she had enjoyed when she checked in to a London clinic in the winter of 1998.

Following the flop of grunge and heroin-chic, glamour once more conquered catwalks and fashion photography. A few of the supermodels, like Claudia Schiffer, Cindy Crawford, Naomi Campbell and Christy Turlington, are still at the top of the fashion business. However, attempts at starting second careers failed even for these superwomen: Claudia flopped as a talk-show host on German television, Naomi's attempt at being a pop singer failed with her first record, and Cindy made a bad movie. Nevertheless, she successfully sold over 5 million copies of her fitness video.

The number of models who have been successful in making the transition to cinema – for example, Andie MacDowell, Rene Russom, and Elle MacPherson – can still be counted on the fingers of one hand. Their role model is Lauren Hutton, who became a supermodel of the 1970s despite a slight squint, a gap in her front teeth, and a crooked nose, and made a career in such movies as *American Gigolo*, not to mention that at the age of 60 she has once again become a much sought-after model, as have her contemporaries Carmen dell'Orefice and Veruschka von Lehndorff. Every year, those girls who do not quite achieve superstatus are discarded ever more efficiently. Although in each season particular girls are elevated to fashion heaven, they are as speedily dropped again. At Chanel, Stella Tennant was replaced by Karen Elson (Karl Lagerfeld certified that she had the Look of the Millennium) and, still in 1999, she in turn was replaced by the Eurasian Devon. Bizarre beauties like Alek Wek from Senegal and androgynous British model Erin O'Connor take turns on the front pages with sporty German girl Heidi Klum and curvy Laetitia Casta from France. In 1998, British designer Alexander McQueen scandalized his audience by featuring a one-legged amputee, model Aimee Mullins, and answered the outraged question of whether this was acceptable with a categorical yes.

Just as, at the start of a new millennium, the fashion world refuses to be pinned down to a single style, the world of modeling is also coming out with new, different faces at high speed. As Karl Lagerfeld succinctly put it when he replaced his muse Claudia Schiffer with British aristocratic punk Stella Tennant: "Stella speaks more of the spirit of the times in fashion than Claudia. Regrettably, this profession is based on unfairness. Fashion is a very hard profession."

Victoire de Castellane, the youngest woman ever to head the list of the best-dressed, is a jewelry designer for Dior. She also belongs to the group of elegant women dressed in black.

Barbara Hutton in Tanger: like a princess from *The Thousand and One Nights* she is seated among the precious objects in her house. This portrait is by Cecil Beaton.

Jewelry designer Paloma Picasso has been in the best-dressed women's Hall of Fame for a long time. Her bright red lipstick became a trademark.

The list of vanities

Who is the most elegant woman in the world? An international jury of designers, fashion professionals, journalists, and celebrities try to answer this question year after year. The result each time is a list featuring 12 names familiar to readers of society pages – also known as gossip columns – at least in the United States. No great surprise there, since the decision as to which of the many nominees eventually makes it on to the list is taken by a committee in New York. For 60 years this committee has been chaired by Eleanor Lambert, a highly talented public relations consultant who began her career looking after modern artists like Jackson Pollock before deciding in 1940 to invest her immense energies in the furtherance of fashion. The idea for the best-dressed woman list was a publicity gimmick born in France in 1922, but since the Paris fashion circus was forced to close during World War II, Eleanor Lambert selflessly decided to carry on with the idea in the United States where, thanks to the large number of emigrants and the lack of competition from France, the textile industry was booming. Miss

Lambert was able to awaken so much press attention for the award – naturally this was purely for glory, there was no money involved – that "the list" became a truly American institution which France never claimed back. And why should it? Most of the couture salons' clients came from the United States anyway, and they were also the ones to get top ranking on the list because, as the now 93-year-old Eleanor Lambert explains, "only those people who spent the most money on clothes were permitted on to the list."

Well, probably money still helps. But contacts are at least as important. Only people who know people in the right circles stand any chance of getting on to the list. It is no coincidence that so many fashion journalists and designers have been nominated; for example, every editor of American *Vogue* has appeared on the list, whereas the ladies who do the same job in Germany or Australia, or even Italy, cannot get anywhere near nomination. Perhaps this is because they cannot attend all the charity balls, award ceremonies, and exhibition

openings that count with the American jurors. After all, what use is the most costly elegance if it is not noticed? The entrepreneur from the German town Aschaffenburg who wears Versace couture to the office every day (she exists!) will forever remain an unknown in the world of fashion. On the other hand, media presence alone will not do the trick either, otherwise one of couture's best clients, the happily divorced ex-wife of a Saudi billionaire, Mouna Ayoub, who generally wears Chanel, would have made it on to the list a long time ago. Yet for so-called oil-princesses and the wives of recently wealthy Russians, the list seems closed for ever.

The most favorable conditions for entering the charmed circle of the listed are provided by a rich husband plus a job on a fashion magazine or in a couture establishment. If one adds to this a photogenic appearance and gracefulness, the scene is set for Eleanor Lambert's approval. Thus it was with the legendary Barbara "Babe" Paley, who was one of the 12 best-dressed women in the world 14 consecutive times before being promoted to the Hall of Fame, introduced in 1958 to make space for fresh names on the annual list. The very first woman to make it to the Hall of Fame, incidentally, was the Duchess of Windsor.

Anjelica Huston, star of the *Addams Family* movies and daughter of director John Huston, was voted the most beautiful and best-dressed woman in the United States.

Tina Chow, jewelry designer, collector of antique clothes, and muse to numerous designers, was admitted to the Hall of Fame. She died of Aids in 1992.

Regrettably, Anna Piaggi, the Italian fashion journalist with the highly individual sense of style and her own hat creations, has not yet been honoured with a nomination.

The elderly Miss Lambert has no difficulty in bringing to her mind's eye every elegant woman of the last six decades, yet for her Babe Paley and her friend Gloria Guinness were the all-time queens of good taste. This was due in great part to the individuality of their style, which did not rely entirely on the art of the couturier. Miss Lambert's preference for originality is also mirrored in the list for the year 1998/99. An honorable first place is awarded to Victoire de Castellane, a refreshingly unconventional young French aristocrat and former long-term employee of Chanel, where she occasionally doubled as a catwalk model dressed in low-cut décolleté and short skirt. The entire list is conspicuous for having been rejuvenated, which was how Eleanor Lambert

wanted it. She knows from experience that only fresh blood can awaken interest in such an old institution as the list of best-dressed women. It is noticeable that three young Hollywood stars have made it on to the list: Cameron Diaz, Gwyneth Paltrow (although she has had to endure a reprimand for the bad fit of her Oscar award ceremony dress), and Uma Thurman. This is practically a renaissance, reminiscent of the 1930s, when all glamour heralded from Hollywood. In those days the glamour was provided by costume designers. Today it is the couturiers who provide the stars with their services; this way, the world of film and fashion provide each other with splendor. Against a zero fee of course. This further reduces the chances for the many women who invest their own

fortunes in clothes in the hope that their name may one day adorn the list of the vanities ... it's not fair. Neither is the "list of the worst-dressed women," in which it is possible to be included without doing very much at all. This is issued annually by the self-styled guru of taste, Mr. Blackwell, who cheerfully includes even the greatest stars on his negative list, only to praise them the following year, perhaps for their unusual sense of style. Among those to whom this has happened are Glenn Close, Julia Roberts, Courtney Love, Demi Moore, Ivana Trump, and even Princess Diana. Mr. Blackwell's favorite victim is Madonna. And yet, might the fact that he always tears apart the ever-transforming diva merely be proof that Mr. Blackwell has no sense of the latest trends in fashion?

Best-dressed women 1998/99:

Victoire de Castellane, member of Parisian society and jewelry designer for Dior.

Mrs. Brooke Douglass de Ocampo, New York and Argentina, American wife of a prominent Argentinian landowner.

Cameron Diaz, American movie actress.

Princess Pavlos (Marie-Chantal) of Greece, New York, social celebrity and philanthropist.

Patricia Herrera, daughter of Reinaldo and

Carolina Herrera, editor of *Vanity Fair*.

Aerin Lauder (Mrs. Eric Zinterhofer), New York, daughter of Mr. and Mrs. Ronald Lauder and head of creative product development at Estée Lauder.

Viscountess Linley (Serena), Great Britain, wife of David Linley, daughter-in-law of Princess Margaret.

Jade Jagger, daughter of Mick and Bianca Jagger and well-known London-based jewelry designer.

Gwyneth Paltrow, American movie actress (although the committee did complain about the bad fit of the dress that she wore to an Oscar awards ceremony).

Uma Thurman, American movie actress.

Marian McEvoy, New York, editor of *Elle Decoration*.

Eliza Reed, young New Yorker, vice-president of business development at Oscar de la Renta.

1990–1999

Toward a minimalist future?

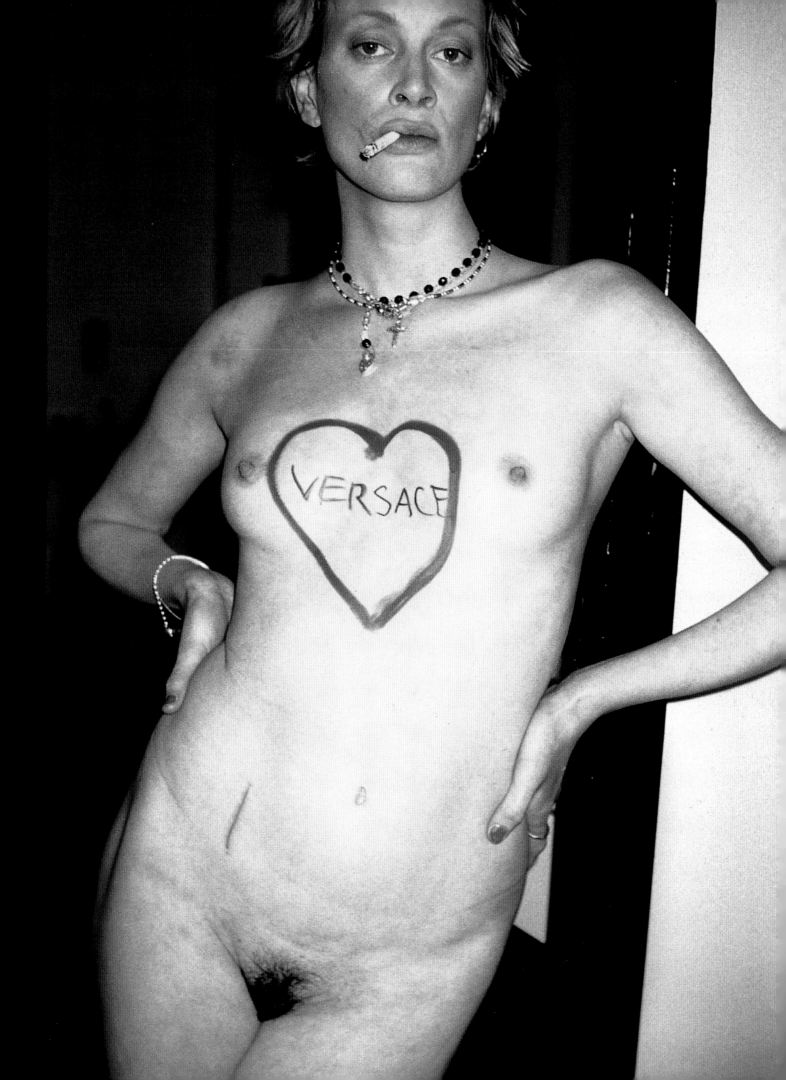

1990–1999

People like to think of the 1990s as a period of calm which followed the overheated glamour of the 1980s, and the last decade before the beginning of the third millennium had indeed many similarities with the *fin de siècle* of the 19th century: fundamental changes caused many people to feel uncertain and there was a general desire for distraction. Computer technology accelerated the rhythm of life and changed the world of work. Consumption remained a leisure pursuit, as it was in the 1980s, and a new search for meaning began. Eternal youth remained the primary goal. And, thanks to increased economic independence, women had more influence than ever, both in their private and public lives.

The 1990s were a period when there were no limits. With the collapse of communism, the ideological wall dividing East and West ceased to exist. America's vision of freedom – everything was "liberal" in the 1990s – also ceased to be obstructed. The influence of the stock exchange literally became boundless.

One of the great idols of the 1990s, the Dalai Lama conquered the world with his optimism and humor: the fact that even a man such as he had something to say on the subject of fashion – he gave an interview to the German newspaper *Süddeutsche Zeitung* in 1997 on footwear fashion – was typical of the decade.

Hollywood and MacDonald's temple to fast food exerted their cultural influence across the world: it was the decade of globalization.

Floods of information became the staple fare of the intellect. People became accustomed to news about environmental and political scandals, violence in the suburbs, Aids, cloned animals, genetically manipulated foods. Bitingly humorous advertisement slogans, such as "All Diesel Jeans have been tested on animals," mirrored the general mood. Most people seemed to yearn for security, truth, and new values. Simultaneously, entertainment became a growing need. The media sought to produce a state of permanent emotion in an era when there was no time left for dreaming. The fatal accident of the charismatic Diana, Princess of Wales was turned into a media spectacle; the world mourned her, and the 36-year-old princess was swiftly enveloped in the aura of a saint.

With the Gulf War in Kuwait in 1990 there began an unexpected

Opposite:
Economic crisis and the Gulf War caused increasing consumer frustration in 1990. The minimalist was born. Her style: unobtrusive basics, noncolors, and discreet jewelry and make-up.

Previous page:
Photographs of top model Kristen McMenamy's emaciated, bruised body shocked the fashion world in 1996. Photographer Jürgen Teller invented heroin-chic in the mid-1990s.

period of consumer frustration. While in Germany the unification of West and East was still cause for euphoric celebration, France and other European countries were beginning to realize that the lack of inhibitions in the golden 1980s now had to be followed by a period of reflection. Sinking consumer spending, record unemployment, economic crisis: the ingredients of the 1990s were not unlike those of the 1920s.

All of a sudden fashion ceased to be fun. Women as well as men learned to be satisfied with fashionably restrained style basics, and in any case everybody agreed their wardrobes were too full. Basics were socially acceptable because they conformed to the mood of the times by being practical, unobtrusive, and unpretentious. Basics, the American term for a kind of emergency gear, were effected in the form of classically cut blazers, pantsuits, narrow skirts, and turtlenecks. Within a short space of time they dominated the shops – and the catwalks. Here, however, a touch of luxury was added to the simple forms by the use of classic, high-quality fabrics made of valuable raw fibers and by the finest craftsmanship. Yet this is not visible from a distance: "Luxury is when the invisible is as luxurious as the visible. The real luxury is found in the lining," declared Karl Lagerfeld in 1992 to the French glossy magazine *Contemporaine*.

In keeping with the spirit of the times, which was encapsulated in the adage "less is more," fashion went environmental in the early 1990s and featured

The girlie look emerged in parallel to minimalism in the mid-1990s, and was immortalized in films like *Clueless*, starring Alicia Silverstone. This look was also popular with more mature women who rebelled against age-specific dress codes by wearing skimpy T-shirts and skirts.

natural colors. Yet this expression of the search for meaning had very little appeal, particularly to southern European women, and rapidly underwent a whole series of recapitulations. In (fashion) design as in music, the search for stability was translated into the past: the ghosts of the 1960s and 1970s haunted fashion for quite a while, flared pants and fringing were once more to be seen, as were the Courrèges look and stylized daisies. The Jackie Kennedy dress became a bestseller and, in 1996, copies of Prada's 1960s geometric patterns and Pucci's psychedelics were prolific.

The search for meaning spread to the catwalks in the form of mystical symbols: the elegance of Gianni Versace's very last couture collection, shortly before his mysterious death in his new luxury villa in Miami later that year, was contained in the rich, golden crosses embroidered on black evening dresses. Balenciaga's designer Nicolas Ghesquière presented monkish black cowl dresses, as seen in *Star Wars II*. It seemed that the high point of fashionable inwardness had been reached. The liberalization in telecommunications in 1993/94 triggered a revolution in Europe: the number of Internet surfers grew rapidly, and reality became virtual.

Lara Croft, the virtual star of the bestselling computer game Tomb Raider, became a fashionable role model for female "kids," with her midriff-

Opposite:
Purely natural: drawstring pants are held up only by a thick cord and a few feathers serve to cover the bosom. This was the image of women held by Belgian avant-garde designer Ann Demeulemeester in the summer of 1992.

Fashion designers worship minimalism in their cool shopping temples: in 1996, Jil Sander opened a boutique on Munich's Maximilianstrasse, designed by Michael Gabellini.

revealing T-shirt, very short shorts, backpack, and paratrooper boots: Belgian designer Walter van Beirendonck presented the colorful, brash, young world of the new media in his Paris shows. The fact that by the end of the 1990s it would be possible to access all manner of things on the Internet, including the contents of mail-order catalogs, still seemed like science fiction in 1993: in the fall of 1998 Jean Paul Gaultier became one of the first designers to sell accessories from his Internet gallery.

Life in the 1990s became very fast thanks to innumerable cable programs, mobile telephones, and e-mail, computerized manufacturing plants, and the digital networking of people and places of work. This acceleration was reflected in fashion design. Whereas in the 1980s the fashionable impetus had emanated from the street rather than couturiers themselves, the flow of information had now become a decisive factor in the fashion industry, which affected all aspects

from the catwalk to the copyists' factories, from the shop cash register all the way back to the garment manufacturer. As a result, low-cost streetwear copies of designer fashions could be manufactured very rapidly, and fashion as a whole became increasingly uniform. The restrained basics style of the mid-1990s rapidly became a huge fashion cult which entered the history of fashion under the name of minimalism. The leading fashion aesthetic for years consisted of simple elegance in black, later in gray. The Austrian Helmut Lang was regarded as one of the most uncompromising and avant-gardist minimalist designers. In 1997, the magazine *Artform* admired his "respect for elegant convention which hits on a decidedly refined sense of the spirit of our times." Fashionable reductionism even went as far as prohibiting accessories. Jewelry became particularly frowned upon. Hair and make-up followed the trend for understatement.

It did not take not long for Sir Terence Conran to celebrate minimalism in his megarestaurants in Paris and London: surrounded by clinical white walls and furniture made of metal and glass, several hundred diners can choose to eat from a Euro-Asian-American menu at any one time. The cult store Colette, which opened in Paris in 1997, is minimal in every respect: inside the pure, white interior, fashion and furnishing items are not presented en masse but in the manner of rare artifacts.

The Parisian couture scene became somewhat remote during this ascendancy of minimalism. Paris complained that everything had become uniform "marketing fashion" and blamed the United States. Thanks to the power of advertising, Ralph Lauren, Calvin Klein, and Donna Karan became irresistible to

Opposite:
Accessories for the modern, 1990s businesswoman: simple basics, discreet jewelry, Filofax, and mobile telephone. Louis Vuitton, the pope of luggage, surprised the world of fashion with his first prêt-à-porter collection, created for fall/winter 1998/99 by US designer Marc Jacobs. He succeeded in reviving the image of the ailing brand to such an extent that the logo is again worn with much enthusiasm.

European women in the 1990s. Ralph Lauren's timeless, middle-class, country-house style was regarded as a safe bet, as were Chanel and Hermès, and interest was concentrated on labels with that kind of image. Behind Calvin Klein lurks a virtual marketing machine. He has propagated a comprehensive, wearable style, produced provocative advertisements aimed at young people, and lent his name to innumerable product licenses. Donna Karan would like to be the first American to prove that fashionable ideas can originate on the other side of the Atlantic. Somewhere in their train, there swims a certain Tommy Hilfiger who has had little more to offer than a preppy-type style in primary colors. Still, timeless design was the in thing and America definitely hit the popularity stakes.

Furthermore, at the end of the century Paris found competition coming from Italy. The Italians, led by Armani and followed later in the mid-1990s by Prada and Gucci, have been the masters of making simple things look very fashionable. Although most people agreed that Milan was too classical, London too mad, and that Paris had the greatest variety and imagination, it was Italian fabric weavers who manufactured the most creative fabrics: in a time of purist, simple fashions, this gave Italy a definite market advantage.

During the second half of the 1990s an earthquake shook the fashion capital, Paris: new owners moved into old couture houses, and new designers and managers followed in their wake. John Galliano from Britain seized the rudder at Christian Dior, his compatriot Alexander McQueen that at Givenchy. An Israeli-American, Alber Elbaz, became Yves Saint Laurent's successor during the latter's lifetime, Cristina Ortiz from Spain renewed Lanvin's style, and the French Canadian Nathalie Gervais took over at Nina Ricci in 1999. Globalization brought a breath of fresh air to Paris's venerable fashion institutions.

John Galliano's first fashion shows for Dior demonstrated his great artistic talent, but his designs looked backward; their inspiration was always in the past. Modern women were not attracted. Despite this, his fashion spectacles had a strong effect on Dior's image.

Conspicuous displays of luxury were not regarded as politically correct in the 1990s yet, paradoxically, luxury labels were more widely distributed than ever. Luxury became democratic. Labels like Hermès, Louis Vuitton, Armani, Gucci, Prada, and Ralph Lauren built colossal global empires in the 1990s. In the race for worldwide recognition by labels and designers, Paris remained in front: American and Italian luxury labels moved to the old Avenue

Opposite:
The frenetic pace at which people experienced the 1990s and the increased importance of technology in everyday life were reflected in fashion photography. This shot was taken by Italian star photographer Andrea Giacobe for Marie Claire Bis.

Above, left to right:
Interpretations of the cyberwoman for the new millennium: a model with aluminum foil head decoration; Vivienne Westwood's aesthetic of the morbid; Nathalie Portman as a galactic princess in George Lucas's movie *Star Wars I: The Phantom Menace*; hood from Thierry Mugler's summer 1999 collection.

In the mid-1990s the desire for domestic security led to the creation of the foundation-garment look – delicate slips worn with jumpers or jackets, to look as if the wearer had just been sitting on the sofa.

In winter, the desire for warmth and comfort means a less seductive look. This layered look by Yamamoto 1996, is reminiscent of a homeless person's outfit.

Montaigne. In 1993 Jil Sander became one of the first non-French designers to make it into the highly desirable Parisian high-class shopping street, and from then on the German designer label was known around the world.

The 1990s minimalist treated herself with bags, eyewear, and shoes by renowned labels as soon as her purse would permit. Prada's black nylon bag was her most desired accessory in 1996/97. Toward the end of the decade, coveted luxury articles were not necessarily labels, but items that demonstrated creative excellence and craftsmanship and so exuded rarity value.

Photogenic extremes occur in fashion from time to time: supermodels became too expensive, too 1980s, and were replaced by delicate, pale mannequins. These had to be superyoung and ultraslim. Baby-dolls were followed on to the catwalk by romantic

nymphs, no older than 16 and symbols of the search for innocence: young Devon, the Eurasian with the doll's face and kissable lips, became the star model of the late 1990s. Yet the defilés also featured hollow-eyed representations of damaged youth. Those who did not look (drug-) damaged enough were made to with a little bit of help from the make-up department. This was another fashionable expression of youthful yearning which became a mass movement in Western society. Youth meant power, fitness, beauty. Youth labor was cheap. The future belonged to youth. Unnerved, Karl Lagerfeld turned to *Le Figaro* in 1999 and mocked "the new racism brought about by the obsession with youth." Milk with added vitamins, face-lifting creams, and the sex pill Viagra all expressed the dream of eternal youth. Young people had more freedom than ever. Young girls and women,

Futuristic bow before the millennium: Hervé Léger's graphically clean fall/winter 1999/2000 collection.

Breakthrough in the decade of understatement: Ralph Lauren presents his summer 1997 collection at the New York ready-to-wear shows.

better educated than any generation before them, enjoyed maximum freedom of movement. Young people now lived at home, did not rebel and frequently had control over not inconsiderable financial means. Their idols were musicians, models, sports personalities. Online chats were a matter of course for them. They may have lacked ideals, but they had an irrepressible desire to have fun.

Young people were not the only ones to make the pilgrimage to Nike Town, the well-known trainer label's giant megastore when it opened in New York in 1996. The store exemplifies the future of shopping. This is not just a place for shopping, it is an experience, a place of fun, wonderment, and surprises. Entertainment shopping caught on and many stores, particularly sportswear stores, began to follow the American example. Lingerie and hosiery

are made to fit in with the desire for the perfect, youthful body. Wonderbras, push-ups, and shape-ups lift bosom and bottom and hold the tummy in. Accessories like the minibackpack have taken on infantile forms, and have a humorous appeal for their young and not so young patrons.

In the late 1990s, even mature women were known to espouse the girlie look, pitched somewhere between baby-doll and Barbie Doll. Satin microskirts and skimpy tops, tiny floral patterns, the occasional pair of knee socks, and shoes that would not seem out of place at a first communion, were essential items for girlies and for those who would have liked to be girlies for ever.

The "kids" let Dad keep his jeans and turned to street fashion inspired by sport and music. Trainers were the epoch's comfort footwear: Rifat Ozbek's 1990

New Age collection featured outsized basketball boots, Karl Lagerfeld decorated them with the CC of the Chanel logo, and Jean Paul Gaultier added high heels. The trainer-generation elevated comfort, once seen as hopelessly square, to the level of fashionable premise.

The minimalists thus moved away from superficiality toward a validity emanating from within, or to be more precise from the fabric. New technology made it possible to make "smart" materials, superseding stretch and supersoftness, which had become standard thanks to microfibers. The new fabrics promise comfort and freedom: they are noniron, microbefree, breathable or thermoactive, UV-resistant, made of antistress fibers, smell nice, and may even dispense moisturizing cream.

1990s minimalist fashion continued to be severe by day and did not become any more expressive until nightfall. The work environment demanded maximum conformity, the pinstripe suit being the standard androgynous uniform. Yet in the evening, privately everything was permitted. Minimalist women turned into *femmes fatales* once more, or went romantic, definitely feminine, sometimes sporty. They revealed a lot of skin, dressed in seductive, figure-hugging or transparent garments, with luster, sequins, feathers, and fur. The third episode of *Star Wars* wallowed in opulence and exuberance long before late 1990s fashion discovered their merits. Judging by the movies' costumes, which represent a mixture of styles and eras, the forecast was not for futuristic cool but sumptuous imagination.

A new generation of young designers suddenly emerged in the late 1990s. They rejected stardom and appeared distrustful of the media. Martin Margiela refuses to give interviews and the label in his garments is white. Belgian shooting star Olivier Theyskens has, at the age of 22, followed the example of his compatriot Margiela, but it is no hard task for him to reject the machinations of PR: ever since Madonna attended an Oscar awards ceremony dressed in his black satin coatdress, his name has been the talk of the town. Two more products of Antwerp's talent school are designers Raf Simons and Véronique Branquinho, who also follow the new trend and do not permit themselves to be photographed. However, they know exactly what they want and how to get it.

In 1999, German designer Bernhard Wilhelm caused quite a stir in Paris when he presented a collection in which he unashamedly and unusually included elements of Black Forest traditional costume. "I wanted to do something German yet fresh," the young fashion designer candidly confessed.

In the prelude to the millennium celebrations, for which long-haul holidays had been booked and vintage champagne stored in the cellar, there was a lack of millennium atmosphere in the fashion world: most women continued to find minimalism attractive and liked the way it exudes efficiency. However, more color – the color for 1999 was shocking pink – did seem to signal a new desire for extravagance. At the same time, men became more adventurous and moved away from the restricting suit. Menswear became a hotly disputed subject; more and more color entered the equation and, for the summer of 1999, the skirt for him was a hot item at the trade fairs.

The craving for security and individual liberty was reflected in sportily styled garments made of hightech fabrics. Protection was also included in the guiding concept of Jean-Charles de Castelbajac's winter 1999/2000 collection, which was entitled State of Emergency. It featured protective clothing like padded coats that looked like polar sleeping bags, and hats shaped like those worn by the UN Security Forces. Optimistically, Castelbajac declared that they looked like Playmobil toy helmets.

Bea Gottschlich

Opposite:
Behind the scenes at Jean-Charles de Castelbajac's show: his fall/winter 1999/2000 collection was shown in a Paris metro station.

Model Helena Christensen and alien in an advertisement for Genny. German photographer Peter Lindbergh is particularly adept at setting 1990s minimalism in unusual and sensual scenarios which always reflect his love of women.

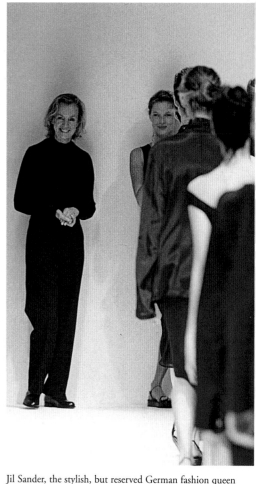

John Galliano and Bar, the prototype for the New Look with which Christian Dior caused an *haute couture* sensation in 1947. Precisely 50 years on, the British designer presented his first collection for Dior.

Outrageous yet successful. Alexander McQueen still causes a stir, even with his collections for Givenchy, as here in 1998, benefiting the renowned company with the headlines that he provokes.

Jil Sander, the stylish, but reserved German fashion queen prefers to take a back seat. She does not need to make a dramatic entrance like other designers – her influence is still strongly felt.

Designers of the decade

In the 1990s, fortress Paris found itself under increasingly heavy assault by foreign designers. Couture in particular, regarded as a national holy relic despite having been founded by the Englishman Charles Worth, was subjected to several shocks, although they did bring new life to the grand old dame, who had been wasting away. The British again played a leading role: John Galliano, the romantic pirate who began his successful plunderings of fashion history at Givenchy and then joined Dior in 1997, and Alexander McQueen, the "bad boy" of Savile Row who succeeded Galliano at Givenchy as the creator of outrageous couture.

In 1993 Oscar de la Renta returned to Paris, where, as a young man, he had spent four years working for Lanvin, to take over couture at the house of Balmain. Unlike the young Brits, this

gentleman, who was born in 1932 in the Dominican Republic and trained with Balenciaga in Madrid, was utterly committed to elegant, feminine, and decorative couture, just like the garments that he had been designing under his own name in the United States since 1965: he created the dress that Hilary Clinton wore at her husband's presidential inauguration.

The Italian Gianni Versace was admitted to the Chambre Syndicale de la Couture in 1990 and was therefore permitted to show his Atelier couture collection in Paris twice a year. Following Versace's murder in 1997, his sister Donatella has maintained the master's tradition, keeping steadfastly to the spirit of her brother's vision, and staging her sexy and glamorous fashion shows at The Ritz hotel before an audience of international show business stars:

hot couture! All other Versace collections continue to be presented in Milan.

The last couture house to be founded under the strict old rules of the Chambre Syndicale was Lecoanet Hemant in 1991. The name represents the Frenchman Didier Lecoanet (b. 1955) and Hemant Sagar (b. 1957), from India. They started their careers by designing ready-to-wear collections for their own store until they made enough money through licensing deals to finance a couture workshop where figure-hugging, extravagant evening gowns are made from precious fabrics.

Couture's strict admittance rules, which had been laid down in 1945, were finally relaxed in 1992. Until then, designers had to have at least 20 permanent members of staff working in their workshop and their salons had to have sufficient

Jil Sander's new financial partner, the Prada group, has bought 75 per cent of her company's shares, leaving her to concentrate solely on design. Jil Sander has created an unusual light and colorful collection for Milan's spring/summer 2000 catwalk.
This picture shows the modern version of a Hawaiian shirt combined with a daisy skirt – the 1960s flower kids, finally become respectable!

capacity for twice-yearly shows featuring a minimum of 50 hand-sewn garments. A new, two-year transition phase for rising couturiers has now been introduced for which they have to employ only ten permanent members of staff and present 25 creations per season.

Bare midriffs featured in Tom Ford's spring/summer 1995 collection for Gucci. Thanks to youthful, innovative designs, the American designer has succeeded in providing the Italian company with a new image and turning it into one of the 1990s' leading fashion houses.

Hervé Léger (b. 1957) began his career in 1992 with a sensational success: he produced a garment of elasticized fabric which emphasized the figure as much as a foundation garment might – not entirely surprising since he spent years designing swimwear with Karl Lagerfeld for Fendi. Despite dire warnings and Azzedine Alaïa's accusation of plagiarism, Léger managed to create ever new and wonderful collections. Nevertheless, 1999 heralded the end for the fashion designer: when his company was sold off, the new proprietors sacked him and hired Jerôme Dreyfuss to take care of the Léger line.

Because eight couture houses were forced to close down within the space of ten years, and the remaining 15 had to fight for survival, Didier Grumbach, the new president of the Paris Chambre Syndicale de la Couture in Paris, further relaxed the rules in 1997 to facilitate entry to couture and to tie talented designers to Paris. For the first time, designers, among them Thierry Mugler and Jean Paul Gaultier, were invited to try their hand at couture collections.

Josephus Melchior Thimister (b. 1962), Balenciaga's design director between 1992 and 1997, was one of those invited to join. The Dutchman who completed five years of training at the Royal Academy of Arts in Antwerp summa cum laude, established himself with two artistic and architectural collections as a trendsetting couturier on whose shoulders rested a great deal of hope. Yet he was still unsure whether "couture is worth it" and signed a contract with the prestigious Italian ready-to-wear house of Genny. His intention is to resume his couture collection in 2000.

Ann Demeulemeester is one of the most influential designers of the avant-garde. She lives and works in Antwerp, where she also trained at the Royal Academy of Arts.

New life has been breathed into the couture scene. The solid and traditional house of Hermès joined up with Jean Paul Gaultier to provide the former *enfant terrible* with enough financial backing to develop promising young couture. And during the couture shows of July 1999, successful designer Tom Ford, who so rapidly restyled the ailing luxury firm Gucci to a cult label, expressed his belief that the time had come to make his own couture: "There are new foundations which are related to garments for personal appearances – because image is becoming more and more important, because Hollywood people want to make a statement when they get out of their cars." There are rumors that Gucci want to take over Saint Laurent – then Tom Ford could replace the weary genius of Yves Saint Laurent.

Yet this may just be one of the many rumors which keep this sensitive industry in a state of perpetual agitation. Thus it is whispered that Bernard Arnault, restless boss of the LVMH (Louis Vuitton Moët Hennessy) group, the largest luxury goods group yet to emerge and owner of several couture houses, has already

had enough of his wunderkind Galliano's capriciousness and is looking to replace him at Dior with Alexander McQueen – whom Givenchy are said to be hoping to replace with Martine Sitbon.

Born in Casablanca in 1951, Frenchwoman Martine Sitbon absorbs every trend, from rock music to literature and painting, which she has allowed to flow into her very personal collections since 1985. Slowly but steadily, she has built up a loyal group of followers and is still treated as a kind of trade secret. Another possible candidate, again French, may be Eric Bergère (b. 1960), who modernized Hermès' ready-to-wear before going it alone with his own small collection. He is a master at making easy-to-wear, simple dresses appear as precious as couture.

It may also be that big boss Bernard Arnault has himself circulated these speculations since people who are talked about stay in business. When he failed to acquire Gucci for the LVMH group, he found himself subject to unexpected and serious competition from the PPR (Pinault-Printemps-Redoute) group. The hotly fought contest for Gucci should have convinced even the greatest skeptics that fashion is all about big business – and that profits rise and fall with the creative head of the organization.

When the Texan Tom Ford (b. 1962) became Gucci's creative director in Italy in 1990, he was still an unknown quantity and Gucci was an unruly family business whose scandals were all too well known. Within three years, Tom Ford successfully endowed the company, which had caused a sensation with its shoes, bags, and belts back in the 1970s, with more renown than it had ever had before. With simple, gleaming, tightfitting garments which look as terrifically arrogant as they look sexy, he increased annual turnover from $250 million to $1 billion.

This is the success story which has inspired everyone since. Indeed, other ailing houses have succeeded in rejuvenating their old names by hiring young designers. For instance, British couture rejuvenators Galliano and McQueen are not the only ones working under the roof of LVMH. There are also three American ready-to-wear designers: Marc Jacobs at Louis Vuitton, Michael Kors at Céline, and Narciso Rodríguez at Loewe.

Hermès has for some time worked successfully with young designers, yet the profession reacted with astonishment when press-shy Belgian Martin Margiela was appointed in 1997 to head the design studio. An uncompromising avant-gardist, who has even

Fashion on its way to the next millennium: the contrast between those who take minimalism as far as possible, like newcomer Ocimar Versolata (*opposite*) and those who prefer a more lavish "baroque" style (*left*) is great. Here the old master Emanuel Ungaro, succeeds by his cautious use of color in outdoing his colleagues' attempts at a hippie-revival.

567

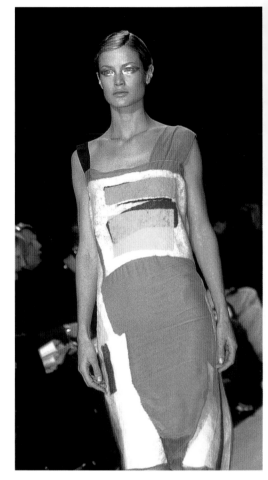

Fall/winter 1998 collection by American ready-to-wear designer Narciso Rodríguez for Loewe.

Figure-emphasizing clothes made him famous: Hervé Léger, 1997.

Still regarded as a red-hot secret tip: Martine Sitbon's fashion designs, fall/winter 1998/99 collection.

been known to send unfinished designs on to the catwalk, teamed with a traditional company renowned for luxury and perfection: is this a good combination? It is.

Old master Karl Lagerfeld, who was creative director at Chloé for two periods, was replaced by 25-year-old Stella McCartney in 1997. At that time all that was known about her was that she was the daughter of ex-Beatle Paul. The fashion world now knows that she is also the creator of featherlight, romantic, young garments.

Very few designers have successfully established their own labels without also working for an already established house, at least part-time. One of the great exceptions is Ann Demeulemeester (b. 1959). The only woman among the Antwerp Six, who all trained at the Royal Academy of Arts in Antwerp, she still works and lives in Belgium. She likes to experiment with bold cutting techniques; her 1997 collection, featuring white shirts that seemed to slip off the shoulder and baggy pants which barely clung to hips, was greatly admired and imitated – this was fashion in movement.

Many people regard the Algerian Jean Colonna (b. 1955) as one big provocation. He lives in a humble part of town, rides a motorbike, and creates cheap garments from primitive materials like PVC. This is exactly what makes him, in the eyes of others, one of the most modern of designers. In 1990 he showed his first collection of wild, seemingly unfinished evening gear for women. His style is slovenly glamour with no respect for convention.

Junya Watanabe (b. 1961), from Japan, stages fashion shows that seem like silent church masses: with great pauses between each appearance on the *défilé*, his models wear futuristic designs as they stride toward an apparently grave future. Watanabe studied at the Bunka School in Tokyo and worked for Comme des Garçons before Rei Kawakubo gave him his own label. He invented "mobile" seams and connecting "joints" for his garments, which are cut close to the contours of the body while providing adequate freedom of movement.

In 1998 American *Vogue* dared to publish a list of the leading 100 fashion houses, thereby

unleashing a storm of indignation. Fashion, according to the voices of protest, could not be judged by annual turnover figures, and creative endeavor could not be squeezed to fit the rigid structure of an order of rank. There is some truth in this; on the other hand, fashion journalists who see all the shows in New York, London, Milan, and Paris and read the larger companies' business reports, have a pretty good idea of the financial or creative power behind a fashion house. The list of big earners – including income from licenses, cosmetics and perfume – is led by Ralph Lauren, Calvin Klein, Tommy Hilfiger, Giorgio Armani, Donna Karan, and Versace. And where are the French, keepers of the Holy Grail of elegance? They are less forthcoming with profit disclosures. In any case, Chanel, Dior, and Saint Laurent are listed among the 20 giants in terms of income, besides the place they deserve at the top of any list in terms of their importance to fashion.

At 29th place in the list of the "Top 100" is the German company Escada, whose design team under the direction of the Scot Brian

New blood for the venerable couture house Balmain – Gilles Dufour uses soft candy colors for the new millennium.

Easy to wear clothes by the "all-American boy" Michael Kors, who also designs for the French brand Céline.

The young Nicolas Ghesquière tries to continue on in Balenciaga's footsteps as their new designer.

Rennie (b. 1963), has succeeded in finding favor among women across the world who have no interest in minimalist fashion and prefer to adorn themselves. Evening gowns by the house of Escada, which produces various lines from couture to sportswear, always feature at the Oscar award ceremonies.

Among all the big players there are designers whose influence is far greater than their income. *Vogue* has therefore scheduled a separate list of "innovators," on which appears Jil Sander at tenth place, above even such worthy names as Galliano, Kawakubo, Yamamoto, and Westwood.

Whereas Germans still think of the cool, northern blond who used to advertise Jil Sander's products in the 1980s, abroad her name is instantly linked to innovative fashion design. She is regarded as a leading designer of the 1990s. Just as Jil Sander's work in the 1980s cannot be reduced to the neat, beige business suit with which she so accurately hit the nerve of the period, so one would now be doing her an injustice by slotting her into the pigeon hole of minimalism. She consistently pursues the

concept of uncurlicued design – even down to the interiors of her stores, where she also inputs her design ideas – but still succeeds in transmitting a sense of opulence because her fabrics are luxurious, the workmanship is perfect, and the clothes are limitlessly comfortable to wear. Jil Sander is not exaggerating when she claims that her garments endow the wearer with self-confidence.

There are other German designers who have made a name for themselves abroad. The most likely to gain professional approbation internationally is Gabriele Strehle (b. 1951) who, like Jil Sander, shows her collections in Milan. She launched the Strenesse label in 1992, featuring an unadorned, slim line, somewhere between Armani and Sander, and aimed at the younger end of the market.

Since 1994 Wolfgang Joop (b. 1944) has been showing his collections in the United States, where his label is very profitable, especially with regard to perfume and jeans. Yet the multitalented designer has not been able to develop a recognizable style of his own.

Helmut Lang who was born in 1956, is considered to be the cult designer of the 1990s. He now occupies sixth place in *Vogue's* list of innovators. The Austrian designer who never set foot in a fashion college, almost single-handedly brought progress to fashion by combining the latest technomaterials with such classic fabrics as silk and lace (melting lace in rubber, for example), by decorating simple shift dresses with holograms or reflective stripes, by decking out T-shirt dresses with feathers as if they were couture, by displacing proportions, and by playing around with cross-dressing. When he quotes from fashion history he does not produce retro clothes but reformulations – for instance, replacing frills with sashes – to adapt them for today's image of the metropolis. Helmut Lang defined the lifestyle of the 1990s as Armani defined the 1980s and Saint Laurent the 1970s. He designs for modern people and therefore moved both his home and workplace to New York where, in his opinion, the fashion music of the future will be playing.

The look of the decade

Like the 1980s, the 1990s began with a great deal of glamour. However, this time it was brought not by squads of new career women, but by the supermodels. They had achieved star status and even outshone Hollywood stars, who had suddenly decided to adopt a "girl next door" stance and be seen in jogging pants and trainers. The supermodels, on the other hand, enjoyed their new opportunities to the full, dressed to the nines, danced at every party, and were as venerated as goddesses.

This almost unattainable model of gleaming perfection was emulated at the very most by a few teenagers hoping to be discovered. The army of working women was exhausted by the demands of the 1980s when they were led to believe, particularly by magazines like *Cosmopolitan*, that they could have it all: career, good sex, a successful husband, and – the most desirable accessory of all – a cute baby. Of course, "having it all" applied only to women who were slim, fit, and groomed from head to toe, as well as witty, charming, and seductive. In 1991, American writer Naomi Wolf exposed this lofty ideal in her book *The Beauty Myth* as being deeply hostile to women, and that same year her colleague Susan Faludi published *Backlash*, in which she bemoaned the setbacks experienced by the women's movement. The spirit of the times was most successfully captured by cinema. Whereas back in 1980 Richard Gere's "American Gigolo" had a benefactress who dressed him in Armani suits, ten years later the roles were reversed: now Richard Gere was the benefactor who bought "Pretty Woman" Julia Roberts expensive designer gear.

The daughters of career women were the first to declare that they had scant interest in the freedom to bear a double or treble load. They rejected their exhausted mothers' ideals as well as their power suits and make-up skills. They preferred a lot of fun over a little career. There was not all that much that could be achieved anyway, given the state of the labor market.

It was not long before the supermodels had to go. They were too expensive for the ailing textile industry and too grand for standard consumers. Also, the countermovement was grouping in the form of grunge. This new variant of the well-known phenomenon of antifashion was marketed even faster than its predecessors by the fashion and beauty industries. Models who looked as if they had been picked up from a street corner, with smudged and smeared make-up and dressed in garments that looked as if they were made up of bits and bobs of old clothes, were first sent across the catwalks by young Belgian designers like Margiela, but quickly found entry to the glossy magazines, who were hungry for new styles.

However, this was not to be seen throughout the entire decade. Instead, every decade that came before was rehashed. Grunge underwent both peak and decline in 1993, although deconstructivism remained a fashion issue, and the yearning for beauty was expressed in the "new glamour," when luster was applied to eyes and lips and even glittering tiaras were worn in the hair. The banished supermodels were brought back, and a few models from the grunge period survived by removing the rings in their noses and the gel in their hair and making themselves look pretty. Not long after that, the make-up had to come off again so that they could look unkempt to portray heroin-chic, which showed the youngest and thinnest models in less than flattering poses. That was enough to cause a healing shock. Consumers began to protest against the look which profited from the (secret) number-one disease of women: anorexia.

Natural freshness subsequently became fashionable again. With shimmering, moist complexions and shiny, clean hair, women had to look as if they had just stepped out of the shower. The less obvious the look the more skilled the make-up artists and hairdressers had to be. Products became ever more specialized, so that only experts were in any position to guess the sequence in which sun protection, moisturizer, color toner, and transparent foundation had to be applied, and whether this "natural" complexion needed to be finished with loose powder or spray, or whether it should be "sealed" by using both. Even on a "just-washed" face, eyelashes were not nude; colorless mascara made them appear as if they retained moisture, and lips were shiny and

As well as hightech products from the laboratory and make-up from health food stores or Body Shop, the 1990s saw the rediscovery of old products: the classic French powder by Leclerc became an overnight bestseller.

This hairstyle was named "Rachael" and became the hairstyle of the outgoing millennium: hair in layers as worn by 30-year-old Jennifer Aniston, who became famous through her part in the American comedy series *Friends*.

shapely despite lacking color. "Really modern make-up should improve a woman's natural appearance without dominating her face or concealing her beauty or personality," says make-up artist François Nars, who works with all the leading fashion photographers. He knows what he is talking about; after all, he assisted Madonna in every one of her transformations without ever making her face unrecognizable.

Supermodel Linda Evangelista also has several transmutations behind her. Each one began with a new hair color or style. Linda started with a long mane of dark blond hair, then she suddenly appeared with short, platinum vamp-waves, closely followed by fire-red curls, and finally, a dark, androgynous pageboy, with the overall result that she is still in business despite being a bit of an old-timer. Small wonder then that hairdressers grew so much in importance during the 1990s that they, and make-up artists, began to be treated like stars in their own right and were able to bring their own product lines on to the market, as did Gerhard Meir and Marlies Möller in Germany. Since hair had to fall naturally, without visible gel or strong spray, the art lay in the cut and the color. The hairstyle of the decade was the much-copied layered look worn by Jennifer Aniston of the television series *Friends*, which is reminiscent of Farrah Fawcett Major's famous blow-dried style, only slimmer and shorter, although with clearly recognizable highlights. Other evergreens that made a comeback were the ponytail and the tied knot.

It is usually nothing more than the tiniest twist that turns an old look into the latest thing. Professional advice is needed to keep up to date. Magazines and television shows demonstrate how to do it; there are waiting lists full of applicants wishing to be made over for popular before-and-after shows. Everyone is chasing the latest or most secret beauty tips, so that the young science of hormone therapy and the ancient potions and lotions are both able to profit. Barely had it become known that make-up artists and models only use powder made by the old-established Pharmacie Leclerc in Paris, there was a run on the old-fashioned tins of loose powder in the flattering shades of banana and apricot. The organic products made by Pharmacie Kiehl, founded in 1851 by German immigrants in New York, also became cult products overnight. Generally, the same trendsetters who use the fashioned beauty remedies also use the "designer hormones"

which promise full hair, toned bodies, and (sexual) energy into old age. Beauty has become a science which is even more dependent on intelligence and information than on genes and money. However, those who can afford just about anything do not necessarily make the best role models: a case in point is millionaire's wife Jocelyne Wildenstein, who, under threat of imminent divorce, literally turned into a panther and lost all her human facial characteristics on the operating table. With regard to pop star Michael Jackson, who had every feature of his appearance which related to his race surgically removed, the question again arises as to whether one should do everything that medicine makes possible. Many women, like *Baywatch* star Pamela Anderson, have had their breast implants removed when huge bosoms went out of fashion. Yet what do those women do who rashly had gaudy tattoos etched into their skin when models like Jenny Shimuzu wowed the world with theirs? The trend for thick lips also came to a rapid end when the collagen naturally broke down. The faster that trends came and went, the more frequently temporary solutions came on to the market: the Wonderbra that replaced silicon and temporary tattoos were the hits of the 1990s.

The manic search for an ideal of beauty to suit the new millennium with its halfhearted revivals distracts from the fact that something decidedly new has been developing for a considerable amount of time: individuality.

The postmodernist mishmash brought to us through fashions and models from around the world have widened our aesthetic horizons. Since we have seen girls featured in the glossy magazines that are perhaps too short or too skinny, too exotic or even rather ugly, the old norms have been suspended. Now we can even accept the perfection of the supermodels once more. Furthermore, designers like Jean Paul Gaultier are smashing the last taboo by sending models from all age groups down their catwalks. The latest advertisement campaign launched by the classic jeans manufacturer Levi features octogenarians wearing their denims, and suddenly we can see that white hair and faces that have lived can also be beautiful. However, this knowledge is not new; it is just being rediscovered – by precisely those people who started the cult of youth in the 1960s and who are now beginning to grow old. They want to enter the new millennium, gray heads held high and still setting the trends.

LARA CROFT

COURTNEY LOVE

SHARON STONE

BJÖRK

SPICE GILRS

LADY DIANA

Idols of the decade

Courtney Love, born in San Francisco in 1965, was dubbed the "Yoko Ono of the 1990s" by malicious gossips. There are indeed parallels between her and the wife of ex-Beatle John Lennon. Neither disguised their ambition for money and power, and both were partly instrumental in the breakup of their respective husbands' bands at the pinnacle of their careers. Well-wishers, on the other hand, maintain that, unlike Yoko, Courtney would have become a star even without her husband. When she married Nirvana's singer Kurt Cobain in 1992, she was already known as the front woman for her own band, Hole, where her extremely obscene stage performance had earned her some attention. She and heroin addict Kurt Cobain were bound together by their excessive drug-taking, until their daughter Frances Bean was nearly taken into care. Her album *Live Through This* was released a week after the suicide of Nirvana's singer, and *Rolling Stone Magazine* voted it 1994 record of the year. On the crest of success and following a Golden Globe nomination for her role in *Larry Flynt*, she was transformed from ill-mannered brat to a platinum blond baby-doll who dressed in extraordinary designer garments, preferably by the Italian Versace.

In 1992, a two-second movie scene catapulted Sharon Stone within weeks to one of Hollywood's most sought-after, top-earning actresses: the scene occurs in the psychological thriller *Basic Instinct* when the alleged murderess Catherine Tramell crosses her legs during a police interview, and reveals that she is wearing nothing underneath her dress. In subsequent years Stone fought unsuccessfully to shed her image as a man-eating vamp, but also enjoyed the reputation of being the most intelligent person in Hollywood, with an IQ of 154. She was admired by all for her beauty, elegant dress sense, and ready wit in interviews, and 1995 finally saw her celebrating her long-awaited success as a serious actress in Martin Scorsese's *Casino*. She married Phil Bronstein, copublisher of the *San Francisco Examiner*, in 1998 and is one of the few superstars who has been able to maintain a happy and intimate private life.

When Geri Halliwell, Melanie Brown, Emma Bunton, Victoria Adams, and Melanie Chisholm were, literally, cast together in the mid-1990s to form a girl group, nobody would have guessed that these five 19-to-25-year-old teenies would become the most successful girl band ever. The Spice Girls stormed the world's pop charts with their first single *Wannabe* in 1996 and within only a few months they were as famous as the Beatles. A series of number-one hits was accompanied by a faultless public relations machine which ensured that the girls filled hundreds of gossip columns every day and thus became so popular that Prince Charles even asked them to tea with his youngest son, Harry. All around the world, from San Francisco to Tokyo, thousands upon thousands of girls copied the five Brits: Union Jack miniskirts, pierced tongues, ponytails, tattoos, and Adidas tracksuits, combined with plenty of make-up and sexual aggression. When Geri, alias Ginger Spice, left the band in 1998, the remaining four apologized to their fans "for what they had to go through." The fans recovered quickly, and at the end of the 1990s the remaining four happily looked forward to the new millennium with undiminished success.

Born in Iceland in 1965, Björk Gudmundsdottir started her first band at 14 and rapidly became the most successful postpunk performer in her home country before achieving her first international successes in the late 1980s with her band the Sugarcubes. In 1993 she catapulted herself into the international charts with her solo album *Debut* and rapidly advanced to be become a dance-music icon of the 1990s. Her complex and extravagant video clips became cult movies, her fashion style – a mixture of streetwear and avant-garde design – inspired trendy magazines like *The Face* and *ID*. Among her admirers can be found such top international photographers as Christophe Kutner and Jürgen Teller as well as Jean Paul Gaultier, who even asked her to take to the catwalk for his collection in the late 1990s.

Lara Croft, the first-ever virtual idol, was born in November 1996. With no childhood, no spotty adolescence, no past, she just was: a powerful woman with stunning curves that were rarely covered by more than a bustier and tiny shorts. And with a gun slung casually from her hip. She beamed through the world, from the South Pole across the entire globe, on the search for magical treasures which endowed people with power and wealth. The only requirement to meet this fascinating figure from far-off worlds was a Sony Playstation or a PC. The Tomb Raider games featuring cyberheroine Lara earned the computer-game company Eidos millions: toward the end of the 1990s, the business magazine *Forbes* listed Lara in a report on the richest world stars as having a turnover worth $425 million, the cult publication *Details* voted her one of the sexiest women of the year 1998, and the pop group U2 featured her in one of their videos. Streetwear companies developed whole collections in the Lara Croft style which millions of young girls bought avidly. Lara's official website was soon followed by unauthorized smut-sites which showed the electronic diva topless or in compromising poses.

Diana Frances Spencer, born in Sandringham, Norfolk, in 1961, had barely turned 20 when she achieved world fame as a result of her marriage to Prince Charles, the heir to the British throne, in July 1981. More than 750 million people watched the wedding of the century take place in London's St Paul's Cathedral live on television. People from every continent were well informed by the gossip press, and followed her transformation from free and easy, etiquette-breaching ex-nursery nurse to confident high-society lady. Billions saw the most famous woman in the world on her skiing holidays, with her sons William and Harry, and shared her marital crisis, her commitment to Aids victims, and her work against poverty, drugs, homelessness, and land mines. They were also aware of the princess' weakness for expensive designer clothes in which she was photographed by such star photographers as Patrick Demarchelier. Her success with the public did not merely bother her mother-in-law; it also distressed her. Her ceaseless attempts to escape the attention of the paparazzi tragically ended her life (and that of her chauffeur and her partner Dodi Fayed) on August 31, 1997, when the car in which she was traveling crashed into a pillar in a Parisian tunnel. No other celebrity of the twentieth century has been as mourned as was Princess Diana, whom the whole world spoke of as the Queen of Hearts after her death.

There were few indications that **Oprah Winfrey**, born in 1954 in the US federal state of Mississippi, would one day become the highest-paid entertainer and the first black woman billionaire in the world: born an illegitimate child, sexually abused by her mother's boyfriends, by the age of 14 she was herself the mother of a child, who died shortly after birth, and on top of everything else she was black. She worked as a radio reporter in Nashville for a while, had a part in Steven Spielberg's *The Color Purple* alongside Whoopi Goldberg, and in 1986 she was given her own television program, the *Oprah Winfrey Show*, which made her world-famous. It was not so much her talk-show guests – prostitutes, porn actors, and psychopaths – who made her the best friend of millions of American women; rather it was the fact that she used her own problems as topics for her shows. Her tearful disclosures regarding her childhood, her drug-taking experiences, and her weight problems, and her skill in persuading her guests to speak of extremely private matters – as in her legendary interview with Michael Jackson – earned her worldwide recognition. In the late 1990s, the Empress of the Media had merely to introduce an unknown author for the latter to find themselves on the American bestseller list within three days. Alternatively, if she dedicated a show to the topic of nutrition, the United States would see thousands of people changing their eating habits.

Hillary Diane Rodham was already a successful lawyer and vehement campaigner for the protection of children before she married Bill Clinton, future president of the United States, in 1975. When, in 1993 and at the age of 46, she became America's first lady and moved into the White House, she made it clear that she would sacrifice her career for the nation but would never be a mere appendage to her husband. Her controversial role when she was appointed to the task force on National Health Care Reform, as well as her dominant public appearances, earned her a great deal of criticism but also worldwide admiration and publicity. The media reproached her for being power-hungry and interpreted her tolerant behavior during the Lewinsky affair as being governed by her lust for power: several indignant feminists agreed. Yet millions of women saw and adored Hillary as a modern woman of the 1990s – and certainly suffered with her – for being as

committed to her profession as she was willing to fight, time and again, for the good and the reputation of her family.

One movie was all that was needed to make **Julia Roberts** the most glamorous and desirable actress of the 1990s: after a string of mediocre cinema successes, the 23-year-old beauty from Atlanta starred alongside Richard Gere in the 1990 hit *Pretty Woman* and became the dream woman of the decade. For a while she was the highest-paid actress in Hollywood, but her subsequent movies never quite matched that of the Pretty Woman fairy-tale. However, her private life fueled the headlines for the next ten years. There is hardly a movie star, from Daniel Day-Lewis via Liam Neeson and Jason Patrick to Robert de Niro, with whom she has not reputedly had an affair. After a broken engagement to actor Kiefer Sutherland, she married musician Lyle Lovett in 1993 and divorced in 1995. In 1999 she made a brilliant comeback in the romantic comedy *Notting Hill*, although in the intervening years fashion magazines around the world used even her most insignificant roles as an excuse to adorn their title pages with Julia Roberts.

More than any other fashion model, **Kate Moss** (b. 1974) achieved "personality" status in the 1990s. Her colleagues, like Claudia Schiffer and Cindy Crawford, were also celebrities, but their private lives were never really separated from their success stories and highly polished faces. Kate was completely different: made famous by the controversial Calvin Klein advertising campaign, she was from the beginning the "anorexic Lolita," thus the idol of every young woman and the hate-object of every parent. Her numerous appearances on the cover of *Vogue* paled in comparison to the innumerable reports about her alcohol problem and drug habits and her tempestuous relationship with actor Johnny Depp.

Since 1988, when she won the first of her seven Wimbledon championships, **Steffi Graf**, born in Brühl in Germany in 1969, was celebrated as the number-one German export. As a result, thousands of parents began to enroll their offspring in tennis clubs in the hope of producing another Graf or Becker.

Idealized across the world for her sporting achievements, toughness and fighting spirit, Steffi was at first regarded as a shy, not very attractive young woman whose gracefulness was limited to center court. This did not change until her domineering father Peter Graf was arrested in 1995 for evading millions of dollars'

worth of tax and then sentenced in 1997 to several years in prison. Suddenly she had to fend for herself, and Steffi made the transformation from remote-controlled tennis ace to a woman who was daring enough to have herself photographed by a top photographer, to chat about her fashion likes and dislikes, to make a public statement about her disappointment with regard to her father, and to take her life into her own hands. When she finally announced in the summer of 1999, on the lawn at Wimbledon, that she was retiring from the international tennis circuit, the sport icon's audience demonstrated their heartfelt respect with standing ovations.

Although familiar to audiences worldwide, actress and model **Isabella Rossellini** and singer **Tina Turner** did not become celebrated icons of their era until the 1990s. The reason: both defied the cult of youth and proved that women over 40 have definitely got what it takes to outshine women half their age.

Isabella Rossellini, born in 1952, daughter of Ingrid Bergman, ex-wife of Martin Scorsese and of his colleague David Lynch, was resplendent on more than 500 magazine covers and was the face of cosmetics giant Lancôme before opening up new paths at the end of the decade when she launched her own cosmetics line with Lancaster.

Even more so than Rossellini, Tina Turner, who was born in 1939, became the best advertisement for divorce and maturity: her big break came in 1969 when she and husband Ike performed as the support band to the Rolling Stones. Following separation from her violent husband in 1975, her audience wrote her off, but within less than ten years she triumphed with her solo album *Private Dancer* and her part in *Mad Max III* as a sexy woman in her mid-40s, in skintight microskirts and giddyingly high heels. Following a creative pause, during which she only did a stint as a lingerie model (this in her mid-50s) she celebrated her 60th birthday in 1999 with a Millennium Tour with which she broke all the rules of aging by being fitter and more attractive than ever before and by luring fans from four decades into the concert halls.

Isabella Rossellini and Tina Turner were the "strong women of the 1990s" who set a trend that was to be felt even on the catwalks of Paris when the most famous models of the 1960s, the legends Veruschka, Lauren Hutton, and Carmen, now mature women, modeled the latest collections of the most sought-after fashion designers.

TINA TURNER

OPRAH WINFREY

STEFFI GRAF

HILLARY CLINTON

JULIA ROBERTS

KATE MOSS

ISABELLA ROSSELLINI

American fashion

Margit J. Mayer

"Sportswear exists because American women were the first to live the modern, fast-paced life." *Michael Kors*

The 1940s are popularly regarded as the period when typical American sportswear began, because this was the period when, thanks to the interrupted flow of information from Nazi-occupied Paris and growing American patriotism, an American style of fashion was able for the first time to develop independently of European couture. The roots of the sportswear idea go back to the 19th century: American women have always had the reputation of being more physically active, independent, and inquisitive than their European sisters, and these qualities also characterized their dress sense. They demanded simple, comfortable clothes that could be worn from morning until evening, and American designers of the 20th century saw their prime task as delivering this type of clothing.

American fashion was traditionally a mixture of hand and machine manufacture in which the trends dictated by Paris were copied and adapted (or simplified). The usual European delimitations between the roles of designer, manufacturer,

and retailer had always been more fluid in the United States, where department stores acted as trend-spotters and filters.

In the 1930s, stores like Lord & Taylor began to mention the names of their house designers in advertisements and through promotional activities. In 1938, the first of American *Vogue*'s "American Fashion" issues was published, and names like Elizabeth Hawes, Clare Potter, Bonnie Cashin, Carolyn Schnurer, Tina Leser, Mildred Orrick, and Tom Brigance began to mean something to the standard consumer on the street: as sportswear designers they created ready-to-wear fashions in the 1940s and 1950s that cost one 40th to one 20th of couture prices of the time. The 1960s then saw the emergence of a new generation of designers who put their own stamp on the concept of sportswear: Calvin Klein, Ralph Lauren, and Donna Karan soon became giants of marketing

who were to make a lasting impression on the market with their designs. In the 1990s American fashion forsook the last vestiges of its insularity and became a global phenomenon. Megalabels like Gap and CK Calvin Klein followed in the footsteps of Coca-Cola and MacDonald's, providing their products with a blanket international market by speedily expanding their networks of outlets.

Transatlantic transfer, with its constantly increasing exchange of goods and ideas, manifests itself in fashion by huge investments in advertising and structures of distribution, and by the appointment of young American designers as creative directors for European luxury labels. The resulting association of European tradition and marketing-conscious American creativity is undoubtedly one of the most interesting phenomena of the decade.

Claire McCardell (1905–58)

Sporty, multifunctional, and chic, this summer combination of swimsuit and skirt is also from 1946. Ideal for the woman who wants it all: fun, action, and to be attractive at the same time. Only one thing had to go: time spent with complicated changes of clothing. As with many of her designs, Claire McCardell was ahead of her time.

It is no coincidence that women dominate America's first generation of designers. Female designers typically put practical considerations before visual effect. The star of the fashion problem-solvers of the 1940s was an inventive young woman from Maryland who, as a student at Parson's School of Design, spent a year in Paris, where she enthusiastically redrafted designs by Chanel and Vionnet, thereby finding her own style.

Claire McCardell worked in the 1930s and 1940s but she thought like a fashion designer of the 1990s: the body determined what a dress should look like. Her style vocabulary – wraparound effects, spaghetti shoulder straps or belts, shorts, dirndls, striped cotton, and denim for evening wear – was characterized by the omission of any form of pretension: no shoulder pads, no restrictive foundation garments, no decoration for the sake of decoration. McCardell's silhouette was youthful; her clothes, made of "honest" materials, were reminiscent of children's wear and beachwear, and this is precisely where she was prophetic: during the decades that followed, adult fashions would become increasingly sporty and thus more childlike in their simplicity. Among McCardell's design classics are the Monastic Dress designed in 1938, a tent dress made of wool jersey which could be worn with or without a belt, and the Pop-over-Dress which was introduced to the market in 1942, a housedress made of quilted denim which had an oven glove attached to it and which was sold by the tens of thousands at the price of $6.96. By comparison the average dress available in the exclusive New York salon of Mainbocher, who was born in Chicago and became famous as a couturier in Paris, would have cost $810 in 1940.

Charles James (1906–78)

Because of the sculptural form of his clothes, Charles James was frequently described as a sculptor of fashion. Born in Britain, James opened a hat shop in Chicago in 1926 and presented his first collection of clothing designs two years later in New York. In 1940 he opened a couture house and was hired by Elizabeth Arden to establish the fashion and accessories salon at Arden on Fifth Avenue. Psychologically unstable and a manic perfectionist, James often spent months working on a garment, which could have the effect of driving his clients to the edge of despair. For his asymmetric silhouettes he preferred to use dramatic fabrics like faille, duchesse satin, and velvet. His specialty was in unusual color combinations – apricot and eggplant, pale pink and cinnamon – which transformed the wearer into a decadent, even obscene, flower. Where Christian Dior's flowers were lilies of the valley and roses, James's aesthetic was in the service of orchids and sea anemones.

In 1948, his best client, American heiress Millicent Rogers, dedicated to him an exhibition at the Brooklyn Museum; in *A Decade of Design*, she showed all the gowns that he had made for her over ten years. Following a failed copyright lawsuit against a blouse manufacturer, James lost every sense of reality with regard to the fashion business, closed his made-to-measure salon in 1958, and spent the rest of his life documenting his old designs.

Opposite:
With their unusual silhouettes and sophisticated draping, Charles James's creations were described as the work of a genius, but he needed months, sometimes years, to finish a single garment. Here photographer Cecil Beaton captured the American couturier at work.

The wife of press baron Randolph Hearst having an evening gown fitted. To own a Charles James creation was regarded as *non plus ultra*. Even Gabrielle Chanel and Elsa Schiaparelli owned dresses made by this fashion designer.

Oleg Cassini

Opposite:
Oleg Cassini worked as an assistant in Hollywood before setting up as fashion designer under his own name. In 1941 he made this dress for actress Gene Tierney.

Cassini presents to a group of fashion editors his design for the dress that the future American first lady was to wear at the inauguration of her husband as president of the United States.

Jacqueline Kennedy became an icon of conservative youth in the 1960s, because the graphic elegance of the dazzling wife of the president of the United States embodied a fusion of girlishness and ladylike demeanor.

In symbiotic collaboration, Jackie and her personal couturier Oleg Cassini (b. 1913) designed a lifestyle uniform for her: chiefly straight dresses with matching coats, suits with short, boxy jackets, and simple yet dramatic evening gowns in a palette of fresh pastel shades such as apricot, sky blue, grass green, pale pink, yellow, beige, and white. The president's wife, with her instinct for the photogenic, would add to these a string of pearls, white gloves, and a white cloth clutch bag. New York's ready-to-wear companies adapted this charming minimalism to suit every woman, and America's enthusiastic women copied the look, including the bouffant hair and low-heeled court shoes.

Rudi Gernreich (1922–85)

The trend for youthfulness, which for men was represented by rebels like Elvis Presley and James Dean, found its American womenswear expression in the college look. Twinsets, kilts, Capri pants, and loafers with bobby socks were worn by such movie stars as Natalie Wood and Audrey Hepburn, who loaded these garments with the power of seduction. Thus, halfway through the century, the prevailing trend made an about turn, which was also reflected in interior design. Until then, the United States had admired Europe's creative output; now Europe began to look toward the United States.

American fashion in the 1960s was also dominated by youth, so that the meaning of the word itself changed. Where it had previously stood for innocence and nonchalance, it acquired during the first half of the decade the meaning of avant-garde and hipness and, at its end, it signified rebellion and experiment. Europe had Courrèges and Mary Quant, America had Rudi Gernreich. He was born in Vienna and in 1938 emigrated to California, where he initially worked as a dancer before founding his fashion label. Gernreich's futuristic designs – dresses featuring plastic inserts, transparent blouses, and a swimsuit with two V-shaped straps forming the top half (3000 Topless Bathing Suits, or monokinis, were sold in total) – pushed the body into view while his models, dressed in military or safari styles, reflected the new fighting spirit of the women's liberation movement.

Gernreich's innovations in the sphere of underwear have had a lasting effect. They include the body stocking of skin-colored polyamide, which he introduced in 1964, or his "no-bra bra" made of unreinforced nylon, which allowed breasts their natural shape.

Roy Halston (1932–90)

Below left:
Roy Halston's name experienced an unexpected comeback under the artistic direction of Randolph Duke Jahren. This top with a cascading neckline featured in his fall/winter 1997/98 collection.

Below right:
Roy Halston was also a trained milliner and designed headgear for other designers, including Charles James. He also created the so-called pillbox hat, which Jackie Kennedy made famous in the 1960s. Here Halston is seen discussing the merits of a variety of hats with Italian actress Virna Lisi.

The quintessential American designer of the 1970s was Roy Halston Frowick, known as Halston. As America's answer to Yves Saint Laurent, he gave sportswear a sophistication which had seemed impossible beforehand. Halston, who had studied art in Chicago, initially worked as a milliner for a luxury department store in New York. By the end of the 1960s he was able to start his own company.

Halston's signature style – halterneck dresses and silk jersey jumpsuits, turtlenecks and simple shirtdresses, ultrasuede blazers and trenchcoats – endowed the sensible all-American look with a hefty dose of jet set decadence, thus making him irresistible to the stars.

Halston became the first American designer of the media era. No longer a mere clothing supplier, he became a style guru, photographed by the paparazzi at receptions or in front of Studio 54 in the company of clients like Liza Minnelli and Bianca Jagger, and his scandals only fueled the publicity surrounding his designs.

Halston's lasting influence is visible right through to Calvin Klein and the minimalist sex of Gucci's 1990s designs (in the mid-1990s Tom Ford seriously cannibalized the 1970s star designer's work for his collections), whereby his cocaine addiction and death from Aids only served to perpetuate the legend. In 1996, a group of financiers relaunched his label.

Bill Blass (1921–74)

When President Reagan took office in January 1981, fashion also saw the return of conservative tendencies. Society designers like Bill Blass supplied the escorts of the new moneyed aristocracy with jewels for the whole body: extravagant cocktail and evening dresses of draped silk taffeta and lace in black, pink, and shades of gemstone. Bill Blass was regarded as the grand old man of American fashion, not only because he was alleged to be the first American whose name was printed on a fashion label, but because he knew how to combine pragmatism with Hollywood glamour. His designs, including those for evening wear, were simply cut, easy to wear, not overladen with decoration yet never unassuming. He loved clear colors, graphic contrasts, and unusual combinations like sporty cashmere jumpers with long satin skirts. His clients appreciated that he knew how to combine American sportswear with European elegance. Even when he based his womenswear collections on men's suits or ethnic national dress, he did so with humor and a sense of chic, and even his short-trousered safari suits were elegant enough to wear in the city. Blass said of himself that his style was influenced by early Hollywood movies and costume designer Adrian.

"Positively Blassfamous" was the advertising slogan for Bill Blass's 1965 collection. For almost 40 years the American designer managed successfully to stay in business. He recognized the trends of the period, as demonstrated by the opulent cut of the dress from 1961 (*below right*) and the simple, reduced form of the coat (*below left*).

Calvin Klein

Calvin Klein's collections do not provide trendsetting visions of the future, but the proprietor of the largest fashion empire in the world succeeds in creating clothes with an equally timeless and contemporary feel about them, which endow the wearer with an erotic presence, as demonstrated by Kate Moss in this low-cut dress of 1995 (*right*) or the flowing dresses from his fall/winter 1998/99 collection (*far right*).

Opposite:
These two creations from Calvin Klein's 1998/99 season have an Asiatic feel about them; the ensemble of simple aesthetic (*right*) and the bound breast (*left*) are reminiscent of traditional Japanese dress.

Like his colleague Ralph Lauren, Calvin Klein (b. 1942) was born in the Bronx, and became a giant of lifestyle marketing in the 1980s. Klein founded his business in the late 1960s. In the 1970s he was part of the generation of designers who dressed women in feminine versions of menswear. The single-breasted blazer with turned-up lapels became a core item of every woman's wardrobe, the cut of pantsuits exactly followed that of their masculine models, and were worn with tailored shirts. Gangster pinstripes, blouses with dress-shirt collars, and white linen three-piece suits satisfied the nostalgia which had been triggered by such movies as *Borsalino*, *The Godfather*, and *The Great Gatsby*. Finally, Calvin Klein's abstract 1980s' designs, his simple pantsuits, T-shirt dresses, and figure-hugging jeans realized a basic tenet of the American look: even the most modest item of clothing can rise to the

Pantheon of chic because the determining criterion for style is not *what*, but *how*. Another aspect which links America's new big designer with Ralph Lauren is the fact that they both consider fashion as an overall work of art: Klein sells not only clothes but a vision of a modern existence which he promotes with advertising campaigns featuring the photography of Bruce Weber, and highly stylized stores which reflect their own lifestyle.

The hub of Klein's aesthetic is sexuality. The advertising for his underwear, jeans, and perfume transferred the body-obsession of gay culture to heterosexual self-consciousness, thereby significantly contributing to a softening of the puritanical foundations of late 20th-century American society. Beginning in the mid-1990s Klein's collections, and Donna Karan's, began to incorporate influences from Japanese avant-garde fashion which diverged from the codex of classic American sportswear.

Ralph Lauren

Ralph Lauren (b. 1939) is regarded as the cowboy among American fashion designers because he appreciates the boots worn by the heroes of the American Western as much as their jeans and fringed suede jackets. He has refined them to such an extent that they are now regarded as the American Look par excellence. However, he also permitted the traditional lifestyle of the British landed gentry, which the white American ruling class has always taken as a model, to come back to life, starting with the comfortable tweed jacket right down to an image of well-tended family life. Who could forget the advertising campaigns which featured Bruce Weber's photographs of several generations of a family, apparently as wealthy as they seemed happy, at leisure on the family's country estate? Lauren was subsequently described as an immensely clever marketer of American sportswear. Yet that is something that he does not understand: "What do they expect of me? I only do what I love to do. I don't like fashion. I like clothes that never look old-fashioned." Under his polo player's trademark, Ralph Laurent joins historic inspiration with an escapist fashion classicism which combines all the potential for glamour that America's cultural heritage has to offer, from the country style à la Gary Cooper to the androgynous nonchalance of Katharine Hepburn. Ralph Lauren's mythical America has no place for losers; it demonstrated to the nouveaux riches of the 1980s just how good money, whether old or new, could look. The hub of his aesthetic is social status. As for himself, the Bronx-born son of Jewish immigrants from Russia, who began his career in fashion by selling neckties, realized the vision of a perfect way of life a long time ago.

Opposite:
Ralph Lauren's fashion spectrum is broad: traditional clothes inspired by English country styles and that of the American Western stand alongside Polo Sport and elegant womenswear, as demonstrated by these two examples of his fall/winter 1997/98 collection.

Norma Kamali

American women designers were also influential trendsetters in the 1980s, although their work covered the full spectrum of styles. Norma Kamali (b. 1945) came to be for sweatshirt fleece what Sonia Rykiel had been for jersey. She developed a functional daywear line out of a material which had previously been reserved for gym wear.

Kamali's mix of retro designs and voluminous "sleeping bag" coats produced an electrifying look which mirrored the schizophrenic mood of the decade's fashion. The former flight attendant, who used to enjoy rummaging around London boutiques like Biba, started with a shop which she and her husband opened in New York in 1968 and which stocked mainly English fashion items. Following her divorce in 1978 she began to work on her own under the abbreviation OMO (On My Own). She was not afraid of inserting huge shoulder pads into her comfortable sweatshirts in order to elevate them to the status of 1980s power suits. Later on she succeeded in working the "sloppy" material to make it look sexy, and she was one of the first to take the leotard out of the fitness center and on to the street.

Donna Karan

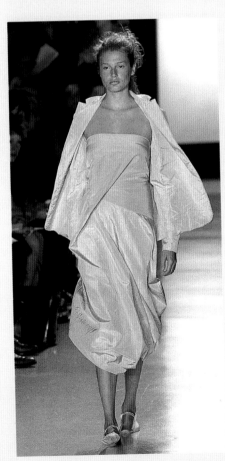

With the advent of 1980s power woman, who replaced the female manager in the tailored suit and blouse as the archetype of emancipated woman, Donna Karan (b. 1948) became the first female American designer to have a global psychological impact.

Karan, who trained with Queen of Sportswear Anne Klein, following whose death she and Louis del'Olio kept the label going, presented her first collection in May 1985. These designs were thoroughly competent and thoroughly sensual, featuring jersey and wool crêpe, opaque black pantyhose, and sculptural jewelry by Robert Lee Morris. Karan had thought of seven items with which the working woman would feel perfectly dressed all day long. The base was the body, which could be worn with pants or a skirt, under a jacket or on its own and to which she was the first to add buttons. Her ensembles were fitted with the sportswear standards of the 1940s: wraparound tops, sarong skirts, bodysuits, wide leather belts, the concept of assembling a wardrobe from various pieces of a jigsaw – a new aggressive touch. Whereas Claire McCardell and others had designed what still seemed like playtime clothes, Donna Karan's sovereign sexiness, which was the result of streamlined influences from Paris, such as Thierry Mugler and Azzedine Alaïa, became the combat fatigues worn in the battle for the boss's chair.

As the designer's alter ego, model Rosemarie McGrotha realized the dream of the first woman president in an advertising campaign – dressed, naturally, in Donna Karan. However, in the late 1990s Donna Karan presented herself as more gentle, contemplative, and sensual, instead of ostentatiously strong and sexy. Again, she has hit the core of women's desires, who feel, just as she does, overpowered by the career trip. She commented on her New York flagship store: "It is about soup and everything that keeps you warm."

Donna Karan at the end of the millennium: she revived the concept of the balloon skirt for the summer of 1999, but in a form which, typically Prima Donna, allows sufficient space for movement. Her winter 1999/2000 collection combines casualness with severity.

Anna Sui

Opposite:
A pinch of Nina Hagen, a pinch of glamour, a pinch of mini-crini: a mixture of styles from the fall/winter 1997 collection.

Anna Sui describes her creations as a jigsaw look, which generally incorporates an echo of the 1960s, whether in Naomi Campbell's patchwork skirt (*below left*) or the pattern of the fabric (*below right*) from her 1999 collection, or the cut of the top (*below center*) modeled by Linda Evangelista in 1995.

With Michael Kors, Marc Jacobs, Isaac Mizrahi, Todd Oldham, and Anna Sui, all of whom were born between 1955 and 1961, a new generation of American designers stepped into the limelight. While Kors and Jacobs followed the modernist tradition, effortlessly finding the transition to the clean lines of the 1990s, Oldham and Sui's aesthetic of fun was rather more suited to the decorative spirit of the 1980s. Isaac Mizrahi's creative new interpretations of the American look of the 1940s and 1950s transformed him into the darling of the media, but his business was unable to keep up with his image. He closed his studio in 1998 in order to concentrate on his other passion: the cinema.

Anna Sui also hesitated between two passions for a long time: should she style a look from existing items or create completely new designs? After graduating from Parson's School of Design, she first worked with her fellow student Steven Meisel, who has since become the fashion photographer of the 1990s. Her knowledge of fashion – she has been devouring glossy magazines since early childhood, during the course of which she has assembled an archive of inspiring photographs – and her talent for putting together a surprisingly contemporary look from individual pieces from various periods and designers, helped her to become a highly sought-after stylist.

After the department store Macy's began to order her designs, Anna Sui finally launched her own label in 1981. Her designs are as eclectic as her styling, but behind the cheerfully wild outfits there are surprisingly wearable and practical individual pieces. Small wonder considering that Anna Sui spent some time working for a sportswear manufacturer.

Left and opposite:
In the United States **Marc Jacobs**
(b. 1963) was one of the young
designers who brought a breath of
fresh air to the world of fashion, and
who were promptly hired by French
fashion houses. Typically of the 1990s,
Jacobs' own collection contains clear
references to the 1950s and 1960s
(*opposite, left and center*).
As the creative director of Vuitton,
he designed clothes for self-confident,
professional women, including a coat
and pullover-scarf (*opposite, right*) and
a fashionable, short-sleeved turtleneck
(*left*) – and, naturally, the obligatory
LV-bag.
His credo is "I love to transform
everyday clothes into luxury items."
In attempting to do this, he has
created the perfect synthesis of
American pragmatism and European
tradition. For him, Paris is the city
of beauty, but "you can only find
energy in New York."

Following pages:
Michael Kors (b. 1960) also
understands the difference between
America and Europe. He has worked
in Paris as the creative director for
Céline since 1997. "French women
treat themselves with goose liver pâte
while Americans share a salad." He
uses this knowledge in his fashion,
which apart from being comfortable,
always retains a certain amount of
lavishness. This has made him
successful not only at Céline in Paris
but also with his own line in New
York, where he was honored in 1999
"designer of the year." *Left* are his
designs for Céline's spring/summer
1999 collection, *right*, his designs for
his own label, which has remained
independent until now. Like Jacobs,
Kors has always had a hand and an eye
for simple elegance and no fear of
contact with new materials and street
fashion. Not surprising that his
designs suited the 1990s so well!

Betsey Johnson

A fashion newcomer in the 1960s, Betsey Johnson attracted attention with her unusual ideas, like this mirror dress of 1966 (*opposite page*). Little has changed since then, as demonstrated by the Lolita look with a frilled skirt (*below left*) and the transparent hobble skirt (*below right*).

Betsey Johnson became established in the 1970s as a specialist for avant-garde sex appeal. Her specialty is brashly colorful printed patterns which are amusing even to those who find them somewhat tasteless. When she had sold a few of her early designs to the cult New York store Paraphernalia, her meteoric rise was unstoppable. And when Julie Christie wore her famous dress with the 10-inch-long retractable collar, Johnson's career was made. The critics waited until 1999 before awarding her a prize for her "timeless talent" – another reason for Johnson to perform her characteristic cartwheel, something she has done after every show.

The permanent future

A conversation with Helmut Lang

The following transcript is an extract from two extensive interviews which Margit J. Mayer held in New York with Helmut Lang in the winter of 1998/99 and which were supplemented by a telephone conversation in the spring of 1999.

MM: Is fashion becoming more democratic or more élitist at the moment?

HL: I am trying to work this out for myself right now. But perhaps all those old rhythms are outdated. It looks like fashion today may be democratic as well as élitist, an organic, inherent contradiction.

MM: Helmut Lang's collection includes a number of basics, but some absolute luxury products as well. What is your most expensive item?

HL: Probably one of the cashmere coats with complex internal lives. When something is particularly detailed it becomes expensive. Nothing costs more than labor. Or the use of very particular fabrics. We have used a fabric for our winter 1999/2000 collection in which pure silver has been woven into silk. The price question is a very personal one ... democratic or élitist, cheap or luxurious – in fact people with fashion sensitivity and money will generally pick and choose from both. Basically, today's limitations in fashion are of a financial nature, even for people with a lot of fashion experience. It all comes down to finances in a brutal way. You can buy a small house in the best area, or a big house in not such a good area.

MM: The small house in the best area wins every time.

HL: Yes [laughs]. Or one in between. In any case, I think that fashion won't lose this, the coexistence of special objects and everyday objects.

MM: What are you wearing today?

HL: What I always wear. A V-necked cashmere sweater, one of my personal basics, over a T-shirt. The T-shirt cost nothing, the cashmere cost a lot. Both are equally important. I expect both to have a decent cut and to make me feel good. My tuxedo, of which I have two versions, a made-to-measure one and another off the peg, is a special item which I rarely wear. What's more important – sweater or tuxedo? Difficult to say. The meaning of the everyday in fashion has changed. Its importance on the fashion scale of value has increased tremendously. Those things that I put on each day without really thinking have a much greater effect on my image than the clothes I only wear to rare events for which I consciously dress up.

MM: I get the impression that the influence on mass fashion of many of the most celebrated designers has been negligible in the last few years. A typical example would be John Galliano. His historicizing Dior look does not seem to have had any effect on the street.

It all comes down to finances in a brutal way. You can buy a small house in the best area, or a big house in not such a good area.

HL: These old systems of classification – couture, prêt-à-porter, street fashion – are no longer applicable. The boundaries have dissolved, the categories no longer exist in their pure form. The currently most influential designer labels use elements from all three categories to make up a single whole. They have taken over the inspirational role which used to be reserved for couture and then, starting in the 1960s, street fashion, and are driving the fashion machine on. The dressmakers who used to copy and reinterpret Dior in the 1950s have been replaced by industrial companies from every price bracket, from chains like Gap or H&M to the high end labels. These absorb the impulses generated by creative labels and then make huge global business with it. This is where direct influences will become visible, season after season.

MM: Helmut Lang's clothes are frequently described as androgynous, but that's not really accurate. Your style treats men and women with the same sense of fairness, although differently for each gender. How do you see the future of sex appeal?

HL: I believe that men and women will always dress differently. What is important is that the basic right to an individual dress style has to remain the driving force. Men and women, that's a natural phenomenon like day and night. We now know that women are feminine and masculine, and that men are feminine and masculine. How much of each there is depends on how much of each one permits there to be. However, there will never be a general suspension of the differences because sex is too strong a basic instinct. The mating game creates these differences all by itself.

We have had all sorts of cyclical variations, but the visual contrast between men and women has survived.

MM: Until a few years ago, men were visually more reserved in the way they dressed, while women were the ones who gave, who exhibited themselves. Since then there has been a marked change in the balance. With the almost unchanged monochrome, preferably dark suit of the last century, men have been more miserly with respect to their physical expression than ever before in history.

HL: That's correct. Yet from an historical perspective this was only a very short period of time. There have been centuries when men were utterly obvious and women were much more restrained ... I think the fashion patterns which have survived so far will be those that continue to survive. We have had all sorts of cyclical variations, but the visual contrast between men and women has survived.

MM: What about revolt and anti-establishment opposition? These were important topics in 20th-century fashion. This impulse seems to have gone rather lame.

HL: The question is whether we are in any position to assess what is revolutionary in our own time. It is true that there do not seem to be any obvious taboos at the moment. Basically, we are just assimilating the breaches of every taboo ever undertaken by fashion. And at the moment there just is no obvious topic, like the emancipation of women was during the course of the last century. That's a fact.

On the other hand, we are currently in the middle of a huge technical revolution and this may possibly bring something new. I don't believe that fashion develops out of itself. This comes from a social level, from major social upheavals. The revolution in communication technology is to us what the Industrial Revolution was 100 years ago. We will probably see the consequences of this in ten years' time.

MM: The Industrial Revolution formed the aesthetic sensibilities of the entire 20th century. From modernist architecture and the "machine for living," to the streamlined ideal for women's bodies – slimmer shape, shorter hair, shorter skirts, agility therefore less volume.

HL: We may assume that the current revolution in communication technology will trigger something like it. Our lifestyle will change, and this will probably give us a new sensitivity and new values as regards dress. However, right now we are still too stuck in the cruel preliminary phase to be able to foresee what the effects will be. To attempt a prognosis now would be as useful as a horoscope in a fashion magazine. The only thing we can say for sure is that things will change, and that it will be far more than a mere trend. We are not dealing here within dimensions of "graphic 1960s now, sloppy hippie 1970s next." The next movement will have a completely different dimension. We have to prepare ourselves for a really big change.

The revolution in communication technology is to us what the Industrial Revolution was 100 years ago. We will probably see the consequences of this in ten years' time.

MM: Returning to everyday fashion in 1999. It looks as if talented young designers are not acknowledged until they go to work for traditional labels which often form part of luxury goods conglomerates.

HL: It is a feature of the 1990s that various designers are organized by larger houses through which they may become well known. Yet there are also many who have chosen to go down a different, individual route. And the phenomenon as such was there before. Saint Laurent started at Dior and then founded his own house. Karl Lagerfeld designed for Chloé from the mid-1960s until the 1980s. Basically, that isn't really very important. The important legitimacy for any designer is provided by continuity and consistency which gradually endows his work with definition and therefore earns him respect. Basically the only important consideration for a designer is to become himself. It is a path which leads past many stations, none of which are that terribly important in the end.

The Prada group and I are now developing a fourth model – a joint venture of independently creative people ... It is a system which enables us to react to new circumstances in a rapidly globalizing economy.

MM: What is your assessment of the growing trend toward fashion houses becoming subsumed by luxury conglomerates? What long-term effect will label empires like Bernard Arnault's LVMH [Louis Vuitton Moët Hennessy] have on the fashion industry?

HL: With Arnault's core fashion properties – Dior, Givenchy, Céline, Loewe – labels whose original designers are either dead or no longer working, or who never had well-known designers working for them, are being continued for business reasons. However, it is quite feasible for fashion houses whose designers still operate within the company to merge, as it would be for two, three, or four designers to get together to form a corporation, just as banks or the automobile industry do now.

MM: You entered into precisely such a joint venture with the Italian Prada group in order to internationalize the Helmut Lang label. What moved you to take this step? You retain full autonomy over both design and image control, and yet there are intense discussions in the industry as to whether and how such a marriage can work.

HL: One advantage is that areas which have nothing to do with the creative process as such – manufacture, accounting, marketing – can be more rationally organized jointly. This enables designers to find a new position of economic power. Fundamentally, I believe that the time has come to get to grips with entirely new business models. We are poised on the threshold of a new validity of the fashion business as a whole, and this also needs to be reflected in the logistics.

MM: Until now there were three opportunities for designers to realize their fashion design visions or bring their designs to the customer: first, the traditional route, which is still the norm among established labels from Armani to Ralph Lauren, via licensing contracts with a variety of manufacturers;

second, the system which was popularized in the 1990s whereby a designer is appointed to create a collection for an existing label – Tom Ford for Gucci, Alexander McQueen for Givenchy, Marc Jacobs for Louis Vuitton, etc.; and third, total independence, i.e. ownership of the entire manufacturing and marketing apparatus, from design studio via various manufacturing plants to marketing and stores. The third model is not really feasible for a single person or company once a certain volume of goods has been surpassed. It only really works for couturiers like Azzedine Alaïa.

HL: The Prada group and I are now developing a fourth model, a joint venture of independently creative people who are seeking to establish a cycle of creation, manufacturing, and retail by means of joint organization. It is a system which enables us to react to new circumstances in a rapidly globalizing economy.

MM: And who has the power? Who controls what, and thus whom?

HL: We have to free ourselves from old ideas of control, which don't work in practice anyway. The process which leads from the design stage to the garment hanging in a store has become too complex for them. The redefinition of independence and creative freedom in a fashion context where manufacture and marketing are spread out all over the planet simply demands new models. As with any change, this is bound up with risks, although the risk inherent in not changing would be much greater. I believe that these individual mergers, if one may call them that, can become a major new factor in the world of fashion.

MM: During the last decade of the 20th century, the influence of the American sportswear aesthetic has increased dramatically. It is apparent that traditional European values – elegance, workmanship – are merging with the traditionally American, i.e. sportiness and versatility. It seems that you are operating at the crossing point of these two traditions. Your company's move in 1998 from Europe to America also fits this context. What effect has the move from Vienna to New York had on your style?

HL: None. In the first place, my aesthetic education was already influenced by America. Like most Europeans of my generation I have grown up wearing jeans and T-shirts. When the time came to wear something else, this provided the basis for finding a new style. On

The permanent future

the one hand there was a central European tradition, an understanding of the value of made-to-measure clothes, a certain instinct for sophistication. And then came the dress code from America. Both are staples of clothing. What is exciting is the mixture of elements from both cultural spheres, and that is what has defined my style. What is interesting, however, is that American basics have always been regarded as special in Europe, whereas they are really only seen as basics in the USA itself.

I believe that there will be a redistribution of values in the fashion landscape as a whole. Not just in terms of the calendar, but also in terms of content. For example, there should soon be a change in the presentation of fashion designers themselves.

MM: Europeans have an emotional response to the classics of American fashion which the Americans don't have. The liberation of Europe from the Nazis by the GIs, who for Europeans cannot be separated from the idea of T-shirts and khaki pants, pop music, and Hollywood movies, have endowed these simple garments with a great deal of glamour in European eyes.

HL: Exactly. On the other hand, there is a certain amount of respect in New York for Europe, especially for Britain, which has spread over to the culture of clothing. This is another romantic vision created by geographic distance.

MM: Your decision, taken after the move, to show your collection before the European collections triggered a minor revolution. American designers like Calvin Klein sided with you and in the spring of 1999, for the first time in history, the New York fashion shows took place before those of Milan, London, and Paris. How does it feel to be a rebel?

HL: The whole thing has developed a dynamic of its own which we observe with some surprise. I guess that's how important changes sometimes have to happen: from the feeling that something needs to change in one's own life. Because it no longer makes sense to follow the system blindly. I believe that there will be a redistribution of values in the fashion landscape as a whole. Not just in terms of the calendar, but also in terms of content. For example, there should soon be a change in the presentation of fashion designers themselves. It could well be that we shall soon cease to be so focused on the personality of the creator, on the cult surrounding the fashion designer as celebrity. It is difficult to assess where exactly it will lead to, but I think it will soon have a new structure.

MM: You were the first designer to show your collection on the Net. How do you see the link between fashion and the Internet in the future?

HL: I think that the Internet is going to be extremely important. Information about collections and designers' philosophies will become accessible across the world, independently of the physical location of stores or showrooms. A designer label's website will have the same role as a catalog at an exhibition – not a replacement for the actual confrontation with the garments, but an introduction or reminder. However, information on the Internet has to be presented properly. Not in the current playful mode like a computer game, but seriously as a new classic means of information. We are currently working on an extension of our website, including information on the fabric for each garment, etc. This will then function as a professional lookbook for the press when they need to order outfits for photographic shoots, and also as a source of information for the wider public, i.e. information on where the items can be purchased. The Internet has given us the opportunity to pass on information directly to the consumer, without detours or interim interpretations.

MM: Will this mean the end of fashion magazines in the long term?

HL: Not at all. However, it will become increasingly important for magazines and television programs to have their own language, their own spirit, for which they are bought or viewed. A signature which attracts people. Because the basic information ...

MM: What's new, where can I buy it, how much is it?

HL: ... will increasingly become available on the Net.

MM: What about selling designer fashion through the Internet? Do you see an opportunity there for designers of avant-garde garments like yourself?

HL: Selling through the Internet is becoming a major topic, and in our market segment as well. It is simply a modern form of the mail-order catalog. This enormous change is already happening with regard to the sale of books, CDs, and videos and the Web will also have a huge impact on the fashion industry.

MM: Although fashion, unlike books or CDs, entails the problem of the body. You can't touch or try these things on before ordering.

Selling through the Internet is becoming a major topic, and in our market segment as well. It is simply a modern form of the order catalog.

HL: Yes, but in fashion too there are many products which we buy repeatedly without trying them on. Simple things like underwear or hosiery, or bed linen that one is familiar with. These are the boring bits of shopping. In fashion too many things are just a question of stocking up and this can be done much more simply and more comfortably via the Internet. Shopping in its real sense, that is, shopping with atmosphere, where one is continuously stimulated and inspired, can still happen. I could imagine that there will one day be a sort of global store. The Internet shows what's available and then there are various points of sale which one can go to. Or you order straight away and have it sent. The Internet is extremely general on the one hand, but also very individual on the other: this dichotomy seems to me to be the perfect precondition for a future.

MM: During the Paris winter 1999/2000 shows there was a palpable tiring of the theatrical retro style which has most recently dominated fashion and the fashion media. Does that mean that modernism has conclusively won and that fashion will in future only be simply cut garments made of luxurious fabrics?

HL: No, I believe that theatricality in fashion will continue, but in a new form. There must always be a counterbalance to modernism. In the end, the problem was not the drama, but the fact that it hadn't really been a new interpretation. It was an antiquated floor show for which things that had once been alive – beading in the 1920s, bias-cut dresses in the 1930s, colors and fabrics in the 1970s – were reissued for show. It would be far more interesting to find a modern version of elegance and opulence. I think this has to be the next challenge. It is now taken for granted that the trend of simplicity equals good taste. The logical countermovement should be eccentricity.

MM: Yet the problem is: what can eccentricity, which after all is a form of rebellion against established style, have to prove in this day and age? What could it rebel against in a period where it seems that everything goes? Fashion today seems to lack intrinsic meaning, and that can't just be blamed on the designers. The roots of this "speechlessness," manifested in visual prattling, must lie in the destruction of social cohesion and in the dramatic changes in the relationship between men and women.

HL: I think that we shall return individuality to the secure net of fashionable codes. Those old words like "eccentric" and "opulence" have to be seen in a completely open context nowadays. The process of self-invention means that one can take a step further in defining the self as soon as one meets too many similar interpretations. People want to be different, unique individuals.

There must always be a counterbalance to modernism. In the end, the problem was not drama, but the fact that it hadn't really been a new interpretation.

MM: During this century, the outward appearance of our bodies and living spaces has provided an enormously fecund topic. Fashion, design, and lifestyle have caught up with traditional artforms like painting and architecture. Could it be that this game of personal expression could soon lose its importance?

HL: If this breaks down, it will mean much more than the collapse of fashion. Shortly after humans discovered that they could use themselves as a surface, there came the idea that this was a way of defining who we were. That we could communicate things with our appearance. This form of communication was used for hierarchies, for power, for seduction, for rebellion, and all these options remain today. I believe that fashion is so elementarily human in this sense that it will never disappear. What will change is the way in which it is manifested. This can shift from the male sphere to the female, and back again. Overall, however, the expression of the self through our surface is evidently a basic human need.

MM: You don't think that our exposure to virtual images will change that? There is a view of the future which holds that we shall soon just be sitting in front of our computers, dressed in pajama-type clothes, and that our skill at composing e-mails will count much more than our clothes or make-up.

HL: I don't think that the developments now taking place in the communications sector will so simply transfer across to fashion. If we look at the ideas that people had of the future in the 1950s and 1960s ... on a technical level much has come true, from space travel to a general increase in supervision. What hasn't come true is how we look and how we live as individuals.

MM: However, the definition of fashion as a whole has changed dramatically since the middle of the century.

As soon as fashion is handed over to the public, it will do something to it. This has nothing to do with advertising but with the actual reaction of each individual at any given moment.

HL: That's true. Fashion has become a given of cultural education. It has ceased to make childish gestures in the sense of "this is the season's color" or "skirts have to be this length." Fashion has become more mature, more global, and also more individual. Charleston in the 1920s, Dior in the 1950s – right up until the 1970s there were always these clearly defined looks. Not until the 1980s did it all start to fan out a bit. Because there was a society which could deal with a much broader fashion spectrum. Fashion always contains some reflection of societal processes. Clothing will not change in its essence until external factors make this necessary. For instance, if clothing, for whatever reason, has to become protective clothing, i.e. when one of those scenarios comes true.

MM: The looks of the 20th century have been strong reactions to the two world wars on the one hand, but also a medium of women's liberation on the other. The latter has been a theme throughout the century, and the process has now been more or less completed. This has created an eerily empty, exhausted situation. As a Western woman I no longer have to fear abuse for wearing pants. On the other hand, pants no longer prove anything and that spoils the fun.

HL: The time for combative activism is over. Things are much more subtle nowadays. In society as a whole there has been a great liberalization, which is a good thing. The revolutionary component is not important at the moment. We prefer to define ourselves in purely personal terms. Somehow, clothes in the fashionable context reflect this quite strongly. Fashion is in fact the medium in which social movements are directly formulated.

MM: Could it be that fashion has already overtaken the spirit of the times and is no longer merely a mirror, but also a crystal ball? That it predicts general tendencies? This is the impression I've been getting lately.

HL: Through its direct links to the media, fashion can very speedily take up societal processes, including those of minorities, and turn them into topics. The work of the designers is publicized immediately and widely. The rhythms are preset; we have to come up with something new at least twice a year. It takes longer to make a movie, or write a book, or construct a building, or exhibit art in such a concentration that new trends become visible. Added to this is the active decision-making involvement of the public. As soon as fashion is handed over to the public, it will do something to it. This has nothing to do with advertising but with the actual reaction of each individual at any given moment. Dior's New Look could just as well have been a huge flop. There was a reason why it worked, namely society's yearning for romanticism after the war.

Fashion always contains some reflection of societal processes. Clothing will not change in its essence until external factors make this necessary.

MM: This means that when designers present new ideas they are perhaps saying more than they know. And they can never know whether the ideas will work.

HL: That is one of the strengths of fashion. This is what made it so interesting to other artforms in the 20th century. Through the unique position of its direct links with the media and public interest, there resulted many crossovers with the cinema, art, literature. The catalyst was frequently provided by fashion, which is unexpected given the standard hierarchies of the arts. But humans want to define themselves. And fashion is just what they need to do so.

Appendix

New textiles

Sarah E. Braddock

During the last century there have been many important breakthroughs in the development of new textiles, with the worlds of science and engineering playing major roles in research. Results – from outside the traditional world of textiles and advanced finishing treatments – include microfibers, microencapsulation, imaginative mixtures of yarn, sophisticated composites, "smart" materials, and new "flexibles."

"I think reinterpreting things with today's influences, today's fabric technology, is what it's all about."[1] Many designers agree, showing that fashion and textiles are being led by technology as well as by social and cultural concerns. From the late 20th century the latest fabrics look luxurious, handle beautifully, feel comfortable, perform well, and are ecologically sound. Research into the study of materials is a fast-growing area worldwide and new technology is allowing diversification in the properties of materials, so that form no longer has to follow function.

The turn of the 19th–20th century saw the invention of viscose rayon; this regenerated fabric is made from woodpulp that is chemically treated to create a lustrous textile. Polyamide was developed by DuPont in 1938 and polyester shortly after, in the 1940s. Originally promoted as artifical silk, viscose rayon has many of the qualities of silk but is significantly cheaper. Polyamide and polyester are lightweight, durable, can take on a variety of looks and textures and are appreciated for their easy-care properties. The development of Lycra (a synthetic rubber fiber) by DuPont in the late 1950s made a significant impact on fashion only in the 1980s. Developed originally for supportive lingerie, it is now used to create body-conscious, streamlined shapes which fit and flatter. Lycra blends well with both natural

and synthetic yarns and its stretch properties have proved immensely popular, making possible one-size garments and allowing shapes which previously would mean complicated tailoring. As we enter the third millennium these textiles are used by both classical and avant-garde fashion designers, who take their performance properties for granted and select them mainly for their aesthetic qualities. Synthetic fabrics are no longer seen as poor relations to the likes of cotton or silk and the customer now chooses to have them in their everyday wardrobe along with natural fabrics. Polyester has been given credibility with the invention of high-performance fabrics such as polar fleece, originally worn by explorers and mountaineers.

The end of the 20th century saw not only a return to vogue of these synthetic fabrics but also the advent of many new. A development in the area of regenerated fabrics has been the group of fibers called lyocell. Here, the manufacturing process of viscose rayon is modified and the result is a beautiful cloth: for example, Tencel (developed by Courtaulds) and Lyocell (by Lenzing), which will remain popular well into the 21st century. Many of the most successful advanced textiles have been developed by the Ministry of Defense and NASA for protective clothing or garments with very specific high-tech end applications. Gore-Tex, Kevlar, and Velcro were all originally developed for the US space program and are now used in everyday wear.

On a micro-level, scientists and engineers are synthesizing fabrics which are extremely fine and can be created to answer very specific needs – for example, Tactel (developed by DuPont), which can be made in a wide range. Microfibers have been big news in recent years, as microtechnology opens up a whole new era in

textiles. Fabrics made from microfibers can provide insulation from heat and cold while offering resistance to wind and rain. They are also breathable, drawing body moisture away from the skin to outside the garment and so ensuring that the wearer remains dry and comfortable and does not experience a chill from a change in temperature. New inroads into microtechnology have also led to the invention of microencapsulation, in which substances such as perfume, vitamins, and seaweed are contained in capsules suspended inside hollow fibers. Originally used in medicine, microencapsulation is now available to the textile industry and therefore fashion. Much of this technology has been developed in Japan, where it was first used for lingerie, hosiery, and sleepwear.

Interest in specialty, health-promoting textiles has given rise to a whole new generation of fabrics – for instance those containing ceramic to help block harmful UV rays, and fibers with antibacterial agents to prevent the growth of bacteria. The combination of a fiber (usually viscose or polyester) and ceramic can provide UV protection up to factor 30+ allowing the wearer to enjoy the psychological benefits of the sun without the physical harm. The antimicrobial fibers Amicor and Amicor Plus (developed by Acordis UK Ltd) have an active ingredient in the core of the fiber which combats odor by controlling bacteria; they are used for high-performance sportswear, lingerie, and bed linen.

One of the latest and much discussed developments in textile technology is the invention of "smart" materials. They are responsive to external stimuli and can adapt accordingly. Pure science fiction though they may appear, these fabrics are being used by designers and architects who exploit their mutant characteristics to great effect.

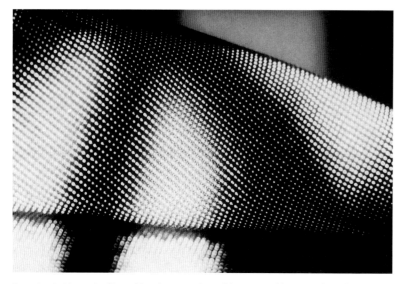

Protective clothing made of heavy fabrics becomes a thing of the past. Scotchlite, a very fine, soft material reflects light up to a distance of 100 meters.

Scotchlite's reflective yarn in detail: a complicated weave protects millions of tiny glass balls from wear.

Textiles can be made out of any fibrous or flexible substance and technology transfer has meant that ceramic, glass, optical fiber, plastic, foam, rubber, metal, and paper can all become textiles. In Japan, Reiko Sudo (cofounder and director of Nuno Corporation and its chief fabric designer), Makiko Minagawa (textile designer at Miyake Design Studio), and Jun'ichi Arai (cofounder of Nuno Corporation and now creator of one-off "art" textiles) are providing the industry with unique fabrics. They often borrow techniques from alternative industries – for instance, the car industry – modifying the equipment to suit their needs. Inventive and creative, their textiles are unlike any that we have previously seen. Using both hand manufacture and industrial processes, Reiko Sudo creates textiles for interiors and fashion from materials including Japanese paper and metal. Research and development in this area is paramount in Japan and innovative textiles are constantly emerging which combine time-honored traditions with the latest sophisticated technology. Materials which were previously considered too delicate or too tough can now be made flexible, with new technology allowing desirable fabrics to be made from such raw materials as paper and metal. Paper – made, for example, of straw, wood and fiber – has a cross-bonded structure. These different materials mean paper can have various looks and textures. Worldwide, paper is used in the manufacture of textiles, such as traditional obi weaving in Japan and woven rugs in Finland. Paper and non-woven materials (which have the same interlacing construction) – for example Tyvek, (developed by DuPont) – are being used worldwide by fashion designers. Tyvek is made of high-density polyethylene fibers which are bonded by heat and pressure. Resistant to many chemicals, it was originally intended for protective clothing but is now being used to create garments with a futuristic appearance. The new "paper" fabrics have a beautiful translucency, good insulating properties, are strong, lightweight, durable, washable, stain-resistant, do not fray (edges and seams do not need finishing), can be subjected to complex cutting, and are recyclable (an important consideration in our ecologically aware society). Indeed, they have a totally new aesthetic; their lack of drape and their crisp quality can be exploited by geometric, origami-like cutting into interesting configurations on the human form. When loosely knitted, paper can have a sensual drape; when woven into high-density cloth, it can take on a definite shape. Even wood is being seriously considered for protective clothing. Its structure makes it naturally resistant to fractures, which could prove ideal for bulletproof and knife-resistant clothing.

Metal in sheet or wire form has long been used in fabric construction but it is only recently, by using the latest technology, that metal textiles can be made which are fluid and comfortable to wear. We can look back to the medieval armor in the world's museums, to the use of metallic thread in the 1920s, to the chain-mail garments of the 1960s, to ecclesiastical textiles with their use of gold and silver wires, and to lamé for stagewear. However, from the end of the 20th century metal is being used in fabrics which are both beautiful and functional, providing us with lightweight, flexible, and thoroughly modern textiles. Nuno has created several fabrics using copper, exploring its soft, ductile properties (a fine polyurethane coating prevents oxidation). Jun'ichi Arai has 36 patents, including ones for his innovative use of metal yarns and metallic finishing treatments. Fabrics lined with metals such as titanium reflect body heat, the latest technologies being used to create performance textiles. The Swiss company Jakob Schlaepfer creates metal fabrics for both fashion and interior decoration. Schoeller Textil AG has developed beautiful metallic fabrics using state-of-the-art technology and has won several awards for its designs. Sumitomo Electric Industries Ltd, a Japanese company, has invented a unique unwoven metal fabric which uses the most advanced microtechnology. Instead of being woven, this textile consists of hollow metal fibers that "communicate" to connect at their joints.

Textile finishing, the final stage in the manufacture of a fabric, is fast becoming as important as its construction. Considered by many to be the future in the development of new textiles, this is where appearance, texture, and performance can be dramatically altered. As with the invention of the latest synthetics, these treatments have often filtered down from research into textiles for space travel, survival, or extreme sportswear where fabric is provided with a shield against uncomfortable or even life-threatening external factors. Momentous advances in finishing technology during the 1990s have given the world of fashion the most futuristic fabrics: for example, Teflon coating (whose very low surface friction prevents anything from adhering to it), rubberized, pearlized, and reflective finishes, and new versions of waxing are enabling wet-weather clothing to be beautiful as well as functional. "Go-faster" stripes of silicone on the back of garments or helmets reduce drag, helping the wearer increase speed by fractions of a second (all that is needed these days to win a race). Worldwide, fashion designers are selecting these finishes for their new aesthetic, their tactile quality, and their enhanced performance.

This precious fabric has been vapor-blasted with aluminum. Its faintly iridescent sheen is reminiscent of precious baroque veils interwoven with gold thread – except that it is much easier to manufacture.

Schoeller dynatic is highly protective and especially well suited for use in motor racing even though it is more economic than traditional materials. The safety factor is provided by its extremely flexible structure.

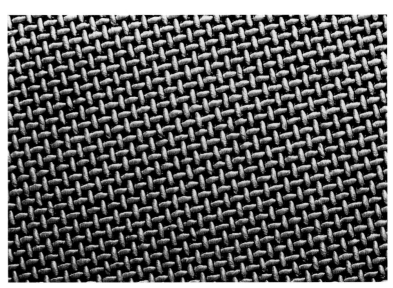

A marvel of durability and ideal for people with allergies, Schoeller's lint-free fabric, Schoeller spirit.

Detail of the anti-lint marvel. The yarn is highly protected and won't fray, even under high pressure and friction.

Visible finishes are often decorative; they include printing, the heat-treatment of synthetics (to create relief surfaces or three-dimensional structures), matt, shiny, or reflective lacquered coatings, spattering, ultrafine membranes for laminates, and various chemical treatments. Sophisticated printing processes can work direct from computer to fabric, eliminating the need for screens and therefore reducing mess and labor. Permanent pleating exploits the thermoplastic nature of synthetics, and new laser cutting, with its intense heat, can fuse or cut to create complex patterns which will not fray. Extremely fine coating creates a new look and performance capability which does not severely affect the drape or texture of the cloth. Spattering is a finish which has a dramatic effect on the finished textile. Minute particles of metal powder are dissolved in a solution and very finely sprayed on to a fabric by means of vacuum-coating. The finish is permanent, so that the material can be hand- or machine-washed, or dry cleaned. Further manipulation using the thermoplastic quality of a synthetic base can produce wrinkles, pleats, or embossed or relief patterns. As well as looking good, a stainless-steel finish protects against many weather conditions and can shield the wearer from some of the radiation emitted from computers and televisions.

The latest finishing technology is also used to create invisible treatments. Membranes can be fused to a substrate (often in between a lining and a surface fabric), adapting the textile to give it a high-performance application. Advanced membrane technology – such as that used in the invisible laminate Gore-Tex – blocks wind and rain yet is breathable. This works by means of a microporous structure in which the Gore-Tex membrane is punctured with tiny holes, too fine to allow air and water in but which allow water vapor out. Another successful laminate, Sympatex (developed by Akzo Nobel), also prevents wind and rain from penetrating and is breathable. Using hydrophilic technology, the water-attracting Sympatex membrane

causes warm water vapor, in the form of perspiration, to move to the generally cooler air outside. Woven cotton, which normally creases readily, can be treated with an invisible laminate which changes its molecular configuration and aligns the fibers in parallel, eliminating creasing. There are numerous finishes, both visible and invisible, on the market today, and much research continues in this area.

Controlling body temperature and offering protection was possible only with layers of clothing made of such textiles as silk or wool. Air trapped between the layers provides insulation but usually means that bulky, heavy clothes must be worn. Advances in fiber and fabric technology made by sportswear companies in the 1990s have changed all this: sport has made an immense impact on everyday clothing. Resulting synthetics are thin and lightweight, giving a slim, contemporary silhouette. These "technofabrics" allow outdoor clothing to be packed away into very small spaces, and reversibility (made more attractive by the latest composites) further enhances their function. Some clothing can be chemically bonded, making seams unnecessary and ensuring totally waterproof clothing, which also feels smooth next to the skin. Without seams there are less places for dirt to collect and the fabric is not weakened by stitching. Both *haute couture* and prêt-à-porter collections use sport textiles such as neoprene (a synthetic polymer similar to rubber), polar fleece, and high-tech performance finishes with Velcro and magnet fastenings to create clothing which is both technical and fashionable. In the United States, with its emphasis on the casual and the functional, designers Calvin Klein, Ralph Lauren, Tommy Hilfiger, and Donna Karan pave the way. Many large fashion houses have added new lines to their collections featuring sports-inspired textiles and garments. Prada has recently launched Prada Sport as well as a new technical skiwear line. "Combining sportswear and citywear is a contemporary phenomenon. It's a necessity of our times. The appeal: modern, cool, dynamic."[2] Dyersburg Corporation USA

produces a range called the Dyersburg ECO collection made from recycled plastic soda bottles which features finely knitted, wind-resistant polar fleece. Yamamoto, a leading manufacturer of neoprene, develops fabrics which are used for wetsuit clothing. Its 3-Dis neoprene (three-dimensional intelligent skin) includes Spherical Carbon, which evenly distributes stresses across the garment, so ensuring that there are no weak areas, and FE Polymer, which enables the neoprene to have a long life. This technical textile feels almost alive, as it responds to any force exerted (either stretch or compression) on the wearer. Fashion sportswear designer Sam de Terán creates sophisticated, functional clothing using high-performance fabrics such as Schoeller's stretch fleece, Sympatex, and Lycra. She has recognized the need for functional clothing which does not forsake style and she fills a gap in the market with her designs which make full use of the latest fiber and fabric technologies.

Fashion, interior, furniture, and product designers, architects and engineers are all looking to soft, flexible materials to answer their needs. At the beginning of the 21st century, new technology has given us smart materials, microfibers, microencapsulation, textiles made with ceramic or spattered with stainless steel – "wearable technology" where digital circuitry is incorporated into clothing and environmentally aware fabrics. The 21st century promises us even more. Responsive and mutant textiles which are beautiful and functional will reveal a different aesthetic, enhanced performance, and a new vision.

1. John Galliano, from "Galliano", an interview with Susannah Frankel, *The Independent Magazine* (London), February 20, 1999.
2. Jil Sander, *Vogue* (London), February 1999.

Fashion illustration

Maria Mester

Paul Poiret was not only an influential couturier of his time; his work also had a determining effect on the presentation of fashion. He was different in that he did not merely depict his designs, as had been the norm until then; his illustrations emphasized the design's special features and evoked a lifestyle and atmosphere. For him the techniques of graphic design were the most effective means of achieving his aims. Given the variety of techniques and styling effects available at the time, graphic art was superior to photography, which was regarded as merely providing an inferior image of reality and not being an art form at all. Poiret, however, wanted art. He wanted imagination, originality and, above all, color. He wanted fashion dreams on paper – idealized images of his designs. So it was that, at the beginning of the 20th century, fashion illustration was much more highly regarded than fashion photography, the latter serving merely as a sketching aid for the actual presentation drawings.

At first Poiret hired the artist **Paul Iribe** (1883–1935), with whom he had already successfully collaborated in the past. In 1908 Iribe produced an album, *Les Robes de Paul Poiret racontées par Paul Iribe*, which made the artist's name. Iribe was truly multitalented. He was a caricaturist, a graphic designer, an interior designer, and a furniture, textile, and jewelry designer. He also created movie costumes, book illustrations, and designs for stage set. Iribe was the first fashion illustrator ever to become an independent artist within this particular field. This was due in large measure to Poiret, who gave him sufficient artistic freedom to develop. This approach bore fruit for both couturier and draftsman: it was their mutual inspiration which made them both so successful. Thus, with the success of Paul Iribe, the great period of fashion illustration thus commenced. (See illustrations on pages 26 and 44.)

Thanks to Poiret's positive experiences with Iribe, he subsequently worked only with professional draftsmen, including **Georges Barbiers** (1882–1932). Barbiers had already made a name for himself in connection with the Ballets Russes. In 1913 he completed two albums of illustrations of dancers from the troupe, depicting their poses and costumes. The quality of these pictures made him instantly famous. Like Iribe, he was multitalented. His major achievement, however, lay in developing new chromatic shades to use in his illustrations.

Like Iribe, **Georges Lepape** (1887–1971) also produced a valuable and very expensive fashion album: *Les Choses de Paul Poiret vues par Georges Lepape*. It is important to note that it was indeed an album and not a catalog. The function of an album was to express the exclusiveness of the clothes. For the same reason, a time-consuming and costly printing process was used that could also guarantee outstanding quality. Due to the cost factor, only few of these albums were produced. (See illustrations on pages 4, 31, and 79)

Of the many artists who worked for fashion tsar Poiret, one stands out in particular: **Erté** (Romain de Tirtoff; 1892–1990). Not beholden to any school, artist, or style, Erté said about his own work: "My work knows no realism – it is an expression of dreams." Born in St Petersburg, the Russian artist went to Paris as a 20-year-old after completing his studies in ballet and painting. There, he began his unparalleled career by working for the man who discovered him, Paul Poiret. Erté was 20 years younger than André-Eduard Marty, who was by then already moving toward a new style, but it was not until Erté's arrival that the theatrical look really became fashionable. Erté was an individualist to the core and an artist who could not be enticed to work for any purpose other than his own. This caused a breach between him and his employer, Poiret, when the latter published Erté's designs under his own name. His infinite inventiveness, impressive line, and masterly use of space and color also impressed *Harper's Bazaar*. The magazine offered him an exclusive contract, and for 25 years Erté designed every one of its covers, until here too disputes arose: a new editor began to exert greater control over his work and demanded to see her ideas realized. Erté resigned. Yet the field needed his virtuosity and mastery. The perfect expression of allegorical fantasies as well as fairy-tale and mythical motifs continued to win the admiration of the public. The fundamental reason underlying his success may well be that he only ever did what he wanted to do, namely to realize his dreams and ideas. (See illustration on page 55.)

The drawings of **André-Eduard Marty** (1882–1974) reflected a new natural, free and easy lifestyle. They also demonstrated the influence of Expressionism on fashion illustration. Marty's simpler style had a strong effect on the look of the period and for many years his work as an illustrator had a critical effect on the appearance of fashion magazines such as *La Gazette du Bon Ton*, *Fémina*, and *Vogue*.

Another proponent of the more natural style was **Eduardo García Benito** (1891–1961): his figures did not adopt stylized poses, nor were his colors brash, for he preferred toning shades. The slimline figure was pivotal in his work, and he liked to use woodcuts to illustrate it. This method permitted him to emphasize contours further, thereby underlining the ideal of the slim, graceful, and elegant woman. This impression is further heightened by the plain backgrounds to the figures. Benito was a major contributor to *Vogue* in the 1920s and 1930s and he designed a number of their covers.

The images created by **Eric** (Carl Ericson; 1891–1958), who came from Sweden but grew up in Illinois, are clearly influenced by Impressionism and may even be described as romantic. Generally, his illustrations exude a mood of calm, harmonious contemplation. Eric used color to accentuate important details that defined or completed the style of dress of his era: a scarf, a hat, gloves, a flower worn in the hair, or a bow. His style was rapidly established at *Vogue*, and helped to determine the magazine's style for 20 years.

Eric's colleagues at *Vogue* during that period were **René Bouet-Willaumez** (1900–74), **Christian Bérard** (1902–49), and **René Bouché** (1906–63). Like Eric, Bouet-Willaumez liked to use color to emphasize the looks illustrated in his graphic works. Yet, in contrast to Eric, he brought out not just the detail but the entire design. (See illustration on page 211.)

Initially, all-rounder **Christian Bérard** (1902–49) declined to work for *Vogue* because he felt that it would have been inappropriate for an artist like himself. The cofounder of the Neohumanist Group and well-known illustrator, who had contacts with the demimonde, became an experienced stage and costume designer for both theater and cinema. He also illustrated books and made a name for himself as an excellent portraitist before finally agreeing to join *Vogue*. His romantic Expressionism and Surrealism had a major influence on the style of draftsmanship at the time.

In contrast to Bérard, who refused at first to work for *Vogue*, **René Bouché** (1906–63) had to persuade the magazine to let him prove himself. He was successful. With his skills of observation and free, expressive style, Bouché convinced *Vogue* and he was soon regarded as one of their most important illustrators.

Like no other, the name of **Cecil Beaton** (1904–80) evokes a period when fashion magazines regarded illustration and photography as equals. He is best known as a photographer and became famous with his images of screen actors and members of high society. Few people are also aware that he was an important fashion illustrator. For 50 years he worked as a  photographer and illustrator for *Vogue*. In this time he used every expressive form offered by the two media. With respect to his drawings he used mainly the stylizing effects of overdrawing right down to malicious caricature. His identifying marks, generally extravagant backgrounds and imaginative details, do not hide the fact that he also designed stage sets and costumes for the Ballets Russes.

Like Beaton, today's Michael Roberts is both a fashion illustrator and photographer. (See illustrations on pages 105, 109, 195, 544, and 572.)

Although **René Gruau** (Count Renato Zavagli Riciardelli delle Caminate; b. 1909) is among the really big names of this genre, he was not immune to the competition posed by photography that began increasingly to push illustration out of fashion publications. As a result Gruau concentrated on advertising graphics and became very successful in this field. He designed almost all the advertisements for  his friend Christian Dior, thereby defining the house's image. In addition he also designed posters for the Moulin Rouge and the Lido. His large expanses of color and sweeping brushstrokes and the horizontal, vertical, and diagonal spatial arrangements in each of his images spontaneously call to mind Toulouse-Lautrec. (See illustrations on pages 256 and 266.)

Unlike Gruau, who regarded himself as a graphic designer, the self-confident draftsmen of today's fashion scene see themselves as artists. **Antonio López** (1943–87) and **Ruben Alterio** (b. 1949) are examples of this trend. López, who worked for *Vogue*, *Harper's Bazaar*, and *Elle*, among others, introduced Pop Art to fashion illustration. He also turned models Grace Jones, Jerry Hall, and Jessica Lange into superstars. Together with Andy Warhol and Karl Lagerfeld, he was a major contributor to the style of the 1970s. López himself wanted his art to be more than a mere mirror of its period; he wanted to be involved in determining trends and he said of himself: "I force modernity to go somewhere else in order that it may become more than

it is." Alterio was born in Argentina and first attracted attention as a painter in 1976. His exhibition of paintings in Paris proved popular because of their inimitable play of light and shade as well as a finely graded richness of color. His roots clearly lie in painting, and the influence of Goya, Delacroix, and Matisse is clearly recognizable. Shortly after the exhibition Alterio began to work regularly for *Marie Claire* and *La Mode*. For Alterio, the street life of Paris, the theater, and music are important sources of inspiration.

Mats Gustafson (b. 1952) is a minimalist. The master of omission emphasizes what is significant: a narrow line and slim silhouette. His highly simplified style generally concentrates on the outlines of a model and has made its way into every major fashion magazine. The Swede studied at Stockholm's Academy of Fine Arts and subsequently worked as a costume designer for Swedish television. Finally he worked regularly for such international fashion publications as *Vogue*, *Marie Claire*, and the *New York Times Magazine*.

Fashion photography

Anne Urbauer

Over the past century, the people who have given us fashion have been referred to as modistes, couturiers or, as now, plain and simple fashion designers. However, the term used to describe the profession that creates the images of fashion has remained almost constant: fashion photographer. Jeanloup Sieff considers it astonishing that his profession's definition of itself is not itself subject to fashion: "We could call ourselves plastic artists or textile social scientists." Fashion photographers are journalists who use images instead of words. If they merely provided a service, they would just take pictures for simple catalogs. Their job is to awaken desires, stir up emotions, and provoke reactions.

Their commentary on the spirit of the times may often be trivial, but the best examples have a visionary and artistic integrity; they are acts of freedom. Photographers at the forefront of developments are frequently reviled: Man Ray's Surrealist images of the 1920s were no less vilified than Jürgen Teller's hyperrealist photographs, criticized by many as "heroin chic."

The 1990s bore scandalous images because fashion photography allowed itself ever greater freedoms. Where fashion, and its depiction, once seemed to be the most ephemeral of all ephemeral things, an expression of evanescence, recent fashion photography has suddenly begun to be seen on gallery walls. It is seen as art, or as a preliminary stage of art. It brings alacrity and freshness to the rigid world of art and derives status and permanence from it. (See illustrations on pages 354 and 364.)

However, fashion photographs can be good only if they say something about their time – through the medium of fashion. They provide a protocol of their society, recording its trends, habits, and collective obsessions. When the desire that they have created has been satisfied and long since forgotten, fashion photographs become portraits of society, visual records of history.

Yet even the most talented photographers cannot produce fine fashion photographs entirely on their own. These must be created in collaboration with the designers who design the clothes, models who can also act as muses and founts of inspiration, and magazine editors who, like truffle hogs, are often the first to sense which new photographer is going to show potential and creativity. The birth of fashion photography was heralded by the establishment of the international publication *Vogue*, an ambitious fashion magazine produced by American publishing company Condé Nast, which made Adolph de Meyer the first salaried fashion photographer.

Without the vision of the editors-in-chief and art directors of magazines such as *Vogue*, *Harper's Bazaar*, *Flair*, *Nova*, *Egoiste*, *Stern*, and, in the 1990s, *Visionaire*, their pictures could never have become so powerful.

This is why the history of fashion photography begins with those people who demanded it and who made it possible – the editorial decision-makers.

Editors and Art Directors

The modernist and very European style which **Alexey Brodovitch** (1898–1971) contributed to fashion photography had a revitalizing effect. In his Design Factory he trained young talents whose new ideas were to provide him with "tools for the future." Photographers like Richard Avedon, the still-life supremo Hiro, and Lillian Bassman blossomed under Brodovitch's tutelage. As art director of *Harper's Bazaar* he gave page layouts greater spontaneity, imbued the magazine with life and movement, and thus invented the modern art director's tools. His motto was "Surprise! Change! Shock!"

Another Russian master of the trade was Ukrainian-born **Alexander Liberman** (1912–99). His influence in the fashion world lasted through six decades, from 1943 as *Vogue*'s art director and then from 1962 as editorial director to the entire stable of Condé Nast publications. Fashion was his habitat of style, a sphere that permitted people to behave in a cultivated manner. Accordingly, fashion photography was a ticket for access to that realm; it was used to take leave of the mundane and to "dive into the heaven of fashion and the impalpable Nirvana of luxury and elegance."

It was to be quite some time before there was another art director who could hold a creative candle to the old masters. The one who came closest is probably **Fabien Baron** (b. 1959), whose sovereign, clear, and typographically robust layouts for Italian *Vogue* in the 1980s and early 1990s seemed to reawaken the spirit of the gifted typographer and groundbreaker Brodovitch. He and photographer Steven Meisel formed a dream team like Brodovitch and Avedon had once been. The first issue of *Vogue* to be produced under Baron's graphic direction, of September 1988, is now a collector's item. Baron subsequently moved on to work for *Interview* and *Harper's Bazaar*, Brodovitch's old haunt. He also directed Madonna's *Erotica* video and designed a frosted glass bottle for Calvin Klein's unisex fragrance CK one, which triggered a wave of imitators.

In her role as editor of *Vogue* (under editor-in-chief Edna Woolman Chase) and then from 1932 as omnipotent editor-in-chief of *Vogue*'s competitor, the Hearst publishing group's *Harper's Bazaar*, Dublin-born **Carmel Snow** (1888–1961) proved to have a unique sense of style. She always appeared to be half asleep at fashion shows. However, if she suddenly awoke on the appearance of a particular garment, legend had it that this outfit would be a guaranteed hit. Cristóbal Balenciaga had much to thank Carmel Snow for. She was the first to understand him and his pure, sculptural form. It was Carmel Snow who gave Dior's postwar collection the name "New Look."

Snow's equal and successor was **Diana Vreeland** (1901–89). As a uniquely dominant and authoritative editor-in-chief of *Harper's Bazaar* and American *Vogue*, she defined fashion and style for 50 years. During the Depression she wrote the short-lived but highly inspiring "Why don't you?" column for *Harper's Bazaar*, where she made suggestions like "Why don't you have your cigarettes monogrammed?" and "Why don't you cut your garden shrubs in the shape of peacocks and poodles?" thereby giving her readers the impression that even in the dreary 1930s there was someone there who could satisfy their yearning for extravagance and style, if only in the imagination. As head of *Vogue*, she turned the magazine into a bastion for her favorite photographers Richard Avedon and Irving Penn. First lady Jacqueline Kennedy used to ask her advice on matters of fashion. In 1972 Diana Vreeland became a consultant to the Costume Institute of the Metropolitan Museum of Art in New York. Her razor-sharp intellect, independent mind, and merciless discernment are legendary. Her aphoristic statements "Elegance is refusal" and "Pink is the navy blue of India" have been quoted so often that they have become fashion clichés. Photographer William Klein's memorial to her, the movie *Who Are You, Polly Magoo?* was not very flattering. Vreeland's traits are also said to have been adopted for the role of the editor-in-chief in the movie *Funny Face*, with Audrey Hepburn and Fred Astaire as Richard Avedon. The stage play *Empress V.* is also dedicated to the Empress of Style.

Baroque and Opulence

During the *belle époque* the aristocracy was losing its power to a rising middle class, born out of industry and trade, that celebrated the good life in grand hotels and on board luxury liners.

In 1909 the young American publisher Condé Nast sold a weekly publication called *Vogue*. In 1914 he employed a permanent photographer who had been raised in Paris and Germany: **Baron Adolph de Meyer** (1868–1949). In those days, society ladies were used for photography instead of professional models. The press portrayed what Mrs e.e. cummings and Mrs Gertrude Vanderbilt Whitney wore in their salons, and released their look for public admiration and imitation. Baron de Meyer went to *Harper's Bazaar* in 1921.

His successor at *Vogue* was **Edward Steichen** (1879–1973), from Luxembourg. Steichen had been an art student and lithographic printer's apprentice. He worked as an aerial photographer for the military during World War I, when he developed the style for which he would subsequently become famous. He put aside the manipulations of "artistic photography," burned all his paintings, and allowed the influences of modern painting to infiltrate fashion photography. He later became the director of the photographic department of the Museum of Modern Art in New York and conceived the legendary exhibition *The Family of Man*, which represented a moral ideal as well as a photographic idea: the unity of man after the Holocaust. This exhibition has found a permanent home in a château in Ardennenort Clervaux (Luxembourg). (See illustrations on pages 21, 83, 124, and 180–181)

Neoclassicism

While art was being rocked by Surrealism and Constructivism in the 1920s, fashion photographers wallowed in the pathos of Greek antiquity.

George Hoynigen-Huene (1900–68), born in St Petersburg, worked as a painter and fashion illustrator before becoming one of the great photographers of the interwar years. In 1920 he went to Paris and studied painting with André Lhote. His fashion illustrations appeared in *Harper's Bazaar* and *Fairchild's Magazine*. On Man Ray's recommendation he then went to *Vogue* to work as a photographic assistant. Hoynigen-Huene is famous for the flawless lighting which imbued models and clothes with structure and sheen. In 1935 he went to New York, where he worked almost exclusively for *Harper's Bazaar*, and in 1946 he moved to Hollywood, where he taught photography at the Art Center School. (See illustrations on pages 48 and 70.)

During his time at *Vogue*, he became friendly with architecture student **Horst P. Horst** (1906–99), who came to photography through this friendship. Horst began to work for *Vogue* in 1932. Combining the ideal of beauty embodied in Greek statues with the decadent elegance of the 1930s, he created images that defined the cutting edge of fashion photography – unapproachable and erotic as, for instance, in his photograph of the Mainbocher corset which was produced in 1939 and proved to be so iconographic that Madonna recreated it 50 years later for her *Vogue* video. (See illustrations on pages 13, 15, 152, and 220.)

Elegance

After World War II, fashion was revolutionized by Dior's New Look. Photographers abandoned the tableaux of the 1920s and 1930s and together they founded a new elegance.

Irving Penn (born in 1917 in Plainfield) and his photography defined the image of *haute couture* in the 1950s. Penn studied design with Alexey Brodovitch and worked for himself in the 1930s. His first cover for *Vogue* came in 1943. Penn's graphic perfection, sharpness, power, and simplicity were captivating. He removed all extraneous props from the picture in order to locate his subject center stage. Penn always worked in the studio using characteristic lighting and the same, gently tinged background, similarly to the later Avedon. This helped him to detach people from their social context, whether he was dealing with Marlene Dietrich, Picasso, or a bunch of carpenters. He endowed his models with a natural yet regal elegance, which is exemplified in the photographs of his Swedish muse and wife, Lisa Fonssagrives, taken in 1950.

The Court Painters

The first fashion photographs portrayed the life of the upper class, but fashion photography soon became an independent discipline which aimed to awaken desires and prescribed what women should look like. This propensity for idealization has been exploited by the British royal family, who for the last 60 years have had the masters of fashion photography take their portraits.

Sir Cecil Beaton (1904–80), born in London, captured the spirit of fashion for 40 years. In 1928 he became a permanent employee of *Vogue*, where he worked as a fashion photographer until the mid-1950s. Despite his advancing years he was a fixture in Swinging London in the 1960s, together with such models as Penelope Tree and Twiggy. Mick Jagger was also photographed by Beaton; he described the master of the aesthetic as "the most stylish celebrity I have ever met." Andy Warhol regarded the dandy as a role model. Following the scandal surrounding the abdication of Edward VIII so that he could marry American mistress Wallis Simpson, whom Beaton had photographed in 1935, the Windsors decided to make good use of Beaton's style and elevated him to the rank of court photographer. He was knighted for his services to the Windsors' image.

After him, **Norman Parkinson** (1923–90) was awarded similar honors. Parkinson and his breathtakingly realistic fashion photographs had been a sensation in Paris in the 1950s, and over the years he developed into a master of color and composition. He was the official photographer at the wedding of Princess Anne and Captain Mark Phillips in 1973, and in 1980 he took a portrait of the Queen Mother on the occasion of her 80th birthday.

Fifty years after Beaton, another member of the British royal family discovered that she needed to work on her public image: Diana, Princess of Wales was seeking a way out of her marriage to Prince Charles and desired a life of her own, as well as a reputation as a modern royal. She had her photograph taken by the Frenchman **Patrick Demarchelier** (born in 1943 in Le Havre). The black and white pictures that he took of her in 1990 had the required effect. Demarchelier combines modernity with grandeur, thereby taking his cue from the great couture photographers of the 1950s.

The official photographs of the wedding of Prince Charles and Lady Diana Spencer in 1981 were taken by **Lord Snowdon**, who himself was a member of the royal family through his (failed) marriage to Princess Margaret. Under the commoner's name Antony Armstrong-Jones, he made a name for himself in the late 1950s as a fashion photographer for *Vogue*.

The Directors

The snapshot is their enemy. Their photographs are posed, minutely constructed, and put together like stage sets: nothing is left to chance. They touch up their photographs in the darkroom, or more recently, with the help of computers. The results are like Surrealist images, perplexing, disturbing, alienating.

Man Ray (Emmanuel Rudnitzky; 1890–1976) was the undisputed master of this genre. He is regarded as the first artist whose photographic work was more important than his painting, thus helping photography to become accepted as an art form. Born in Philadelphia, Man Ray studied art at night school and soon made close contacts with the European avant-garde. In 1917 he founded the New York branch of Dadaism. In 1921 he went to Paris, where he worked for *Harper's Bazaar* and *Vogue*. Man Ray freed fashion photography from the formal boundaries of standard poses. Together with the American Lee Miller, his colleague, model, and lover, he invented pseudosolarization, which was based on the Sabatier effect, and produced an impression of three-dimensionality which made the images look as if they were drawn. (See illustrations on pages 29, 111, 124, 144, 169, and 172.)

In the 1950s, Man Ray recommended a young Parisian photographer to French *Vogue*: **Guy Bourdin** (1928–91). Bourdin's big time came in the schizoid, self-centered 1970s. His images are technically brilliant. They have an incredible depth of field and they are pure precision engineering devoid of any romanticism. Nothing is superfluous; nothing unclear is permitted. Yet, his photographs are full of erotic puzzles.

Bourdin's great competitor at French *Vogue* was a man who was equally meticulous in his arrangement of sexually charged tableaux. Unlike the tortured and compulsive Bourdin, the German-born Australian **Helmut Newton** (b. 1920) has always gone about his work with maximum lightheartedness and joy – and an enormous rate of productivity. Since producing his first pictures for Australian *Vogue*, he has filled some 3000 editorial magazine pages with his images – for *Vogue*, *Vanity Fair*, *Nova*, *Stern*, and *Playboy* – as well as advertising campaigns for numerous companies, including the hosiery company Wolford. The omnipresent thrill of latent perversion sold copies but it also caused scandal. Newton takes his photographs along an exposed nerve of society: the power of definition over the role of women. He does not take pictures of fashion. Newton invites viewers to continue his pictorial stories in their heads. (See illustration on page 257.)

A much freer image of women is contained in **Peter Knapp**'s photographic work. Born in 1931 in Zurich, he studied painting, photography, and graphic design. When he was appointed art director of *Elle* in 1959, at an extremely young age, he was still much more interested in painting than in photography. It was only the fact that he could not find a photographer to realize his fresh, new ideas that forced him to take his place behind the camera. Reality is always well organized in his fashion photographs: nothing is left to chance, especially not line and contour which, for him, are more important elements than light. Knapp never entirely gave up painting and he continues to exhibit his work as a painter.

Ines van Lamsweerde and **Vinoodh Matadin**, from Holland, also cross the boundaries between art and fashion and, not unlike Newton, they became famous with their photographs of window dummies. *Thank You Thigh Master*, a series of images of naked women whose sexual attributes had been erased by computerized manipulation, was created in 1992. Their "posthuman" effect was the result of the digital transfer of "real" skin on to the faces of 1970s window dummies. The bodies appear hermetically sealed. In 1994 Lamsweerde and Matadin became known thanks to a feature on the designs of Veronique Leroy in *The Face*. This was followed by assignments from *Vogue* and others. In record time Lamsweerde and Matadin succeeded in becoming established in the fashion and art worlds. Their work has also inspired fashion designers like Vivienne Westwood and Thierry Mugler. "Fashion photographs are something like a sketchbook for our art," says Lamsweerde, who admits to being interested in neither computers nor cameras: "Both are just stages between concept and finished work."

The Ironists

For many photographers, fashion is just one of many genres that they work in. They may also be photojournalists (like Richard Avedon), painters and movie directors (like William Klein), or artists (like Wolfgang Tillmans). Their attitude to fashion can be decidedly ambivalent.

In the case of **Erwin Blumenfeld** (1897–1969), born in Berlin, this ambivalence was the source of sensationally iconographic images. Blumenfeld was a dissident through and through, a master at invoking conflicts. Initially he completed an apprenticeship in a ladies dress shop. He subsequently came to know such people as Georg Grosz, Else Lasker-Schüler, and the Herzfelde brothers. After the Nazis took power, he went to Amsterdam, where he opened a leather goods shop, in the back room of which he began his photographic career. His style turned away from neoclassicist photography toward a modern language of images influenced by Cubism which was consciously decadent,

which distorted and deconstructed. Cecil Beaton secured for Blumenfeld his first one-year contract with *Vogue*. Blumenfeld mastered the transition from black and white to color photography in the 1940s and in the late 1940s became the world's highest-paid photographer. His images are highly artificial, the gestures exaggerated, the lighting reminiscent of Hollywood. (See illustration on page 232.)

In 1946, **William Klein** (b. 1928) was stationed in Germany, where he was put in charge of art by the US Army in Munich. He decided not to go back. In 1948 Klein began to study painting with Fernand Léger in Paris. In the early 1950s he discovered a passion for photography and in 1954 he was employed by the legendary art director Alexander Liberman at *Vogue*. Although Klein always regarded fashion photography as the opposite of "serious photography," he worked for *Vogue* until 1966. In order to make "proper pictures" for his lucrative fashion jobs, he made his couture models rush through the city traffic, pose in the wax works museum, had them stand on the roofs of houses next to large mirrors. This produced pictures that were elegant, startling, eccentric, and that made him famous. In 1961 he gave up photography in favor of the cinema; his 1966 movie *Who Are You, Polly Magoo?* was a contemptuous fashion satire and parody of *Vogue*'s editor-in-chief Diana Vreeland. Klein's verdict on his tumultuous life: "I had my fun."

The Frenchman **Jean-Paul Goude** (b. 1940) created his very own aesthetic territory in the 1980s. Occupying a gray zone between comedy and couture, between movie, theater, and photography, his work has generally consisted of extended jokes at the expense of Goude's friends. Because this circle included designer Azzedine Alaïa and one of his women was model Grace Jones, one of the things that came out of it was fashion photography: ironic, comic, and told in theatrical stories. Goude, a trained draftsman, was appointed art director of the American magazine *Esquire* in the 1970s and returned to Paris in the early 1980s. The images that he created with the diminutive designer Alaïa and the towering model Farida Khelfa became famous. Goude, who demonstrated an overwhelming talent for show business with his dramatic parade designs for the 200th anniversary of the French Revolution in 1989, generally remains aloof from the fashion world. "I am not interested in fashion but in style. I am interested in setting trends, not in following them like the fashion industry does." Goude created the image of the androgynous black woman/machine Grace Jones, with her flat-top hairstyle, geometric face, and dangerous glance. The first-ever pop video is attributed to him. He also directed the first advertising shots to be characterized by the ironic spirit of the 1980s, for Chanel's fragrances Egoiste and Coco. (See illustration on page 486.)

However, there is no one who has taken irony to such extremes as **David LaChapelle** (b. 1964), whose "bombastic images brim over with absurdity and offensiveness" (*Die Woche*). For the American whose first job was waiting at tables in New York's Studio 54 disco, there is "nothing more boring than taking pictures of a beautiful girl in a beautiful bikini on a beautiful beach." LaChapelle prefers to use his computer to enable the beautiful girl to sit on the back of a giant butterfly. James Truman, of the Condé Nast publishing company, describes his visual rides at full speed as a mixture of "Dadaism, Surrealism, 1950s kitsch, 1970s bad taste, and elements of cyberspace culture."

The Pop Stars

To be in the right place at the right time, to create, either by chance or through talent, something unique and iconographic, and to be endowed with the status of a hero from then on: very few photographers are so fortunate. Their rank is unsurpassed today, and not necessarily on account of their fashion photography, although this was often the starting point for their unusual careers.

Richard Avedon (born in 1923 in New York) studied philosophy at Columbia University. In 1944 he met Alexey Brodovitch, the gurulike art director, who trained him and employed him at *Harper's Bazaar*. Under his aegis, Avedon developed into a revolutionary fashion photographer in the 1950s. His most famous image has been published and praised innumerable times and yet, *Dovima with Elephants*, taken in 1955, retains its freshness, boldness, and overwhelming elegance. (The dress was one of Yves Saint Laurent's first creations for Dior). In those days couture was photographed in the studio. Avedon took his models out on to the street – in anticipation of emancipation. In the 1960s, Avedon brought pace and movement into his images; for example, he captured model Penelope Tree in the middle of a joyful leap while dressed in an Ungaro suit. Avedon's fashion photography subsequently became increasingly bare and drifted back to the studio. Avedon had long since secured special status, which has guaranteed that he is granted absolute freedom: involvement in the layout of his images and no discussions about fees. In the 1990s Tina Brown took him to the *New Yorker*, where Avedon publishes pictures to his own taste – here too without competition, the king in the empire of photography. (See illustration on page 265.)

It was fate that helped **Bert Stein** (born in 1929 in New York) achieve his unique status: when he met Marilyn Monroe in July 1962, in a Los Angeles hotel for a fashion shoot for British *Vogue*, he could not have anticipated that these would be the last pictures ever to be taken of the legendary actress. Within the space of three days, Stern shot around 2700 pictures, including those which feature Marilyn wearing Dior and which were later published by British *Vogue*. At the time of this shoot, Stern, who had developed from an art director to a photographer, had long outgrown the world of fashion. He led a magnificent life as a highly paid advertising photographer. Among his clients were such renowned names as Polaroid, Pepsi, Volkswagen, and Smirnoff. (See illustration on page 380.)

Despite his outstanding *œuvre*, **David Bailey** would probably be almost forgotten by now had it not been for *Blow-up*, Michelangelo Antonioni's cinematic depiction of the lifestyle of the 1960s, which captured David Bailey's fast-paced, beautiful existence. The dyslexic child of the less salubrious East End of London drove a convertible, lived with Jean Shrimpton, the "face of the Sixties," and later married Marie Helvin, another of his favorite models. He did not want to enter the annals of history as a fashion photographer – Jean Shrimpton said that he photographed "women who wear clothes" – and he subsequently earned a living as an advertising photographer. Yet the image created by Antonioni's movie proved to be stronger.

The Playful

There can never be a trend without a countertrend: alongside hard, glamorous, and staged pictures there will always be another school of softer, more diffuse images that exude calm, evoke a dream world, or have the appearance of playful snapshots.

At the height of neoclassicism in the 1930s, **Toni Frissell** (1907–88), born in New York, photographed the carefree upper class at leisure: on the beach, playing tennis, on their yachts. Her images combine the vitality and emotion of the snapshot with classical composition, and the models acted as if they were unobserved on the sunny side of life. Her photographs of the wedding of Jacqueline Bouvier and John F. Kennedy, future president of the United States, became world-famous.

Lillian Bassmann (born in 1917 in New York) was a fashion illustrator before she was discovered and trained by Alexey Brodovitch. She did not photograph subjects but sensuous, dreamlike moods.

Sarah Moon (born in 1941 in Paris) is almost inseparable from Biba, the boutique for which she produced advertisements and which embodied the mood of the early 1970s. Following a modeling career in the 1960s, she began her career as a photographer with an advertising campaign for Cacharel: unfocussed, dreamlike, shadowy, nostalgic with doll-like models who could have stemmed from the 1920s, the campaign was a break with the aesthetics of the 1960s and marked the beginning of a new style. (See illustration on page 422.)

Ellen von Unwerth (born in 1954 in Frankfurt-am-Main) is another model who took to the other side of the camera and then had a fabulous career creating erotic fashion photographs. Today she is regarded as the rightful heir to Helmut Newton. For an advertising campaign for the jeans label Guess, she styled the then almost unknown model Claudia Schiffer as a young Bardot in black and white, thus inventing the modern pinup for a young generation of men. Numerous assignments by major magazines from *Vogue* to *The Face* and even *Playboy* have made Unwerth a woman who has shaped the images of the 1990s. They are pleasing photographs, which contain a zest for life, relaxed sexuality, and humorous little scenes, quite as if snapshots had been taken among friends or lovers.

The Zen Craftsmen

Serene, good-humored, and clear: **Tyen** (b. 1950), originally from Vietnam, found his way to fashion photography via his profession of make-up artist. While studying painting at the École des Beaux-Arts in Paris he also worked part-time at the Paris Opéra, where he stood in during a strike by make-up artists. He was subsequently appointed creative director first at Revlon, then at Christian Dior. He believes that he exists to capture beauty, to enhance and define it. "I have loved beautiful things ever since I was young – flowers, clothes, people in the street." He has produced advertisements for Dior – his image for the innovative cellulite product Svelte became famous – and fashion and cosmetic spreads for magazines, mainly *Vogue*.

In 1963 **Hiro** (Yasuhiro Wakabayashi; b. 1930) photographed the black hoof of a steer which he decorated with a glittering ruby necklace by Harry Winston. This picture revolutionized still-life photography and made an instant celebrity of Avedon's Japanese assistant, who was raised in China. This was followed by sensational works for Italian *Vogue* and portraits for *Vanity Fair*. Hiro is admired for his artful lighting, experiments with double exposure, and idiosyncratic points of view.

The Image-Makers

Image is everything. Image campaigns by major fashion labels have been turned into stage shows and a small group of photographers have become extremely successful and wealthy thanks to this. Their work blurred the distinctions between editorial spreads and advertising campaigns. These moved closer together because they were shot by the same photographer.

Steven Meisel (b. 1954) is one of the most successful image-makers: this highly intelligent New Yorker, who sees himself as a "mirror of his era," changed the image of the designers whose garments he photographed. Italian *Vogue* gave him free reign over 30 pages of a single issue. In a society that has been highly sensitized to the issue of child abuse, his advertising campaign for Calvin Klein caused grave offense, depicting as it did lascivious teenagers in underwear in tacky basement dens, a setting all too reminiscent of child pornography and Meisel's only misjudgment of the public's response.

Without causing offense but being no less effective, the German **Peter Lindbergh** (b. 1944) shaped the profile of the supermodels. Some discovered their photographic personality through him, because his grainy black and white images inspired by classical portrait photography guide the eye toward the person. Fashion is of secondary importance. The calm realism, reportagelike authenticity and lack of artifice in his pictures may be influenced by Lindbergh's origins in the Ruhr, the heartland of Germany's working class. Lindbergh studied painting at the art college in Krefeld and was 27 before he first held a camera in his hands. In 1978 the German magazine *Stern*, at the forefront of progressive fashion journalism at the time, published a fashion spread which launched Lindbergh's international career. Lindbergh has taken pictures for all the great fashion magazines, and he has produced advertising campaigns for Armani, Prada, Karan, Calvin Klein, and Jil Sander. His 1999 portraits of the newly elected German chancellor in a Brioni suit were very similar to fashion photographs, and earned the Social Democrat Gerhard Schröder the nickname "cashmere chancellor." (See illustrations on pages 560–561.)

Smoother and more open in its erotic allusions is the black and white photography with which **Herb Ritts** (born in 1952 in Los Angeles) won the favor of fashion magazines in the 1980s. Ritts, the son of wealthy parents and once a neighbor of Steve McQueen, is a self-taught photographer. His career began with a sensual image of the young actor Richard Gere. From the late 1970s, Ritts published in all the fashion magazines his pictures, which perfectly articulate the spirit of the 1980s. Their calculated glamour found an echo in the designs of Gianni Versace, which Ritts frequently photographed. Ritts has increasingly shifted his work to advertising. His black and white testimonials for the chain The Gap are now regarded as the high art of advertising. In a similar way to his compatriot Bruce Weber, Ritts has produced impressive work with his myth-building star portraits and gently homoerotic studies of young men.

The Neorealists

Starting in London, a protest against the gloss and luxury of photography in the 1980s developed as a reaction to the supermodel era. *Shocking*. Because the new images avoided any semblance of a will for beauty and poise. Zits, red-rimmed eyes, and hairy armpits were photographed in close-up. Women refused to be coquettish; men withheld their muscles and machismo from observers. The role models came from British pop culture. The fashion equivalent was grunge, a street fashion which based its style on secondhand shops, military surplus stores, and cheap off-the-peg clothes and which took the responsibility for fashion away from the editors-in-chief of the big glamour publications. Soon, new magazines grew out of the fertile soil of the London underground scene, with street cred and an understanding of the new realism. *i-D* magazine was an underground pop music magazine and organ of the indie scene in the 1980s, which increasingly became a trendsetting fashion magazine in the second half of the 1990s. This was supplemented by new publications such as *Dazed and Confused* and *Sleazenation*, whose titles signalized that competition to *Vogue* and *Elle* was coming out of the gutter.

The expressive, unstyled images of **David Sims** (b. 1966) heralded the birth of grunge. Another pioneer of pallid coolness, **Craig McDean** (b. 1964) moved from Manchester to London in the late 1980s, where he worked as an assistant to Nick Knight before becoming one of the creators of heroin chic: tired, haggard, impassive models with dark shadows under their eyes, which were denounced for glorifying drugs by alarmed observers and populists such as US president Bill Clinton.

Juergen Teller (b. 1964), a graduate of Munich's Academy of Photographic Design, became famous through his pictures of model Kristen McMenamy: written on her naked body were words like "Fashion" and "Versace." A McMenamy torso photographed in 1996 was already on show at the great art exhibition in Munich in 1998. Teller's advertising work, for example for Strenesse, proves that even a protagonist of trash is capable of developing modern glamour. Stylist Venetia Scott, who lives with Teller, has been a major contributor to this development. (See illustrations on pages 547 and 606–614)

Nick Knight (b. 1958) uses pictures like *Jerome in Elevator* to pass ironic comment on the dirty pathos of the younger hyperrealists, but avoids classification. In 1992 he permitted a sudden blast of glamour to light up a Jil Sander advertisement for which he was photographing Tatjana Patitz in a white dress, with a photograph of dried flowers full of decaying poetry. In 1996 there were images of model Devon with a Japanese hairstyle and a gown by Alexander McQueen which was computer-enhanced to create a surreal mixture of tradition and of a posthuman vision of the future. "If you want reality, why don't you look out of the window," says Knight. (See illustration on pages 10–11).

Wolfgang Tillmans (b. 1968) has consistently refused to allow his style to be commercially exploited. Like Nick Knight, the photographer from Remscheid studied in Bournemouth. He worked for magazines like *Tempo*, *i-D*, and *The Face*, then for *Vogue*, in order, as he says, "to hijack fashion photography."

In his incorruptible way, Tillmans is closest to the mother of hyperrealism, the American **Nan Goldin** (b 1953), who portrayed the damaged lives of her friends, some of whom suffered from Aids or were drug addicts, as if in a diary, merciless and loving at the same time. Despite her obvious technical deficiencies, Nan Goldin became established as an influential contemporary photographer with several large exhibitions devoted to her work.

Fashion schools

How do you become a fashion designer?

Those who have become established always seem to give the same answer to this question:

There are two classic routes. The first, as ever, is to go work directly for a fashion house, where you gradually learn by doing, as an apprentice, work experience student, left or right hand, and by looking over the shoulders of everyone who works there. Even without previous training this path is still available if applicants have something to show: their own designs, drawn or sewn, handmade creative accessories such as hats or costume jewelry.

The second classic route is to train at one of the established fashion colleges from which the fashion houses traditionally recruit their young talents.

The best known of the fashion schools are listed below:

Meisterschule für Mode, München
Alumni: Gabriele Strehle, Gabriele Blachnik, Peter Bäldle
Info: Roßmarkt 15, D-80331 München
Tel.: (0) 89-23 32 24 23

Academie voor Schone Kunsten, Antwerp
Alumni: Martin Margiela, Ann Demeulemeester, Dries van Noten, Olivier Theysken
Info: Mutsaardstraat 31, B-2000 Antwerp
Tel.: 00 32-32 32 41 61

Lette-Verein, Berlin
Alumni: Susanne Wiebe
Info: Victoria-Luise-Platz 6, D-10777 Berlin

Esmod, Paris
Info: 16 Boulevard Montmartre, F-75009 Paris

Esmod, München
Info: Frauenhoferstrasse 23 h, D-80469 München
Tel.: (0) 89-2 01 45 25
http:\\www.esmod.de

Hochschule für Künste in Bremen
Info: Am Waldrahm 23, D-28195 Bremen
Tel.: (0) 4 21-30 19-0

Central Saint Martin's School of Art and Design, London
Alumni: John Galliano, Alexander McQueen

Goldsmiths University of London
Info: http:\\www.goldsmith.ac.uk

Royal College of Art, London
Info: http:\\www.rca.ac.uk
Very prestigious

Domus Academy, Milan
Info: http:\\www.moda.italynet.com

Ecole de Chambre Syndicale de la Couture, Paris
Alumni: Yves Saint Laurent, Valentino
Info: 45, rue Saint Roch

Parson's School of Design, New York and Paris
Alumni: Donna Karan
Info: http:\\www.parsons.edu

Fashion Institute of Technology (FIT), New York
Info: FITinfo@suny.edu

Tama University of Fine Arts, Tokyo
Alumni: Issey Miyake
Info: http:\\www.tamabi.ac.jp

Bunka Fukuso Gakuin, Tokyo
Alumni: Kenzo, Yamamoto

Glossary

Accessory: fashionable item that complements clothes, e.g. a handbag, shoes, scarf, or jewelry.

Accordion bag: classic handbag with several internal compartments, expandable like an accordion (illustration 1).

Acetate: chemical fiber based on cellulose, first manufactured in 1864 and in mass production since 1920.

Ajouré: collective term for fine openwork embroidered fabric. Much in evidence in 1998 at Missoni and Julien MacDonald.

Aléoutienne: rigid, bright silk fabric.

A-line: dress shaped in outline like the letter A, which flares from narrow shoulders and a low waist to a wide skirt. Created by Christian Dior, the A-line has returned to *haute couture* and was seen in Chanel's 1998/99 collection.

Alta moda: Italian *haute couture*.

American shoulder: obliquely cut armhole that reveals the shoulder (illustration 2).

Ankle boot: any type of ankle-high boot.

Anorak: Scandinavian-style weatherproof jacket, hooded and zipped with cuffed or elasticized sleeves; originally a drawstring waist-length cagoule, the anorak came into general use after the 1936 Winter Olympics and is available today in a variety of forms and weatherproof fabrics.

Arabesque: widely used folkloric pattern of stylized leaf or flower ornamentation (illustration 3).

Arafat scarf or Palestinian scarf: square headscarf with geometric patterns (*keffijeh*), worn folded into a triangle, popularized in the 1970s and 1980s by Yassir Arafat, founder of the Palestinian Liberation Organization and worn by young Europeans.

Argyll or **Argyle:** diamond pattern most often seen on woolen socks and pullovers; named for an area of western Scotland.

Armani sleeves: turned-up sleeves made of two different fabrics.

Baby doll: two-piece nightwear consisting of a loose top with puff sleeves and short bottom half. It was made popular by the 1956 movie of the same name and its star, Caroll Baker, and was adapted by couturier Jacques Griffe for day wear, the top being elongated to form a dress (illustration 4).

Baby Jane: strapped shoe, named for children's strapped shoes.

Baggy pants: extremely wide, overlong pants adopted from the techno music trend and worn low at the hip, thus exposing the top of underwear.

Baguette bag: long, narrow handbag carried under the arm like a baguette of French bread; designed by Karl Lagerfeld for Fendi and the fashionable handbag shape of 1999.

Baker's check: pattern similar to gingham but twice the size → Vichy-check.

Balconette: strong uplift brassiere with removable straps for a low décolleté; frequently a half-cup brassiere with straps (illustration 5).

Ballerina length: hem length of skirt or dress, reaching to just above the ankles.

Ballerinas: flat ladies' shoes with or without ties around the ankles, similar in appearance to ballet dancers' training shoes, though fitted with stronger soles; popularized by movies of the 1950s in which Audrey Hepburn appeared and back in fashion during the 1980s.

Ballerina skirt: short, very wide skirt, often with tulle frills; popularized by Madonna and Cindy Lauper in the 1980s.

Balloon skirt: wide skirt hemmed so as to curve inward at the knees; fashionable in cocktail dresses until 1958, revived in the late 1980s and again as part of the → retro look in the late 1990s.

Balloon sleeve: very full sleeve held in place at the wrist by a cuff; created in 1890 and revived by Nina Ricci (illustration 6).

Bandanna: printed cotton scarf worn around the neck or as a headscarf; originally the neckerchief worn by North American settlers and cowboys; popular as part of leisurewear and Western wear (as a pirate-style head scarf) in the 1990s.

Bandeau: strapless brassiere in the form of a flat piece of fabric; worn to flatten the bust.

Bangle: rigid circular bracelet, inspired by African tribal jewelry and popular in Europe since 1900 (illustration 7).

Bateau neckline: → boat neck.

Bathrobe coat: lightweight coat with a tie belt, similar to a bathrobe; usually made of cashmere, wool, or velvet; often worn with softly draped pants and high heels.

Batik: Javanese textile printing technique in which tying the fabric or applying wax to it keeps selected areas free of color during the dying process.

Battle dress: loose suit with a bomber jacket, modeled on British fighter pilots' uniform.

Battle jacket: waist-length, military-type zipped jacket with patch pockets.

Batwing sleeve: sleeve set very deep in the armhole, tapering toward the wrist (illustration 23).

Belgravia shoe: open lace-up shoe; became popular in 1870 and frequently inspires modern designers, e.g. John Galliano for Dior.

Bermuda shorts: narrow pants for men and women that end just above the knee: popular, colorful beachwear in the United States since the 1950s, part of general leisurewear since the 1960s.

---

1 Accordion bag

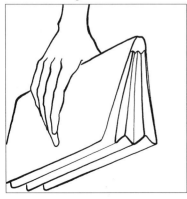

2 American shoulder

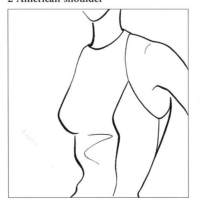

3 Arabesque

4 Baby Doll

Bias cut: cut across the grain of the fabric, a technique introduced by Madeleine Vionnet in the 1920s.

Block heel: wide, square heel of various heights.

Bloomers: loose, full shorts or ankle-length harem pants with elasticized waist and cuffed legs. Introduced by the feminist Amelia Bloomer in the mid-19th century, they became popular among women cyclists and for children and were briefly revived in the late 1970s to early 1980s.

Blouson: hip-length sports jacket with a drawstring around the bottom which creates gathers at the hips; popular in the 1950s.

Boa: long, narrow scarf made of fur or feathers and named after the snake of the same name; in and out of European fashion since 1800.

Board shorts: extremely short, figure-emphasizing shorts designed for freedom of movement and worn for yachting.

Boat neck or **bateau neckline:** collarless, boat-shaped neckline running from shoulder to shoulder (illustration 9).

Bodice: top half of a garment, close-fitting and often reinforced, without sleeves or straps.

Body: one-piece item of clothing or foundation garment usually fastened at the crotch by means of snaps or hooks; nowadays it is usual for the closefitting or blouselike top half to be visible.

Body-slimmer: figure-shaping foundation garment.

Body stocking: one-piece closefitting garment made of elastic material and covering the whole body, originally worn mainly by dancers and mannequins, popular during the disco craze of the 1970s and still worn today by sportspeople.

Body suit: → Jumpsuit.

Bolero: 1. waist-length, open jacket adopted from Spanish national costume (illustration 8); 2. small, round hat with upturned brim.

Bomber jacket: blouson-type, US military-style jacket, usually made of nylon; the olive-green version is frequently worn by skinheads.

Boob tube: strapless tubelike top covering the bust.

Boot-cut pants: lightly flared pants that fall over the shoe; narrower than a full flare and comfortable to wear with boots.

Bord-à-bord jacket: ladies' jacket in which the front edges do not cross but abut each other and are held together with frogs or toggles, etc.

Borsalino: elegant soft felt gentleman's hat named after Milanese hat-maker Giovanni Borsalino; also worn by ladies; popular until the 1930s but has sporadically reappeared ever since.

Boule shape: shape of skirt that is full below the waist and tighter at the hem,

reminiscent of Paul Poiret's → hobble skirt (illustration 10).

Boxer shirt or **muscle shirt:** sleeveless T-shirt worn by boxers, popular with women since the 1970s.

Box skirt: straight skirt with a waistband, with two thick, often quilted monk's seams along both front and back which make the skirt appear very square.

Bumster: hipster pants worn low so as reveal the top of the buttocks; introduced by Alexander McQueen in the 1990s.

Burberry: gabardine raincoat with small collar and covered buttons, the material patented by Thomas Burberry; a typical characteristic is the removable plaid wool lining.

Bustier: strapless, corsetlike top of variable length above the waist; worn as an undergarment, or since the 1970s as a summer garment.

Bustle: pad, stuffing, or hoops serving as a base over which the rear of a skirt is draped so as emphasize the derrière; came into fashion around 1785 and found new popularity in the late 19th century; later adapted by Christian Dior.

Butterfly sleeve: short frilled sleeve.

Caddy pants: short pants, similar to knickerbockers but narrower.

Caftan: loosely cut, straight dress with buttons.

Camel hair: short soft undercoat of the camel used to make soft woolen fabric; camel-hair coats are especially well known.

Camisole: item of underwear that covers the body from the bust to the waist, with narrow straps and straight neckline; the camisole dress, which is derived from it, is similar to a negligée with narrow shoulder straps, is often made of semitransparent material, and is worn in any length (illustration 13).

Camouflage look: garments made of army camouflage material, popular with hippies in the 1960s and 1970s and with hip-hoppers in the 1990s.

Cancan look: style of crinolinelike skirts, usually decorated with lace, inspired by the skirts worn by cancan dancers.

Cape: outer garment, often with slits for the arms and with a hood.

Capri pants: three-quarter-length, narrow ladies' pants with a small slit at the side of the hem, either left open of fastened with buttons, a zipper, or similar; inspired by the trousers worn by Italian fishermen and created by Emilio Pucci in the 1950s (illustration 14).

Cardigan: casual, hip-length knitwear jacket for men and women, collarless and frequently V-necked.

Cargo pants: loose pants with patch pockets and drawstring waist.

Caribbean look: style of hip-hugging dresses or skirts flaring out at the knee → Folkloric; → Carmen look.

5 Balconette

6 Balloon sleeve

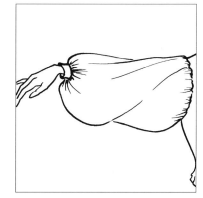

7 Bangles

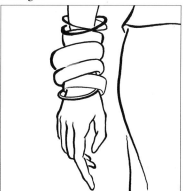

8 Bolero

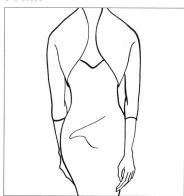

Carmen look: style of dresses modeled on Spanish flamenco costume, usually narrow at the hips, thighs, and knees, and ending in a wide skirt; bare shoulders and lace or frills at the neckline (Carmen décolleté); particularly popular in 1977 as part of → folkloric fashion.

Carrot pants: sharply tapered pants popular in the 1980s.

Carryall: large handbag.

Casaque: hip-length blouse worn over a skirt, fashionable in the 1920s, 1930s, and 1950s, and also worn like a pinafore over pants around 1965–70 (illustration 29),

Cascade neckline: neckline with narrow straps and a cascade of fabric at the front (illustration 48).

Cashmere: soft, lightweight wool made from the hair of the Kashmir goat.

Casual look: look made up of coordinates, contrasting with the business or city look, but no less expensive.

Catsuit: figure-hugging one-piece garment made of wool or stretch fabric, so named because it gives a sleek outline.

Catwalk: elongated, raised podium along which models walk at a fashion → show, wearing clothes from the latest couture or ready-to-wear collections.

Cauterization: the application of acid to a blended fabric so as to destroy part of one the types of fibers in the fabric, thereby creating a pattern, e.g. as in devoré velvet.

Chalk stripes: pale stripes on a dark background, less defined and spaced further apart than pin stripes.

Champagne-glass dress: cocktail dress shaped like an upturned cocktail glass, close fitting around the body and with a projecting, usually short skirt (illustration 42).

Chanel suit: slightly boxy, simple yet elegant tweed suit, designed by Coco Chanel in 1954 and an almost instant classic; typical are the trimmings along the edges of the top, which is either a → bord-à-bord jacket or single breasted, with gold buttons and patch pockets.

Changeant: iridescent material

Chantilly lace: fine black bobbin lace, usually with swags of flowers or motifs in the Baroque and Rococo style.

Chasuble pleat: pleat covering the top seams of sleeves and broadening the appearance of the shoulders.

Chauffe-cœur: sleeveless vest made of warm fabric with low-cut, round neck, barely waist-length; adapted from ballet clothes.

Chelsea boots: ankle boots with elasticized sides instead of laces or a zipper, popularized by the Beatles in the 1960s.

Chenille yarn: yarn that has been cut in the warp of a fabric, the fibers standing proud thus producing an effect similar to velvet; used as velour and corduroy fabrics, and toweling and carpets.

Cheongsam: close-fitting Suzy Wong shift dress with a mandarin collar and a vent at the side of the skirt (illustration 15).

Chiffon: light, translucent fabric with an uneven surface, made of natural silk or synthetic fibers.

Chinos: straight-cut casual pants made of tough fabric, e.g. cotton gabardine, with front side pockets and, usually, pleats.

Choker: collar of pearls or band of velvet or similar fabric worn around the neck (illustration 16).

Circular skirt: skirt based on a circular or semicircular cut, narrow at the hips and flowing at the hem; frequently supported by → godets.

Clam-diggers: narrow knee-length or calf-length pants; popular in the 1950s.

Clean look: clean-cut clothing with understated details → college style.

Clogs: slipperlike shoes with thick wooden or cork soles, the uppers of leather or synthetic material, fashionable in the 1960s and 1970s, and revived in the late 1990s.

Cocktail dress: short dress, usually with a low neckline; when worn with a bolero or short jacket, it is suitable for variety of occasions; came into fashion in the 1940s.

Colitair: close-fitting necklace with solitaire diamond.

Collection: a collection of designs prepared for a single season by a couturier or designer, to be shown to the public, usually during a → show.

College style: casual style derived from American college dress, typical features being shirtdresses with white collars, pleated skirts, blazers, and twin sets, popular in European fashion since the 1950s and now a classic style → Clean look.

Collier de chien: → choker.

Colonial style: → safari look.

Color blocking: contrasting expanses of color on fabric which endow clothes with a graphic quality, as in → Courrèges look.

Coolie pants: three-quarter-length, straight, wide-legged pants.

Coordinates: various fabrics or items of clothing which are matched by color or fabric type.

Corduroy pants: wide-legged corduroy pants.

Corsair pants: narrow trousers with slits below the knees, cut slightly wider than → Capri pants.

Corselette: lightweight → corset

9 Bateau neckline

10 Boule shape

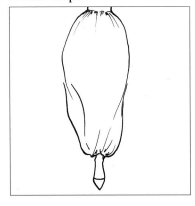

11 Pea jacket

12 Wraparound top

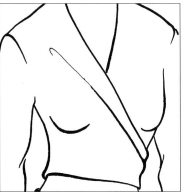

without stiffening, more usually known as a → bodice.

Corset: bodice used to shape a woman's body by means of stiffening or lacing.

Cossack pants: baggy, ankle-length or calf-length pants with a wide waist held by a belt (illustration 18).

Cossack style: style adopted from the Cossack costume, featuring stand-up collars, fur-trimmed hems, and toggles (illustration 32).

Country look: style of classic British casual dress in which wool and tweeds, often in traditional → Glen check or Tartan pattern, are characteristic materials; was taken up by *haute couture* in the 1970s.

Courrèges look: style created by André Courrèges and influenced by → Op Art and space travel; popular in the mid- and late 1960s.

Couture: hand-sewn, made-to-measure garments, designed as unique pieces by couturiers and made of high-quality fabrics.

Cowl neck: wide piece of fabric tubing attached to the neck of a garment.

Crêpe: fabric which has been given a crinkled surface by means of heat and a crêpe weave.

Crêpe de Chine: delicate, sheer, crinkled fabric made from natural or synthetic silk.

Crêpe sole: thick, rubber shoe sole first used for golf shoes in the 1920s and then for sports shoes in general after 1936; later also used in fashion footwear.

Crinoline: rigid petticoat originally made of horsehair, later of steel hoops which gave skirts extraordinary width; went out of fashion around 1870 and reappeared in 1984 in Vivienne Westwood's mini crinis.

Crystal mesh: material made of fine particles of crystal, developed by Daniel Swarovski.

Culottes: divided skirt.

Cup collar: stand-up collar open at the front, set at back to enable the fabric to fall in cup-like arches.

Cutout: area cut out of evening dresses, pant, or tops (illustration 19); characteristic of the 1960s.

Cut steel: filigree jewelry; became fashionable in the late 18th century as a substitute for diamonds.

Cycling pants: tight-fitting, elastic, above-the-knee shorts adopted from the dress of cyclists.

Deauville Style: → *nautical style.*

Delphos gown: floor-length, loose-fitting, pleated silk gown, designed by couturier Mariano Fortuny, in which the shoulders and sleeves are held together with glass beads.

Derrière: French for "behind"; the

derrière was emphasized by such devices as the → bustle.

Diana décolleté: asymmetric neckline with one bare shoulder; first seen in the second half of the 19th century, it was adopted by Elsa Schiaparelli in the 1930s and by Madame Grès in the 1950s, and regained popularity in the late 1970s and mid-1990s (illustration 20).

Dior vent or **Dior pleat:** short vent designed by Christian Dior in 1948 for his tight → pencil line skirt.

Dirndl: full skirt gathered into the waistband.

Disco fashions: style of clothes worn to discotheques, strongly influenced by the cult movie *Saturday Night Fever* (1977) with John Travolta and Olivia Newton John; characterized by glittering and shiny materials like metallic fabrics, sequins, and lurex; came back into fashion in the 1990s.

Dolman sleeve: sleeve cut as an extension of the bodice, probably copied from the Turkish dolman; in 1968 Emanuel Ungaro designed an angular version known as the Ungaro dolman.

Double sace: 1. fabric in which both sides are equally usable; 2. reversible jacket and coat of the 1920s, one side being camel-hair, the other gabardine.

Drainpipe pants: tight pants with narrow, straight legs.

Drawstring waist: waistband in which a

belt is drawn through a tube formed by two layers of fabric laid one next to the other.

Duchesse: expensive, shiny satin made of silk, viscose, or acetate.

Duffel coat: short, casual coat with a hood and fastened with toggles; originally worn by men of the British Royal Navy (calf-length, camel-colored) it was adapted after World War II (knee-length, usually navy blue) and became popular with women and children.

Elizabethan collar: type of collar based on the high lace collars of 16th-century court dress; the lace may be replaced by feathers or wool threads.

Empire line: style of dress fashionable during the French Napoleonic Empire (1804–14); the cut of Empire-style dresses and coats, which are gathered beneath the bust and fall loosely to the feet, frequently reappears in contemporary fashions.

Encrustment: pieces of fabric, e.g. lace, leather, or trimmings, inserted into another; distinct from appliqué.

End-and-end weave: small dotted pattern produced by alternating light and dark warp and weft threads in black, gray, or brown with white.

Epaulet: shoulder-piece originally designed to prevent slippage of shoulder-slung rifles and later developed into a symbol of rank; it gives clothes a military touch and

13 Camisole

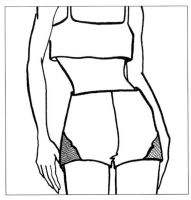

14 Capri pants

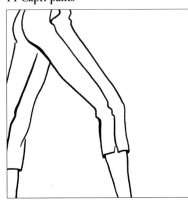

15 Cheongsam

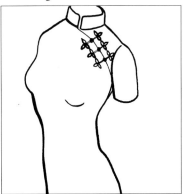

16 Choker

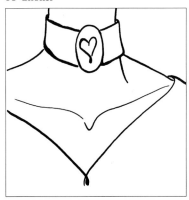

appeared in ladies fashions of the 1930s.

Ethnic: fabrics and patterns based on tribal dress.

Fancy: 1. dense flannel, napped on both sides; 2. type of printed pattern on fabric.

Fancy cord: corduroy with varying shapes of rib (e.g. wide and narrow, or open and closed).

Fedora: felt hat named for a stage play by Victorien Sardou, written in 1882 (illustration 22).

Fish tail: taillike extension of the back hem of a skirt.

Flammé: fabric into which yarns of varying thickness have been woven.

Flannel: generic term including weaves napped either on one or both sides, and made of cotton, wool, or viscose.

Flapper dress or **Charleston Dress:** dress, fashionable in the 1920s, with narrow shoulder straps and a low waist often tied with a belt or scarf.

Flared pants: hipster pants, tight-fitting to the knee and flaring to the ankle; fashionable in the 1970s (illustration 45).

Flip-flops: flat sandals with strap between the big and second toe, usually made of plastic or rubber.

Floppy hat: flat ladies' hat with very wide brim, fashionable around 1910 and in the 1950s (illustration 47).

Flyback: → halter neck.

Folkloric: style of dress which assimilates elements of national costumes from around the world; popularized by Yves Saint Laurent in 1976 and revived in the ethno-mix of the 1990s.

French cuffs: double cuffs.

French knickers: loosely cut panties with lace trimmings, worn with matching → camisole; created by Janet Reger in the late 1960s and modeled on historic precedent.

French leg: high-cut leg in underwear or swimwear giving the illusion of longer legs.

French pocket: pocket set in the side seams of pants or skirt.

Frock coat: long-sleeved, knee-length garment which appeared in several 1998/99 collections as a basic element of pantsuits.

Frou-frou: intentional rustling noise of petticoats made of fabrics such as silk or taffeta; particularly fashionable during the late 19th century, it was a successful element of cancan costumes around 1885–1900. Today four-four is understood as any kind of playful frilliness on clothes.

Gandoura dress: → trapeze line caftan dress, often decorated with sequins, companion piece to the tent coat.

Garçonne: severe, masculine style of dress of the 1920s, named for the

title of a novel by Victor Margueritte, *La Garçonne* (mannish girl) and regarded as an expression of emancipation; characteristic of this style were the tuxedo suit, greatcoat, and masculine jackets.

Garter: band of elastic worn around the thigh to hold up stockings.

Gaucho pants: calf-length, wide-bottomed ladies' pants, based on those worn by South American cowboys (gauchos); became fashionable in the early 1970s.

Georgette crêpe: delicate, translucent crêpe fabric; keeps its shape.

Gigot sleeve or **leg-of-mutton sleeve:** sleeve that is tight-fitting from cuffed wrist to elbow, then puffs up from elbow to shoulder.

Girlie look: look adopted in the 1990s by young girls, especially by fans of the Spice Girls, and intended as an expression of girl power; consists of girly yet sexy clothes, e.g. → transparent or → lingerie style, worn with boots, the hair often worn in bunches or braids.

Gladiator sandals: flat sandals with narrow laces, modeled on the footwear worn by gladiators in ancient Rome.

Glen check or **Prince of Wales check:** woven tartan pattern, traditionally used for suits, now also used for dresses and long skirts.

Godet: triangular piece of fabric sewn into a skirt to produce fullness.

Granny style: romantic, intentionally old-fashioned style, often inspired by garments obtained from secondhand clothing shops and including such accessories as shawls and beaded bags.

Greatcoat reverse: wide lapel on coats or blouses, named for the lapel of the greatcoat, which is produced by undoing the top button.

G-string: → tanga with a very slim back that is invisible under skirts or pants.

Guard style: severe, military style of coats and suits.

Gypsy look: style modeled on Gypsy costume and characterized by frilly or unevenly hemmed skirts worn with blouses tied above the waist or with a Carmen neckline, and with copious jewelry → Carmen Look; became popular in 1976/77, at the same time as the → Folkloric look.

Halter neck: dress or top with straps that are tied at the nape of the neck, leaving shoulders and back exposed (illustration 24).

Harness top: high-necked sleeveless top, fashionable in leather, piqué, or shantung.

Haute couture: exclusive garments made by couturiers and presented to the public twice a year, which are regarded as setting fashion styles in general; invented by Charles Frederick Worth in the second half of the 19th century; its major centers are Paris and Rome (where it is known as *alta moda*); the rise of ready-to-wear in the 1960s and

17 Peter Pan collar

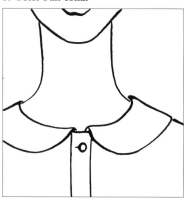

18 Cossack pants

19 Cutouts

20 Diana décolleté

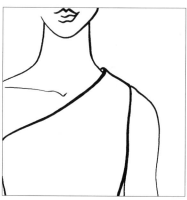

the influence of youthful trends on fashion have modified the role of *haute couture*, and new trends are increasingly set by ready-to-wear.

Herringbone: pattern of diagonal lines resembling the skeleton of a herring, produced by a broken twill weave and often emphasized by the use of different-colored yarns.

Hipster: narrow, midriff-revealing pants or skirt worn by hippies.

Hipster skirt: skirt cut to fit around the hips, usually elasticized.

H-line: slightly tailored → Princess line, with a slender top and narrow hips; launched by Christian Dior in 1954/55.

Hobble skirt: ankle-length skirt created by Paul Poiret in 1910, cut and draped to narrow below the knee with a hem or fur border, thus allowing only small steps to be taken; in order to avoid tearing the material, foot-cuffs (wide ribbons used to the calves together to an appropriate tightness) could be worn.

Hot pants: extremely brief shorts that barely cover the bottom; came into fashion in the early 1970s; in velvet or lurex for eveningwear (illustration 25).

Houndstooth check: small check pattern of two or more colors (traditionally black and white); distinguishable from → Pepita by the pattern linking individual checks.

I-line: extremely narrow line of clothing, created by Cristobal Balenciaga in 1954/55.

Informals: abstract patterns on fabric, e.g. wild white lines on a red background, as devised at Missoni and Calvin Klein.

Inverness coat: mid–19th-century sleeveless men's coat with hip-length cloak; also worn by women; refined versions were made with covered buttons, silk collars, and linings. The Inverness coat later became popular as an evening coat for men; the design reemerged in the form of a sports coat in the 1970s, with the addition of sleeves and a shorter cape.

Iridescent fabric: fabric with a mother-of-pearl sheen.

Italian length: skirt length which just permits a view of the knees; also known as a lady mini.

Jabot: decorative frill used to cover buttons on blouses or dresses; originally worn by men, it became popular with women from the late 19th century and remained so until the late 1950s; in a modified form it became fashionable again in 1980.

Jeans: originally the hard-wearing pants for gold diggers allegedly invented by German-born Levi Strauss around 1850 in the United States; initially confined to work wear, jeans became popular in the 1930s for leisurewear. They crossed the Atlantic after World War II and became established as youth leisurewear in the 1950s. Today jeans are socially acceptable for both male and female everyday wear and have become a

fashion fixture. The traditionally blue denim trousers are available in all shapes and colors.

Jersey: 1. now generic term for various types of knitwear: jersey is particularly stretchable without losing its shape and feels soft to the skin; after the British actress Lillie Langtry created the jersey costume, the material became popular for outer garments; also used in *haute couture* since Coco Chanel introduced it in 1916/17; 2. knitted pullover.

Jesus sandals: plain, flat leather sandals.

Jet pants: narrow-cut pants suitable for the ski slopes, made of bi-elastic material with padded knees and straps; first appeared in the 1970s.

Jodhpurs: riding breeches, very full from hip to knee, narrow on the calves, and usually with a leather insert on the inside leg; modeled on early 20th-century Indian riding pants and named after the city of Jodhpur, they have enjoyed periodic revivals since the 1970s (illustration 27).

John Wayne collar: cowboy-style collar with asymmetric button fastening; named for the famous movie star.

Jumpsuit: one-piece pantsuit, usually with short legs made of an elastic material such as jersey; introduced in 1969.

Jungle look: Rastafarian and military-style clothes worn by followers of early 1990s jungle music.

Kangaroo pocket: large patch pocket often seen on the front of cagoules (illustration 28).

Kelly bag: ladies' handbag first sold by Hermès in the 1930s and made popular by Grace Kelly in the 1950s.

Khaki pants: pants made of hard-wearing khaki fabric; frequently part of uniforms; also used to describe khaki-colored cotton pants.

Kilt: pleated tartan skirt with a flat front piece, often secured with a large safety pin and a leather strap; the kilt is based on the Scottish national costume (illustration 30).

Kimono sleeve: straight sleeve attached at right angles to a garment, as in the Japanese kimono.

Kitten heels: delicate high heels, like those worn by Audrey Hepburn in Billy Wilder's film *Sabrina* (1954).

Knickerbockers: loose, full breeches gathered below the knee, narrower than → plus fours; in leather, part of the German national costume and occasionally revived for ladies' fashions, i.e. in the 1960s (illustration 31).

Knitwear: knitted garments.

Kotze: rough loden cloak; part of Alpine traditional costume.

Label: trademark under which a collection is marketed.

Lamé: fabric interwoven with metallic threads.

21 Sheath dress

22 Fedora

23 Batwing sleeve

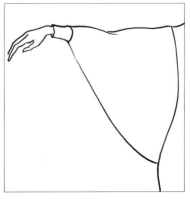

24 Halter neck

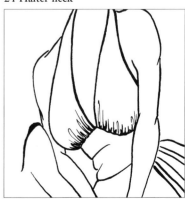

Lara look or **Zhivago look:** Cossack style inspired by the movie *Dr. Zhivago* (1965).

Lavallière: loosely tied bow, named for the Comtesse de Lavallière, a mistress of Louis XIV; fashionable in Bohemian circles during the 19th century, it was again popular in the mid-20th century.

Layered look: dress style of the 1990s, featuring several layers of clothes worn one over the other.

Leg-of-mutton sleeve: → gigot sleeve.

Leggings: footless leg covering made of elastic material; in a variety of colors and patterns, became part of ladies' wear during the 1980s.

Liberty: 1. British textile and fashion company, famous for its cotton floral prints; 2. term for dress and lining fabric made of shiny silk or synthetic satin.

Liberty floral: small floral pattern.

Ligne corolle: → New Look

Lingerie: generic term for fine nightwear and underwear.

Lingerie style: style of outfits modeled on nightdresses, especially popular in the 1990s (e.g. Studio Versace).

Liquette: shirt with rounded slits at the sides.

Loden: sturdy woolen fabric used mainly for national costumes and coats; typical colors are green, gray, and brown.

Lounge wear: various outfits that developed from nightwear for wearing around the house, e.g. wide pants with casual top.

Louver pleats: horizontal pleats (illustration 26).

Lumber jacket: waist-length or hip-length jacket with close-fitting, often knitted waistband and cuffs, loose but not baggy, similar to → blouson shape; its origins in the working clothes of North American tree fellers and it later became a military uniform jacket; the cut has been used since the 1930s for sports and leisure jackets.

Lurex®: metallic fabric developed in the United States after World War II.

Lycra®: extremely elastic synthetic fiber.

Madras: fabric in large, colorful checks.

Maillot: classic tight-fitting swimsuit.

Mancheron: short sleeve.

Mandarin collar, or **Chinese collar,** or **Nehru collar:** stand-up collar, open at the front (illustration 33).

Mannequin or **model:** 1. window dummy; 2. attractive, generally very young woman who demonstrates the latest fashions on the → catwalk.

Manolos: shoes designed by "King of Shoes" Manolo Blahnik; usually refers to his sexy slingbacks.

Mao suit: suit modeled on Chinese workers' suits as worn during the rule of Mao Zedong, with a single-breasted, high-collared jacket and skirt or pants; briefly popular in Britain in the late 1960s.

Marlene Dietrich pants: extremely wide-legged ladies pants cut like men's trousers, as worn by Marlene Dietrich in the 1930s, although she wore genuine men's suits.

Martha Graham dress: calf-length, flowing jersey dress named for the diva of modern dance; adopted by Armani and Calvin Klein.

Mary Janes: ankle-strap button shoes, popular in the 1920s, 1970s, and again in the 1990s. Mary Janes were originally designed for children.

Maxiskirt: ankle-length or floor-length skirt popular around 1970, along with → miniskirts and → midiskirts; maxicoats were often worn with miniskirts and maxiskirts with hot pants; → slit look.

Mermaid train: narrow train that tapers off at the end.

Midiskirt: calf-length skirt, distinct from the → miniskirt and → maxiskirts; although the word is no longer current, this length has been dominant since 1973.

Military style: look inspired by men's and women's military uniforms, often in shades of khaki shades.

Millefleurs: classic floral pattern, usually on cotton fabrics, the finest produced by → Liberty in London, and thus also known as Liberty prints.

Minaudière: small metallic evening bag, first presented by Cartier in 1900; today also decorated with paste or jewels and worn either with or without a shoulder chain.

Miniskirt: very short skirt; the minimum distance between hem and knee being 4 inches; Mary Quant, who introduced the line in 1959, is regarded as the inventor of the miniskirt and André Courrèges first showed his *haute couture* version in 1964/65; the fashion for miniskirts peaked in the second half of the 1960s.

Miranda pumps: slingback shoes with platform soles and high heels as worn by Carmen Miranda in the 1940s; came back into fashion in the late 1960s and again in the 1990s following the success of the movie *Evita.*

Moccasin: flat shoe made of soft leather, modeled on Native American footwear; a fashionable shoe for both men and women since the 1930s.

Model: contemporary, internationally acknowledged term for → mannequin, especially someone who works in front of the camera (photographic model).

Moiré: watered effect on fabric, formerly silk and also acetate; generally used for formal eveningwear.

Monokini: 1. swimwear influenced by topless fashion, where only the bottom half of a bikini is worn; 2. One-piece swimsuit in which the top and bottom parts are connected by straps of varying widths.

---

25 Hot pants

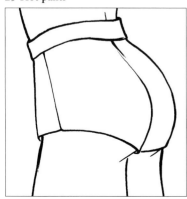

26 Louver pleats

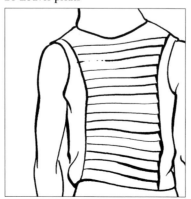

27 Jodhpurs

28 Kangaroo pocket

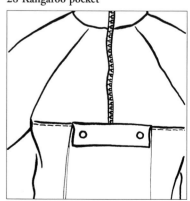

Moon boots: voluminous snow boots, modeled on astronauts' footwear; first appeared in the 1970s after the first men landed on the moon.

Muff: fur or fabric cylinder designed to keep the hands warm.

Mule: backless slipper with a high or low heel, usually made of suede or silk; nowadays a leather summer shoe.

Musketeer collar: wide lace collar, reminiscent of that in musketeer's uniform.

Muslin: lightweight, loosely woven cotton or woolen fabric; named for the city of Mosul, in Iraq.

Narrow line: → pencil line.

Nautical style or **Deauville style:** style of leisurewear and sportswear, generally navy blue and white, which first appeared in 1880; features navy blazers with gold buttons, white trousers, etc. modeled on naval uniforms.

Neck bag: small bag designed by Tom Ford for Gucci that is worn slung around the neck on a long strap.

Negligée: 1. comfortable yet elegant item of morning wear or house wear; 2. lightweight dressing gown or throw in the style of elegant nightwear.

New Edwardian style: 1950s style of menswear reminiscent of the Edwardian era, consisting of single-breasted jacket with waistcoat, narrow pants, bowler hat, tie pin, and pocket handkerchief.

New Look or **ligne corolle:** line created by Christian Dior in 1947 which made him world-famous; very feminine look with narrow, rounded shoulders, emphasized bust, narrow waist and wide, calf-length skirt.

No-bra-bra: brassiere designed by American designer Rudi Gernreich in 1963; made of unstructured nylon, it permits the breasts to keep their rounded form and does not squeeze them into a pointed shape.

Nylon: polyamide fiber, patented in the United States in 1937; after World War II, it became available in Europe, where initially it was used mainly in the manufacture of underwear and hosiery.

Op Art: art style characterized by geometric, abstract patterns and strong colors, especially black and white; it influenced 1960s fashion; → Courrèges look.

Organdy: a very lightweight, fine, sheer, stiffened cotton fabric (now synthetic), usually in pastel colors.

Organza: fabric similar to → organdy, originally made of silk.

Origami: Japanese art of paper-folding which has inspired designers to include artistic folds in their fashion designs.

Overknee: long sock reaching above the knee.

Over look/under look: multifaceted combination of simple coordinates, e.g. calf-length dress over narrow pants.

Overset: combination of jacket and sweater which, unlike the → twin set, are not of the same fabric or color.

Oversize look: garments that appear several sizes too large; in vogue during the 1980s and revived by Jean Paul Gaultier in the late 1990s.

Oxford bags: men's pants worn by students at Oxford University around 1920, with, unusually for the period, long and wide legs that flared out from the knee; the Oxford, or brogue, lace-up shoe became equally popular.

Page panties: waist-high panties with straight leg openings.

Pagoda shoulder: emphasized shoulder inspired by the shape of Asian pagodas; launched by Elsa Schiaparelli in 1933 (illustration 34).

Paisley: fabric pattern reminiscent of a rolled-up palm leaf without a stem.

Paletot: single- or double-breasted coat with lapels and patch pockets.

Panne: silk velvet.

Pant coat: coat or jacket designed to be worn over pants.

Parallelo: horizontally knitted jacket or jumper, very fashionable in the 1950s.

Para boots: hard-wearing lace-up boots, usually black, styled on short military boots.

Parka: comfortable, lined, long outer garment with large pockets, usually made of tough cotton fabric with removable lining; initially designed as an all-weather jacket for soldiers (therefore usually in olive fabric), it became very popular with young people in the 1970s.

Pashmina: lightweight cashmere and silk fabric used mainly for scarves and blankets; Donatella Versace favored this fabric for her 1998/99 eveningwear collection.

Passementerie: generic term for all types of trimmings on garments and furniture, essential absolute requirements for Coco Chanel's suits.

Passe-partout jacket: jacket similar to → bolero.

Paste: glass containing lead used to make artificial gemstones.

Patchwork: pieces of material, often of different colors, sewn together; also printed fabrics that look like patchwork; generally used for bedspreads, patchwork for clothes was popularized thanks to the → Gypsy look of the 1960s.

Pea jacket: man's double-breasted, hip-length jacket made of heavy, usually uniformly colored, fabric; popular during the Beatles era and revived by Tom Ford at Gucci (illustration 11).

Pedal pushers: → cycling pants.

Peek-a-boo: openwork earring design.

Pelerine: coat with a cape attached at the shoulder → Inverness coat.

---

29 Casaque

30 Kilt

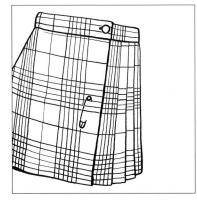

31 Knickerbocker

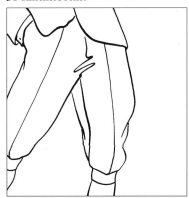

32 Cossack style

Pencil line: figure-emphasizing line created by Christian Dior in 1948, whereby the skirt is cut in one straight line from the hips, narrowing down to the hem like a pencil and frequently with a slit → Dior vent.

Pendant: piece of jewelry suspended from a long metal, leather, or silk band and worn around the neck; the strictly purist form was created in the 1980s by Robert Lee Morris and was reissued by Gucci.

Pennant collar: triangular collar.

Penny loafer: flat college shoe with a strap across the instep in which there is an opening that could perhaps hold a penny, which may once have been enough for a student's bus ride or telephone call.

Pepita: woven, very small check pattern with diagonal connecting lines, usually in black and white or navy and white.

Peplum jacket: short tailored ladies' jacket with flounces or flared flaps sewn into the waist (illustration 41).

Peter Pan collar: small, flat, round collar (illustration 17).

Petticoat: wide, rigid, frilly underskirt worn under the wide skirts of the 1950s and early 1960s (illustration 35).

Piqué: cotton fabric with relief pattern, usually honeycombed or waffled.

Pillbox: small, round or oval brimless hat worn perched on the head, created for Greta Garbo in the 1930s;

Jacqueline Kennedy made it famous and brought it up to date in the 1960s (illustration 36).

Pinafore dress: sleeveless, collarless dress based on the design of a chasuble.

Platform soles: shoes with extremely thick soles and heels, very fashionable in the 1970s and late 1990s.

Pleated pants: pants with pleats below the waistband; popularized in the 1920s and widely worn ever since with sewn-in pleats under the waistband.

Plissé: pleats pressed into fabric.

Plus fours: breeches, gathered below the knee with fabric falling below the knee-band.

Polka dots: fabric pattern of evenly spaced dots; the name was invented by German fashion designer Heinz Oestergaard.

Polo shirt: sport and leisure jersey shirt with short row of buttons and soft collar; usually short-sleeved.

Pompadour: small fabric bag named after the Marquise de Pompadour.

Poncho: woolen garment with an opening in the middle for the head, as worn by Native Americans in Central and South America.

Première: forewoman in an *haute couture* salon.

Prêt-à-porter or **ready-to-wear:** youthful, avant-garde designs produced

by couturiers and distinct from the made-to-measure, exclusive clothes of → *haute couture*; prêt-à-porter came about in the 1960s when young designers emerged who created fashion without referring to the prescribed line of *haute couture*; today trends are set by prêt-à-porter.

Prince of Wales check: → Glen check.

Princess line: dress or coat without a waist seam, the tailoring being achieved by working in the vertical seam; it was launched by Charles Frederick Worth in 1863 and became popular again in 1900, in the 1930s and again between 1955 and 1965.

Puff sleeves: balloon-like short sleeve gathered just above the elbow.

Pullover: long-sleeved woolen top derived from the knitted garments worn by seamen; became popular in Europe in the 1920s when Coco Chanel included it in several *haute couture* collections.

Pumps: ladies' strapless shoes without laces, variable height of heel; generally popular form of ladies shoe since the 1920s.

Quilting: fabric made of two layers of material enclosing a layer of padding secured by cross-stitching; extremely popular in the 1999/2000, e.g. Jean Paul Gaultier's quilted long skirts.

Raglan sleeve: sleeve that extends from the neckline to the wrist (illustration 37).

Rational dress: following the discussions surrounding the negative effects on health of tight corsets and heavy skirts, a dress was designed in 1898 that was loosely cut and did not emphasize the waist, fell loosely from the shoulders with wide sleeves; although this dress did not become popular itself, it had a long-term effect on the way dresses were cut.

Rayon: name for viscose, used between the early 1950s and the 1970s.

Redingote: tailored coat or long jacket, usually flared toward the hem, often fitted with a shawl collar; can be worn with or without a belt.

Retro: style of an earlier time that is revived, sometimes in modified form.

Reversible: 1. fabric with a shiny and a matte side; 2. clothes that can be worn inside out.

Rio panty: high leg panty with V-shaped waist exposing the navel.

Rivière: tennis bracelet.

Romantic look: dress style of the 1960s and 1970s incorporating folkloric elements and featuring frills, loose, long cotton dresses, and corset tops.

Ruffle: gathered, loosely falling decorative frill on dresses or skirts.

Sabrina heel: → kitten heels.

Sabrina neckline: square décolleté, name for Audrey Hepburn's clothes in the movie

33 Mandarin collar

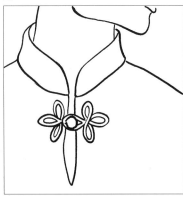

34 Pagoda shoulder

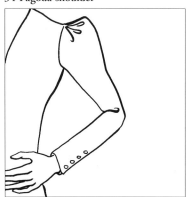

35 Petticoat

36 Pillbox

Sabrina (1954) (illustration 38).

Safari look or **colonial style:** style of sportswear made of strong, lightweight fabrics, modeled on tropical clothes, and characterized by the colors beige, brown, and khaki and by patch pockets and shoulder flaps; adopted in the mid-1960s.

Safari jacket: ladies' jacket in the → safari style, usually fitted with a belt and patch pockets (illustration 39).

Sailor collar: collar and neckline modeled on those in naval uniforms.

Sailor neck: turtleneck with zipper fastening (illustration 40).

Sari neckline: draped décolleté based on the sari.

Sarong: piece of fabric tied around the waist as in traditional dress of Malaysia and Indonesia.

Sarouel: pants that are as wide as a skirt down to the knee and close-fitting from knee to ankle; modeled on Middle Eastern pants for men.

Satin: lightweight, lustrous fabric.

Sautoir: originally any long chain or necklace; the term now denotes Coco Chanel's favorite jewelry, a string of pearls more than 40 inches long.

Self-cling bra: reusable bra cups, without straps or sides, that stick to the body and are worn with low necklines.

Sequins: small, shiny disks used to decorate garments, available separately or sewn on to finished fabric.

Serafino: collarless, buttoned T-shirt.

Shake pants: pants that have no seam at the sides but that are sewn together on the front and back crease.

Shatush: very fine wool made from the coat of the Himalayan mountain goat; fabrics made of the yarn are so fine they can be threaded through a ring; trade in this material is strictly forbidden.

Sheath dress: collarless, usually knee-length dress, close-fitting, straight, and cut from a single piece of fabric, with an oval or round neckline; also an evening dress with décolleté and shoulder straps; launched in 1918 and popular in the 1920s; it became known as the "Jackie-O dress" (after Jacqueline Kennedy Onassis) in the 1960s and was revived in the late 1990s (illustration 21).

Shantung: hand-woven silk with irregular, therefore less shiny, surface than regular silk.

Shift: loosely falling, unstructured dress, → tank suit; various forms have been fashionable, especially in the 1920s and mid-1960s.

Shirtwaister: loose dress, the upper part modeled on a man's shirt, with collar, buttons to the waist, and cuffs; popularized by Coco Chanel; adapted to suit contemporary fashion and frequently back in fashion.

Shopper: large bag modeled on a shopping bag.

Shoulder pads: pads designed to emphasize the shoulders; very fashionable in the 1980s.

Shows: abbreviated term for the fashion shows held twice a year in Paris, London, Milan, and New York at which couturiers (in January and July) and designers (in March and October) present their new → collections.

Silk: fine fibers from the cocoon of the silkworm and the fabric woven from them; silk is said to have been in use in China since the 3rd millennium BC.

Ski pants: ankle-length pants secured with an elasticized strap under the instep; fashionable off the piste in the 1950s and briefly revived in 1980 and in the early 1990s.

Skort: cross between a skirt and shorts which from the front has the appearance of a short wraparound skirt.

Slacks: straight-legged pants with a central, pressed pleat.

Slingbacks: → pumps with a strap across the heel.

Slinky look: sinuous clothes made of fluid fabrics, fashionable in the early 1970s and harking back to the 1930s.

Slipper: → moccasin.

Slit look: hot pants or a miniskirt worn under a maxiskirt or midiskirt left open at the front; fashionable in the early 1970s.

Sloppy Joe: oversize knitted pullover.

Slouch hat: hat with a small, soft brim, as worn by Greta Garbo in the 1930s; a crocheted version of the hat came back into fashion in the 1970s, and also in the 1990s in the form of a velvet hip-hop hat.

Smock: straight, narrow dress with front, back, and sleeves attached to a yoke collar.

Smocking: material which has been tightly gathered with decorative stitching (usually using elastic thread) to form geometric patterns; smocking is frequently featured in folkloric garments.

Sneaker: originally a rubber-bottomed, two-tone shoe with canvas uppers, now any type of sports footwear.

Spectator pumps: ladies' shoes in the style of the two-tone shoes that gentlemen once wore to horse races.

Spencer: short, waist-length jacket.

Sportswear: generic term for comfortable leisurewear, based on various types of sports clothing but which can be worn anytime, without the wearer engaging in sporting activities.

Step shorts: cross between hot pants and a miniskirt.

Stiletto: thin high heel on ladies' shoes.

Stole: large long scarf worn draped across the shoulders.

37 Raglan sleeve

38 Sabrina neckline

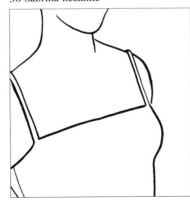

39 Safari jacket

40 Sailor neck

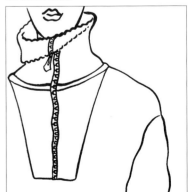

Stretch fabric: stretchable fabric made of elastic materials; produced since World War II after the development of synthetic fibers.

St. Tropez pants: navel-revealing hipster pants.

Sweater: roll-neck pullover modeled on British naval wear: in the 1940s, pinup girls wore figure-hugging sweaters over cornet-shaped brassieres designed by Howard Hughes.

Sweatshirt: comfortable, loose, long-sleeved, round-necked cotton top, fleecy on the inside; originally part of the jogging suit, it is now an accepted item of casual wear.

Swinger: type of A-line coat, shorter than knee length and with narrow sleeves and shoulders.

Taffeta: fine, stiff fabric made of silk or synthetic fibers, often made of → changeant.

Tailored suit: suit distinguishable from the → tailleur in that the jacket is modeled on a sports jacket.

Tailleur: ladies' suit distinguishable from the → tailored suit in that the jacket is tailored; in French all ladies' suits are referred to as tailleurs.

Tanga: very brief bikini bottom or panties made of two triangles of fabric connected by ties at the sides.

Tank suit: sporty swimsuit with a high neckline and wide straps.

Tartan: Scottish plaid cloth or pattern (illustration 43).

Tassel loafer: → moccasin with tassel.

T-bars: ladies' pumps with a T-shaped strap cut from the uppers.

Tea gown: loose gown cut in the → princess line, created by Charles Frederick Worth in 1864 as a → negligée dress; with long sleeves and elaborately decorated front, it became fashionable as an elegant and luxurious housedress.

Teddy: loose one-piece undergarment consisting of bodice and knickers, usually with lace decoration.

Tiara: semicircular, jewel-encrusted hair decoration (illustration 44).

Toga: loose outer garment of Roman antiquity, worn draped over the left shoulder from the front, across the back, then back to the front and across the left shoulder.

Toile: fabric woven from fine (synthetic) silk yarns, used mainly for blouses and underwear.

Top: any type of a short ladies' T-shirt or sleeveless shirt.

Topless fashion: ladies' fashion designs which do not cover the bust; presented by designer Rudi Gernreich in 1964 topless fashions influenced swimwear designs, to which the topless → monokini was introduced in the 1970s; the → transparent look picked up on this trend.

Topper: short, straight jacket with sloping shoulders, and front edge forming a right angle with the hem

Toque: rigid, usually flat, brimless and beautifully draped hat, often decorated with feathers, stringed beads, or veils, etc.

Torso dress: plain dress, pleated or gathered beneath the hipline, with a figure-hugging bodice.

Transparent look: look produced by outfit made partly or entirely of transparent fabric, revealing either bare skin or underwear.

Trapeze line: line of dress or coat with narrow shoulders and either a high waist or no waist, flaring out toward the hem; it first appeared during World War I; Yves Saint Laurent successfully presented his trapeze line in 1958; it remained popular throughout the 1960s.

Triangle bra: featherweight bra made of two triangles, without reinforcements or decorations.

Trim: narrow decorative ribbon, etc. used, for example, on the edges of garments.

Tube line: line of garment with a straight, elongated outline and a comfortable, casual cut.

Tulle: netting or lacelike fabric.

Tunic: simple type of dress or pinafore modeled in the loose, often sleeveless garment of ancient Rome; the armholes

either form part of the side seams or are attached at right angles.

Turban: long scarf worn wound around the head.

Tutu: short tulle skirt worn by ballerinas; fashionable as a multicolored miniskirt in 1982 and reappeared in cocktail dresses of the late 1980s.

Tuxedo shoe: black patent leather shoe.

Tuxedo style: 1. ladies' dinner jackets designed for day wear; 2. pants with satin trimming worn with cashmere pullovers or combined with colorful tops, as presented by Versace and Paco Rabanne.

Tweed: rough-textured woolen fabric in a variety of colored patterns, used especially for coats and suits; particularly well known as the material for → Chanel suits.

Twin set: matching knitted cardigan and sweater.

Twist line: outline with narrow hips and slightly flared, pleated skirt which flares as the wearer moves.

Umbrella skirt: skirt made up of 12 or more long sections, like an umbrella.

U-neckline: U-shaped neckline with wide shoulder straps.

Vamp style: shoulderless garment style.

Velcro fastening: fastening consisting of two pieces of rough material that adhere to each other when pressed together and

---

41 Peplum jacket

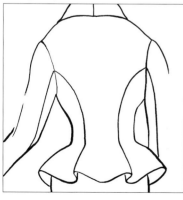

42 Champagne-glass dress

43 Tartan

44 Tiara

can be opened and closed by pulling and pressing.

Velour: fabric with a D velvetlike surface.

Velvet: short-piled, soft-textured fabric, usually cotton.

Vichy check: check pattern similar to → gingham but with larger checks (illustration 46).

Viennese seam: seam running from one armhole across the bust and to either the waist seam or hem, thus obviating the need for darts; introduced by Viennese dressmakers.

Viscose: synthetic fiber made of cellulose.

Voile: sheer, lightweight fabric.

Waspie: short corset.

Wasp waist: extremely narrow, corseted waistline.

Westover: sleeveless knitted waistcoat worn with suits in the 1920s and now over blouses and shirts.

Wet look: appearance of materials with a very high shine, giving the illusion that they are wet.

Wing collar: collar with upper corners that turn down.

Witzschoura: fur-lined ladies' coat with fur trimmings on hems; originates from Russian influence on western European coat styles in the early 19th century.

Wraparound dress: wrap-over dress introduced by Diane von Fürstenberg in the 1970s.

Wraparounds: close-fitting eyewear curving around the sides of the head, e.g. as made by Chanel; very popular form of sunglasses in the late 1990s.

Wraparound top: small jersey or knitwear top adapted from the practice clothing of ballet dancers (illustration 12.)

Wrapover skirt: skirt made of rectangular piece of fabric and fastened at the waist.

Y-line: garment line created by Christian Dior in 1955/56, with narrow skirts or dresses and wide lapels or other V-shaped neckline, thus forming the letter Y.

Zhivago Look: → Lara look.

Zouave jacket: short, waist-length, collarless ladies' jacket, open at the front, with three-quarter-sleeves, modeled on the traditional dress of the Zouaves, an Algerian Berber tribe.

45 Flared pants

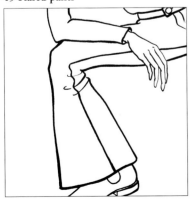

46 Vichy check

47 Floppy hat

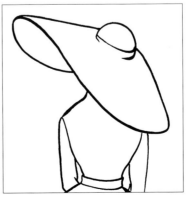

48 Cascade neckline

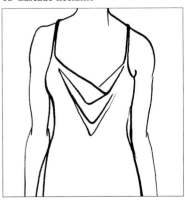

Index of names

Index of subjects

Headscarf 286
Helmet 227 (illus)
Henna 46
Hermès scarf135 (illus)
High heels 399
High-tech materials 569
Hip belt 239 (illus), 269
Hippies 409, 419, 436, 446 (illus), 523 (illus)
Hobble skirt 27, 28 (illus)
Hollywood 521
    Hollywood look 456
Home collection 32
Hot pants 393
Hourglass 192, 236, 261, 263 (illus), 291
Housedress 580

I

Inspiration 301
International Wool Secretariat 355, 382, 382 (illus)
Internet 613
Italy 493, 518, 555

J

Jabot blouse 134 (illus)
Japan, the Japanese 420, 436, 437, 438, 495, 508, 511
Jazz-Babe (the Hottest Baby) 96, 125
Jeans 200, 413 (illus), 590
Jersey 457, 60, 96, 99, 103 (illus), 390, 504 (illus)
Jet 59
Jodhpurs 100
Joy 170 (illus)
Jumpsuit 34 (illus), 53 (illus), 202 (illus), 368
Jungle red 186

K

Kelly bag 286, 286 (illus), 291
Kohl 79, 123, 125
Kimono 28, 44, 80, 240 (illus), 420, 436
Knitwear 528 (illus)
Knickerbockers 65 (illus)
Knossos scarf 36

L

La Vague 24, 54
Label 512, 555, 578
Lace 191
Lamé 163
Lampshade tunic 31 (illus)
Lastex 135
Leather 429, 458, 530
Leather blouson 413

Leggings 493
Leg-of-mutton sleeve see Gigot sleeve
Leotard 368
License 568
Ligne Corolle 212 (+ illus), 253
Ligne serpentine 44
Lingerie 526
Little black dress 75 (illus), 99, 116–121 (+ illus), 174, 400 (illus)
London 555
Luxury 487, 550, 555
    Luxury label 578
LVMH (Louis Vuitton Moët Hennessy) 565, 609
Lycra 130, 301, 493, 497
    Lycra stretch 504

M

Made-to-measure workshop 565
Mainstream 569 (illus)
Maison Rouff 44
Maison Walteau 61
Makeup 79
Mannequin 308, 556
Man's jacket 467
Man's suit 526 (illus)
Material 302, 567
Micro fiber 559
Minimalist, minimalism 549 (illus), 550 (illus), 552 (illus), 555, 569
Miniskirt 348, 350, 352, 368, 372 (illus), 395 (illus), 396, 399, 399 (illus), 403
Model 330 (illus), 541, 562
Musée des Arts Décoratifs 210

N

Natural fibers 550
New Look 110, 164, 164 (illus), 192, 212 (illus), 214, 235, 245, 246 (illus), 249 (illus), 253, 261 (illus), 272, 291, 355, 372, 562 (illus)
No-bra-bra 580
Nylons 138, 229

O

Op Art 528
Opulence 614
Organdy 162, 169
    Organdy dress 192
Ostrich feathers 18, (illus), 19, 45 (illus), 57, 93, 131, 376, 379 (illus)
Overall 62, 200

P

Pageboy 79, 85, 86 (illus), 86, 123, 123 (illus), 227

Pagoda umbrella 88 (illus)
Pancake 170, 227
Pants 62, 446, 615
Pantsuit 163, 523, 590
Pantyhose 399
Patron 305
Paris 519, 552, 555, 562
Passementerie 309, 316 (illus), 308, 359 (illus)
    Passementerie fastenings 140
Paste 138, 249, 286
Patches 197
Pattern mix 436 (illus), 503 (illus), 556 (illus)
Pearls
    Cascade of 99
    String of 238 (illus), 285, 286, 291, 402 (illus), 403
Pelerine coat 100
Permanent wave 446 (illus)
Petticoat 246, 247, 254 (illus), 269
Piercing 46
Pinups 46 (illus), 231 (illus)
Piping 103 (illus), 368
Plastic 419
Platform shoes 197, 140, 207 (illus), 209 (illus), 409 (illus), 415
Platinum blond 170, 173
Pleating 36
Plus fours 28, 54
Polka dots 381
Poof 500 (illus)
Power suit 182
PPR (Pinault-Printemps-Redoute) 565
Première 320 (illus)
Première d'Atelier 305
Première Vision 302
Preppy look 416
Prêt-à-Porter 144, 353, 372, 382, 420, 565, 607
Princess dress 131
Proportions 420, 479, 508 (illus), 569
Protection 559
Prototype 305, 309
Puff sleeve 162, 489
Punks 419, 420, 429, 458, 487, 500
Puzzle look 598 (illus)
PVC 393

R

Rayon 91, 192
Ready-to-wear 452
Retail network 578
Retro look 569
Rhodium-iodine platelets 376 (illus)
Rhodophane 154
Robe d'Ambassade 206
Robe de Style 40 (illus), 96, 452
Rococo 458
Role image 458

Romantic 487, 507
Rosalba crepe 75
Rosettes 269
Rue Cambon 60 (illus), 61, 101, 109 (illus), 110, 382
Rue de la Paix 38
Ruffles 214, 269, 272, 381

S

Sabrina heel 286
Sack dress 214, 245
Sari 512 (illus)
Sarong 512 (illus)
Saucer Eyes 285
Sautoir 19
Scarves 249
Seam 512, 568
Season 309
Secondary collection 526
Serge 168 (illus)
Sequins 191, 192
    Sequined sheath dress 173
Sexy 504
Shawl collar 59, 68 (illus), 93
Sheath dress 403
Shift dress 103, 186, 206, 269 (illus)
Shocking 152 (illus), 153 (illus), 154
Shopping 552, 557
Shorts 64 (illus)
Shoulders 429, 489, 512
    Padded shoulders 191
Silhouette 508 (illus), 511 (illus)
Silk 307 (illus)
Silk duchesse 16 (illus)
Silk, printed 306 (illus)
Silk printing 307 (illus)
Silk scarf 135
Sketch 302 (illus)
Skirt 493, 503 (illus)
Slacks 138, 157
Slingbacks 99, 110
Snakeskin 415
Society 615
Space-age look 352
Spats 23 (illus)
Special collection 452
Sportswear 68, 139, 144, 428, 578, 589, 590
S-shape 27 (illus)
Stiletto heels 395, 286, 289 (illus), 348
Stockman 305
Strap shoe 86 (illus), 90 (illus)
Street fashion 271, 399, 495, 552, 607
Stretch 559
Studio 54, 416–417
Style russe 103
Sultry chic 537
Sunglasses 138, 416 (illus)
Supermodels 530 (illus), 541, 569

Sources of illustrations

The publishers have made every effort to trace the copyright-holders of the illustrations used in this book. Any persons or institutions who have not been contacted are invited to notify the publishers.

Cover: Nick Knight, New York/Art Direction: Marc Ascoli/Catalog for Yohji Yamamoto Advertising Campaign 1987/88
P.4: UP/Edimedia/Georges Lepape/VG Bild-Kunst, Bonn 1999
P.8: Nick Knight, New York/Art Direction: Marc Ascoli/Catlog for Yohji Yamamoto 1986
PP.10–11: D. Simon/Gamma/Studio X

1900–1909:

P.13: Horst P. Horst/Hamiltons Photographers Ltd, The Mainbocher Corset, Paris 1939
P.14: Hulton Getty/Tony Stone
P.15: Portrait: Hulton Getty/Tony Stone; Label: Emmanuel de Lepervanche
P.16: Musée de la Mode et du Textile, collection UFAC
P.17: Roger-Viollet
P.18: Fächer: Plaisir de France, 12/38, P.49; A.L., A.R. and B.L.: Hulton Getty/Tony Stone; B.R.: Patrice Stable/Lesage Archive
P.19: Roger-Viollet
P.20: Roger-Viollet
P.21: Edward Steichen/Museum Ludwig Cologne/ Rheinisches Bildarchiv/Courtesy Carusel Research
P.22: Lipnitzki-Viollet
P.23: A.R.: Roger-Viollet; U.: Lipnitzki-Viollet; Label: Musée de la Mode et du Textile, collection UFAC
P.24: Lipnitzki-Viollet
P.25: L.: Roger-Viollet; R.: Lipnitzki-Viollet
P.26: Drawing: Raoul Dufy for Bianchini-Férier, (Drawing Nr. 51170 from 1913) 1999 Ill.: Paul Iribe/Gerstenberg Archive
P.27: A.: Roger-Viollet; B.: Mary Evans Picture Library
P.28: Ill.: Musée de la Mode et du Textile, collection UFAC; Harlingue-Viollet
P.29: Drawing: Bracken Books, London; Télimage/ Man Ray Trust, Paris/VG Bild-Kunst, Bonn 1999
P.30: Drawing: Karin Heßmann/Könemann Verlagsgesellschaft mbH, Cologne; A.L.: Kövesdi Presse Agentur (KPA); A.R.: Roger-Viollet; B.L.: Angeli/Pandis/Telepress; B.R.: Studio Holle-Suppa, Frankfurt.
P.31: Archiv for Kunst und Geschichte (AKG)/ Georges Lepape/VG Bild-Kunst, Bonn 1999
P.32: Lipnitzki-Viollet
P.33: Lipnitzki-Viollet
P.34: Ill.: Benito/Musée de la Mode et du Textile, colection UFAC; Roger-Viollet

P.35: L.: Lipnitzki-Viollet; R.: Marcio Madeira, Paris
P.36: Portrait: Countess Elsie Lee Gozzi, Venice; Label: Musée de la Mode et du Textile, collection UFAC; Ill.: Musée de la Mode et du Textile, collection UFAC/Courtesy Museum Fortuny
P.37: Drawing: Countess Elsie Lee Gozzi, Venice; Nell Dorr
P.38: Portrait and Label: Musée de la Mode et du Textile, collection UFAC; Keystone-Sygma
P.39: Mary Evans Picture Library
P.40: Portrait: Roger-Viollet; Ill.: Patrimoine Lanvin
P.41: Ill.: Patrimoine Lanvin; Studio Holle-Suppa, Frankfurt
PP.42–43: Patrimoine Lanvin
P.44: Portrait: Roger-Viollet; Label: Emmanuel de Lepervanche; Georges Barbier/Bridgeman-Giraudon
P.45: Hulton Getty/Tony Stone; Ill.: Paul Iribe/ Roger-Viollet
P.46: A.L., B.L. and F.R.: Hulton Getty/Tony Stone; R.: Charles Dana Gibson/Archive Photos/KPA
P.47: Boyer-Viollet; L: Helena Rubinstein Archive
P.48: A.L.: AKG; A.C.: Hulton Getty/Tony Stone; A.R. and B.L.: Interfoto; B.C.: Ullstein Bilderdienst; B.R.: George Hoyningen-Huené/Vogue, Condé-Nast Publications, Inc.
P.49: Corbis/Picture Press

1910–1919:

PP.51–54: Hulton Getty/Tony Stone
P.55: L. and A.R.: Tajan/Edimedia/Erté/VG Bild-Kunst, Bonn 1999; B.R.: Leon Bakst/AKG
S: 56: A.L. and B.L.: Hulton Getty/Tony Stone; Roger-Viollet
PP.57–58: Hulton Getty/Tony Stone
P.59: A.R.: Museum für Glas und Bijouterie, Gablonz/ Neiße; AKG
P.60: A.L. and B.: Roger-Viollet; R.: Hulton Getty/Tony Stone
P.61: Courtesy Klüver/Martin, Montparnasse Archive
P.62: L. and C.: Hulton Getty/Tony Stone; R.: Roger-Viollet
P.63: Hulton Getty/Tony Stone
P.64: A.L.: Roger-Viollet; M.L.: Lipnitzki-Viollet; Hulton Getty/Tony Stone
P.65: Hulton Getty/Tony Stone
P.66: Portrait: Roger Schall, Paris; Label: Emmanuel de Lepervanche; Musée de la Mode et du Textile, collection UFAC
P.67: F. Kollar/Ministère de la Culture, France
P.68: Portrait and Ill.: Musée de la Mode et du Textile, collection UFAC; Label: Emmanuel de Lepervanche; L.: AKG; R.: Hulton Getty/Tony Stone
P.69: C. Demiston/Bridgeman-Giraudon
P.70: George Hoyningen-Huené/Vogue, Condé-Nast Publications, Inc.

P.71: Label: Musée de la Mode et du Textile, Collection UFAC; Interfoto
P.72: Musée de la Mode et du Textile, collection UCAD
P.73: Ill.: Musée de la Mode et du Textile, collection UFAC; Lipnitzki-Viollet
PP.74–75: Musée de la Mode et du Textile, collection UFAC
P.76: Musée de la Mode et du Textile, collection UCAD
P.77: Studio Holle-Suppa, Frankfurt
P.78: Hulton Getty/Tony Stone
P.79: A.: Victoria & Albert Museum, London/ Bridgeman-Giraudon/Georges Lepape/ VG Bild-Kunst, Bonn 1999; B.: Helena Rubinstein Archive
P.80: L.: Corbis/Picture Press; C. and R.: Hulton Getty/Tony Stone
P.81: Nelson Evans/Interfoto

1920–1929:

P.83: Edward Steichen/Interfoto
P.84: Hulton Getty/Tony Stone
P.85: Corbis/Picture Press
P.86: L.: Harlingue-Viollet; R.: Hulton Getty/Tony Stone
P.87: Hulton Getty/Tony Stone
P.88–89: Bridgeman-Giraudon
P.90: A.L. and R.: Hulton Getty/Tony Stone; B.L.: Roger-Viollet; C.: Hulton Getty/Tony Stone
P.91: Hulton Getty/Tony Stone
P.92: Lipnitzki-Viollet
PP.93–94: Hulton Getty/Tony Stone
P.95: Ill.: Tejan/Edimedia/Georges Lepape/ VG Bild-Kunst, Bonn 1999; Workman Publishing/ Photograph: Andreas Bleckmann
P.96: Musée de la Mode et du Textile, collection UFAC
P.97: L.: Hulton Getty/Tony Stone; A.R. and B.R.: Lipnitzki-Viollet
P.98: Roger Schall, Paris
P.99: Hulton Getty/Tony Stone; Label: Emmanuel de Lepervanche
P.100: L.: Musée de la mode et du Textile, collection UFAC; R.: Hulton Getty/ Tony Stone
P.101: Collection Bernstein-Gruber
P.102: Ill.: Union Française des Arts du Costume et Centre de Documentation du Costume/ Roger-Viollet; A.: Hulton Getty/Tony Stone; B.: Lipnitzki-Viollet
P.103: L.: Frères Seeberger/Bibliothèque Nationale de France; C.: Privatbesitz; "D.R."; B.L.: Roger Schall, Paris
P.104: F. Kollar/Ministère de la Culture, France

P.105: Cecil Beaton/Interfoto
P.106: A.R.: Privatbesitz; B.L.: Roger Schall, Paris;
B.R.: Kirkland/Sygma/Pandis/Telepress
P.107: Roger Schall, Paris
P.108: F. Kollar/Ministère de la Culture, France
P.109: Cecil Beaton/Camera Press, London/
Marion Schweitzer
P.110: Lipnitzki-Viollet
P.111: Télimage/Man Ray Trust, Paris/VG Bild-Kunst,
Bonn 1999
P.112: Angeli/Pandis/Telepress
P.113: Chanel Archive
P.114: A.L.: Tom Roch, Munich;
B.L., C. and A.R.: Musée de la Mode et du Textile,
collection UFAC; C.L.: Eduard Noack, Cologne;
C.R.: Jo Magrean, Paris;
B.R.: O. Mauffrey/Boutique Chanel, Frühjahr/
Sommer 1999
P.115: Drawing: Musée de la Mode et du Textile,
collection UFAC; A.L. and A.F.R.: Angeli/Pandis/
Telepress; Studio Holle-Suppa, Frankfurt
P.116: Lipnitzki-Viollet
P.117: Vogue, Condé Nast Publications, Inc.
P.118: A.F.L.: Studio Holle-Suppa, Frankfurt;
C.F.L.: Interfoto; C.L.: P/Interfoto;
B.L.: Lipnitzki-Viollet; C.R.: Pandis/ Telepress;
B.R. and B.R.: Corbis/Picture Press;
Hulton Getty/Tony Stone
P.119: Interfoto
P.122: Hulton Getty/Tony Stone
P.123: Hulton Getty/Tony Stone; Bourjois Archive,
Paris
P.124: A.L. and A.C.: Eugene Robert Richee/Interfoto;
A.R.: Télimage/Man Ray Trust, Paris/VG Bild-Kunst,
Bonn 1999;
B.L.: Edward Steichen/ Vogue, Condé-Nast
Publications, Inc.;
B.C.: Roger-Viollet; B.R.: Corbis/Picture Press
P.125: Hulton Getty/Tony Stone

1930–1939:

P.127: Hulton Getty/Tony Stone
P.128: F. Kollar/Ministère de la Culture, France
P.129: Lipnitzki-Viollet
P.130: F. Kollar/Ministère de la Culture, France
P.131: L.: E. Hoinkis/Interfoto;
R.: Hulton Getty/Tony Stone
P.132: L. main picture: F. Kollar/Ministère de la
Culture, France;
L. inset: Studio Holle-Suppa, Frankfurt;
R.: Hulton Getty/Tony Stone
P.133: Plaisir de France, 12/38, P.74
P.134: L.: Hulton Getty/Tony Stone;
R.: Martin Munkacsi/Interfoto
P.135: A.: Lipnitzki-Viollet; B.: Roger-Viollet
P.136: Lipnitzki-Viollet

P.137: Hulton Getty/Tony Stone
P.138: Lipnitzki-Viollet
P.139: L.: Hulton Getty/Tony Stone;
C. and R.: Lipnitzki-Viollet
P.140: Lipnitzki-Viollet
P.141: Schönecher/Interfoto
P.142: F: Kollar/Ministère de la Culture, France
P.143: Label: Musée de la Mode et du Textile,
collection UFAC; Ill.: Vertès/Schiaparelli Archive;
Roger-Viollet
P.144: Schiaparelli Archive
P.145: Télimage/Man Ray Trust, Paris/VG Bild-Kunst,
Bonn 1999; R.: Schiaparelli Archive
PP.146–147: F. Kollar/Ministère de la Culture, France
P.148: Musée de la Mode et du Textile,
collection UFAC
P.149: L.: UP/Edimedia; R.: Lipnitzki-Viollet;
Schmetterling: Musée de la Mode et du Textile,
collection UFAC
P.150: Musée de la Mode et du Textile,
collection UFAC
P.151: Drawing: Lesage Archive;
Ill.: Musée de la Mode et du Textile, collection UFAC
P.152: Horst P. Horst/Hamiltons Photographers Ltd;
A.R.: Musée de la Mode et du Textile,
collection UFAC; B.R.: Tom Roch, Munich
P.153: Ill.: Vertès/Schiaparelli Archive; Interfoto
P.154: Hulton Getty/Tony Stone
P.155: Brooklyn Museum of Art, New York
P.156: A.L. and A.R., and C.L., and C.C. and U.M.O.:
Hulton Getty/Tony Stone;
A.C.: AKG/ VG Bild-Kunst, Bonn 1999;
C.R., B.L. and B.R.: Roger Schall, Paris;
Snark/UP/ Edimedia
P.158: Portrait: F. Kollar/Ministère de la Culture,
France; Label: Emmanuel de Lepervanche;
L.: Musée de la Mode et du Textile,
collection UFAC;
R.: Cireuse/Nina Ricci Archive
P.159: Keystone-Sygma
P.160: Lipnitzki-Viollet
P.161: Label: Emmanuel de Lepervanche;
Lipnitzki-Viollet
P.162: Label: Emmanuel de Lepervanche;
Lipnitzki-Viollet
P.163: Portrait and L.: Lipnitzki-Viollet;
Label: Emmanuel de Lepervanche;
R.: Angeli/Pandis/Telepress
P.164: Portrait and Label: Musée de la Mode et
du Textile, collection UFAC;
B.L.: Hulton Getty/Tony Stone;
B.C. and B.R.: Lipnitzki-Viollet
P.165: Corbis/Picture Press
P.166: Hulton Getty/Tony Stone
P.167: Musée de la Mode et du Textile,
collection UFAC
P.168: Label: Musée de la Mode et du Textile,
collection UFAC;

L.: Austrian Archives/Christian Brandstätter, Vienna;
R.: Lipnitzki-Viollet
P.169: Portrait and R.: Austrian Archives/
Christian Brandstätter, Vienna; Label: Emmanuel de
Lepervanche;
L.: Télimage/Man Ray Trust, Paris/VG Bild-Kunst,
Bonn 1999
P.170: A.: Monteil Archive; B.: The Advertising
Archives
P.171: Roger-Viollet
P.172: C.: Télimage/Man Ray Trust, Paris/VG
Bild-Kunst, Bonn 1999;
A.R.: Hulton Getty/Tony Stone;
B.C.: Roger-Viollet; Interfoto
P.174: Everett Collection/KPA
P.175: Interfoto; R.: Angeli/Pandis/Telepress
P.176: L.: Studio Holle-Suppa, Frankfurt;
R.: Roger-Viollet
P.177: Hulton Getty/Tony Stone
P.178: Drawing: Tony Stone;
L. and R.: Lipnitzki-Viollet;
C.: Roger-Viollet
P.179: L. and C.: Angeli/Pandis/Telepress;
R.: Marcio Madeira, Paris
P.180–181: Edward Steichen/Vogue, Condé-Nast
Publications, Inc.
P.182: Interfoto
P.183: Everett Collection/KPA
P.184: Hulton Getty/Tony Stone
P.185: Archive Photos/KPA
P.186: L.: Paramount/Kobal/KPA;
R.: Everett Collection/KPA
PP.187–189: Interfoto
P.190: A.L., B.C. and B.R.: Archive Photos/KPA;
A.C.: Paramount/Kobal/KPA;
C.L.: Everett Collectio/KPA;
A.L., C. and C.R.: Interfoto
P.192: L.: Archive Photos/KPA;
C.: Everett Collection/KPA; R.: Interfoto
P.193: Interfoto

1940–1949:

P.195: Cecil Beaton/Courtesy Sotheby's,
P.196: Musée de la Mode et du Textile, collection
UFAC
P.197: The Advertising Archives
P.198: 3 A.L., : Lapi-Viollet; 2 R.A. and
B.: Roger-Viollet
P.199: Lapi-Viollet
P.200: Interfoto
P.201: L.: Interfoto; C.: Lapi-Viollet;
R.: Roger-Viollet
P.202: L.: Roger-Viollet; R.: Musée de la Mode
et du Textile, collection UFAC
P.203: Hulton Getty/Tony Stone;
R.: The Advertising Archives

PP.204–205: Lapi-Viollet
P.206: Hulton Getty/Tony Stone
P.207: Roger-Viollet; Ill.: Jean Paul Gaultier Archive
P.208: Roger Schall, Paris
P.209: Studio Holle-Suppa, Frankfurt;
  Schuh: Lapi-Viollet
PP.210–211: L.: Hulton-Getty/Tony Stone;
  A. Benainous/Gamma/Studio X
P.212: Henri Cartier-Bresson/Magnum/Focus
P.213: Assoc. Willy Maywald/VG Bild-Kunst,
  Bonn 1999
P.214: Portrait: Lipnitzki-Viollet; Label: Emmanuel de
  Lepervanche; Balenciaga Archive
P.215: Bert Stern/Vogue, Condé-Nast Publications Inc.
P.216: L.: Interfoto; R.: F. Kollar/Ministère de la
  Culture, France
P.217: Kublin/Balenciaga Archive
P.218: Portrait: Roger-Viollet; Label: Musée de la Mode
  et du Textile, collection UFAC; Roger-Viollet
P.219: L.: Hulton Getty/Tony Stone;
  R.: Interfoto
P.220: Horst P. Horst/Hamiltons Photographers Ltd.
  Gertrude Stein at a Balmain fashion show, in the
  background: Rosamond Bernier and Carl Erickson,
  Paris 1949
P.222: Portrait: Roger-Viollet;
  Label: Emmanuel de Laervanche;
  Roger Schall, Paris
P.223: Assoc. Willy Maywald/VG Bild-Kunst,
  Bonn 1999
P.224: Gerstenberg Archive
PP.225–227: Hulton Getty/Tony Stone
P.228: L.: The Advertising Archives;
  R.: Advertisement from *Harper's Bazaar* (NY),
  April 1939/AKG
P.229: A.: Hulton Getty/Tony Stone; B.: Interfoto
P.230: A.R.: Roger-Viollet; Interfoto
P.231: Interfoto

1950–1959:

P.233: Erwin Blumenfeld/VG Bild-Kunst, Bonn
  1999/Vogue, Condé-Nast Publications Inc.
P.234: Interfoto
P.235: Keystone-Sygma
P.236: The Advertising Archives
P.237: Interfoto
P.238: A.L., A.C., C.L. and C.R.: Hulton Getty/Tony
  Stone; C.C.: Interfoto;
  A.R. and B.L.: Gerstenberg Archive
P.239: Archive Photos/KPA
P.241: Interfoto
P.242-243: Hulton Getty/Tony Stone
P.244: Interfoto
P.246: L.: Sygma/Pandis/Telepress;
  R.: Hulton Getty/Tony Stone

P.247: A.: Interfoto; B.: Hulton Getty/Tony Stone
P.248: Interfoto
P.249: Archive Photos/KPA
P.250: Hulton Getty/Tony Stone
P.251: Interfoto
P.252: Roger-Viollet
P.253: Label: Emmanuel de Lepervanche
P.254: Dior Archive
P.255: L.: Interfoto; R.: Angeli/Pandis/Telepress
P.256: René Gruau/Dior Archive
P.257: Hulton Getty/Tony Stone
P.258: B.L.: Assoc. Willy Maywald/VG Bild-Kunst,
  Bonn 1999; Hulton Getty/Tony Stone
PP.259–260: Assoc. Willy Maywald/
  VG Bild-Kunst, Bonn 1999
P.261: Dior Dior
PP.262–263: Assoc. Willy Maywald/
  VG Bild-Kunst, Bonn 1999
P.264: Hulton Getty/Tony Stone
P.265: Photography by Richard Avedon *Dovima with
  Elephants*. Evening dress by Dior. Cirque d'hiver,
  Paris August 1955
P.266: René Gruau/Dior Archive
P.267: Drawing: Tim Davis/Tony Stone;
  A.L. and A.C.: Marcio Madeira, Paris;
  A.R.: Angeli/Pandis/Telepress;
  B.: Norbert Schmitt/Interfoto
P.268: Christoph Kicherer, Paris
P.269: L.: Interfoto; Hulton Getty/Tony Stone
PP.270–271: Robert Doisneau/Rapho/Focus
P.272: Portrait: Givenchy Archive;
  Label: Emmanuel de Lepervanche;
  C.L. and B.L.: Angeli/Pandis/Telepress;
  B.R.: Gerstenberg Archive
P.273: Givenchy Archive
P.274: Portrait: Louis Féraud Archive;
  Label: Emmanuel de Lepervanche;
  L.: Louis Féraud Archive; R.: Roger-Viollet
P.275: Roger-Viollet
P.276: Portrait: Angeli/Pandis/Telepress; Label:
  Emmanuel de Lepervanche; L. and R.: Valentino
  Archive; C.: Barry Lategan/Courtesy Vogue 1970
  Edizioni Condé-Nast P.p.A.
PP.277–279: Valentino Archive
P.280–281: Hulton Getty/Tony Stone
P.282: L.: Angeli/Pandis/Telepress;
  R.: Hulton Getty/Tony Stone
P.283: Hulton Getty/Tony Stone
P.284: Walter Lautenbacher/Interfoto
P.285: A.: The Advertising Archives;
  B.: Hulton Getty/Tony Stone
P.286: A.: Hulton Getty/Tony Stone; B.: Interfoto
P.287: Foodfoto, Cologne
P.288: Hulton Getty/Tony Stone
P.289: C. and B.: Ferragamo Archive;
  L.: Workman Publishing
P.290: A.R.: Everett Collection/KPA,

A.F.R.: AKG; Interfoto
PP.291–292: Interfoto
P.293: Hulton Getty/Tony Stone
P.294: Everett Collection/KPA
P.295: Hulton Getty/Tony Stone
PP.296–297: Eric Robert/Sygma
P.298: A.L.: Lipnitzki-Viollet;
  A.M., B.F.L. and B.F.L.: Pat-Arnal/Stills/Studio X;
  A.R.: Angeli/Pandis/Telepress;
  C.: Pandis/Telepress;
  B.L.: Enzo Signorelli/Gamma/Studio X;
  B.R.: Sygma/Pandis/Telepress
P.299: A.F.L., A.F.R. and
  B.R.: Pat-Arnal/Stills/Studio X;
  A.L.: Sygma/Pandis/Telepress;
  A.R., B.L. and C.R.: Angeli/Pandis/Telepress;
  C.L.: Studio Holle-Suppa, Frankfurt

From design to finished garment

P.300: Jacques Torregano, Paris
P.302: L&M Services B.V. Amsterdam 991116
P.303: Jacques Torregano, Paris
P.304: A.: Harlingue-Viollet; B.: Jo Magrean, Paris
P.305: Jacques Torregano, Paris
PP.306–307: Fabric Frontline Archive
P.308: Jacques Torregano, Paris
P.309: L.: Sygma; R.: Palisse/Lesage Archive
PP.310–311: Erik Sampers/Lesage Archive;
  R: Palisse/Lesage Archive
P.312: B.R.: Sygma; Lesage Archive
P.313: Sygma
PP.314–316: Jacques Torregano, Paris
P.317: Sygma/Pandis/Telepress
PP.318–333: Jacques Torregano, Paris

1960–1969:

P.335: Roger-Viollet
P.336: Studio Bokelberg
P.337: AKG
P.338: Interfoto
P.339: Yurek/Marie-Claire/Studio X
PP.340–344: Hulton Getty/Tony Stone
PP.345–346: Yurek/Marie-Claire/Studio X
P.347: Josh Westrich, Essen
P.348: L.: Hulton Getty/Tony Stone;
  R.: The Everett Collection/KPA
P.349: Archive Photos/KPA
P.350: Edinger/Gamma/Studio X
P.351: Corbis/Picture Press/UPI
P.352: Peter Knapp, Paris
P.353: Hulton Getty/Tony Stone
P.354: Jeanloup Sieff/Maconochie Photography,
  London

P.355: Label: Emmanuel de Lepervanche; Paul Popper Photo/Interfoto
P.356: Yves Saint Laurent Archive
P.357: Helmut Newton/Maconochie Photography, London
PP.358–362: Yves Saint Laurent Archive
P.363: A.L. and B.L: Angeli/Pandis/Telepress; A.R. and B.R.: Yves Saint Laurent Archive
P.364: Jeanloup Sieff/Maconochie Photography, London
P.365: A.L. and A.R.: Jo Magrean, Paris; A.C.: Hulton Getty/Tony Stone; B.: Sygma/Pandis/Telepress
PP.366–367: Yves Saint Laurent Archive
P.368: Portrait: Hulton Getty/Tony Stone; Logo: Courrèges; Peter Knapp, Paris
PP.369–371: Peter Knapp, Paris
P.372: Portrait: Ciro Cappellari/Interfoto; Label: R. Stempell Photographie, B. Holefleisch, Cologne; L.: Y. Takata/Cardin Archive; C.: Dalmas/Sipa Press/Pandis/Telepress; R.: Angeli/Pandis/Telepress
P.373: L.: Lipnitzki-Viollet; R.: Studio Holle-Suppa, Frankfurt
PP.374–375: Cardin Archive
P.376: Portrait: Roger-Viollet; Label: R. Stempell Photographie, B. Holefleisch, Cologne; L.: UP/Edimedia; R.: Interfoto
P.377: UP/Edimedia
P.378: Angeli/Pandis/Telepress
P.379: Interfoto
P.380: Bert Stern/Vogue 1969/Ungaro Archive
P.381: Portrait: Ungaro Archive; Label: Emmanuel de Lepervanche; L.: Peter Knapp, Paris/Ungaro Archive; R.: D. Simon/Gamma/Studio X
P.382: Portrait: Angeli/Pandis/Telepress; Label: R. Stempell Photographie, B. Holefleisch, Cologne; L. and C.: Angeli/Pandis/Telepress; R.: D. Simon/Gamma/Studio X
P.383: Keystone-Sygma
P.384: Hulton Getty/Tony Stone
P.385: Portrait: Roger-Viollet; Corbis/Picture Press
P.386: F. C. Gundlach, Hamburg
P.387: Portrait: Guy Laroche Archive; Label: Emmanuel de Lepervanche; Corbis/Picture Press
PP.388–389: Guy Laroche Archive
P.390: Portrait: Angeli/Pandis/Telepress; Label: R. Stempell Photographie, B. Holefleisch, Cologne; L.: Angeli/Pandis/Telepress; R.: Sonia Rykiel Archive
P.391: Sonia Rykiel Archive
P.392: Hulton Getty/Tony Stone
P.393: Portrait: Interfoto; Logo: Mary Quant;

Hulton Getty/Tony Stone
P.394: Roger Viollet
P.395: R.: Hulton Getty/Tony Stone; B.C.: Roger-Viollet
P.396: L. and R.: Advertising Archives; C.: Bourjois Archive
P.397: Yurek/Marie-Claire/Studio X
P.398: Gamma/Studio X
P.399: Hulton Getty/Tony Stone
P.400: A.F.R.: Corbis/Picture Press; Hulton Getty/Tony Stone
P.401: Hulton Getty/Tony Stone
P.402: 1 and 3: Greek Photo Agency/Pandis/Telepress; 6: Pandis/Telepress; 2 and 5: Interfoto; 4: PPP/Interfoto; 7: Manfred Kreine/Interfoto
P.404: L.: F. C. Gundlach, Hamburg; R.: Interfoto
P.405: B.L.: Interfoto; Hulton Getty/Tony Stone

1970–1979:

P.407: AKG/Advertisement for Servas in *twen*, 12. Jg., Nr. 3, Munich, 3. March 1970
P.408: Corbis/Picture Press
P.409: Ullstein Bilderdienst
P.410: P. Vigeveno/Gamma/Studio X
P.411: Willy Rizzo/Marie-Claire/Studio X
P.412: N. Quidu/Gamma/Studio X; A.C., A.R. and B.R.: Corbis/Picture Press; B.L.: B. Lacombe/Gamma/Studio X
P.414: F. C. Gundlach, Hamburg
P.415: L.: Sygma; R.: Rodgers/Gamma/Studio X
P.416: L.: Interfoto; C. and R.: Corbis/Picture Press
P.417: L.: Hulton Getty/Tony Stone; C.: Pandis/Telepress; R.: F. Quinto/Olympia/Pandis/Telepress
P.418: Rex Features
P.419: L. and C.: Sipa Press; R.: Bennett/Gamma/Studio X
P.421: D. Simon/Gamma/Studio X
PP.422–423: Sarah Moon/Marie-Claire/Studio X
P.424: Portrait: Sygma; Label: R. Stempell Photographie, B. Holefleisch, Cologne; B.L.: Studio Holle-Suppa, Frankfurt; B.M. and B.R.: D. Simon/Gamma/Studio X
PP.425–427: A. Duclos-Stevens/Gamma/Studio X
P.428: Portrait: Sygma/Pandis/Telepress; B.L.: D. Simon/Gamma/Studio X; B.R.: Studio Holle-Suppa, Frankfurt
P.429: Portrait: Angeli/Pandis/Telepress; Label: R. Stempell Photographie, B. Holefleisch, Cologne; B.L.: Gamma/Studio X; B.R.: D. Simon/Gamma/Studio X
P.430: Portrait: Angeli/Pandis/Telepress; Label:

R. Stempell Photographie, B. Holefleisch, Cologne; B.L. and B.C.: Jean Paul Gaultier Archive; B.R.: Mail Newspapers p.l.c./Pandis/Telepress
P.431: J. Andanson/Sygma/Pandis/Telepress
P.432: Jean Paul Gaultier Archive
P.433: A.L.: Jean Paul Gaultier Archive; A.C. and B.R.: Sygma/Pandis/Telepress; A.R.: D. Simon/Gamma/Studio X; B.L. and B.M.: Angeli/Pandis/Telepress
P.434: Studio Holle-Suppa, Frankfurt
P.435: L.: Interfoto; R.: Studio Holle-Suppa, Frankfurt
P.436: Portrait: A. Benainous/Gamma/Studio X; Label: R. Stempell Photographie, B. Holefleisch, Cologne; B.L.: D. Simon/Gamma/ Studio X; B.R.: D. Simon – W. Stevens/Gamma/Studio X
P.437: Portrait and R.: A. Benainous/Gamma/Studio X; L.: D. Simon/Gamma/Studio X
P.438: Portrait: Sygma/Pandis/Telepress; Label: R. Stempell Photographie, B. Holefleisch, Cologne; L.: Holle-Suppa, Frankfurt; R.: D. Simon – W. Stevens/Gamma/Studio X
P.439: Studio Holle-Suppa, Frankfurt
P.440: D. Simon/Gamma/Studio X
P.441: L.: Angeli/Pandis/Telepress; A. and C.R.: D. Simon – W. Stevens/Gamma/Studio X; B.C. and B.R. Sygma/Pandis/Telepress
PP.442–443: Yasuaki Yoshinaga/Issey Miyake Inc./Fondation Cartier pour l'Art contemporain/Exposition Issey Miyake Making Things/13.10.1998 – 28.02.1999
P.444: Loewenstein/Marie-Claire/Studio X
P.445: A.: Horth/Marie-Claire/Studio X; B.: Interfoto
P.446: A.L., A.R. and C.L.: The Advertising Archives; R.: Hulton Getty/Tony Stone
P.447: Novick/Marie-Claire/Studio X
P.448: A.L.: Thuan/Sipa Press; A.C. and A.R.: Interfoto; C.F.L.: Forum Press/Pandis/Telepress; C.L. and B.C.: Corbis/Picture Press; C.R.: Sygma; C.F.R.: Nova Press/Pandis/Telepress; B.L.: Hulton Getty/Tony Stone; B.R.: Sygma/Pandis/Telepress
P.450: Corbis/Picture Press
PP.451–457: Hulton Getty/Tony Stone
P.458: Portrait: D. Simon – W. Stevens/Gamma/Studio X; Label: R. Stempell Photographie, B. Holefleisch, Cologne; L.: Big Pictures/Pandis/Telepress; R.: Angeli/Pandis/Telepress
P.459: P. Massey/Gamma/Studio X
PP.460–461: Studio Holle-Suppa, Frankfurt
P.462: Olivier Claisse, Paris
S.463: A.L., B.C. and B.R.: Angeli/Pandis/Telepress; A.C. and B.L.: Marcio Madeira, Paris; A.R.: Mail Newspapers p.l.c./Pandis/Telepress
P.464: L.: Interfoto; R.: Marcio Madeira, Paris
P.465: Angeli/Pandis/Telepress
P.466: Portrait: Hulton Getty/Tony Stone; Sygma

P.467: Portrait: Sipa Press;
  L. and C.: Marineau/Stills/Studio X;
  R.: Gamma/Studio X
P.468: Rex Features
P.469: dpa
P.470: Marineau/Stills/Studio X
P.471: Portrait: Sygma;
  L.: E. Signorelli/Gamma/Studio X;
  R.: Sygma/Pandis/Telepress
P.472: Portrait and R.: Angeli/Pandis/Telepress;
  C.: P. Massey/Gamma/Studio X;
  L.: Studio Holle-Suppa, Frankfurt
P.473: Sygma/Pandis/Telepress
474: P. Massey/Gamma/Studio X
P.475: L.: P. Massey/Gamma/Studio X;
  R.: Angeli/Pandis/Telepress
P.476: Studio Holle-Suppa, Frankfurt
P.477: Sygma/Pandis/Telepress
P.478: Angeli/Pandis/Telepress
P.479: Portrait, L. and C.: Angeli/Pandis/Telepress,
  R.: Sygma/Pandis/Telepress
P.480: A.L.: Angeli/Pandis/Telepress;
  A.R.: Marcio Madeira, Paris;
  B.L.: Studio Holle-Suppa, Frankfurt;
  B.R.: A. Duclos/Gamma/Studio X
P.481: A.L. and B.R: Angeli/Pandis/Telepress;
  A.R.: Studio Holle-Suppa, Frankfurt;
  B.L.: Bruno Pellerin/Givenchy Archive
P.482: Portrait: Pandis/Telepress,
  L. and R.: D. Simon/Gamma/Studio X;
  C.: Angeli/Pandis/Telepress
P.483: Portrait: K. Lathigra/Gamma/StudioX;
  L. and R.: G. Marineau/Stills/Studio X

1980–1989:

P.485: Roxanne Lowit, New York
P.486: Jean-Paul Goude, Paris
P.487: Corbis/Picture Press
P.488: L.: Interfoto; R.: B. Edelhajt/Gamma/Studio X
P.489: Sacha/Marie-Claire/Studio X
P.490: L. and R.: Gamma/Studio X;
  C.: D. Simon/Gamma/Studio X
P.491: Sygma/Pandis/Telepress
P.492: Pierre et GilleP. Courtesy
  Galerie Jérôme de Noirmont, PariP.
P.493: Sygma/Pandis/Telepress
P.494: Sichow/Sipa Press
P.495: Studio Holle-Suppa, Frankfurt
P.496: Platon/Fiore Crespi for Moschino –
  Werbekampagne Fall/Winter 1995/96
P.497: Michael Heeg, Munich
P.499: Angeli/Pandis/Telepress
P.500: Portrait: Jacques Torregano, Paris;
  Label: R. Stempell Photographie,
  B. Holefleisch, Cologne;

L.: Sygma/Pandis/Telepress;
  R.: D. Simon/Gamma/Studio X
P.501: D. Simon/Gamma/Studio X
P.502: Studio Holle-Suppa, Frankfurt
S.503: A.L.: Sygma/Pandis/Telepress;
  A.C., A.R., B.C. and B.R.: Studio Holle-Suppa,
  Frankfurt; B.L.: Guy Marineau/Lacroix Archive
P.504: Portrait: Sygma/Pandis/Telepress;
  Label: R. Stempell Photographie,
  B. Holefleisch, Cologne,
  L.: T. Ryan/Gamma/Studio X;
  R.: Sacha/Marie-Claire/Studio X
P.505: G. Gorman/Gamma/Studio X
P.506: L.: Arnal-Garcia/Stills/Studio X;
  R.: D. Simon/Gamma/Studio X
P.507: Portrait: Sygma/Pandis/Telepress;
  Label: R. Stempell Photographie, B. Holefleisch,
  Cologne; D. Simon/Gamma/Studio X
P.508: Portrait: C. Leroy/Gamma/Studio X;
  Label: R. Stempell Photographie, B. Holefleisch,
  Cologne; L.: J. Casano/Stills/Studio X;
  R.: D. Simon/Gamma/Studio X
P.509: Studio Holle-Suppa, Frankfurt
P.510: A. Duclos/Gamma/Studio X
P.511: Portrait: Agostini/Gamma/Studio X;
  Label: R. Stempell Photographie, B. Holefleisch,
  Cologne; L.: A. Duclos/Gamma/Studio X;
  R.: D. Simon/Gamma/Studio X
P.512: L.: W. Stevens/Gamma/Studio X;
  C.: D. Simons/Gamma/Studio X;
  R.: Gastaud/Sipa Press
P.513: Sygma/Pandis/Telepress
P.514: Sygma
P.515: A.: The Advertising Archives; B.: Sygma
P.516: C. Sherman: Abe Frajndlich/Focus;
  F. Griffith-Joyner: Sipa Press;
  I. Adjani: Niviere/Barthelemy/Villard/Sipa Press;
  G. v. Thurn und Taxis: Villard/Sipa Press;
  Cher: Weber/Sipa Press;
  I. and I. Trump: Angeli/Pandis/Telepress;
  C. Streep: P. Adenis/Sipa Press;
  Madonna: Sygma/Pandis/Telepress
P.518: L.: Hulton Getty/Tony Stone;
  C.: Yasuaki Yoshinaga/Issey Miyake Inc./Fondation
  Cartier pour l'Art contemporain/Exposition Issey
  Miyake Making Things/13.10.1998 – 28.02.1999;
  A.R.: Werbekampagne Benetton/Toscani/
  Gamma/Studio X; B.R.: Ullstein Bilderdienst
P.519: L.: Hulton Getty/Tony Stone;
  R.: Sygma/Pandis/Telepress
P.520: Portrait and R.: Interfoto;
  L.: Roger-Viollet
P.521: Interfoto
P.522: Marion Schweitzer Bildarchiv
P.523: Label: R. Stempell Photographie,
  B. Holefleisch, Cologne;
  Hulton Getty/Tony Stone

P.524: Portrait and R.: Gucci Archive; Label:
  R. Stempell Photographie, B. Holefleisch, Cologne;
  L.: Studio Holle-Suppa, Frankfurt
P.525: Studio Holle-Suppa, Frankfurt
P.526: Portrait: Sygma; Label: R. Stempell
  Photographie, B. Holefleisch, Cologne;
  L.: Studio Holle-Suppa, Frankfurt;
  R.: Sygma/Pandis/Telepress
P.527: G. Marineau/Stills/Studio X
P.528: Portrait: Thomas Marcel/Sipa Press;
  Label: R. Stempell Photographie, B. Holefleisch,
  Cologne; L.: Romaniello/Olympia/Gamma/Studio X;
  C.: E. Signorello/Gamma/Studio X;
  R.: Olympia/Gamma/Studio X
P.529: Portrait, L. and C.: Angeli/Pandis/ Telepress;
  R.: P. Guerrini/Gamma/Studio X
P.530: Label: R. Stempell Photographie,
  B. Holefleisch, Cologne; Pandis/Telepress
P.531: A.C.: Pandis/Telepress;
  A.R.: A. Duclos/Gamma/Studio X; Angeli/Pandis/
  Telepress
PP.532–533: D. Simon/Gamma/Studio X
P.534: Portrait: Don Iron/Sipa Press; Label:
  R. Stempell Photographie, B. Holefleisch, Cologne;
  L.: Romaniello/Olympia/Gamma/Studio X;
  C. and R.: E. Signorelli/Gamma/Studio X
P.535: E. Signorelli/Gamma/Studio X
P.536: Gamma/Studio X
P.537: Portrait: Mullan/Gamma/Studio X;
  Label: R. Stempell Photographie, B. Holefleisch,
  Cologne; L.: G. Marineau/Stills/Studio X;
  R.: Romaniello/Olympia/Gamma/Studio X
P.538: Portrait: Agostini/Gamma/Studio X;
  Label: R. Stempell Photographie, B. Holefleisch,
  Cologne; Tasche: Prada Catalog; L.: Angeli/Pandis/
  Telepress; R.: G. Marineau/Stills/Studio X
P.539: A. Carrara/Marie-Claire/Studio X
P.540: Sygma/Pandis/Telepress
P.542: L.: Lipnitzki-Viollet;
  C.: Roger Schall, Paris; R.: Roger-Viollet
P.543: L.: Lipnitzki-Viollet;
  C.: Studio Holle-Suppa, Frankfurt;
  R.: Jo Magrean, Paris
P.544: L.: P. Chevalier/Christian Dior Archive;
  C.: Cecil Beaton/Camera Press/Marion Schweitzer
  Bildarchiv; R.: Sygma
P.545: L.: Sygma; C.: Sheila Metzner, New York;
  R.: Jo Magrean, Paris

1990–1999:

P.547: Juergen Teller/Z Photographic, London
P.548: Kaj Blunck/Model: Fionda/Visagistin:
  Katrin Baier
P.549: G. de Keerle/Sygma/Pandis/Telepress
P.550: Interfoto

P.551: Ann Demeulemeester Archive
P.552: Paul Warchol/Jil Sander Archive
P.553: L: Studio Holle-Suppa, Frankfurt;
R: Tom Roch, Munich
P.554: G. Andrea/Marie-Claire/Studio X
P.555: G.L.: Tobey Corney/Tony Stone;
L.: Olivier Claisse, Paris; R.: I.P.A./Stills/Studio X;
G.R.: A. Duclos – W. Stevens/Gamma/Studio X
P.556: L.: A. Duclos/Gamma/Studio X;
R.: Studio Holle-Suppa, Frankfurt
P.557: L.: D. Simon – W. Stevens/Gamma/
Studio X; R.: Agostini/Gamma/Studio X
P.558: A. Duclos/Gamma/Studio X
PP.560–561: Peter Lindbergh
P.562: L.: and C.: Angeli/Pandis/Telepress;
R.: Jil Sander Archive
P.563: Jil Sander Archive
P.564: L.: Gucci Archive
R.: Ann Demeulemeester Archive
P.565: Ann Demeulemeester Archive
PP.566–567: D. Simon – W. Stevens/Gamma/
Studio X
P.568: L.: Studio Holle-Suppa, Frankfurt;
C.: Corbis/Picture Press;
R.: A. Duclos/Gamma/Studio X
P.569: L.: A. Duclos – W. Stevens/Gamma/Studio X;
C.: D. Simon/Gamma/Studio X;
R.: D. Lecca/Balenciaga Archive
P.570: Frank Peinemann, Cologne
P.571: T. LeClerc Archive
P.572: Corbis/Picture Press
P.573: Corbis/Picture Press
P.574: A.L.: Eidos Interactive;
A.R., C.L. and B.L.: Sygma;
C.R.: Scorcelletti/Gamma/Studio X;
B.R.: Sygma/Pandis/Telepress
P.577: A.L.: Mail Newspapers PLC/Pandis/Telepress;
A.C.: Einhorn/Gamma/Studio X; O.R.: Sipa Press;
C.: Sygma U.L.: Agostini/Gamma/Studio X;
B.C.: F. Apesteguy/Gamma/Studio X;
B.R.: Corbis/Picture Press
P.578: L. and A.R.: A. Duclos/Gamma/
Studio X; A.C.: Interfoto;
B.R.: Benali/Gamma/Studio X
P.579: Hulton Getty/Tony Stone
PP.580–581: Corbis/Picture Press
P.582: Cecil Beaton/Courtesy Sotheby's London
PP.583–587: Corbis/Picture Press
P.588: L.: Marineau/Stills/Studio X;
Corbis/Picture Press
P.589: Portrait: Hulton Getty/Tony Stone;
L.: Agostini/Gamma/Studio X;
R.: Corbis/Picture Press
P.590: Portrait: Angeli/Pandis/Telepress;
Label: R. Stempell Photographie, B. Holefleisch,
Cologne; L.: Calvin Klein Archive;
C.: Sygma/Pandis/Telepress;

R.: Angeli/Pandis/Telepress
P.591: Angeli/Pandis/Telepress
P.592: Bruce Weber/Ralph Lauren Archive
P.593: Portrait: Corbis/Picture Press;
Label: R. Stempell Photographie, B. Holefleisch,
Cologne; L.: Angeli/Pandis/Telepress;
C.: Ralph Lauren Archive;
R.: Angeli/Pandis/Telepress
P.594: Portrait: Sipa Press; Benali/Gamma/Studio X
P.595: Benali/Gamma/Studio X
P.596: Studio Holle-Suppa, Frankfurt
P.597: Portrait: Corbis/Picture Press;
Label: R. Stempell Photographie, B. Holefleisch,
Cologne; Studio Holle-Suppa, Frankfurt
P.598: Portrait: Sipa Press; Label: R. Stempell
Photographie, B. Holefleisch, Cologne;
L. and R.: J. Barth/Gamma/Studio X;
C.: Somoz-Tumo/Stills/Studio X
P.599: Sygma/Pandis/Telepress
P.600: Drawing and R.: W. Stevens /Gamma/
Studio X; L.: Angeli/Pandis/Telepress;
C.: A. Duclos/Gamma/Studio X
P.601: W. Stevens/Gamma/Studio X
P.602: L.: Studio Holle-Suppa, Frankfurt;
R.: W. Stevens/Gamma/Studio X
P.603: L.: Studio Holle-Suppa, Frankfurt;
R.: J. Barth/Gamma/Studio X
P.604: Portrait and L.: Corbis/Picture Press;
R.: A. Duclos/Gamma/Studio X
P.605: Corbis/Picture Press

**The permanent future,
or ready-to-future:**
P.606: Elfie Semotan/
Archive: Helmut Lang
PP.610–611, 614: Juergen Teller/
Archive: Helmut Lang

Appendix:
PP.616–617: A. Duclos/Gamma/Studio X

New textiles:
PP.618–620: Schoeller Archive

Fashion illustration:
P.621: A.L.: Paul Iribe/Gerstenberg Archive;
B.L.: Georges Barbier/Bridgeman/Giraudon;
A.R.: AKG/Georges Lepape/VG Bild-Kunst Bonn,
1999
P.622: L.: Cecil Beaton Kamera Press, London/
Marion Schweitzer;
R.: René Gruau/Dior Archive

Glossary:
PP.628–639: Yris Kayser

Abbreviations:

L.: = Left
R.: = Right
C.: = Center

A.L.: = Above left
B.L.: = Below left
F.L.: = Far left

A.R.: = Above right
B.R.: = Below right
F.R.: = Far right

A.C.: = Above center
B.C.: = Below center

L. and R.: = Left and right

C.L.: = Center left
C.M.: = Center right

C.F.L.: = Center far left
C.F.R.: = Center far right
A.F.L.: = Above far left
A.F.R.: = Above far right

The authors

Charlotte Seeling (Editor)
After completing her training as a journalist, Charlotte Seeling worked as a freelance writer, contributing to newspapers and magazines including *Quick, Stern,* and *Geo.* She traveled around the world as a reporter and became famous for her sensitive interviews with people ranging from Indira Gandhi to Federico Fellini and from Patricia Highsmith to Giorgio Armani. In the 1980s she was editor-in-chief of *Cosmopolitan, Vogue, Marie Claire,* and French *Marie France* in Paris. Since the mid-1990s she has been concentrating on writing books and working as a consultant on the subjects of lifestyle and fashion.

Margit J. Mayer
Born in 1960 near Vienna. Studied drama and history of art at Vienna University followed by stage design course at Vienna's School for Applied Arts in 1982/83 and took part in the Erich Wonder master class. From 1983 she worked for *Wiener* magazine, first as theater critic, later as fashion editor and author. From 1986 to 1999, she worked for Condé Nast in Munich, first at *Männer-Vogue,* then as a consulting editor at W-Europe (Fairchild Publications) in Paris. She has also contributed to French *Vogue,* the *Süddeutsche Zeitung* color supplement, *Artforum,* and *Frank.*

Katharina Tilemann
Born 1963. Freelance academic and author, worked for many years as an editor for a publishing company and is currently working on fashion photography in the 1920s and 1930s.

Maria Mester
Born 1966. Studied education, German, and philosophy. Subsequently trained as a public relations consultant and worked as a product manager for a public relations agency.

Bonizza Giordani Aragno
Fashion historian. She was the curator of several exhibitions in Italy and abroad and editor of their respective catalogs. Some of her work for Italian television has included the documentary *Storia della moda italiana dal 1940 al 1980* and the program Valentino trent'anni di magia for the television series *Le grandi Mostre.* She has contributed to the magazines *Linea Capital, Imago* and *Mondo Uomo.* She is now the editor-in-chief of the quarterly magazine *Audrey.*

Bea Gottschlich
Born 1957. Since 1980, after a course in Business Studies, she has worked in the trade fashion press field, initially at the German trade publishers *Textil Wirtschaft* and at Burda (*Freundin*). In 1987 she went to Paris to take up the editorship of the trade magazine for young fashions *Sportswear International.* Since 1990 she has been the French correspondent of *Textil-Wirtschaft.*

Elke Reinhold
Born 1964. She studied history at the Sorbonne and subsequently spent many years working as a foreign correspondent for German newspapers and magazines, reporting on fashion and lifestyle in Paris. She was also the deputy editor of *Cosmopolitan* and today works as a freelance author in Munich and Paris.

Anne Urbauer
Journalist. Since 1989 she has been working in Hamburg where, as the head of the lifestyle departments of *Tempo, Stern,* and *Die Woche,* she has been in charge of fashion and fashion photography. Born in Bavaria, her first fashion experiences were gained with the dresses of her three older sisters and the splendid robes of the village priest: "That's enough to give anyone a life-long obsession." She wrote her first pieces on fashion for the *Münchner Abendzeitung.* A pivotal experience was Helmut Lang's 1986 show during Munich's fashion week. She has also worked as a consultant and writer for television. As well as working for *Die Woche,* she is currently a Contributing Editor for the London weekly *Wallpaper.*

Sarah E. Braddock
Sarah E. Braddock is a lecturer in textiles at the Goldsmith College, University of London. Her main field of expertise is in fiber and textile technologies and their applications in fashion and art. She trained in textiles and fashion, graduating with a BA honours degree from Winchester School of Art, Great Britain. There she was awarded an exchange with the Fashion Institute of Technology in New York City and then gained her master's degree in fiber (MFA) at the University of Michigan, USA. Sarah Braddock was cocurator of the international exhibition *2010: Textiles and New Technology* and coeditor of the book of the same title (Artemis, London, 1992). She is coauthor of *Techno Textiles: Revolutionary Fabrics for Fashion and Design* (Thames and Hudson, London, 1998). In 1998 she was invited to join the panel of judges for the Sixth International Textile Competition, Kyoto, and in 1999 she co-organized a major symposium as part of International Textile Week in Frankfurt. Sarah Braddock lectures internationally on fashion, textiles, and textile as art with an emphasis on new technology and worldwide developments.

Katharina Hesedenz
Born in 1961 in the Saar, Germany. She studied German, glassmaking, and dressmaking, and has been working as a fashion journalist since 1986 for publications including *Vogue, Elle,* and *Marie Claire.* This passionate salsa dancer and mother of a five-year-old daughter has an iridescent idea for a book on cheesy pickup lines which has been thwarted by numerous trips to Costa Rica.

Acknowledgments

The editor would like to thank:

Fabric Frontline: André Stutz
Christian Lacroix

Special thanks to the models and their agencies for their support.

The publisher and the picture editor would like to thank the following people and institutions
for their generous assistance in illustrating this book:

AKG: Karen Müller-Kühne; Ann Demeulemeester: Benjamin; Archiv Gerstenberg; Association Willy Maywald: Jutta Niemann; Balenciaga; Benjamin Holefleisch; Bert Stern; Billy Klüver: Julie Martin; Bourjois: Michèle Duhamel; Calvin Klein: Dagmar Laemmle and Jennifer Yu; Cardin: Jean-Pascal Hesse; Centre de Documentation du Musée de la Mode et du Textile: Marie-Hélène Poix; Chanel: Katja Wilde and Odile Premel; Christian Brandstätter Verlagsgesellschaft mbH; Christian Dior: Philippe Le Moult; Christine Steutelberg; Christoph Kicherer; Clara Lempert; Città di Bologna, Cologne; DPA; Edimedia: Laurence Touffait; Eduard Noack;Eidos Interactive; Emmanuel Ungaro: Cordelia de Castellane; F. C. Gundlach; Focus; Frank Peinemann; Gamma: Caroline; Gertraude Holle-Suppa; Guillermo de Osma; Giraudon: Muriel and Penelope; Gisela Wiegert; Givenchy: Mylène Lajoix; Guy Laroche: Fabien Larchez; Hamiltons Photographers Ltd: Leigh Yule; Helena Rubinstein: Nicola Noack; Hermès: Annelise Catineau and Nathalie Vidal; Interfoto: Magdalena Gadaj; Jacques Torregano; Jaja Deffe for Marcio Madeira; Jean-Frederic Schall; Jean-Paul Gaultier: Sylvie; Jil Sander; Jo Magrean; Josh Westrich; Kaj Blunck; KPA: Gabriele Mast; La Fondation Cartier; Lanvin: Odile Fraigneau; L'Association Française pour la Diffusion du Patrimoine Photographique: Anne-Catherine Bidermann; Lesage: Madame Vibert; Louis Féraud: Ghislaine Brégé; Louis Vuitton; Maconochie Photography: Tiggy Maconochie for Jeanloup Sieff and Helmut Newton; Manolo Blahnik: Frau Hirschmann; Marc-O-Textilgroßhandel GmbH, Cologne; Marie-Claire: Evelyne Reingwitz; Marion Schweitzer; Mary Evans Picture Library: Mark Vivian; Michael Heeg; Michele Filomeno: Hélène for Peter Lindbergh; Monika Bergmann; Monteil: Frédérique Leng; Moschino: Stefania Vismara; Museo Salvatore Ferragamo: Chiara Casalotti; Network Public Relations: Christine Sticken; Nick Knight and Emma; Nina Ricci: Caroline Grabbe; Peter Knapp; Picture Press: Frau Hahn and Frau Tresp; Rainer Langhans; Ralph Lauren: Caroline Laurens; Renate Niebler; Rex Features: Gertrud; Richard Avedon; Roger-Viollet: Madame Comminges and Madame Rabec; Sarah Moon and her agent Renate Gallois-Monbrun; Scala; Schiaparelli; Schoeller Textil AG: Frau Signer; Sheila Metzner; Sipa: Petra; Sonia Rykiel: Safia Bendali; Studio Bokelberg; Studio X: Nicole Bergmann; Sygma: Philippe Mériaux and Nathalie Claveau; Sylvie Flaure for Jean-Paul Goude; Télimage: Frank; T. LeClerc; The Advertising Archives: Suzanne Viner; The Brooklyn Museum: Ruth Janson; Tom Roch; Tony Stone: Roswitha Salzberger and Katrin Baars; Ullstein Bilderdienst; Uta Brandes; Valentino: Olivia Berghauer; VG Bild-Kunst: Frau Hilger; Vogue Permissions: Michael Stier; Workman Publishing: Anita Dickhuth; Yohji Yamamoto: Angie Rubini; Ypsilon Boutique, Cologne; YSL: Dominique Leroche; Z Photography: Olivia Funnell for Juergen Teller

The publishers like to extend their particular thanks to the following people for their assistance on the original German book:

Aicha Becker (Picture research); Mareile Busse (Design); Katharina Tilemann (Captions and Glossary);
Silke v. Schönfeld (Corrections to text and index); argus Korrekturservice (Typesetting);
Christine Kalkhof (Research); Christine Dobbs (Index); Wolfgang Müller (Typesetting of appendix);
Ina Kalvelage, Bernhard Schreyer, Vera Brauner (Typesetting and corrections);
Jana Hallberg (Research and liaison with model agencies)